A·N·N·U·A·L E·D·I·T·I·O·N·S

Psychology

Thirty-Third Edition

03/04

D1410976

EDITOR

Karen G. Duffy

SUNY at Geneseo (Emerita)

Karen G. Duffy holds a doctorate in psychology from Michigan State University, and she is an emerita Distinguished Service Professor of State University of New York at Geneseo. Dr. Duffy continues to work on her books and research, and she is also involved in several community service projects both in the United States and Russia.

McGraw-Hill/Dushkin

530 Old Whitfield Street, Guilford, Connecticut 06437

Visit us on the Internet
http://www.dushkin.com

DAVID GLENN HUNT
MEMORIAL LIBRARY
GALVESTON COLLEGE

Credits

1. **The Science of Psychology**
   Unit photo—© 2003 by PhotoDisc, Inc.
2. **Biological Bases of Behavior**
   Unit photo—Medical World News photo.
3. **Perceptual Processes**
   Unit photo—Courtesy of Pamela Carley.
4. **Learning and Remembering**
   Unit photo—© 2003 by Cleo Freelance Photography.
5. **Cognitive Processes**
   Unit photo—United Nations photo by Milton Grant.
6. **Emotion and Motivation**
   Unit photo—© 2003 by Cleo Freelance Photography.
7. **Development**
   Unit photo—Courtesy of Pamela Carley.
8. **Personality Processes**
   Unit photo—© 2003 by Cleo Freelance Photography.
9. **Social Processes**
   Unit photo—Courtesy of Pamela Carley.
10. **Psychological Disorders**
    Unit photo—© 2003 by PhotoDisc, Inc.
11. **Psychological Treatments**
    Unit photo—Courtesy of Louis P. Raucci.

Copyright

Cataloging in Publication Data
Main entry under title: Annual Editions: Psychology. 2003/2004.
1. Psychology—Periodicals. I. Duffy, Karen G., *comp.* II. Title: Psychology.
ISBN 0–07–254829–0   658'.05   ISSN 0272–3794

© 2003 by McGraw-Hill/Dushkin, Guilford, CT 06437, A Division of The McGraw-Hill Companies.

Copyright law prohibits the reproduction, storage, or transmission in any form by any means of any portion of this publication without the express written permission of McGraw-Hill/Dushkin, and of the copyright holder (if different) of the part of the publication to be reproduced. The Guidelines for Classroom Copying endorsed by Congress explicitly state that unauthorized copying may not be used to create, to replace, or to substitute for anthologies, compilations, or collective works.

Annual Editions® is a Registered Trademark of McGraw-Hill/Dushkin, A Division of The McGraw-Hill Companies.

Thirty-Third Edition

Cover image © 2003 PhotoDisc, Inc.
Printed in the United States of America   1234567890BAHBAH543   Printed on Recycled Paper

Editors/Advisory Board

Members of the Advisory Board are instrumental in the final selection of articles for each edition of ANNUAL EDITIONS. Their review of articles for content, level, currentness, and appropriateness provides critical direction to the editor and staff. We think that you will find their careful consideration well reflected in this volume.

EDITOR

Karen G. Duffy
SUNY at Geneseo (Emerita)

ADVISORY BOARD

Jeffery L. Arbuckle
Hood College

Michael Atkinson
University of Western Ontario

Timothy Barth
Texas Christian University

John Cross
St. Louis University

Linda K. Davis
Mt. Hood Community College

Joan F. DiGiovanni
University of Arizona

Mark J. Friedman
Montclair State University

Rebecca Ganes
Modesto Junior College

Florine A. Greenberg
Northern Virginia Community College

Robert L. Hale
Shippensburg University

C. Harry Hui
University of Hong Kong

Angela J.C. LaSala
Community College of Southern Nevada

Nancy G. McCarley
Mississippi State University

Carroll Mitchell
Cecil Community College

Quentin Newhouse
Tennessee State University

Paul Nochelski
Canisius College

Terry F. Pettijohn
Ohio State University

Janice Rafalowski
County College of Morris

Edward Raymaker
Eastern Maine Technical College

Mitchell W. Robins
New York City Technical College

Virginia F. Saunders
San Francisco State University

Stephen P. Stelzner
College of Saint Benedict

Harry Strub
University of Winnipeg

David W. Wolfe
Ocean County College

Staff

EDITORIAL STAFF

Ian A. Nielsen, Publisher
Roberta Monaco, Senior Developmental Editor
Dorothy Fink, Associate Developmental Editor
Iain Martin, Associate Developmental Editor
Addie Raucci, Senior Administrative Editor
Robin Zarnetske, Permissions Editor
Marie Lazauskas, Permissions Assistant
Diane Barker, Proofreader
Lisa Holmes-Doebrick, Senior Program Coordinator

TECHNOLOGY STAFF

Richard Tietjen, Senior Publishing Technologist
Jonathan Stowe, Executive Director of eContent
Marcuss Oslander, Sponsoring Editor of eContent
Christopher Santos, Senior eContent Developer
Janice Ward, Software Support Analyst
Angela Mule, eContent Developer
Michael McConnell, eContent Developer
Ciro Parente, Editorial Assistant
Joe Offredi, Technology Developmental Editor

PRODUCTION STAFF

Brenda S. Filley, Director of Production
Charles Vitelli, Designer
Mike Campell, Production Coordinator
Laura Levine, Graphics
Tom Goddard, Graphics
Eldis Lima, Graphics
Nancy Norton, Graphics
Juliana Arbo, Typesetting Supervisor
Karen Roberts, Typesetter
Jocelyn Proto, Typesetter
Cynthia Powers, Typesetter
Cathy Kuziel, Typesetter
Larry Killian, Copier Coordinator

To the Reader

In publishing ANNUAL EDITIONS we recognize the enormous role played by the magazines, newspapers, and journals of the public press in providing current, first-rate educational information in a broad spectrum of interest areas. Many of these articles are appropriate for students, researchers, and professionals seeking accurate, current material to help bridge the gap between principles and theories and the real world. These articles, however, become more useful for study when those of lasting value are carefully collected, organized, indexed, and reproduced in a low-cost format, which provides easy and permanent access when the material is needed. That is the role played by ANNUAL EDITIONS.

Ronnie's parents couldn't understand why he didn't want to be picked up and cuddled as did his older sister when she was a baby. As an infant, Ronnie did not respond to his parents' smiles, words, or attempts to amuse him. By the age of two, Ronnie's parents knew that he was not like other children. He spoke no English, was very temperamental, and often rocked himself for hours. Ronnie is autistic. His parents feel that some of Ronnie's behavior may be their fault. As young professionals, they both work long hours and leave their children with an older woman during the weekdays. Ronnie's pediatrician assures his parents that their reasoning, while logical, holds no merit because the causes of autism are little understood and are likely to be biological rather than parental. What can we do about children like Ronnie? What is the source of autism? Can autism be treated or reversed? Can it be prevented?

Psychologists attempt to answer these and other complex questions using scientific methods. Researchers, using carefully planned research designs, try to discover the causes of complex human behavior—normal or not. The scientific results of psychological research typically are published in professional journals, and therefore may be difficult for the lay person to understand.

Annual Editions: Psychology 03/04 is designed to meet the needs of lay people and introductory level students who are curious about psychology. This *Annual Edition* provides a vast selection of readable and informative articles primarily from popular magazines and newspapers. These articles are typically written by journalists, but a few are written by psychologists and retain the excitement of the discovery of scientific knowledge.

The particular articles selected for this volume were chosen to be representative of the most current work in psychology. They were selected because they are accurate in their reporting and provide examples of the types of psychological research discussed in most introductory psychology classes. As in any science, some of the findings discussed in this collection are startling, while others confirm what we already know. Some articles will invite speculation about social and personal issues; others will encourage careful thought about potential misuse of research findings. Readers are expected to make the investment of effort and critical reasoning necessary to answer such questions and concerns.

I believe that you will find *Annual Editions: Psychology 03/04* readable and useful. I suggest that you look at the organization of this book and compare it to the organization of your textbook and course syllabus. By examining the *topic guide* the *table of contents*, you can identify those articles most appropriate for any particular unit of study in your course. Your instructor may provide some help in this effort or assign articles to supplement the text. As you read the articles, try to connect their contents with the principles you are learning from your text and classroom lectures. Some of the articles will help you better understand a specific area of research, while others are designed to help you connect and integrate information from diverse research areas. Both of these strategies are important in learning about psychology or any other science. It is only through intensive investigation and subsequent integration of the findings from many studies that we are able to discover and apply new knowledge.

Please take time to provide me with some feedback to guide the annual revision of this anthology by completing and returning the *article rating form* in the back of the book. With your help, this collection will be even better next year. Thank you.

Karen Grover Duffy

Karen Grover Duffy
Editor

Contents

UNIT 1
The Science of Psychology

Three articles examine psychology as the science of behavior.

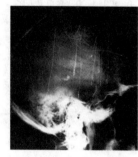

UNIT 2
Biological Bases of Behavior

Three selections discuss the biological bases of behavior. Topics include brain functions and the brain's control over the body.

The concepts in bold italics are developed in the article. For further expansion, please refer to the Topic Guide and the Index.

UNIT 3
Perceptual Processes

Seven articles discuss the impact of the senses on human perceptual processes.

The concepts in bold italics are developed in the article. For further expansion, please refer to the Topic Guide and the Index.

UNIT 4
Learning and Remembering

Five selections examine how operant conditioning, positive reinforcement, and memory interact during the learning process.

UNIT 5
Cognitive Processes

Four articles examine how social skills, common sense, and intelligence affect human cognitive processes.

The concepts in bold italics are developed in the article. For further expansion, please refer to the Topic Guide and the Index.

UNIT 6
Emotion and Motivation

Four articles discuss the influence of stress, mental states, and emotion on the mental and physical health of the individual.

Unit Overview 100

UNIT 7
Development

Five articles consider the importance of experience, discipline, familial support, and psychological aging during the normal human development process.

Unit Overview 112

The concepts in bold italics are developed in the article. For further expansion, please refer to the Topic Guide and the Index.

UNIT 8
Personality Processes

Three selections discuss a few of the processes by which personalities are developed. Topics include self-esteem, empathy, and the secrets of happiness.

The concepts in bold italics are developed in the article. For further expansion, please refer to the Topic Guide and the Index.

UNIT 9
Social Processes

Six selections discuss how the individual's social development is affected by genes, stereotypes, prejudice, and relationships.

UNIT 10
Psychological Disorders

Six articles examine several psychological disorders. Topics include unexpected behavior, the impact of depression on a person's well-being, and phobias.

The concepts in bold italics are developed in the article. For further expansion, please refer to the Topic Guide and the Index.

UNIT 11
Psychological Treatments

Three selections discuss a few psychological treatments, including psychotherapy to alleviate depression, self-care, and the use of drugs.

The concepts in bold italics are developed in the article. For further expansion, please refer to the Topic Guide and the Index.

Topic Guide

This topic guide suggests how the selections in this book relate to the subjects covered in your course. You may want to use the topics listed on these pages to search the Web more easily.

On the following pages a number of Web sites have been gathered specifically for this book. They are arranged to reflect the units of this *Annual Edition*. You can link to these sites by going to the DUSHKIN ONLINE support site at *http://www.dushkin.com/online/*.

ALL THE ARTICLES THAT RELATE TO EACH TOPIC ARE LISTED BELOW THE BOLD-FACED TERM.

World Wide Web Sites

The following World Wide Web sites have been carefully researched and selected to support the articles found in this reader. The easiest way to access these selected sites is to go to our DUSHKIN ONLINE support site at *http://www.dushkin.com/online/*.

AE: Psychology 03/04

The following sites were available at the time of publication. Visit our Web site—we update DUSHKIN ONLINE regularly to reflect any changes.

General Sources

APA Resources for the Public
http://www.apa.org/psychnet/

Use the site map or search engine to access *APA Monitor,* the American Psychological Association newspaper, APA books on a wide range of topics, PsychINFO, an electronic database of abstracts on scholarly journals, and the HelpCenter.

Health Information Resources
http://www.health.gov/nhic/Pubs/tollfree.htm

Here is a long list of toll-free numbers that provide health-related information. None offer diagnosis and treatment, but some do offer recorded information; others provide personalized counseling, referrals, and/or written materials.

Mental Help Net
http://mentalhelp.net

This comprehensive guide to mental health online features more than 6,300 individual resources. Information on mental disorders and professional resources in psychology, psychiatry, and social work are presented.

Psychology: Online Resource Central
http://www.resourcehelper.com/qserpsychology.htm

Thousands of psychology resources are currently indexed at this site. Psychology disciplines, conditions and disorders, psychiatry, assistance, and self-development are among the most useful.

School Psychology Resources Online
http://www.schoolpsychology.net

Numerous sites on special conditions, disorders, and disabilities, as well as other data ranging from assessment/evaluation to research, are available on this resource page for psychologists, parents, and educators.

Social Psychology Network
http://www.socialpsychology.org

The social Psychology Nrtwork is the most comprehensive source of social psychology information on the Internet, including resources, programs, and research.

UNIT 1: The Science of Psychology

Abraham A. Brill Library
http://plaza.interport.net/nypsan/service.html

Containing data on over 40,000 books, periodicals, and reprints in psychoanalysis and related fields, the Abraham A. Brill Library's holdings span the literature of psychoanalysis from its beginning to the present day.

American Psychological Society (APS)
http://www.psychologicalscience.org/links.html

The APS is dedicated to advancing the best of scientific psychology in research, application, and the improvement of human conditions. Links to teaching, research, and graduate studies resources are available.

Psychological Research on the Net
http://psych.hanover.edu/APS/exponnet.html

This Net site provides psychologically related experiments. Biological psychology/neuropsychology, clinical psychology, cognition, developmental psychology, emotions, health psychology, personality, sensation/perception, and social psychology are some of the areas covered.

UNIT 2: Biological Bases of Behavior

Adolescence: Changes and Continuity
http://www.personal.psu.edu/faculty/n/x/nxd10/adolesce.htm

A discussion of puberty, sexuality, biological changes, cross-cultural differences, and nutrition for adolescents, including obesity and its effects on adolescent development, is presented here.

Division of Hereditary Diseases and Family Studies, Indiana University School of Medicine
http://www.iupui.edu/~medgen/division/hereditary/
hereditary_diseases.html

The Department of Medical and Molecular Genetics is primarily concerned with determining the genetic basis of disease. It consists of a multifaceted program with a variety of interdisciplinary projects. The areas of twin studies and linkage analysis are also explored.

Institute for Behavioral Genetics
http://ibgwww.colorado.edu/index.html

Dedicated to conducting and facilitating research on the genetic and environmental bases of individual differences in behavior, this organized research unit at the University of Colorado leads to Genetic Sites, Statistical Sites, and the Biology Meta Index, as well as to search engines.

Serendip
http://serendip.brynmawr.edu/serendip/

Serendip, which is organized into five subject areas (brain and behavior, complex systems, genes and behavior, science and culture, and science education), contains interactive exhibits, articles, links to other resources, and a forum area.

UNIT 3: Perceptual Processes

Five Senses Home Page
http://www.sedl.org/scimath/pasopartners/senses/welcome.html

This elementary lesson examines the five senses and gives a list of references that may be useful.

Psychology Tutorials and Demonstrations
http://psych.hanover.edu/Krantz/tutor.html

Interactive tutorials and simulations, primarily in the area of sensation and perception, are available here.

UNIT 4: Learning and Remembering

Mind Tools
http://www.psychwww.com/mtsite/

Useful information on stress management can be found at this Web site.

The Opportunity of Adolescence
http://www.winternet.com/~webpage/adolescencepaper.html

According to this paper, adolescence is the turning point, after which the future is redirected and confirmed. The opportunities and problems of this period are presented with quotations from Erik Erikson, Jean Piaget, and others.

Project Zero
http://pzweb.harvard.edu

The Harvard Project Zero has investigated the development of learning processes in children and adults for 30 years. Today, Project Zero's mission is to understand and enhance learning, thinking, and creativity in the arts and other disciplines for individuals and institutions.

UNIT 5: Cognitive Processes

Chess: Kasparov v. Deep Blue: The Rematch
http://www.chess.ibm.com/home/html/b.html

Clips from the chess rematch between Garry Kasparov and IBM's supercomputer, Deep Blue, are presented here along with commentaries on chess, computers, artificial intelligence, and what it all means.

Introduction to Artificial Intelligence (AI)
http://www-formal.stanford.edu/jmc/aiintro/aiintro.html

A description of AI is presented here along with links to other AI sites.

UNIT 6: Emotion and Motivation

CYFERNET-Youth Development
http://www.cyfernet.mes.umn.edu/youthdev.html

CYFERNET presents many articles on youth development, including a statement on the concept of normal adolescence and impediments to healthy development.

Emotional Intelligence Discovery
http://www.cwrl.utexas.edu/~bump/Hu305/3/3/3/

This site has been set up by students to talk about and expand on Daniel Goleman's book, *Emotional Intelligence*. There are links to many other EI sites.

John Suler's Teaching Clinical Psychology Site
http://www.rider.edu/users/suler/tcp.html

This page contains Internet resources for clinical and abnormal psychology, behavioral medicine, and mental health.

Nature vs. Nature: Gergen Dialogue with Winifred Gallagher
http://www.pbs.org/newshour/gergen/gallagher_5-14.html

Experience modifies temperament, according to this TV interview. The author of *I.D.: How Heredity and Experience Make You Who You Are* explains a current theory about temperament.

UNIT 7: Development

American Association for Child and Adolescent Psychiatry
http://www.aacap.org

This site is designed to aid in the understanding and treatment of the developmental, behavioral, and mental disorders that could affect children and adolescents. There is a specific link just for families about common childhood problems that may or may not require professional intervention.

Behavioral Genetics
http://www.ornl.gov/hgmis/elsi/behavior.html

This government backed Web site includes helpful information on behavioral genetics.

UNIT 8: Personality Processes

The Personality Project
http://personality-project.org/personality.html

This Personality Project (by William Revelle) is meant to guide those interested in personality theory and research to the current personality research literature.

UNIT 9: Social Processes

National Clearinghouse for Alcohol and Drug Information
http://www.health.org

Information on drug and alcohol facts that might relate to adolescence and the issues of peer pressure and youth culture is presented here. Resources, referrals, research and statistics, databases, and related Net links are available.

Nonverbal Behavior and Nonverbal Communication
http://www3.usal.es/~nonverbal/

This fascinating site has a detailed listing of nonverbal behavior and nonverbal communication sites on the Web, including the work of historical and current researchers.

UNIT 10: Psychological Disorders

American Association of Suicidology
http://www.suicidology.org/top.htm

The American Association of Suicidology is a nonprofit organization dedicated to the understanding and prevention of suicide. This site is designed as a resource to anyone concerned about suicide.

Anxiety Disorders
http://www.adaa.org/mediaroom/index.cfm

Anxiety disorders in children, adolescents, and adults are reviewed by the Anxiety Disorders Association of America (ADAA). A detailed glossary is also included.

Ask NOAH About: Mental Health
http://www.noah-health.org/english//illness/mentalhealth/mental.html

Information about child and adolescent family problems, mental conditions and disorders, suicide prevention, and much more is available here.

Mental Health Net Disorders and Treatments
http://www.mentalhelp.net/

Presented on this site are hotlinks to psychological disorders pages, which include anxiety, panic, phobic disorders, schizophrenia, and violent/self-destructive behaviors.

Mental Health Net: Eating Disorder Resources
http://www.mentalhelp.net/poc/center_index.php/id/46

This mental health Net site provides a complete list of Web references on eating disorders, including anorexia, bulimia, and obesity.

National Women's Health Resource Center (NWHRC)
http://www.healthywomen.org

NWHRC's site contains links to resources related to women's substance abuse and mental illnesses.

www.dushkin.com/online/

UNIT 11: Psychological Treatments

The C.G. Jung Page
http://www.cgjungpage.org

Dedicated to the work of Carl Jung, this is a comprehensive resource, with links to Jungian psychology, news and opinions, reference materials, graduate programs, dreams, multilingual sites, and related Jungian themes.

Knowledge Exchange Network (KEN)
http://www.mentalhealth.org

Information about mental health (prevention, treatment, and rehabilitation services) is available via toll-free telephone services, an electronic bulletin board, and publications.

NetPsychology
http://netpsych.com/index.htm

This site explores the uses of the Internet to deliver mental health serices. This is a basic cybertherapy resource site.

Sigmund Freud and the Freud Archives
http://plaza.interport.net/nypsan/freudarc.html

Internet resources related to Sigmund Freud, which include a collection of libraries, museums, and biographical materials, as well as the Brill Library archives, can be found here.

We highly recommend that you review our Web site for expanded information and our other product lines. We are continually updating and adding links to our Web site in order to offer you the most usable and useful information that will support and expand the value of your Annual Editions. You can reach us at: *http://www.dushkin.com/annualeditions/.*

UNIT 1
The Science of Psychology

Unit Selections

1. **A Dance to the Music of the Century: Changing Fashions in 20th-Century Psychiatry**, David Healy
2. **Good and Evil and Psychological Science**, Ervin Staub
3. **Exploring a Controversy**, George W. Albee

Key Points to Consider

- Which area of psychology (biological psychology, social psychology, human development, etc.) do you think is the most valuable and why? Many people are aware of clinical psychology by virtue of having watched films and television where psychotherapists are depicted. Is this the most valuable area of the discipline? About which other areas of psychology do you think the public ought to be informed?

- How do you think psychology is related to other scientific disciplines, such as sociology, biology, and human medicine? Are there nonscience disciplines to which psychology might be related, for example, philosophy and mathematics? How so?

- Is there one psychological theory to which you are especially attracted? Why? Which theories do you think will continue to be important to the field of psychology? Do you think psychologists will ever be able to piece together a single grand theory of human psychology? Do you have your own theory of human behavior? If yes, on what do you base your theory—your own observations? In developing a theory of human behavior, should psychologists rely extensively on research?

- Why is research important to psychology? What kinds of information can be gleaned from psychological research? What types of research methods do psychologists utilize? Can research results from psychology be used for both "good" and "evil"? Can you provide some examples of both beneficial and harmful use of research results in psychology? What about other disciplines; can their results be used in both ways, too?

- Do you think editors of psychological journals should publish results "as is" or should they exclude certain types of research or results from their journals? If yes, what types? If you answered no, why? What role do you think the media should play in disseminating the results and interpretations of psychological research?

 **Links: www.dushkin.com/online/**
These sites are annotated in the World Wide Web pages.

Abraham A. Brill Library
http://plaza.interport.net/nypsan/service.html

American Psychological Society (APS)
http://www.psychologicalscience.org/links.html

Psychological Research on the Net
http://psych.hanover.edu/APS/exponnet.html

Little did Wilhelm Wundt realize his monumental contribution to science when in 1879 in Germany, he opened the first psychological laboratory to examine consciousness. Wundt would barely recognize modern psychology compared to the way he practiced it.

Contemporary psychology is defined as the science or study of individual mental activity and behavior. This definition reflects the two parent disciplines from which psychology emerged: philosophy and biology. Compared to its parents, psychology is very much a new discipline. Some aspects of modern psychology are particularly biological, such as neuroscience, perception, psychophysics, and behavioral genetics. Some aspects are more philosophical, such as the study of personality, while others approximate sociology, as does social psychology.

Today's psychologists work in a variety of settings. Many psychologists are academics, teaching and researching psychology on university campuses. Others work in applied settings such as hospitals, mental health clinics, industry, and schools. Most psychologists also specialize in psychology after graduate training. Industrial psychologists specialize in human performance in organizational settings, while clinical psychologists are concerned about the assessment, diagnosis, and treatment of individuals with a variety of mental disorders. Each specialty typically requires a graduate education and sometimes requires a license to practice.

There are some psychologists who think that psychology is still in its adolescence and that the field is experiencing growing pains. Since its establishment, the field has expanded to many different areas. As mentioned above, some areas are very applied; other areas appear to emphasize theory and research. The growing pains have resulted in conflict over what the agenda of the first national psychological association, the American Psychological Association, should be. Because academics perceived this association as mainly serving practitioners, academics and researchers established their own competing association, the American Psychological Society. Despite its varied nature and growing pains, psychology remains a viable and exciting field. The first unit of the book is designed to introduce you to the study and history of psychology.

In the first article, "A Dance to the Music of the Century: Changing Fashions in 20th-Century Psychiatry," David Healy reviews the history and theories of psychology and psychiatry. He also anticipates where these disciplines are headed and which

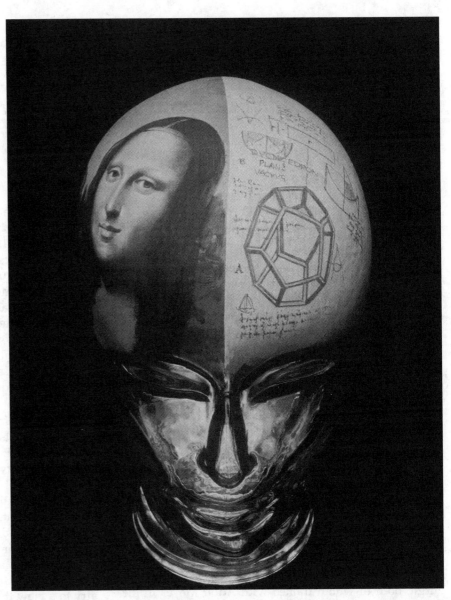

theories will continue to play an important role in shaping psychological thought.

The next article also pertains to psychological science. The author asks a cogent question, "Can psychology be used for both good and evil?" The answer is "yes." Author Ervin Staub, using his own research on several different topics, demonstrates the uses and misuses of findings from psychological research.

The third introductory article is also about psychological research. In 2002, editor George Albee decided to publish an extremely controversial article in the leading journal *American Psychologist*. The article covered research pertaining to sexual abuse of children. Albee reviews why he published the article and challenges critics to place the neutrality and significance of scientific methods and results ahead of their own personal values.

A dance to the music of the century:

Changing fashions in 20th-century psychiatry

David Healy, Director

North Wales Department of Psychological Medicine,
Hergest Unit, Bangor LL57 2PW

Modern psychiatry began in the early 19th century from a social psychiatric seed. The early alienists, Pinel and Tuke, Esquirol and Connolly believed that managing the social milieu of the patient could contribute significantly to their chances of recovery. These physicians produced the first classificatory systems in the discipline. At the turn of the century, university psychiatry, which was biologically oriented, began to impact on psychiatry, especially in Germany. This is seen most clearly in the work and classificatory system of Emil Kraepelin (Healy, 1997). At the same time, a new psychodynamic approach to the management of nervous problems in the community was pioneered most notably by Sigmund Freud. This led to yet another classification of nervous problems.

In the first half of the century, unlike German and French psychiatry, British psychiatry remained largely aloof from the influences of both university and psychodynamic approaches. It became famously pragmatic and eclectic. Edward Mapother, the first director of the Maudsley Hospital, typified the approach. Aubrey Lewis, who succeeded him, as well as David Henderson in Edinburgh, both of whom trained with Adolf Meyer in the USA, were committed to Meyer's biopsychosocial approach (Gelder, 1991). The social psychiatry that stemmed from this was to gain a decisive say in European and world psychiatry in the decades immediately following the Second World War.

Things at first unfolded no differently in that other bastion of English-speaking psychiatry—America. In the first decade of the 20th century, Meyer introduced Kraepelin's work to North America, where it had a modest impact, failing to supplant Meyer's own biopsychosocial formulations. In 1909, Freud visited the USA. He appears to have regarded it as an outpost of the civilised world, one particularly prone to enthusiasms. At this point, Freudian analysis restricted itself to handling personalities and their discontents. It initially made little headway in the USA.

There was another development in the USA that was to have a decisive impact on British and world psychiatry in due course. In 1912, the USA legislature passed the Harrison's Narcotics Act, the world's first piece of legislation which made drugs available on prescription only, in this case, opiates and cocaine. While substance misuse was not at the time a part of psychiatry, which confined itself worldwide almost exclusively to the management of the psychoses, this move to prescription-only status by involving medical practitioners in managing the problem almost by necessity meant that the issue of personalities and their disorders would at some point become part of psychiatry.

The years before the Second World War led to two sets of developments. First, there was a migration of psychoanalysts from Europe to North America, so that by the 1940s a majority of the world's analysts lived there. In America, what had been a pessimistic worldview was recast with an optimistic turn, in part perhaps because the War demonstrated that nervous disorders could be environmentally induced and at the same time genetic research was temporarily eclipsed. This new remodelled psychoanalysis abandoned Freud's reserve about treating psychosis. It triumphed and drove American psychiatry to a view that everyone was at least latently ill, that everyone was in need of treatment and that the way to put the world's wrongs right was not just to treat mental illness, but to resculpt personalities and promote mental health (Menninger, 1959).

Second, sulphonamides were discovered and the War stimulated research, which made penicillin commercially available. The success that stemmed from these led to explosive growth in the pharmaceutical sector. The search for other antibiotics led to the discovery in France of antihistamines, one of which turned out to be chlorpromazine. The Food and Drug Administration in the USA responded to these new drugs by making all new drugs available on prescription only. European countries followed suit. This was to bring not only problems of personality but also the vast pool of community nervousness within the remit of non-analytic psychiatry.

The psychoanalysts gained control of American psychiatry in the decade before the introduction of the psychotropic drugs. By 1962, 59 of 82 psychiatric departments were headed by analysts, all graduate programmes were based on analytical principles and 13 of the 17 most recommended texts were psychoanalytical (Shorter, 1996). As a director of the National Institute of Mental Health put it:

> "From 1945 to 1955, it was nearly impossible for a non-psychoanalyst to become a chairman of a department or professor of psychiatry" (Brown, 1976).

As early as 1948, three-quarters of all committee posts in the American Psychiatric Association (APA) were held by analysts (Shorter, 1996).

One of the features of these developments was that a rootless patois of dynamic terms seeped out into the popular culture to create a psychobabble, with untold consequences for how we view ourselves. Another feature that is regularly cited was the way the analytical totalitarianism that resulted handled failures of patients to get well or of critics to come on side. These were turned around and viewed as further indicators of the psychopathology afflicting patients and critics respectively (Dolnick, 1998).

Walter Reich (1982) argued that this style was a defence against pessimism that stemmed at least in part from America's peculiar needs for solutions to complexity. He was writing at a time of change, just after the publication of DSM-III (American Psychiatric Association, 1980). DSM-III, which is commonly cited as marking the triumph of a neo-Kraepelinian revolution in American psychiatry, was widely seen as changing the rules to favour a newly emerging biological psychiatry. Its message, that psychiatry's business was to treat diseases, was a counter to perceptions that the analytical agenda had become a crusade that had taken "psychiatrists on a mission to change the world which had brought the profession to the verge of extinction" (Bayer & Spitzer, 1985).

Part of the stimulus to DSM-III had come from participation in the International Pilot Study of Schizophrenia, where American psychiatrists had felt keenly the disdain with which their diagnostic views were regarded by their European counterparts, who were British or who, like Norman Sartorius, Assen Jablensky and others, had close links with the Maudsley (Spitzer, 2000). The DSM-III was fiercely resisted in the UK, whose leading authorities had been the key figures behind the international system of classification (ICD) for several decades. The new system was dismissed—"serious students of nosology will continue to use the ICD" (Shepherd, 1981). But an empire was slipping from British hands (Spitzer, 2000). The World Psychiatric Association took as its banner for its 1996 meeting the slogan "One World, One Language". Few people, attending the meeting at least, thought this language was anything other than biological or neo-Kraepelinian.

Reich (1982) commented on the change in American psychiatry from analysis to a more biologically-based discipline but this change, he suggested, was likely to be governed by similar dynamics to those that drove the earlier turn to psychoanalysis. By the 1990s, the rise of psychopharmacology and biological psychiatry was complete. The chances of a non-neuroscientist becoming a head of a psychiatric department in the USA was highly unlikely and not much more likely in the UK. The standard textbooks were heavily neuroscientific in their emphasis. Where once the APA was controlled by analysts, annual meetings now generated millions of dollars—largely from pharmaceutical company sponsored satellite symposia, of which there were 40 in 1999, at approximately $250 000 per symposium in addition to fees for exhibition space and registration fees for several thousand delegates brought to the meeting by pharmaceutical companies, as well as several million dollars per annum from sales of successive versions of the DSM.

The UK, which had once stood dismissive of American trends and diagnoses, increasingly followed American leads. Fashions in recovered memory therapies or fluoxetine-taking rapidly crossed the Atlantic, influenced in part perhaps by the ever-increasing attendance of British psychiatrists at APA meetings. By 1999, it was possible that greater numbers of British psychiatrists, sponsored largely by pharmaceutical companies, attended the APA meeting than the annual meeting of the Royal College of Psychiatrists, a development that would have been incredible a decade before.

Biological psychiatry, meanwhile, had not restricted itself to the psychoses from whence it came. By the end of the century, the complete transformation of personality rather than simply the treatment of disease was becoming the goal. This was most clearly articulated in Peter Kramer's *Listening to Prozac* (Kramer, 1993). Where once the psychiatric concern had been for symptoms as these reflected diseases, the emphasis was increasingly on the management of problems by biological means. The extent to which community nervousness stems from social arrangements rather than diseases is clearly uncertain, but where the best estimates of annual prevalence rates of depressive disease stood at between 50 and 100 per million in 1950, by the mid-1990s they had risen to 100,000 per million for depressive disorders as defined by the DSM, with even higher rates for depressive symptoms (Healy, 1997).

Despite the neo-Kraepelinian revolution, some American opinion leaders were beginning to argue that the profession faced disaster if it did not stop offering to solve social ills and if it did not pull back to a medical focus (Detre & McDonald, 1997). Where once blame had been put on families, or mothers in particular, the 1990s became the decade of blaming the brain (Valenstein, 1998). By the end of the decade, the psychobabble of yesteryear was fast being replaced by a newly minted biobabble. *The Guardian* newspaper ran a feature on "Oh no! We're not really getting more depressed are we?" in which a psychologist, Oliver James, pondered whether the British have become a low-serotonin people (James, 1997). Finally, an ever increasing emphasis on long-term treatment with psychotropic agents, along with difficulties with withdrawal from them (a perennial British concern), inevitably recalls Karl Kraus' quip about analysis becoming the illness it purported to cure.

The mass treatment of problems with psychotropic drugs could not but in itself run into problems. Reports of suicides, homicides and other events while taking fluoxetine (Healy *et al*, 1999) led Eli Lilly to devise a strategy to manage criticism which involved blaming the disease, not the drug (Cornwell, 1996). On 20 April 1999, two students took firearms into a high school in Littleton, Colorado, killing 12 students, one staff member and then themselves. Within days of suggestions that one of the teenagers had an antidepressant in their blood stream, the APA Website carried a statement from the Association's president:

> "Despite a decade of research, there is little valid evidence to prove a causal relationship between the use of antidepressant medications and destructive behavior. On the other hand, their [sic] is ample evidence that undiagnosed and untreated mental illness exacts a heavy toll on those who suffer from these disorders as well as those around them" (American Psychiatric Association, 1999).

Many of those who take up psychiatry as a career might be thought to do so for fairytale or romantic reasons. At some point they will have nourished fantasies of helping patients with neuroses or psychoses to recover to the point of being invited to participate in the ball of life once more. In the course of a century, psychiatrists attending the ball have elegantly changed partners on a number of occasions. It is less clear that those who are not invited to the ball have seen much difference as a consequence of changes on the dance floor. When the clock strikes for the new millennium, are any of the dancers likely to be bothered by a stray glass slipper or does that just happen in fairytales?

References

AMERICAN PSYCHIATRIC ASSOCIATION (1980) *Diagnostic and Statistical Manual of Mental Disorders* (3rd edn.) (DSM-III). Washington, DC: American Psychiatric Association.

AMERICAN PSYCHIATRIC ASSOCIATION (1999) *Online News Stand*, release no. 99–19. www.psych.org/news.stand/nr.990428.html.

BAYER R. & SPITZER, R. L. (1985) Neurosis, psychodynamics and DSM-III. *Archives of General Psychiatry*, **25**, 123–130.

BROWN, B. S. (1976) The life of psychiatry. *American Journal of Psychiatry*, **133**, 489–495.

CORNWELL, J. (1996) *The Power to Harm. Mind, Medicine and Money on Trial*. London: Viking Press.

DETRE, T. & McDONALD, M. C. (1997) Managed care and the future of psychiatry. *Archives of General Psychiatry*, **54**, 201–204.

DOLNICK, E. (1998) *Madness on the Couch. Blaming the Victim in the Heyday of Psychoanalysis*. New York: Simon & Schuster.

GELDER, M. (1991) Adolf Meyer and his influence in British psychiatry. In *150 Years of British Psychiatry 1841–1991* (eds. G. E. Berrios & H. Freeman), pp. 419–435. London: Gaskell.

JAMES, O. (1997) Oh no! We're not really getting more depressed are we? *The Guardian*, G2, pp. 1–3. Monday 15 September.

HEALY, D. (1997) *The Antidepressant Era*. Cambridge, MA: Harvard University Press.

HEALY, D., LANGMAACK, C. & SAVAGE, M. (1999) Suicide in the course of the treatment of depression. *Journal of Psychopharmacology*, **13**, 94–99.

KRAMER, P. (1993) *Listening to Prozac*. New York: Viking Press.

MENINGER, K. (1959) Hope. *American Journal of Psychiatry*, **116**, 481–491.

REICH, W. (1982) American psychoideology. *Psychiatric Bulletin*, **6**, 43.

SHEPHERD, M. (1981) Diagnostic and Statistical Manual, 3rd Edition. American Psychiatric Association Press. *Psychological Medicine*, **11**, 215.

SHORTER, F. (1996) *A History of Psychiatry. From the Age of the Asylum to the Era of Prozac*. New York: John Wiley & Sons.

SPITZER, R. (2000) A manual for diagnosis and statistics. In *The Psychopharmacologists*, volume 3 (ed. D. Healy). London: Arnold.

VALENSTEIN, E. S. (1998) *Blaming the Brain*. New York: Free Press.

From *Psychiatric Bulletin*, January 2000, pp. 1-3. © 2000 by the American Psychological Association. Reprinted by permission.

Good and Evil and Psychological Science

ERVIN STAUB
Guest Columnist

To me, evil means great human destructiveness. Evil can come in an obvious form, such as a genocide. Or it can come in smaller acts of persistent harm doing, the effects of which accumulate, like parents being hostile and punitive, or a child being picked on by peers day after day for a long time. Goodness means bringing about great benefit to individuals or whole groups. It too can come in an obvious form, like a heroic effort to save someone's life, or great effort in pursuit of significant social change, or in smaller, persistent acts.

Nations often act in selfish and destructive ways. But goodness by groups, small and large, does exist. In the case of nations, goodness often comes from mixed motives, as in the case of the Marshall Plan that rebuilt Europe, but also was aimed at preventing the spread of Communism. At other times, as in Somalia—where intervention to help reduce starvation ended in violence and confusion—seemingly altruistic motives come to bad ends. The work of the Quakers in the abolition of slavery, and the village of LaChambon in France saving thousands of Jews during the Holocaust, illustrate goodness born of humane values and altruism.

What is the role of psychology in relation to goodness and evil? One obvious role is to study the influences that lead to great or persistent acts of harm or benefit. We can study the psychological processes, such as anger, hostility, the devaluation of groups of people, empathy or its absence, and a feeling of responsibility for others' welfare, that make a person act in destructive or caring ways. We can study the characteristics of persons, cultures, social/political systems and existing conditions that make either destructive or benevolent behavior likely. What are these processes and characteristics and how do they evolve?

Cultures and social systems influence not only group behavior but also shape individual psychology. Until not long ago, children were seen in many Western cultures as inherently willful. It was thought that to become good people, their will must be broken early, using severe punishment to do so. Such practices enhance the potential for both individual and group violence.

I will briefly discuss role of psychological science in a few specific domains of "good and evil": child rearing; the origins of genocide; and healing and reconciliation.

RAISING CARING, NOT VIOLENT, CHILDREN

On the basis of my own research on child rearing and the research of many others, and my own experiences with the application of research, I believe that we know a great deal about raising caring and nonaggressive children. Affection and nurturance that help fulfill a child's important needs; guidance that is both firm and responsive to the child, democratic and nonpunitive, based on values that are explained to children; and leading children to actually engage in behavior that benefits others are among the important elements.

So are positive peer relations. In our recent work in evaluating children's perception of their lives in school, from second grade to high school, we found, as have others, that even in good schools some children are the object of negative behavior, of bullying by others. Other children are excluded. Both groups report that they experience fewer positive emotions and more negative emotions in school. Bystanders, peers and teachers mostly remain passive. When they act, children who receive some protection feel better. So do the active bystanders themselves.

Psychologists ought to move, at this point, from piecemeal studies to holistic interventions, carefully evaluated, that aim to foster the development of caring, helpful and nonaggressive children. Doing so requires working not only with children but also with adults, since it is adults who have to provide affection, nurturance and guidance.

Intervention can center on creating caring schools, with communities that include every child and promote positive peer relations and constructive bystandership. Such intervention would help children who are badly treated and disconnected from people at home, and protect children in school. It may even stop such horrors as school shootings. Schools can also call on parents as allies, provide training, and help parents create a supportive community that fosters positive socialization.

An important point for me is that "intervention" is an essential aspect of the work of psychological science. Intervention aims to create a better world. But it is also a means of essential new learning. Only by combining the influences explored, usually individually, in controlled research, can we learn whether the whole is what we expect from a combination of the parts, whether the combination of influences usually required to create real change in the world actually does so. Our observation and experience in the course of such interventions—and careful evaluation with controls—can confirm old knowledge, but is almost certain to also give rise to new knowledge.

ORIGINS OF GENOCIDE AND OTHER GROUP VIOLENCE

I have studied the origins of genocide and other group violence for a long time. Psychologists, who with some exceptions have just begun paying attention to this realm, have a great deal to do. Their research has to extend beyond the laboratory. The data we need include economic and political conditions in a society; a history of relationships between groups such as conflict and enmity; characteristics of cultures—such as devaluation of another group, strong respect for authority, past woundedness and the absence of pluralism; the actions of leaders; the evolution of increasing harmdoing; and the behavior (passivity versus action) of bystanders. All of these have important roles (Staub, 1989; 1999).

It is essential to understand the characteristics and psychological processes of individuals and groups: Turning to a group for identity; scapegoating; ideologies or visions of life that iden-

tify enemies; changes in individuals and in group processes in the course of the evolution of increasing harmdoing; the psychology of leaders; and reasons for the passivity of internal and external bystanders. These are the proximal influences leading to violence.

Just as important is the issue of prevention. Understanding origins points to avenues for prevention. Some of these origins are not traditionally in the realm of psychology, but ought to be. For example, the passivity of nations encourages perpetrators. But such passivity has psychological elements, for example, the way leaders combine values and "interests" in decision making. Or the way leaders of genocidal groups make decisions. It is often assumed, by political scientists and sociologists, that such leaders act to enhance their own power and influence. But I strongly believe that they are impacted by social conditions and culture, as are other members of their group. Their actions are the results of complex psychological processes that arise under violence-generating conditions. We must understand these to ultimately deal with them in preventive ways.

HEALING AND RECONCILIATION

My work in Rwanda, in collaboration with Laurie Anne Pearlman, Alexandra Gubin and Athanase Hagengimana, has focused on helping people heal and reconcile in the aftermath of genocide, as a way of preventing renewed violence there (for early partial reports, see Staub 2000; Staub and Pearlman, in press).

Without healing, people so victimized will feel extremely vulnerable and see the world as dangerous. They may engage in violence, believing that they need to defend themselves, but in the process become perpetrators (Staub, 1998). Healing by them is essential. So is healing by perpetrators. Past victimization and other traumatic events are among the influences that contribute to perperation. In addition, perpetrators of mass violence are wounded by their own horrible actions. Perpetrator and victims groups, or two groups that have inflicted violence on each other, both need to heal if they are to overcome hostility, reconcile, and stop a continuing cycle of violence.

In Rwanda we trained people who worked for organizations that work with groups in the community. We talked to them and with them about the origins of genocide, about basic human needs—the frustration of which contributes to genocide and which are deeply frustrated in survivors of a genocide, about the traumatic effects of genocide on people, and about avenues to healing. We had them talk to each other in small groups about their painful experiences during the genocide.

Afterwards, some of the people we trained worked with groups in the community. In both training and application, Hutus and Tutsis participated together. The people in these community groups reported fewer trauma symptoms after this intervention and a more positive orientation to people in the other ethnic group. These changes occurred both over time and in comparison to changes in people who participated in groups led by facilitators we did not train, or were in control groups that received no treatment.

Doing such work is difficult and demanding, but highly rewarding. Working on the prevention of group violence is a field with newly emerging theories, limited experience, and little research. Psychological scientists are much needed to contribute to our knowledge, as well as to actually reduce evil and promote goodness.

REFERENCES

Staub, E. (1989). The roots of evil: The origins of genocide and other group violence. New York: Cambridge University Press.

Staub, E. (1998). Breaking the cycle of genocidal violence: Healing and reconciliation. In J. Harvey (ed.). Perspectives on loss: A sourcebook. Philadelphia: Taylor and Francis.

Staub, E. (1999). The origins and prevention of genocide, mass killing, and other collective violence. Peace and Conflict: Journal of Peace Psychology, 5(4), 303–336.

Staub, E. (2000). Genocide and mass killing: Origins, prevention, healing, and reconciliation. Political Psychology, 21(2), 367–382.

Staub, E., & Pearlman, L.A. (In press). Healing, reconciliation and forgiving after genocide and other collective violence. Forgiveness and Reconciliation, Radnor, PA. Templeton Foundation Press.

ERVIN STAUB is Professor of Psychology at the University of Massachusetts. He is President of the International Society for Political Psychology. His books include Positive Social Behavior and Morality *Vol 1, 1978; Vol 2, 1979, Academic Press, and* The Roots of Evil. *He is currently working on* A Brighter Future: Raising Caring and Nonviolent Children.

From *APS Observer*, May/June 2001, pp. 32-33. © 2001 by the American Psychological Society. Reprinted by permission.

EDITOR'S NOTE

Exploring a Controversy

George W. Albee

University of Vermont and University of South Florida

When the American Psychological Association (APA) Board of Directors asked me to serve as the editor of the *American Psychologist* for this special issue, I agreed in spite of being largely unfamiliar with the issues and events that apparently so strongly inflamed the passions of the participants and others. I was told that the editor-in-chief, the regular editor, and the special issue guest editor could not be the overall editor of this issue because they were all involved in the events to be discussed. Perhaps I was chosen by the board because I am 80 and I do not own a computer. Because of the latter fact, I was not part of the extensive e-mail discussions in May of 2001. Broadly defined, this special issue is about the opportunities and challenges that exist when scientists and policymakers (and the media) interact.

I have a long history of involvement in APA affairs. I worked in the APA Central Office from 1951 to 1953, when the Association was small and the Central Office was housed on the third floor (non-air-conditioned walk-up) of the old American Association for the Advancement of Science (AAAS) building. Later, I was APA president in 1969–1970, when major crises involving the demands of Black psychologists and women psychologists threatened to disrupt the established ways. I negotiated with both groups and helped find compromises all could live with.

My duties as editor have been quite simple and straightforward. I have read all the articles, made modest suggestions for changes in the interest of clarity or tone, made the final determination of the order in which the articles appear, and written this introductory piece. The major responsibility for initiating this special issue and making the initial invitations to potential contributors of regular articles was handled by the guest coeditors Nora S. Newcombe and Richard McCarty. Contributors initially received a manuscript copy of the Lilienfeld (2002, this issue) article with their invitation, but they were invited to focus broadly on the interface between scientists and policymakers. During the final revision process, contributors also received a manuscript copy of the Garrison and Kobor (2002, this issue) article. Finally, I invited a couple of individuals to comment on specific aspects of the controversy.

The integrity of psychological science is based on the academic freedom to explore fundamental questions about the nature of human behavior, thoughts, feelings, and social processes. Certain standards for the conduct of scientific inquiry must be adhered to, and the resulting report prepared for potential publication must go through strict editorial review by peers for the evaluation of methodology, analysis, and interpretation of findings. Along with academic freedom of inquiry goes the academic responsibility to present one's results clearly, drawing out the implications and noting cautions about what cannot be concluded. The latter is particularly important when the findings are sensitive, controversial, or potentially inflammatory.

Academic freedom is fundamental for science and scholarship. Political and economic forces often try to influence scientific findings and scholarly speculations to make them conform to conventional beliefs and practices. Historically, in America, the tenure system has evolved whereby one's faculty peers across several disciplines make recommendations about retention, promotion, and tenure. Violation of such peer evaluation and recommendations may subject an educational institution to widely noted censure. In the 1950s, the Regents of the University of California, Berkeley, demanded that all faculty members sign a loyalty oath swearing that they were not Communists. The resulting opposition to the oath, with refusal to sign, included distinguished psychologists E. C. Tolman and Nevitt Sanford. The APA was the first national society to urge that its members not apply for positions at Berkeley. Soon, the APA was joined by dozens of other academic–scientific disciplines, and, after great turmoil, the university dropped the requirement that the oath be signed.

Psychological science collectively should make a difference. That is, the results of the collected body of psychological research should be used to benefit individuals and society. This is part of the process that George Miller described as "giving psychology away." To do this, organized psychology has moved into activities often referred to as *media relations* and *government relations.* Movement into such activities is a normal development in the maturing of a discipline (and an association). The APA became more involved with the media in the early 1950s (I describe this in more detail below). The APA involvement in public policy formation came later, with the so-called starting date varying from the early 1960s, according to some authors, to the early 1980s, according to others.

Involvement in media relations and involvement in government relations, however, are strikingly different arenas of activities from those most psychologists are familiar with. These arenas have audiences, purposes, goals, and common practices different from those of scholarly research and publishing. Thus, both individual psychologists and the APA as an organization must adapt to the differing environment. The challenge, in many ways, is finding the right balance between working effectively in a new arena and operating in a manner consistent with the basic procedures and values of one's own discipline. Perhaps, more importantly, it is critical to keep the three worlds partially separate, so that assumptions and common practices from the media and political worlds do not inappropriately affect the academic world. As psychologists, we, of course, hope that our scientific approach and logic will influence the media and political worlds because it is for that reason that organized psychology became involved in such activities.

It is clear conceptually what the APA wishes to do on the media front and the public policy front—provide the best scientific information possible to the public and policymakers so that the nation has a psychologically informed population and federal policies that are based on the most solid research possible. However, the challenge is doing this through the media and public policy lenses—lenses that are very different from that of the research community. This is where the core of the current controversy lies. This special issue makes an archival record of an important set of problems and controversies that will be studied over time and that will lead to constructive changes in ways psychology responds to future crisis.

Psychologists would all agree that the news media, the public, and politicians must become better informed about psychological science, about its scientific methods, about the importance of open discussion, and about the self-correcting nature of carefully peer reviewed scholarly publications. Psychologists are also more aware today than ever before of the hunger of the media for emotional and controversial issues that will attract the maximum number of listeners, viewers, and readers. The same desire for the controversial is true of politics, where appeals to emotions appear to be valued equally with logic and data.

In 1953, the APA hired an experienced science writer, Michael Amrine, to work half time as an in-house science writer and media relations contact. He stayed on for many years. Amrine had written a science column for the North American Newspaper Alliance, had been editor of the *Bulletin of the Atomic Scientists,* had with scientists including Albert Einstein and Leo Szilard written explanatory pamphlets for the public, and was friendly with Oppenheimer, Fermi, and others. He ran the first APA newsroom at the 1953 convention. Over the years,

he built trusting relationships with the principal science writers of the time. In those days, half a century ago, most science reporting was in newspapers and newsmagazines.

With the growth of television news and the tightening of newspaper budgets, specially qualified science writers largely disappeared for a while, although there has been a reemergence in the 1990s. As fierce competition for viewers (and advertising revenue) has developed, more sensational stories interpreting science findings have replaced thoughtful and balanced reports in some (often highly visible) media outlets. With the proliferation of new types of news media, including especially the 24-hour video news programs, the supermarket weeklies, and shock radio, there is intense competition for readers and viewers. The more readers or viewers, the greater the advertising revenues. So, successful articles and programs are those that maximize emotional issues, celebrities' sexual peccadilloes, and controversy involving religion and morality. Although it is interesting and important to point out the logical errors and distortions of pop media talkers and writers, it is most unlikely that they will change the formula that makes them so highly successful.

There are still war correspondents who reveal in their questions and writing a sophisticated knowledge of weaponry and military matters, and there are other reporters sophisticated in specific areas of the law. However, by the mid-1970s, science reporters were rarely in evidence, particularly in psychology. Since that time, there has been steady but slow improvement. Several universities have established graduate programs in science writing. The AAAS has developed a Media Fellows program that provides scientists with an opportunity to gain firsthand experience in an array of media outlets. National Public Radio now has several well-trained science writers on its staff, and most major newspaper outlets, such as *The New York Times, The Washington Post, USA Today,* and *The Los Angeles Times,* among others, have specialized science writers on staff, some of whom specialize in writing on psychological topics. During the fall of 2001, the United Press International added seven additional science writers. In addition, *Science News* has on its staff a full-time psychologist–reporter, Bruce Bower, and *The New York Times* features a science section every Tuesday that often includes Jane Brody's informed articles on health and mental health.

As science and scientific findings become more important in affecting major national and political policy decisions, there is increasing political pressure on science and scientists. Examples are the issues of cloning, global warming, decisions about air quality, water pollution and deforestation, and genetic engineering of crops and animals. The list is extensive, and all its items are based on scientific findings whose implications are enormous. The rapid changes in human sexual behavior from procreational to recreational, for example, based on scientific findings that have led to effective contraception, have resulted in profound societal disagreements about what is acceptable sexual behavior.

Some observers suggest that the social and behavioral sciences are more subject to popular criticism and misunderstanding than other fields of science. This may not be true. The field of biology has been a major target of attacks by conservatives because of its strong reliance on a foundation of evolution. A recent 2001 Public Broadcasting System (PBS) series of evolution showed the current passionate attacks on the teaching of evolution in the public schools and the frequent demands for presenting the creation story as described in Genesis along with, or instead of, the theory of evolution. Sometimes, this conflict leads to bitter campaigns for election or defeat of members of school boards depending on their view on life's (and human) origins. The PBS series reported that currently, 2,000 public school boards across the nation, along with a large majority of private religious schools, insist on equal time in presenting the creation story (with some even forbidding the "evolution story").

An important point, it seems to me, is that science ultimately wins out. Scientific findings may elicit passionate opposition, censorship, and official (religious and secular) condemnation, but scientific findings that are valid and reliable persist, whereas their critics do not. It took 500 years for the Catholic Church to publicly admit that it was wrong in its opposition to Galileo's findings. Contrariwise, a political insistence on invalid, supposedly scientific conclusions does not survive empirical scientific ongoing evaluation. Lysenko's genetics, supported by powerful political authority, were doomed from the start.

I personally have experienced federal censorship of academic inquiry. For many years, the Vermont Conference on Primary Prevention of Psychopathology planned and hosted conferences on factors thought to be involved in producing stresses and other variables leading to emotional disorders in groups at risk. The papers presented were edited and appeared as books. Topics like family stress, child foster care, school programs, neighborhood changes, genetic and prenatal problems, the stresses of aging, delinquency, gender inequality, and marital disruption were covered in detail. Many of the conferences received financial support from the National Institute of Mental Health (NIMH). Yet, when I called to ask about support for a planned conference on the stresses of heterosexism and homophobia, my NIMH contact laughed at length and told me to forget about receiving any federal funding. He named several members of Congress who would block any such funding because it would be seen, incorrectly, as supporting homosexuality. Legislators themselves have a range of religions and moral views, and they are sensitive to the views of important blocks of constituents. They obviously do not always support research on sensitive topics or the publication of scientific findings that contradict conventional beliefs.

It upsets me when contemporary federal scientists remain silent, for example, when their leader, a powerful scientist–administrator, states as proven, "Mental illness can be cured with drugs," or says, "We now know that schizophrenia is genetic," or "All mental illnesses are diseases of the brain." Why is there no outcry about these politically correct scientific inaccuracies? It is sometimes dangerous to speak truth to power. How can psychology, as a discipline, work to see that true facts are ultimately made publicly available?

Everyone agrees that, as psychologists, we must do a better job of educating the public about science and scientific

methods, as well as about the ways science corrects itself. However, it is probably the case that such activities will not totally solve the problem. To suggest that psychology (or biology) must educate the media or politicians on scientific methods, as though such information would change their readiness to attack views that contradict deeply held attitudes, is not realistic.

There is also another way for psychology to educate the public. That is through the traditional educational process. Nearly everyone going to college takes at least one course in psychology. This is usually a broad survey of the field. When I took Introductory Psychology more than 60 years ago, the first half-dozen classes were devoted to establishing psychology's credentials as a science. There was detailed consideration of scientific methods, including hypothesis testing and the logic of the experiment. The concepts of reliability and validity were stressed. Today's introductory course has much more content to cover, but instructors should be encouraged and prepared to emphasize the discipline of scientific research and to be sure undergraduates understand the logic and power of scientific methods.

More and more, psychology is being offered as an elective in the high schools, and high school teachers of psychology are being recognized, included, and supported by the APA. Here is another large and significant path to reaching young people with solid information about scientific psychology and its methods. Efforts within the APA Education Directorate, as well as portions of the Year 2002 Presidential Initiative to develop an APA high school psychology textbook, should prove useful in this area.

Graduate students in scientific fields of psychology and applied areas like clinical psychology (as well as in social work and related disciplines) should receive thorough education in scientific logic and methods. However, it may be worth noting that the defense of the peer review system in the current controversy was made by people with solid scientific credentials who were not listened to or believed. Though the best preparation in science is highly desirable, there are sometimes circumstances that challenge reason and weaken resolve. The present controversy should provide a warning and may well provide material for further education of tomorrow's leaders in psychology.

Long ago, as a student, I learned that science insists on framing its hypotheses as falsifiable sentences and then tries mightily to falsify them. Science then holds onto the statements it cannot disprove, even if they run counter to widespread beliefs. However, nothing is ever accepted as certain; the null hypothesis must always be rejected at some level of certainty less than absolute. Scientists must defend the hypotheses they hold onto from the criticism and rejection of those who find them unacceptable for political, religious, or economic reasons.

All of this sounds good in the abstract. In the real world, though, where religious or political or economic power may control one's funding, one's job security, even one's personal freedom and the well-being of one's field, one's choices may not be easy. Scientists are fundamentally correct in saying they must not reject or deny their findings because they are not acceptable to groups with enormous power. Yet it is also true that one may sometimes retreat to fight another day. Eventually, however, scientists believe scientific truth endures and false knowledge does not.

With the appearance of this special issue, the published exploration of these events in the pages of the *American Psychologist* is concluded. As promised, moderated discussion of new ideas and perspectives will appear at the *American Psychologist* Web site, beginning this month. The URL is http://journals.apa.org/comments. Interested parties should offer reasoned comments no more than once a month per person.

It is my expectation that this controversy, like earlier controversies in psychology, will have a positive effect on focusing the attention of psychologists on critically important issues. I believe there will be major efforts at better informing the public about science. Also, there will be increased sensitivity to the power of and anger from exploiters of controversial issues.

References

Garrison, E. G., & Kobor, P. C. (2002). Weathering a political storm: A contextual perspective on a psychological research controversy. *American Psychologist, 57,* 165–175.

Lilienfeld, S. O. (2002). When worlds collide: Social science, politics, and the Rind et al. (1998) child sexual abuse meta-analysis. *American Psychologist, 57,* 176–188.

George W. Albee is Professor Emeritus of the Department of Psychology at the University of Vermont and is currently also Courtesy Professor with the Department of Mental Health Law and Policy, Louis de la Parte Florida Mental Health Institute, at the University of South Florida.

Correspondence concerning this article should be addressed to George W. Albee, 7157 Longboat Drive North, Longboat Key, FL 34228.

From *American Psychologist,* March 2002, pp. 161-164. © 2002 by the American Psychological Association. Reprinted by permission.

UNIT 2
Biological Bases of Behavior

Unit Selections

4. **The Tangled Skeins of Nature and Nurture in Human Evolution**, Paul R. Ehrlich
5. **Altered States of Consciousness**, Susan Greenfield
6. **Brain-Based Learning**, Ruth Palombo Weiss

Key Points to Consider

- What do you think contributes most to our psychological make-up and behaviors: the influence of the environment, the expression of genes, or the functioning of the nervous system? Do you believe that perhaps some combination of these factors accounts for psychological characteristics and behaviors? How are these contributors to behavior studied?

- How do we study the human brain? What parts of the brain control various aspects of our behavior? That is, how does the brain influence human behavior and psychological characteristics? If an individual experiences brain damage, can other parts of the brain take over functions controlled by the damaged area? Explain.

- Describe the brain's role in promoting attention, understanding patterns and emotions, facilitating memory and recall, and enhancing motivation.

 **Links: www.dushkin.com/online/**
These sites are annotated in the World Wide Web pages.

Adolescence: Changes and Continuity
   http://www.personal.psu.edu/faculty/n/x/nxd10/adolesce.htm
Division of Hereditary Diseases and Family Studies, Indiana University School of Medicine
   http://www.iupui.edu/~medgen/division/hereditary/hereditary_diseases.html
Institute for Behavioral Genetics
   http://ibgwww.colorado.edu/index.html
Serendip
   http://serendip.brynmawr.edu/serendip/

As a child, Angelina vowed she did not want to turn out like either of her parents. Angelina's mother was very passive and acquiescent about her father's drinking. When Dad was drunk, Mom always called his boss to report that Dad was "sick" and then acted as if there was nothing wrong at home. Angelina's childhood was a nightmare. Her father's behavior was erratic and unpredictable. If he drank just a little bit, most often he was happy. If he drank a lot, which was usually the case, he frequently became belligerent.

Despite vowing not to become her father, as an adult Angelina found herself in the alcohol rehabilitation unit of a large hospital. Angelina's employer could no longer tolerate her on-the-job mistakes nor her unexplained absences from work, and he therefore referred her to the clinic for help. As Angelina pondered her fate, she wondered whether her genes preordained her to follow in her father's inebriated footsteps or whether the stress of her childhood had brought her to this point in her life. After all, being the child of an alcoholic is not easy.

Psychologists also are concerned with discovering the causes of human behavior. Once the cause is known, treatments for problematic behaviors can be developed. In fact, certain behaviors might even be prevented when the cause is known. But for Angelina, prevention was too late.

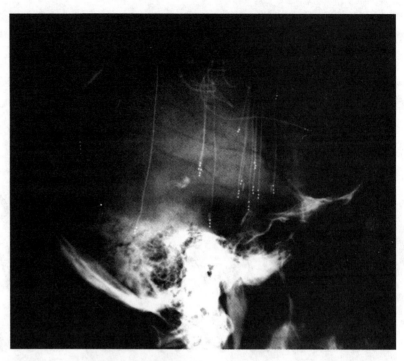

One of the paths to understanding humans is to understand the biological underpinnings of their behavior. Genes and chromosomes, the body's chemistry (as found in hormones, neurotransmitters, and enzymes), and the nervous system (comprising the brain, spinal cord, nerve cells, and other parts) are all implicated in human behavior. All represent the biological aspects of behavior and ought, therefore, to be worthy of study by psychologists.

Physiological psychologists and psychobiologists are often the ones who examine the role of biology in behavior. The neuroscientist is especially interested in brain functioning; the psychopharmacologist is interested in the effects of various pharmacological agents or psychoactive drugs on behavior.

These psychologists often utilize one of three techniques to understand the biology-behavior connection. Animal studies involving manipulation, stimulation, or destruction of certain parts of the brain offer one method of study. There is also a second available technique that includes the examination of unfortunate individuals whose brains are malfunctioning at birth or are damaged later by accidents or disease.

We can also use animal models to understand genetics; with animal models we can control reproduction as well as manipulate and develop various strains of animals if necessary. Such tactics with humans would be considered extremely unethical. However,

by studying an individual's behavior in comparison to both natural and adoptive parents or by studying identical twins reared together or apart, we can begin to understand the role of genetics versus environment in human behavior.

The articles in this unit are designed to familiarize you with the knowledge psychologists have gleaned by using these and other techniques to study physiological processes and other underlying mechanisms in human behavior. Each article should interest you and make you more curious about the role of biology in human activities.

The first article in this unit reviews almost all aspects of the biological bases of behavior. In "The Tangled Skeins of Nature and Nurture in Human Evolution," the author discusses the nature-versus-nurture debate, which questions whether genetics or the environment (in the form of learning) contribute to our psychological make-up. The author suggests that both nature and nurture are intricately intertwined to produce the characteristics of each individual.

The next article covers information about the central nervous system, another important biological aspect of human behavior. In "Altered States of Consciousness," author Susan Greenfield does a thorough job of examining the functioning of various parts of the brain. She details the neurochemistry and organization of this complex and important structure. Ruth Palombo Weiss, in the last article in this unit, "Brain-Based Learning," connects the relationship of the brain to various psychological phenomena that affect the ability to learn.

The Tangled Skeins of Nature and Nurture in Human Evolution

By Paul R. Ehrlich

Wᴴᴱɴ we think about our behavior as individuals, "Why?" is a question almost always on the tips of our tongues. Sometimes that question is about perceived similarities: why is almost everyone religious; why do we all seem to crave love; why do most of us like to eat meat? But our differences often seem equally or more fascinating: why did Sally get married although her sister Sue did not, why did they win and we lose, why is their nation poor and ours rich? What were the fates of our childhood friends? What kinds of careers did they have; did they marry; how many children did they have? Our everyday lives are filled with why's about differences and similarities in behavior, often unspoken, but always there. Why did one of my closest colleagues drink himself to death, whereas I, who love wine much more than he did, am managing to keep my liver in pretty good shape? Why, of two very bright applicants admitted to our department at Stanford University for graduate work, does one turn out pedestrian science and another have a spectacular career doing innovative research? Why are our natures often so different, and why are they so frequently the same?

The background needed to begin to answer all these *whys* lies within the domain of human biological and cultural evolution, in the gradual alterations in genetic and cultural information possessed by humanity. It's easy to think that evolution is just a process that sometime in the distant past produced the physical characteristics of our species but is now pretty much a matter of purely academic, and local school board, interest. Yet evolution is a powerful, ongoing force that not only has shaped the attributes and behaviors shared by all human beings but also has given every single individual a different nature.

A study of evolution does much more than show how we are connected to our roots or explain why people rule Earth—it explains why it would be wise to limit our intake of beef Wellington, stop judging people by their skin color, concern ourselves about global warming, and reconsider giving our children antibiotics at the first sign of a sore throat. Evolution also provides a framework for answering some of the most interesting questions about ourselves and our behavior.

When someone mentions evolution and behavior in the same breath, most people think immediately of the power of genes, parts of spiral-shaped molecules of a chemical called DNA. Small wonder, considering the marvelous advances in molecular genetics in recent decades. New subdisciplines such as evolutionary medicine and evolutionary psychology have arisen as scientists have come to recognize the importance of evolution in explaining contemporary human beings, the network of life that supports us, and our possible fates. And the mass media have been loaded with stories about real or imagined links between every conceivable sort of behavior and our genes.

Biological evolution—evolution that causes changes in our genetic endowment—has unquestionably helped shape human natures, including human behaviors, in many ways. But numerous commentators expect our genetic endowment to accomplish feats of which it is incapable. People don't have enough genes to program all the behaviors some evolutionary psychologists, for example, believe that genes control. Human beings have something on the order of 100,000 genes, and human brains have more than one *trillion* nerve cells, with about 100–1,000 trillion connections (synapses) between them. That's at least one *billion* synapses per gene, even if each and every gene did nothing but control the production of synapses (and it doesn't). Given that ratio, it would be quite a trick for genes typically to control more than the most general aspects of human behavior. Statements such as "Understanding the genetic roots of personality will help you 'find yourself' and relate better to others" are, at today's level of knowledge, frankly nonsensical.

The notion that we are slaves to our genes is often combined with reliance on the idea that all problems can be solved by dissecting them into ever smaller components—the sort of reductionist approach that has been successful in much of science but is sometimes totally unscientific. It's like the idea that knowing the color of every microscopic dot that makes up a picture of your mother can explain why you love her. Scientific problems have to be approached at the appropriate level of organization if there is to be a hope of solving them.

There are important "coevolutionary" interactions between culture and genetics. For example, our farming practices change our physical environment in ways that alter the evolution of our blood cells.

That combination of assumptions—that genes are destiny at a micro level and that reductionism leads to full understanding—is now yielding distorted views of human behavior. People think that coded into our DNA are "instructions" that control the details of individual and group behavior: that genetics dominates, heredity makes us what we are, and what we are is changeable only over many generations as the genetic endowment of human populations evolves. Such assertions presume, as I've just suggested, that evolution has produced a level of genetic control of human behavior that is against virtually all available evidence. For instance, ground squirrels have evolved a form of "altruistic" behavior—they often give an alarm call to warn a relative of approaching danger. Evidence does indicate that this behavior is rooted in their genes; indeed, it probably evolved because relatives have more identical genes than do unrelated individuals. But some would trace the "altruistic" behavior of a business executive sending a check to an agency helping famine victims in Africa, or of a devout German Lutheran aiding Jews during the Holocaust, to a genetic tendency as well. In this view, we act either to help relatives or in the expectation of reciprocity—in either case promoting the replication of "our" genes. But experimental evidence indicates that not all human altruistic behavior is self-seeking—that human beings, unlike squirrels, are not hereditarily programmed only to be selfish.

ANOTHER FALSE ASSUMPTION of hereditary programming lies behind the belief that evolution has resulted in human groups of different quality. Many people still claim (or secretly believe), for example, that blacks are less intelligent than whites and women less "logical" than men, even though those claims are groundless. Belief in genetic determinism has even led some observers to suggest a return to the bad old days of eugenics, of manipulating evolution to produce ostensibly more skilled people. Advocating programs for the biological "improvement of humanity"—which in the past has meant encouraging the breeding of supposedly naturally superior individuals—takes us back at least to the days of Plato, more than two millennia ago, and it involves a grasp of genetics little more sophisticated than his.

Uniquely in our species, changes in culture have been fully as important in producing our natures as have changes in the hereditary information passed on by our ancestors. Culture is the nongenetic information (socially transmitted behaviors, beliefs, institutions, arts, and so on) shared and exchanged among us. Indeed, our evolution since the invention of agriculture, about 10,000 years ago, has been overwhelmingly cultural because, as we shall see, cultural evolution can be much more rapid than genetic evolution. There is an unhappy predilection, especially in the United States, not only to overrate the effect of genetic evolution on our current behavior but also to underrate that of cultural evolution. The power of culture to shape human activities can be seen immediately in the diversity of languages around the world. Although, clearly, the ability to speak languages is a result of a great deal of genetic evolution, the specific languages we speak are just as clearly products of cultural evolution. Furthermore, genetic evolution and cultural evolution are not independent. There are important "coevolutionary" interactions between them. To take just one example, our farming practices (an aspect of our culture) change our physical environment in ways that alter the evolution of our blood cells.

Not only is the evolution of our collective nongenetic information critical to creating our natures, but also the rate of that evolution varies greatly among different aspects of human culture. That, in turn, has profound consequences for our behavior and our environments. A major contemporary human problem, for instance, is that the rate of cultural evolution in science and technology has been extraordinarily high in contrast with the snail's pace of change in the social attitudes and political institutions that might channel the uses of technology in more beneficial directions. No one knows exactly what sorts of societal effort might be required to substantially redress that imbalance in evolutionary rates, but it is clear to me that such an effort, if successful, could greatly brighten the human prospect.

Science has already given us pretty good clues about the reasons for the evolution of some aspects of our natures; many other aspects remain mysterious despite a small army of very bright people seeking reasons. Still others (such as why I ordered duck in the restaurant last night rather than lamb) may remain unanswerable—for human beings have a form of free will. But even to *think* reasonably about our natures and our prospects, some background in basic evolutionary theory is essential. If Grace is smarter than Pedro because of her genes, why did evolution provide her with "better" genes? If Pedro is actually smarter than Grace but has been incorrectly evaluated by an intelligence test designed for people of another culture, how did those cultural differences evolve? If I was able to choose the duck for dinner because I have free will, what exactly does that mean? How did I and other human beings evolve that capacity to make choices without being complete captives of our histories? Could I have exercised my free will to eat a cockroach curry had we been in a restaurant that served it (as some in Southeast Asia do)? Almost certainly not—the very idea nauseates me, probably because of an interaction between biological and cultural evolution.

Trying to separate nature and nurture is like trying to separate the contributions of length and width to the area of a rectangle, which at first seems easy. When you think about it, though, it proves impossible.

Every attribute of *every* organism is, of course, the product of an interaction between its genetic code and its environment. Yes, the number of heads an individual human being possesses is specified in the genes and is the same in a vast diversity of environments. And the language or languages a child speaks (but not her capacity to acquire language) is determined by her environment. But without the appropriate internal environment in the mother's body for fetal development, there would be no head (or infant) at all; and without genetically programmed physical structures in the larynx and in the developing brain, there would be no ca-

pacity to acquire and speak language. Beyond enabling us to make such statements in certain cases, however, the relative contributions of heredity and environment to various human attributes are difficult to specify. They clearly vary from attribute to attribute. So although it is informative to state that human nature is the product of genes interacting with environments (both internal and external), we usually can say little with precision about the processes that lead to interesting behaviors in adult human beings. We can't partition the responsibility for aggression, altruism, or charisma between DNA and upbringing. In many such cases, trying to separate the contributions of nature and nurture to an attribute is rather like trying to separate the contributions of length and width to the area of a rectangle, which at first glance also seems easy. When you think about it carefully, though, it proves impossible.

Diverse notions of inherited superiority or inferiority and of characteristic innate group behaviors have long pervaded human societies: beliefs about the divine right of kings; "natural" attributes that made some people good material for slaves or slave masters; innate superiority of light-skinned people over dark-skinned people; genetic tendencies of Jews to be moneylenders, of Christians to be sexually inhibited, and of Asians to be more hardworking than Hispanics; and so on. Consider the following quote from a recent book titled *Living With Our Genes*, which indicates the tone even among many scientists: "The emerging science of molecular biology has made startling discoveries that show beyond a doubt that genes are the single most important factor that distinguishes one person from another. We come in large part ready-made from the factory. We accept that we *look* like our parents and other blood relatives; we have a harder time with the idea we *act* like them."

In fact, the failure of many people to recognize the fundamental error in such statements (and those in other articles and books based on genetic determinism, such as Richard J. Herrnstein and Charles Murray's famous *The Bell Curve*) is itself an environmental phenomenon—a product of the cultural milieu in which many of us have grown up. Genes do not shout commands to us about our behavior. At the very most, they whisper suggestions, and the nature of those whispers is shaped by our internal environments (those within and between our cells) during early development and later, and usually also by the external environments in which we mature and find ourselves as adults.

How do scientists know that we are not simply genetically programmed automata? First, biological evolution has produced what is arguably the most astonishingly adaptable device that has ever existed—the human nervous system. It's a system that can use one organ, the brain, to plan a marriage or a murder, command muscles to control the flight of a thrown rock or a space shuttle, detect the difference between a 1945 Mouton and a 1961 Latour, learn Swahili or Spanish, and interpret a pattern of colored light on a flat television screen as a three-dimensional world containing real people. It tries to do whatever task the environment seems to demand, and it usually succeeds—and because many of those demands are novel, there is no way that the brain could be preprogrammed to deal with them, even if there were genes enough to do the programming. It would be incomprehensible for evolution to program such a system with a vast number of inherited rules that would reduce its flexibility, constraining it so that it could not deal with novel environments. It would seem equally inexplicable if evolution made some sub-groups of humanity less able than others to react appropriately to changing circumstances. Men and people with white skin have just as much need of being smart and flexible as do women and people with brown skin, and there is every reason to believe that evolution has made white-skinned males fully as capable as brown-skinned women.

A SECOND TYPE OF EVIDENCE that we're not controlled by in-nate programs is that normal infants taken from one society and reared in another inevitably acquire the behaviors (including language) and competences of the society in which they are reared. If different behaviors in different societies were largely genetically programmed, that could not happen. That culture dominates in creating intergroup differences is also indicated by the distribution of genetic differences among human beings. The vast majority (an estimated 85 percent) is not between "rac-es" or ethnic groups but *between individuals within groups*. Hu-man natures, again, are products of similar (but not identical) inherited endowments interacting with different physical and cultural environments.

Thus, the genetic "make-brain" program that interacts with the internal and external environments of a developing person doesn't produce a brain that can call forth only one type of, say, mating behavior—it produces a brain that can engage in any of a bewildering variety of behaviors, depending on cir-cumstances. We see the same principle elsewhere in our de-velopment; for instance, human legs are not genetically programmed to move only at a certain speed. The inherited "make-legs" program normally produces legs that, fortu-nately, can operate at a wide range of speeds, depending on circumstances. Variation among individuals in the genes they received from their parents produces some differences in that range (in any normal terrestrial environment, I never could have been a four-minute miler—on the moon, maybe). Envi-ronmental variation produces some differences, too (walking a lot every day and years of acclimatization enable me to climb relatively high mountains that are beyond the range of some younger people who are less acclimatized). But no amount of training will permit any human being to leap tall buildings in a single bound, or even in two.

Similarly, inherited differences among individuals can influ-ence the range of mental abilities we possess. Struggle as I might, my math skills will never approach those of many pro-fessional mathematicians, and I suspect that part of my inca-pacity can be traced to my genes. But environmental variation can shape those abilities as well. I'm also lousy at learning lan-guages (that may be related to my math incompetence). Yet when I found myself in a professional environment in which it

would have been helpful to converse in Spanish, persistent study allowed me to speak and comprehend a fair amount of the language. But there are no genetic instructions or environmental circumstances that will allow the development of a human brain that can do a million mathematical calculations in a second. That is a talent reserved for computers, which were, of course, designed by human minds.

Are there any behavioral instructions we can be sure are en-graved in human DNA? If there are, at least one should be the urge to have as many children as possible. We should have a powerful hereditary tendency to maximize our genetic contri-butions to future generations, for that's the tendency that makes evolution work. Yet almost no human beings strictly obey this genetic "imperative"; environmental factors, espe-cially cultural factors, have largely overridden it. Most people choose to make smaller genetic contributions to the future— that is, have fewer children—than they could, thus figura-tively thwarting the supposed maximum reproduction "ambi-tions" of their genes.

If genes run us as machines for reproducing themselves, how come they let us practice contraception? We are the only ani-mals that deliberately and with planning enjoy sex while avoiding reproduction. We can and do "outwit" our genes— which are, of course, witless. In this respect, our hereditary en-dowment made a big mistake by "choosing" to encourage human reproduction not through a desire for lots of children but through a desire for lots of sexual pleasure.

There are environments (sociocultural environments in this case) in which near-maximal human reproduction has appar-ently occurred. For example, the Hutterites, members of a Men-nonite sect living on the plains of western North America, are famous for their high rate of population growth. Around 1950, Hutterite women over the age of 45 had borne an average of 10 children, and Hutterite population growth rates exceeded 4 per-cent per year. Interestingly, however, when social conditions changed, the growth rate dropped from an estimated 4.12 per-cent per year to 2.91 percent. Cultural evolution won out against those selfish little genes.

Against this background of how human beings can over-whelm genetic evolution with cultural evolution, it becomes ev-ident that great care must be taken in extrapolating the behavior of other animals to that of human beings. One cannot assume, for example, that because marauding chimpanzees of one group sometimes kill members of another group, selection has pro-grammed warfare into the genes of human beings (or, for that matter, of chimps). And although both chimp and human ge-netic endowments clearly can interact with certain environ-ments to produce individuals capable of mayhem, they just as clearly can interact with other environments to produce individ-uals who are not aggressive. Observing the behavior of nonhuman mammals—their mating habits, modes of communication, inter-group conflicts, and so on—can reveal patterns we display in common with them, but those patterns certainly will not tell us which complex behaviors are "programmed" inalterably into our genes. Genetic instructions are of great importance to our natures, but they are not destiny.

THERE are obviously limits to how much the environment ordinarily can affect individual characteristics. No known environment, for example, could have allowed me to mature with normal color vision: like about 8 percent of males, I'm colorblind—the result of a gene inherited from my mother. But the influence on many human attributes of even small environmental differences should not be underestimated. Consider the classic story of the "Siamese twins" Chang and Eng. Born in Siam (now Thailand) on May 11, 1811, these identical twins were joined at the base of their chests by an arm-like tube that in adulthood was five or six inches long and about eight inches in circumference. They eventually ended up in the United States, became prosperous as sideshow attractions, and married sisters. Chang and Eng farmed for a time, owned slaves before the Civil War, and produced both many children and vast speculation about the circumstances of their copulations. They were examined many times by surgeons who, working before the age of X-rays, concluded that it would be dangerous to try to separate them.

From our perspective, the most interesting thing about the twins is their different natures. Chang was slightly shorter than Eng, but he dominated his brother and was quick-tempered. Eng, in contrast, was agreeable and usually submissive. Although the two were very similar in many respects, in childhood their differences once flared into a fistfight, and as adults on one occasion they disagreed enough politically to vote for opposing candidates. More seriously, Chang drank to excess and Eng did not. Partly as a result of Chang's drinking, they developed considerable ill will that made it difficult for them to live together—they were constantly quarreling. In old age, Chang became hard of hearing in both ears, but Eng became deaf only in the ear closer to Chang. In the summer of 1870, Chang suffered a stroke, which left Eng unaffected directly but bound him physically to an invalid. On January 17, 1874, Chang died in the night. When Eng discovered his twin's death, he (although perfectly healthy) became terrified, lapsed into a stupor, and died two hours later, before a scheduled surgical attempt was to have been made to separate the two. An autopsy showed that the surgeons had been correct—the twins probably would not have survived an attempt to separate them.

Chang and Eng demonstrated conclusively that genetic identity does not necessarily produce identical natures, even when combined with substantially identical environments—in this case only inches apart, with no sign that their mother or others treated them differently as they grew up. Quite subtle environmental differences, perhaps initiated by different positions in the womb, can sometimes produce substantially different behavioral outcomes in twins. In this case, in which the dominant feature of each twin's environment clearly was the other twin, the slightest original difference could have led to an escalating reinforcement of differences.

The nature-nurture dichotomy, which has dominated discussions of behavior for decades, is largely a false one—all characteristics of all organisms are truly a result of the simultaneous influences of both. Genes do not dictate destiny in most cases (exceptions include those serious genetic defects that at present cannot be remedied), but they often define a range of possibilities in a given environment. The genetic endowment of a chimpanzee, even if raised as the child of a Harvard professor, would prevent it from learning to discuss philosophy or solve differential equations. Similarly, environments define a range of developmental possibilities for a given set of genes. There is no genetic endowment that a child could get from Mom and Pop that would permit the youngster to grow into an Einstein (or a Mozart or a García Marquez—or even a Hitler) as a member of an isolated rain-forest tribe without a written language.

Attempts to dichotomize nature and nurture almost always end in failure. Although I've written about how the expression of genes depends on the environment in which the genes are expressed, another way of looking at the development of a person's nature would have been to examine the contributions of three factors: genes, environment, *and* gene-environment interactions. It is very difficult to tease out these contributions, however. Even under experimental conditions, where it is possible to say something mathematically about the comparative contributions of heredity and environment, it can't be done completely because there is an "interaction term." That term cannot be decomposed into nature or nurture because the effect of each depends on the contribution of the other.

To construct an artificial example, suppose there were a gene combination that controlled the level of a hormone that tended to make boys aggressive. Further, suppose that watching television also tended to make boys aggressive. Changing an individual's complement of genes so that the hormone level was doubled and also doubling the television-watching time might, then, quadruple some measure of aggressiveness. Or, instead, the two factors might interact synergistically and cause the aggression level to increase fivefold (perhaps television is an especially potent factor when the viewer has a high hormone level). Or the interaction might go the other way—television time might increase aggression only in those with a relatively low hormone level, and doubling both the hormone level and the television time might result in only a doubling of aggression. Or perhaps changing the average *content* of television programming might actually reduce the level of aggressiveness so that even with hormone level and television time doubled, aggressiveness would decline. Finally, suppose that, in addition, these relationships depended in part on whether or not a boy had attentive and loving parents who provided alternative interpretations of what was seen on television. In such situations, there is no way to make a precise statement about the contributions of "the environment" (television, in this case) to aggressiveness. This example reflects the complexity of relationships that has been demonstrated in detailed studies of the ways in which hormones such as testosterone interact with environmental factors to produce aggressive behavior.

The best one can ordinarily do in measuring what genes contribute to attributes (such as aggressiveness, height, or I.Q. test score) is calculate a statistical measure known as heritability. That statistic tells how much, on average, offspring resemble their parents in a particular attribute *in a particular set of environments*. Heritability, however, is a measure that is difficult to make and difficult to interpret. That is especially true in determining heritability of human traits, where it would be unethical or impossible to create the conditions required to estimate it, such as random mating within a population.

Despite these difficulties, geneticists are gradually sorting out some of the ways genes and environments can interact in experimental environments and how different parts of the hereditary endowment interact in making their contribution to the development of the individual. One of the key things they are learning is that it is often very difficult for genetic evolution to change just one characteristic. That's worth thinking about the next time someone tells you that human beings have been programmed by natural selection to be violent, greedy, altruistic, or promiscuous, to prefer certain facial features, or to show male (or white) dominance. At best, such programming is difficult; often it is impossible.

T ODAY'S DEBATES about human nature—about such things as the origins of ethics; the meanings of consciousness, self, and reality; whether we're driven by emotion or reason; the relationship between thought and language; whether men are naturally aggressive and women peaceful; and the role of sex in society— trace far back in Western thought. They have engaged thinkers from the pre-Socratic philosophers, Plato, and Aristotle to René Descartes, John Locke, Georg Wilhelm Friedrich Hegel, Charles Sanders Peirce, and Ludwig Wittgenstein, just to mention a tiny handful of those in the Western tradition alone.

What exactly *is* this human nature we hear so much about? The prevailing notion is that it is a single, fixed, inherited attribute—a common property of all members of our species. That notion is implicit in the universal use of the term in singular form. And I think that singular usage leads us astray. To give a rough analogy, *human nature* is to *human natures* as *canyon is to canyons*. We would never discuss the "characteristics of canyon." Although all canyons share certain attributes, we always use the plural form of the word when talking about them in general. That's because even though all canyons have more characteristics in common with one another than any canyon has with a painting or a snowflake, we automatically recognize the vast diversity subsumed within the category *canyons*. As with *canyon*, at times there is reason to speak of human nature in the singular, as I sometimes do when referring to what we all share—for example, the ability to communicate in language, the possession of a rich culture, and the capacity to develop complex ethical systems. After all, there are at least *near*-universal aspects of our natures and our genomes (genetic endowments), and the variation within them is small in relation to the differences between, say, human and chimpanzee natures or human and chimpanzee genomes.

I argue, contrary to the prevailing notion, that human nature is not the same from society to society or from individual to individual, nor is it a permanent attribute of *Homo sapiens*. Human natures are the behaviors, beliefs, and attitudes of *Homo sapiens* and the changing physical structures that govern, support, and participate in our unique mental functioning. There are many such natures, a diversity generated especially by the overwhelming power of cultural evolution— the super-rapid kind of evolution in which our species excels. The human nature of a Chinese man living in Beijing is somewhat different from the human nature of a Parisian woman; the nature of a great musician is not identical with that of a fine soccer player; the nature of an inner-city gang member is different from the nature of a child being raised in an affluent suburb; the nature of someone who habitually votes Republican is different from that of her identical twin who is a Democrat; and my human nature, despite many shared features, is different from yours.

The differences among individuals and groups of human beings are, as already noted, of a magnitude that dwarf the differences within any other nondomesticated animal species. Using the plural, *human natures*, puts a needed emphasis on that critical diversity, which, after all, is very often what we want to understand. We want to know why two genetically identical individuals would have different political views; why Jeff is so loud and Barbara is so quiet; why people in the same society have different sexual habits and different ethical standards; why some past civilizations flourished for many centuries and others perished; why Germany was a combatant in two horrendous 20th-century wars and Switzerland was not; why Julia is concerned about global warming and Juliette doesn't know what it is. There is no single human nature, any more than there is a single human genome, although there are features common to all human natures and all human genomes.

But if we are trying to understand anything about human society, past or present, or about individual actions, we must go to a finer level of analysis and consider human nature*s* as actually formed in the world. It is intellectually lazy and incorrect to "explain" the relatively poor school performance of blacks in the United States, or the persistence of warfare, or marital discord, by claiming that nonwhites are "naturally" inferior, that all people are "naturally" aggressive, or that men are "naturally" promiscuous. Intellectual performance, aggression, and promiscuity, aside from being difficult to define and measure, all vary from individual to individual and often from culture to culture. Ignoring that variance simply hides the causative factors—cultural, genetic, or both—that we would like to understand.

Permanence is often viewed as human nature's key feature; after all, remember, "you can't change human nature." But, of course, we *can*—and we do, all the time. The natures of Americans today are very different from their natures in 1940. Indeed, today's human natures everywhere are diverse products of change, of long genetic and, especially, cultural evolutionary processes. A million years ago, as paleoanthropologists, archaeologists, and other scientists have shown, human nature was a radically different, and presumably much more uniform, attribute. People then had less nimble brains, they didn't have a language with fully developed syntax, they had not developed formal strata in societies, and they hadn't yet learned to attach worked stones to wooden shafts to make hammers and arrows.

Human natures a million years in the future will also be unimaginably different from human natures today. The processes that changed those early people into modern human beings will continue as long as there are people. Indeed, with the rate of cultural evolution showing seemingly continuous acceleration, it would be amazing if the broadly shared aspects of human natures were not quite different even a million *hours* (about a hundred years) in the future. For example, think of how Internet commerce has changed in the past million or so minutes (roughly two years).

As evolving mental-physical packages, human natures have brought not only planetary dominance to our species but also great triumphs in areas such as art, music, literature, philosophy, science, and technology. Unhappily, though, those same packages—human behavioral patterns and their physical foundations—are also the source of our most serious current problems. War, genocide, commerce in drugs, racial and religious prejudice, extreme economic inequality, and destruction of society's life-support systems are all products of today's human natures, too. As Pogo so accurately said, "We have met the enemy, and they is us." But nowhere is it written that those problems have to be products of tomorrow's human natures. It is theoretically possible to make peace with ourselves and with our environment, overcome racial and religious prejudice, reduce large-scale cruelty, and increase economic equality. What's needed is a widespread understanding of the evolutionary processes that have produced our natures, open discourse on what is desirable about them, and conscious collective efforts to steer the cultural evolution of the more troublesome features of our natures in ways almost everyone would find desirable. A utopian notion? Maybe. But considering progress that already has been made in areas such as democratic governance and individual freedom, race relations, religious tolerance, women's and gay rights, and avoidance of global conflict, it's worth a try.

Paul R. Ehrlich is a professor of population studies and of biological sciences at Stanford University. This essay is adapted from his Human Natures: Genes, Cultures, and the Human Prospect, *published by Island Press in August 2000.*

From *The Chronicle of Higher Education,* September 22, 2000, pp. B7-B11. © 2000 by The Chronicle of Higher Education. Reprinted with permission of the author. This article may not be posted, published, or distributed without permission from *The Chronicle.*

Altered states of consciousness

Abstract:
Greenfield questions how the range of mental activities that people are capable of performing are embedded and related to the structural variation in the brain. One idea is that each brain region has its own function.

Susan Greenfield

EVERYONE would claim to be an individual; everyone would claim they were different from everyone else. And yet the macabre idea is that if we all took our brains out, they would look pretty much the same. Just looking at the brain is not very helpful. If you were to look at the heart, you would see it pumping, and if you saw the lungs, they would be inflating like bellows, and that would inspire some idea as to how both function. But if you look at the brain, it does not move. The brain has no intrinsic moving parts, so you cannot actually guess by looking at it how it is working, and, even worse, you certainly cannot tell how one person might be individual from another.

What you can see clearly, if you do look at the brain, are the different bits to it. So you have that cauliflower thing on the back, like a little brain, that is called the cerebellum; you have the stalky part, continuous with the spinal cord, and the "cortex," so named after the Latin for bark because it wraps around the brain like its arboreal namesake around a tree. But what do these structures actually do? That is the first question if we are to understand how brains work or how an individual's brain works:

How are the functions that we have, the awesome range of mental activities that we are capable of performing, embedded and related to this structural variation?

One idea is that each brain region has its own function—that the brain is really a set of minibrains. But with this idea we would simply enter an infinite regress that miniaturizes the problem but does not solve it.

Instead, we know that the brain functions like an orchestra, where different instruments each play a different part. Or it is like a stew or some complex food, where each ingredient plays its own part. With the advent of scanning techniques, this holistic organization has become clear. In a test a subject was asked to passively view, listen to, and speak words, or to generate verbs—all fairly subtle. But even a single "function" like language is, in terms of the brain, subtly different. Scans show that the brain divides different aspects of the task according to constellations of different brain regions. But the important take-home message is that there is no single brain area lighting up for language, and there is certainly, no single brain area lighting up even for aspects of language. The regions are working

like instruments in an orchestra or like ingredients of some complex dish.

How is this organized? Let us look at how the brain is put together, because there is far more to your brain than mere gross brain regions. We start with consciousness. That is the ultimate and blanket function of the brain. What is consciousness? We will come to that later, because it is a very hard question. It is the first-person world as it seems to you. It is the world that no one can hack into directly. No one knows what you are experiencing or feeling at this moment.

Of course you can have aspects of consciousness that go wrong, dysfunctions such as depression, schizophrenia, or anxiety that would be described as a constellation of different features that would then be described as forms of consciousness. And language, or your memory, or the way you think, or even sometimes your senses, which can become distorted, are indeed functions of the brain. These can be divided even further; for example, vision has 30 different brain regions in the brain. And even within those regions one has so-called parallel processing, where the brain processes vision in parallel, dealing with form, color, and motion simultaneously. We have yet to discover how those different aspects of vision are brought back together again but we know that it is shared around.

We come then to the brain regions themselves that we have looked at. If you were to open up a brain region, you would arrive at large-scale assemblies of brain cells or neurons. These could be broken down further to isolated circuits. And then, beyond the circuits, you could look at one connection between one brain cell and another, across a narrow gap, which is called a synapse. And across the synapse you could start looking at the machinery that enables one brain cell to communicate with another. And then, finally—and only finally—do you come to the subject of much biomedical science, which is causing such delirium at the moment, and that is the gene. The genes will express a protein that is part of the biochemical machinery for working across the synapse.

So the brain is organized in a nested hierarchy. It is not just a brain region functioning as some final unit; you can break it down further and further and further. Let us look at how far you can break it down and try to discover where the secret of your individuality might lie, because it does not lie at the level of the gross brain regions. Instead, let us look at the networks of neurons that make up a brain region. You have 100 billion neurons, as many trees as there are in the Amazon rain forest. But even more awesome than that are the connections between your brain cells.

You have up to 100,000 connections onto any one brain cell. If you were to count them at one a second in the outer layer of the brain, in the cortex alone, it would take 32 million years to accomplish the task. If you wanted to work out the permutations and combinations, it would exceed the particles in the universe.

Why are they so important? Let us go back again to see where they fit in. I will remind you they are midway between the genes and the gross brain regions. The number of genes you have is about 10^5. Even if one makes the assumption—which is completely wrong—that every single gene in your body was accounting for a brain connection, you can see that you have about 10^{15} brain connections, so you would be out by 10^{10}. You just do not have enough genes to determine your brain connectivity. People who hope one day to manipulate their genes so that they are good at housekeeping or cooking or being witty or not being shy—all these other things that people fondly hope they can start targeting with molecular biology—should bear this number in mind. There is far more to your brain than your genes.

I am not saying that genes are not important and I am not saying that if a gene goes wrong you will not have some kind of terrible malfunction. What I am saying is that there is far more above and beyond the single genes that is really important. And I am talking, of course, about nurture, not just nature, because the most marvelous thing about being born human is that as you grow your brain connections grow with you. So, although you are born with pretty much all the brain cells you will ever have, it is the growth of the connections after birth that accounts for the growth of your brain.

The reason this is so exciting, and the reason I have been emphasizing the connections, is because this means, if the connections are growing as you are growing, then they will mirror what happens to you. This means that even if you are a clone (that is, even if you are an identical twin), you will have a unique configuration of brain cell connections that will trigger your reactions to events and will mirror your experiences such that you will see the whole world in terms of your brain cell connections.

Let us look at some evidence for that. London taxi drivers, as you may know, are masters at remembering. Every working day they must remember how to get from one place to another—and not only the configurations of the streets but also the one-way systems and how best to navigate round the streets of London. In a fascinating study, scientists scanned the brains of London taxi drivers and compared them with scans of other people of a similar age. Surprisingly, they found that the hippocampus was enlarged in taxi drivers compared to people of a similar age. Now, could it be that people with an enlarged hippocampus are disposed to become taxi drivers? No, because it was found that the longer they had been plying their trade the more marked this structural difference was. It was a result of what they were doing—what they were physically doing—that their brains had physically changed.

Your brain will relate to whatever you do. Here is another simple example. Human subjects were asked to practice five-finger piano exercises. The study found that with physical practice of even only five days, an enormous enhancement occurred in areas of the brain relating to the digits—just by engaging in five-finger piano exercises. But more remarkable still is a comparable change in brain territory when people were not practicing the piano but were imagining they were practicing. In real terms you can see that brain territory reflects every mental processes, and it is physically measurable, which is why we now wish to shoot down the myth between mental activity and brain activity, as if airy fairy thoughts were something that floated free, beamed in from Planet Zog or somewhere. Everything that happens to you, everything you are thinking, has a physical basis rooted in your physical brain. What we are realizing now is how exquisitely sensitive the brain is to your experiences and what you do, and therefore how it makes you the individual you are.

Even into old age, one's brain remains continuously "plastic"; that is, it is constantly dynamic, constantly evolving and changing, mirroring whatever happens to you. Sadly, sometimes things can go wrong. For example, dementia (which is a name for confusion and memory loss that characterizes Alzheimer's disease) is not a natural consequence of aging; when it strikes a brain cell in the vulnerable region, the main part of the cell (the cell body) remains, but the branches (dendrites) with which it makes contact with other cells have atrophy. Therefore, as one becomes senile—and I stress this is not going to happen to everyone, it is a particular illness—it is almost like becoming a child again. As the brain connections are dismantled, you retrace back. Where, just as in childhood the world means more and more, so this time the world means less and less. It means less because you cannot see things in terms of other things anymore because the connections are no longer there.

This prompts me to ask the question—which is not a scientific question at all, but is one I think puzzles many people: What is a mind? We are clear what brains are, but why do people now talk about minds as opposed to brains? I myself do not subscribe to the idea that it is some alternative to the biological squalor that scientists work in. I would like to suggest that mind has a very clear physical basis in the brain. We have seen that you are born with almost all your brain cells. The growth of the connections between cells accounts for the growth of the brain after birth. These connections reflect your experience, and in turn they will influence your further perception so that you see the world in terms of what has happened to you. You are born, in the words of the great William James, into a world that is a "booming, buzzing confusion," where you judge the world in terms of how sweet, how fast, how cold, how hot, how loud, how bright. You judge it in terms of its pure sensory qualities. But as you get older, the sweet, the bright, the noisy, the loud, the fast, the cold, the hot acquire labels; they become objects or people or processes or phenomena.

They have labels, then they have memories and associations attached to them, and gradually you can no longer deconstruct the world (unless you are some brilliant artist) in terms of colors and noises and abstract shapes; instead, you see it with a meaning, a meaning that is special to you. That is how it continues to occur and, as we have seen, the brain connections remain highly dynamic. I think this is what the mind is: the personalization of the brain.

As you go through life the world acquires a highly personalized significance, built up by "hardwired circuits" in the brain. But although we have this mind rooted in personalized circuits in the brain and we therefore see the world in a certain way, this organization is not always accessed.

Let us consider "blowing the mind." Here people are not using their mind: they are engaged in a mindless pursuit. Sadly, with dementia you are losing your mind on a permanent basis, but, amazingly, some people pay money to lose their minds or "let themselves go." The very word ecstasy means "to stand outside of yourself." I think phrases like "lose your mind," "blow your mind," "out of your mind," "let yourself go" are exactly what we are talking about.

But what about accessing the mind or otherwise? I think this is the real challenge to anyone with aspirations to model the brain on a computer and, indeed, to neuroscience in general. Because what I am talking about is of course "consciousness." Consciousness and the mind are very different things, although of course one will be related to the other. You can lose your mind but still be conscious. Tonight, when you lose your consciousness, I imagine you are not expecting to lose your mind. So the two concepts are separate and can be differentiated. What I want to turn to now—having looked at how the brain is hardwired and how it is reflecting experience—is the much harder question: Why do we sometimes access those connec-

tions but sometimes not? For people at a rave, for example, what is actually changing in the brain? That really is the much harder question.

Some people, like MIT AI expert Marvin Minsky, believe that it is going to be possible to build computers that are conscious. My own view is that at the moment biological brains are not like computers—and I am using the word "computer" to mean in general artificial intelligence and not just the laptop. I am not saying that in the future it is not going to be possible, since that would be an arrogant assertion; you cannot say something is not going to happen. But I cannot see how it is going to happen, especially in light of the way people are dealing with the problem at the moment.

First, the brain is based on chemicals. Chemical transmission is the absolute cornerstone of brain function; it is the most basic principle there is, and yet it is not allowed for in modeling. This is important because it gives a qualitative dimension, because you have many chemical messengers that are not found in computer modeling, and, more important, we have access to manipulating those chemicals with drugs. If you are to start manipulating at this level, which is a basic level, imagine how you would be manipulating the mind quite dramatically, and hence perhaps even consciousness, by doing that. Every psychoactive drug works on the principle of modifying chemical transmission in the brain in different ways to different extents. We thus have chemically based events in the brain and we know that if you take a drug like morphine, it will give you a dreamlike euphoria; it is manipulating your emotions. We know it works at the chemical level, and therefore emotions must be chemically based, which is something as yet not modeled in computers. As Stuart Sutherland, the psychologist, once said, he would believe a computer was conscious when it ran off with his wife. It is not good enough to have learning and memory machines. We already have that—a Cray Computer makes a very good learning and memory machine—but it is not conscious. Are we not missing the point here that it is not all about learning a memory and building up the mind? That it is about something that you had before you have a mind even—when you are a one-day-old baby—and that is an emotion?

The final important point about biological brains and computers is the issue of responses. I am sure you may be familiar with the so-called Turing test devised by the great computer pioneer Alan Turing. He said a computer would be conscious if it satisfied the following test: if a person given impartial access to a computer or a person and allowed to ask any question he or she liked could not tell from the answers whether it was a computer or a person, then the computer would have succeeded in being conscious. At the moment there are modified versions of the Turing test because the test is still too hard for a computer to do, but the modified versions make it easy by having limited subject matter to ask the computer. But even then there is no computer yet that has passed the Turing test (although, rather amusingly, there is a human being who has failed it). My own worry is that you do not even have to point to the Turing test because responses are not key. Therefore, you can be conscious without making responses, and, indeed, as we know from speak-your-weight machines, responses can occur without consciousness. The fact that you have a computer that does things is not a testament to the fact that there is a consciousness inside the computer. Instead, we have this wonderful personal world that only you can experience firsthand.

What unique property is in the brain that generates consciousness? It is not the hardwired connections; it is not our learning ability. It might have something to do with chemicals; my own contention is that it has a lot to do with feelings—but then,

of course, feelings and consciousness are very similar, if not often synonymous.

So what is the basis for that? Why is it unique to the brain and why is it not possible in machines? We have seen that there is no such thing as a center for this or a center for that, and certainly, therefore, there is no such thing as a center for consciousness. We have seen already that autonomous brains within brains make no sense. Now I can show you, scientifically, additional evidence against this idea. If you look at brain imaging again and give subjects anesthesia, thus removing their consciousness, you can see that no single area of the brain shuts down. There is no one brain area that has just stopped. There is no center for consciousness.

If there is no center for consciousness, where is it? Let me compound this by introducing another concept. Is a dog conscious? If so, what is the difference between dogs and us? And how does that give us a clue as to what is special about the brain for generating consciousness?

More controversially, let us extend the riddle to that of the fetus. It is still a commonly held belief that the fetus is not conscious. But if it is not conscious, when does it become conscious? When does a baby become conscious? At the time of birth? Fine, but when is a baby born? Some babies are born prematurely, and they are conscious. You would not for two months just ignore the baby in the incubator in the hospital and say, "Ah, 40 weeks are up, it is going to be conscious today. Now we can go and visit." That would not be likely. Even less likely would you do it after the birth and say, "Ah, a few weeks have gone now, it is coming up to six months from birth, it might be conscious." It does not make sense.

Or is it the manner of birth, squeezing down the birth canal? That is tough on babies born by Caesarean section, if this is the case, because they will never be conscious. Clearly the manner and the timing of birth, because it is so variable, cannot

determine, cannot be the trigger, for consciousness. To my mind, it is a much more logical deduction that the fetus must be conscious.

But, for our purposes, we say, "OK, so this is a bit like the problem with cats and dogs or, indeed, rats or other animals: How is it different from consciousness?" When would the fetus become conscious? What would it be conscious of? I think the big problem here, and one that stops us from developing the idea, is that we normally think of consciousness as all or none. I myself defined it as "the thing you are going to lose tonight." But what if I was wrong? What if instead of consciousness being all or none, on or off, what if consciousness grew as brains grew? What if, therefore, it gradually developed? And so a fetus was conscious, but not as conscious as a child, and a baby was conscious but not as conscious as an adult, and a cat was conscious but not as conscious as a primate, and a monkey was conscious but not as conscious as a human.

If consciousness grows as brains grow, two interesting issues are raised. One is that you as an adult human being are more conscious at some times than at other times. If you think about it, we talk about raising our consciousness or deepening our consciousness—it does not matter which way you go, you can go up or down—consciousness is something that is variable. If that is the case, science finally has purchase on the problem, because, instead of looking for some magic brain region or some magic gene or some magic chemical, we can look for something that varies in degree, something we can measure. We can look for something conceivably that ebbs and flows within your brain, something that changes in size within your brain. Now, what could that be?

Let us look at the properties of consciousness. We have seen there is no special brain region; consciousness is spatially multiple, many brain regions must be contributing to it, but you have only one consciousness at any time. I would like to think that you see only one thing at one time. Although it is a complex pattern, you will see it as a pattern. Think of those famous vases and profiles, where either you see the profiles or you see the vase; which is true? Both are valid, but looking at it one way negates for that moment looking at it the other. You have only one at a time. I have just suggested to you that it is continuously variable.

Finally, we are always conscious of something. When we become very sophisticated, of course, we have an inner hope, fear, dream, thought, or fantasy: you can close your eyes and have consciousness triggered internally. But in the simplest form we have momentary states triggered by the changing input from the sensory world.

Let me suggest a metaphor to capture how these properties might be accommodated in the brain. Imagine a stone falling in a puddle. The stone is fixed; if the "stone" in the brain is a hub of brain circuits, then it could be, if you like, hardwired. You can see where this is leading. It could be a fixed thing, but, when a stone is thrown, it generates, just for a moment, ripples that are highly transient, that are vastly bigger in their extent than the size of the stone itself; and those ripples can vary enormously according to the size of the stone, the height from which it is thrown, the force with which it is thrown, and the degree of competition from other stones coming in. All these factors will determine the extent of the ripples. What I am suggesting is that in the brain you do have the equivalent of stones: hardwired little circuits, as we have seen, riddling your adult brain, which are sometimes accessed, sometimes not. The equivalent of throwing the stone would be, for example, me seeing my husband. That would then go through certain parts of my brain and start activating the circuitry that is related to my husband. Still, I would not be conscious of him. What would happen

then? How could we now get ripples occurring in the brain? Amazingly enough, you have something very special in your brain: you have chemical fountains, not just circuits, and these chemical fountains actually emanate from those primitive parts of your brain and access the cortex and other areas. These are the chemicals that are targeted, for example, by Ecstasy or by Prozac, and these are the chemicals that vary during sleep-wakefulness and during high arousal, and these chemicals fulfill a very special function: they put brain cells on red alert. Imagine I see my husband. That is the equivalent of throwing the stone. It activates the hub of hardwired circuitry, established over long experience of married life. If that is coincidental with a group of brain cells being sprayed upon by a fountain of chemicals related to arousal, then that would predispose those adjacent cells to be corralled just for that moment, and just for that moment this very active hub will activate a much larger group of cells, and that larger group of cells will determine the extent of my consciousness at that particular moment. That is the model.

How do we know the brain works like that? How do we know that you can get ripples in the brain. I was very fortunate to visit Israel and meet Arnivam Grinvald, who works at the Weizmann Institute. He showed me experiments—not on humans because it is invasive—but using optical dyes that register the voltage of brain cells. Arnivam showed that even to a flash of light there is indeed the neuron equivalent of ripples. These ripples (in this particular experiment to a simple flash of light) are extending over 10 million neurons, and they are extending very quickly, in less than a quarter of a second, or about 230 milliseconds. So this means that in your brain you can have tens, even hundreds of millions of brain cells corralled into transient working assembly in less than a quarter of a second and then it is all gone again, just

like a ripple. That, in my view, is the best place to look if we are trying to find out about consciousness.

As a kind of interim thought on the physical basis of consciousness, I would like to suggest that there is no magic ingredient. The critical factor is not qualitative but quantitative: the larger the assembly of brain cells, the greater the depth of your consciousness.

Let us play around with that idea. What would happen if you had an abnormally small assembly of brain cells? Let us just think about what kind of consciousness you might have, because the advantage of this model is that there are different reasons for which you could have an abnormally small assembly of brain cells. For example, if the connectivity was modest, or if the epicenter was weak or only weakly activated (as a tiny pebble laid very gently on the surface of the water), or if the fountains of chemicals malfunctioned, or, indeed, if there was competition from new, rapidly forming assemblies—all these factors could give you different types of consciousness. Modest connectivity occurs in childhood, as we have seen. What do we know about children? Very young children are living in the moment. They are not doing vast learning and memory tasks, the world does not "mean" much to them; they judge the world literally at face value, on how fast and cold and sweet and so on. They have a literally sensational time. They are judging the world not in terms of associations but on the impact of their senses at that very moment. Let's look at an example of when the center is weakly activated. A particular example is one that we are most likely to experience tonight, and that is a dream. A dream could be a small assembly because in your sleeping state your senses are not working heavily, so they are therefore not able to recruit a very large assembly and you are thus dependent on the small spontaneous activity of brain cells. That is why in dreaming the world seems to be highly emotional, not very logical;

you have ruptures in your logic like with schizophrenic states.

We know also that children have a much greater predisposition to dreaming than people who are older. It seems that these different states all have one element in common. They are caused for different reasons, but dreaming, along with fast-paced sports and childhood, are all characterized by living in the moment, by having a strong emphasis on the senses, and by not putting a great premium on anything you have learned or remembered; that is, not using your mind. The mind is not accessed in any of these states.

Let me summarize: childhood, dreaming, schizophrenia, fast-paced sports, and, dare I say it, raves are all examples of where the mind is not being accessed. It is not being accessed for different reasons: lack of connectivity (childhood), lack of strong sensory stimulation (dreams), an imbalance with those fountains of chemicals (schizophrenia), or a degree of competition from other stimulations (fast-paced sports and also raves, where, for good measure, people are flooding their brains with a drug that deliberately confuses those fountaining chemicals).

This brings us to pleasure—indeed, it brings us to the opposite of that—to what would occur if you had a large neuronal assembly. It would be where the world seems gray and remote, where you feel cutoff from other people, where, instead of the senses imploding in on you, as they do in dreaming or fast-paced sports or childhood or in schizophrenia, you feel numb and remote, and your emotions are turned down—you perhaps feel nothing at all or you do not think you feel anything. That, of course, you might recognize as the features of clinical depression: the outside world is remote, the senses are understimulated, and a continuity of thought exists, even a persistent thought. In such conditions people do not feel pleasure. It is not that they feel desperately sad; they just feel nothing. They suffer from something clinically called anhe-

donia, meaning literally "not enjoying yourself." A depressed person may have the sun on her face or the grass between her bare toes but she does not feel that sensual pleasure that I would like to think we all feel to some measure and certainly children feel considerably. They are completely cutoff from it. In clinical depression, then, we have an imbalance of the fountains of the modulating chemicals and therefore a lack of pleasure and a lack of emotion. I would like to suggest, because of that, the greater the neuronal assembly, the fewer emotions you have. High emotional states, like childhood, dreaming, or schizophrenia, are associated with small assemblies and the emotions therefore must be the basic form of consciousness, not learning and memory.

This has all been a rather long-winded way to get round to the question: How we are going to model this on a computer if, indeed, we wish to? Let us go the other way round and say: What kind of consciousness could we have? How would we interpret that in terms of this model? Sadly, something everyone has experienced is pain. Most people think of pain as rather boring, as something that surely we would all feel the same if, for example, we put our hands over a flame. But nothing could be further from the truth.

First, we know pain is expressed as other associations: pricking, stabbing, burning, chilling. We know that it can vary, interestingly enough, throughout the day. There are some particularly sadistic experiments where volunteers had electrical shocks through their teeth and had to report when they felt the pain. Amazingly, if that happens, you find that throughout the day your so-called pain threshold (when you report that the pain is particularly intense) varies. But the conduction velocity of your pain fibers has not changed, so something in the brain is changing, something in its chemical landscape; something transient is changing if you as the same individ-

ual do not experience the same pain depending on what time of day it is. We know that the more people anticipate pain, the more they will perceive it as painful, and I would suggest that this is because there is a buildup of the connections. If you are anticipating pain that is because more and more assemblies are being recruited before you feel it. And, incidentally, the diurnal threshold occurs because throughout the day those chemical fountains are changing. We know that phantom limb pain is felt by people who do not have the limb but feel as though they do. That is because a so-called neuronal matrix—which I would call "assembly"—corresponds to the severed limb that would be stimulated by the lack of input from signals resulting from it. Pain is absent in dreams—which, we have seen, would be a small assembly state. Similarly, morphine, which is a strong analgesic or painkiller, creates a dreamlike euphoria that works through a natural opiate that makes the brain cell assemblies less efficient at being corralled. People will therefore often say they feel the pain but it no longer "matters," it is no longer significant to them. With schizophrenia, which I have suggested is a small assembly state, people have a higher threshold for pain. For people who are depressed, it is the opposite: they feel pain more. Finally, anesthetics—which have always proved a puzzle to understand how they work because there are many different types of anesthetics chemically—could work by depressing the activity, so that in the end gradually it reduced the size of your assembly to such a small one that you did not have appreciable consciousness. If that were the case, you would expect, as the assembly was shrinking, you would go through the small assembly state and have some form of delirium, some madness, or some kind of euphoria or pleasure—a rather odd idea if you are going under an anesthetic. Nowadays it is not possible because anesthetics are so efficient that they work very quickly,

Article 5. Altered states of consciousness

but in the old days people would actually have "ether frolics" or inhale nitrous oxide at fun fairs to have the pleasure of taking the anesthetic. (Even Ketamine, which is an anesthetic in high doses, is a drug of abuse in low doses.) So, paradoxically, a link exists just as you are going under: because it is less efficient, you go through that period of euphoria where suddenly you are experiencing a sensual time.

One can actually work out the different factors that will determine the size of a brain cell assembly, and they can be expressed bilingually, in neuroscientific or phenomenological terms, so we can talk about the "intensity'" of our senses, and that is the degree to which your neurons are active. We can talk about "significance," and that can be the existence of preexisting associations. We can talk about how "aroused" you are, and that is the availability of those chemical fountains that are called amines. I have not talked about predisposition or mood but they can be modified by other chemicals that also put cells on red alert, such as hormones. And, finally, we can talk

about "distraction," which bilingually one could refer to as the formation of competing assemblies.

What I have done in this paper is relate that which you feel to that which could be happening in the brain so you can build up some kind of match. I think in the future we could image these brain cell assemblies and manipulate those factors differentially and make predictions as to the type of consciousness someone might have according to how big their assembly was or vice versa. I am not suggesting this model is right, but its strength is that it can be tested one day.

Finally, we must remember—and this is another problem for computer modeling—that the brain is an integral part of the body, that your central nervous system, your hormones, and your immune systems are all interlinked; otherwise you would have biological anarchy. So these brain cell assemblies that I am suggesting are related to consciousness are merely an index of consciousness. If you put one in a dish, you would not have consciousness. Somehow that causes a readout to the rest of the

body and somehow the rest of the body signals back through chemicals that will influence the size of the assembly and hence the consciousness. One candidate group of chemicals is the peptides, which can also function as hormones and could coordinate the immune, endocrine, and nervous systems.

In conclusion, we will never be able to get inside someone else's brain. Yet science is starting to make a contribution by being a little more modest, by actually saying, "Well, let's match up physical brain states with what people are feeling and then perhaps we will have some insight into why people take drugs, what happiness is, and, perhaps most important of all, why people go bungee jumping or to raves."

Susan Greenfield is Professor of Pharmacology at the University of Oxford and Director of the Royal Institution of Great Britain. She is also cofounder of a spin-off company specializing in novel approaches to neurodegeneration, Synaptica Ltd. Her books include Journey to the Centres of the Mind (1995) and The Private Life of the Brain (2000).

From *Social Research*, Fall 2001, pp. 609-626. © 2001 by The New School for Social Research.

Brain-Based Learning

The wave of the brain

By Ruth Palombo Weiss

It's a jungle out there! We have all heard and probably uttered that phrase. Well, the Nobel Prize winning neurobiologist Gerald Edelman postulates that it's a jungle inside there as well. Edelman, director of the Neuroscience Institute at the Scripps Research Institute, compares our brains to a dense web of interconnecting synapses. His metaphor gives us insight into current, sometimes confusing, research on how the brain works and its connection to learning theory.

Many of us use the Internet daily and are astounded by the vast and seemingly endless connections we can make. The brain's interconnections exceed the Internet's by an astronomical number. The typical brain has approximately 100 billion neurons, and each neuron has one to 10,000 synaptic connections to other neurons. Says Edelman, "The intricacy and numerosity of brain connections are extraordinary."

Our brains are suffused with a vast number of interdependent networks. We process all incoming information through those networks, and any information already stored influences how and what we learn.

"The human brain is the best-organized, most functional three pounds of matter in the known universe," says educator Robert Sylwester in his book, *A Celebration of Neurons: An Educator's Guide to the Human Brain*. "It's responsible for Beethoven's Ninth Symphony, computers, the Sistine Chapel, automobiles, the Second World War, *Hamlet*, apple pie, and a whole lot more."

Increasingly, educators such as Sylwester are relying on brain-based learning theory to take advantage of the growing body of evidence that neurologists are uncovering about how humans learn. He says, "To learn more about the brain, scientists had to discover how to perform intricate studies that would provide solid information on its most basic operations—the normal and abnormal actions of a single neuron, the synchronized actions of networks of neurons, and the factors that trigger neuronal activity."

It's clear that no two human brains are alike. Every nerve cell (neuron) serves as a relay station. Neurons not only receive signals from other cells, but they also process the signals and send them on to other cells across tiny gaps called synapses. Chemicals called neurotransmitters (there may be as many as 100) cause the signals to flow from one neuron to another. That electrochemical process is the basis of all human behavior. Every time we speak, move, or think, electrical and chemical communication are taking place between tens of thousands of neurons.

"As a nerve cell is stimulated by new experiences and exposure to incoming information from the senses, it grows branches called dendrites. Dendrites are the major receptive surface of the nerve cell. One nerve cell can receive input from as many as 20,000 other nerve cells. If you have 100 billion cells in your brain, think of the complexity! With use, you grow branches; with impoverishment, you lose them.

"The ability to change the structure and chemistry of the brain in response to the

The Gist
❏ The human brain's interconnections exceed the Internet's by an astronomical number.
❏ Educators are increasingly relying on brain-based learning theory.
❏ Imaging technologies such as MRIs are helping scientists understand memory, recall, and how the brain manages information and information overload.

environment is what we call plasticity," says Marian Diamond, a neuroscientist and professor of neuroanatomy at the University of California at Berkeley.

As we might imagine, for a subject as vast and complicated as brain research and learning theory there are a variety of views. Some scientists feel that there are fundamental differences between learning and education. They insist that brain-based research on learning isn't the same as research done on education theory. They also note that many of the initial neurological inquiries into learning have been done on animals and that it's an iffy proposition to extrapolate from animals to humans.

But during the past 10 years, known as the Decade of the Brain, a number of scientists have been using new technologies such as Magnetic Resonance Imaging (MRI), Functional MRI (fMRI), and Positron Emission Topography (PET) scans. Those tests help scientists explore how human brains process memory, emotion, attention, patterning, and context—

A Few Brain Facts

❑ Weight: 3 pounds
❑ Shape: walnut
❑ Color: uncooked liver

The brain is divided into two hemispheres called the *cerebral cortex* (commonly known as the conscious thinking center), covered in a thin skin of deeply wrinkled gray tissue, and separated by the *corpus callosum*. That curved band of white tissue acts as a bridge between the two halves, shuttling information back and forth at such a rate of speed that for all practical purposes the two hemispheres act as one. With the exception of the *pineal gland*, every brain module is duplicated in each hemisphere—another of nature's creative duplication systems.

The areas lying beneath the corpus callosum make up the *limbic system*, the area that relates to the unconscious and yet profoundly affects our experience. Its job is to feed information upward to the conscious cortex. Emotions are generated in the limbic system along with many urges that direct our behavior and usually help in survival. Within this limbic system, are the

❑ *thalamus*. Directs incoming information to the appropriate part of the brain for further processing.

❑ *hypothalamus*. and *pituitary*
❑ *thalamus*. Directs incoming information to the appropriate part of the brain for further processing.
❑ *hypothalamus*. and *pituitary glands*. Adapt the body to environment by constantly adjusting hormones.
❑ *amygdala*. Registers and generates fear.

Last, the *brainstem* carries information from the body into the brain and establishes general levels of alertness and such automatic tasks as breathing, blood pressure, and heartbeat.

A few additional terms are needed to understand the brain's physiology:

❑ *neuron*. The primary building block of the brain. Neurons carry electrical charges and make chemical connections to other neurons.
❑ *axons*. Long fibers (extending from the cell body) that receive messages.
❑ *dendrites*. Short fibers (surrounding the cell body) that receive messages.
❑ *synapses*. Tiny gaps between axons and dendrites (with chemical bridges) that transmit messages.
❑ *myelin* A sheath that serves as insulation and allows electricity to flow between the axons and dendrites.

The definitions come from Mapping the Mind *by Rita Carter.*

---

among other areas in this vast area of inquiry.

Renate Numella Caine and Geoffrey Caine, in their book *Unleashing the Power of Perceptual Change: The Potential of Brain-Based Teaching*, confirm the idea that our brains are whole and interconnected. "Even though there are a multitude of specific modules with specific functions, thought, emotion, physical health, the nature of our interactions with others, even the time and environment in which we learn, are not separated in the brain. They are not dealt with one thing at a time."

Says Edelman: "The nervous system behavior is to some extent self-generated in loops: Brain activity leads to movement, which leads to further sensation and perception and still further movement. The layers and loops between them are the most intricate of any object we know, and they are dynamic. They continually change. Parts of the brain (indeed, the major portion of its tissues) receive input only from other parts of the brain, and they give outputs to other parts without intervention from the outside world. The brain might be said to be in touch more with itself than with anything else."

There are several areas/topics that brain-based learning theories are examining. As we will see, they are intercon-

nected in much the same way as our own complex neuronal groups.

Attention

It appears that the thalamus, in the center of the brain, plays an especially important role in attention. According to Sylwester, the thalamus is the "relay center between our sense organs and the cortex.... This process holds the important information within our attentional and short-term memory systems by ignoring the less important information, and thus seems to create the visual awareness we experience." Eric Jensen, author of *Teaching With the Brain in Mind*, points out that our bodies have high-low cycles of about 90 to 110 minutes. When students are at the top of those cycles, they're more attentive. At the bottom of the cycle, people's energy drops along with their level of attention. Jensen suggests that if educators and trainers "learn to ride with the cycles," they'll have fewer problems.

Renate Caine talks about the different types of motivators and what happens in our brains depending on the source of motivation. "When we encounter high stress in learning, there is a psychophysiological response to the threat, accompanied by a feeling of helplessness or fatigue. This type of response keeps people from using

their higher order, more complex thinking, and creativity."

During high-stress situations, physiologically the information takes the primary pathway through the thalamus and amygdala and then moves into the cerebellum. Memorization of isolated facts can be accomplished under high-stress conditions, but higher order and creative thinking may be lost. We tend to respond with either a primitive mode of behaving or to rely solely on early programmed behavior.

In situations that may involve stress but in which we have a sense of control or choice, the physiology shifts. The primary path is no longer directly through the amygdala but through other paths of the cortex, the parts that are involved in higher-order functioning. Thus, we avoid a "knee jerk response."

Learning situations that are low stress favor reflection and analytic thinking. Says Renate Caine, "The thalamus, hippocampus, and cortex (where stored memories are housed and higher-level thinking takes place) are involved. With this system, you can translate factual elements and make connections. Furthermore, you can make inferences based on other things you know. That higher-order thinking includes synthesizing information and integrating it to come up with new ideas."

Context and patterns

"Without context, emotions, or patterns, information is considered meaningless. There's a tendency to try to form some kind of meaningful pattern out of our learning—this process seems innate," says Jensen.

He adds, "While the brain is a consummate pattern maker, intellectual maturity often enriches the process. PET scans indicate that a novice chess player burns more glucose (has to work harder) and uses the step-by-step sequential left side of the brain. A master chess player uses less glucose and engages larger patterns from the right side of the brain."

A lot of recent memory research involves pattern-making abilities. One study that has been replicated several times involves reading a long list of words to a subject. When the subject is asked to remember certain words on the list, an interesting thing happens. Let's say the list has 25 words strung together, including cake, cookie, sugar, train, candy, tree, car, dog. If asked whether the word *sweet* is on the list (it wasn't), most subjects say *yes* because of the words *cake, cookies,* and *sugar.* Interestingly, the same area of the brain that registered other words on the list lights up on an MRI.

That clearly illustrates the economy of brain-processing mechanisms. The brain makes a connection and generalizes even though the generalization might be wrong. One conclusion is that detail isn't efficient and generalization is, though not always correct. The brain doesn't have values; it's an information organ. It isn't an arbiter of values, of right and wrong. What we do have is a system that puts related events together in hierarchies and categories.

Geoffrey Caine states: "The brain-mind naturally organizes information into categories. We can generically call that 'patterning.' These patterns always involve interpreting information in context. There's a great deal of research to show that we learn from focused attention as well as from peripheral perception. When people are forming patterns, a lot of the information that brings the pattern together is peripheral or contextual information."

Emotion

The amygdala, an almond-shaped structure in the brain's center, seems most involved with emotions. According to Jensen, it has 12 to 15 distinct emotive regions and often exerts a tremendous influ-

ence on the cortex. "Information flows both ways between the amygdala and the cortex, but many other areas are involved in subtle emotions," he says.

"Making daily decisions based on emotions is not an exception; it's the rule," says professor Antonio Damasio, a neurologist at the University of Iowa, in his book *Descartes's Error: Emotion, Reason, and the Human Brain.* "While extremes of emotion are usually harmful to our best thinking, a middle ground makes sense. Appropriate emotions speed up decision making enormously."

Brain research shows that emotions and thought are deeply interconnected. In *Molecules of Emotion,* Candace Pert wrote that on the surface of every cell in the body are receptors that respond to molecules such as various peptides and neurotransmitters. Scientists used to think that those neurotransmitters were found only in neurons in the brain, but it turns out they're in every part of the body. When we have a thought, many of the peptides and neurotransmitters interact with cells throughout the body, and those interactions trigger what we call "the experience of emotions."

"Good learning engages feelings. Rather than viewing them as an add-on, emotions are a form of learning. Emotions also engage meaning and predict future learning because they involve our goals, beliefs, biases, and expectancies. Emotions drive the threesome of attention, meaning, and memory," says Renate Caine.

According to Daniel Schacter of Harvard University, author of *Searching for Memory,* there are two possible explanations for the way emotionally charged events are emblazoned in our memories. One is that stress hormones and chemical messengers, or neurotransmitters, are released at such times, which "tag" the event with special significance and give it prominence in the memory pathways. The other explanation for what are commonly known as flashbulb memories is that even though they don't need to be rehearsed or reiterated, they usually are. "People tend to discuss and go over the things in their lives that are important to them, and that strengthens the memory," says Schacter.

Renate Caine points out that the climate of the workplace is critical to the kind of product you're going to get. If we feel supported in that environment, the physiological effect is a slight increase in dopamine, which releases the right amount of acetylcholine (another neurotransmitter) that stimulates the hippocampus. People with increased dopamine show improved epi-

sodic memory, working memory, verbal functioning, flexibility in thinking, creative problem solving, decision making, and social interactions.

Memory and recall

One of the most spectacular uses of recently improved imaging technologies such as CAT scans, MRIs, and fMRIs is to show the brain at work—thereby helping scientists understand memory, recall, and how we manage information and information overload.

"Memory is the ability to repeat a performance. In the nervous system, it is a dynamic property of populations of neuronal groups. Unlike computer-based memory, brain-based memory is inexact. But it's also capable of great degrees of generalization. Memory would be useless if it couldn't in some way take into account the temporal succession of events—of sensory events as well as patterns of movement," says Edelman.

Rita Carter, who wrote *Mapping the Mind,* says that new neural connections are made with every incoming sensation and old ones disappear as memories fade.

"Each fleeting impression is recorded for a while in some new configuration, but if it's not laid down in memory, the pattern degenerates and the impression disappears like the buttocks-shaped hollow in a foam rubber cushion after you stand up. Patterns that linger may in turn connect with, and spark off, activity in other groups—forming associations (memories) or combining to create new concepts.

"Little explosions and waves of new activity, each with a characteristic pattern, are produced moment by moment as the brain reacts to outside stimuli. That activity creates a constantly changing internal environment, which the brain then reacts to as well. That creates a feedback loop that ensures constant change. The loop-back process, sometimes referred to as neural Darwinism, ensures that patterns that produce thoughts (and thus behavior) and that help the organism thrive are laid down permanently while those that are useless fade. It's not a rigid system."

According to Carter, it seems that incoming information is split into several parallel paths within the brain, each of which is given a slightly different treatment depending on the route it takes. Information that's of particular interest to one side of the brain will activate that side more strongly than the other. You can see that happen in a brain scan: The side that's in charge of a particular task will light up while the matching area on the other side will glow more dully.

For More About the Brain and Learning

❏ ascd.org
❏ brainconnection.com
❏ cainelearning.com
❏ dana.org
❏ 21learn.org
❏ lern.org
❏ newhorizons.org/blab.html
❏ thebrainstore.com

Geoffrey Caine reminds us that when we can connect rote memory with ordinary experience, we understand and make sense of things and remember more easily. To transfer information effectively, we need to see the relevance of what we're learning.

Motivation

Richard Restak, a neurobiologist, writes in his book *The Brain:* "Learning is not primarily dependent on a reward. In fact, rats—as well as humans—will consistently seek new experiences and behaviors with no perceivable reward or impetus. Experimental rats respond positively to simple novelty. Studies confirm that the mere pursuit of information can be valuable by itself and that humans are just as happy to seek novelty."

Robert Aitken at the Vancouver British Columbia Community College points out that we choose to stay motivated. "One of the things becoming clear is that our brains have been built for survival. That hasn't changed in 30,000 years. If something helps us survive, we're motivated to learn.

"Trainers have to find ways to convince learners that this is vital to their survival. If we get an emotional buy-in then learning takes place."

We can approach motivation from several different points of view, says Geoffrey Caine. "The distinction is between intrinsic and extrinsic motivation. Intrinsic motivation has to do with what we want, need, and desire. It's deeply grounded in our values and feelings. Extrinsic motivation is often an attempt by someone else trying to make us want to do something. In terms of learning and creativity, we know there's a positive correlation between creativity and intrinsic motivation. When we're organizing information in our minds, the way we form patterns is deeply motivated by what we're interested in."

We have all heard the phrase *Use it or lose it.* That's the ultimate truth of the healthy brain's capability to learn, change, and grow as long as we're alive.

"The most exciting discovery about all of this work is that education should continue for a lifetime. With enrichment, we grow dendrites; with impoverishment, we lose them at any age," concludes Diamond.

Ruth Palombo Weiss *is a freelance writer based in Potomac, Maryland; pivotal@ erols.com*

From *Training & Development*, July 2000, pp. 20-24. © 2000 by ASTD Magazines. Reprinted by permission.

UNIT 3
Perceptual Processes

Unit Selections

Key Points to Consider

- Why would psychologists be interested in studying sensations and perceptions? Can you differentiate the two? Isn't sensation the domain of biologists and physicians? Can you rank-order the senses, that is, place them in a hierarchy of importance? Can you justify your rankings?

- What role does the brain play in sensation and perception? Can you give specific information about the role of the brain for each sense? Are some senses "distant" senses and some "near" senses in terms of how we perceive a stimulus, despite whether the stimulus is physical or social? Can you think of other ways to categorize the various senses?

- Do you think vision is the most important human sense? Is it the dominant sense in other animals? How is the brain involved in vision? Does stem cell transplantation help blind people to see? Why or why not? If you were blind, would you want a stem cell transplant? Explain.

- What is deafness; is it complete hearing loss? What are some of the causes of deafness? Are Americans at risk for deafness? How much noise is too much noise? What can be done to reduce noise levels so that they are not detrimental to us?

- What is synesthesia? Can you provide some sensory examples of what a synesthete might experience? Would you want to experience synesthesia? Why or why not? How are the brain and heredity involved in synesthesia?

- What are phantom limbs? Why do people experience phantom limbs? How does the brain play a role in phantom limb experiences? Did you try the exercises in the article on phantom limbs? What was your experience like?

- What is congenital analgesia? How do most people experience pain? What are scientists discovering about what causes pain and how it can be reduced?

- What is REM sleep? What is NREM sleep? What are some of the problems dream researchers encounter? What do dreams mean? Was Freud's theory that dreams are repressed wishes correct? Or, on the other hand, are dreams about events we would rather remember? What are some of the other theories that attempt to explain why we dream?

 **Links: www.dushkin.com/online/**
These sites are annotated in the World Wide Web pages.

Five Senses Home Page
http://www.sedl.org/scimath/pasopartners/senses/welcome.html
Psychology Tutorials and Demonstrations
http://psych.hanover.edu/Krantz/tutor.html

Marina and her roommate have been friends since freshman year. Because they share so much in common, they decided to become roommates in their sophomore year. They both want to travel abroad one day. Both date men from the same college, are education majors, and want to work with young children after graduation from college. Today they are at the local art museum. As they walk around the galleries, Marina is astonished at her roommate's taste in art. Whatever her roommate likes, Marina hates. The paintings and sculptures that Marina admires are the very ones to which her roommate turns up her nose. "How can their tastes in art be so different when they share so much in common?" Marina wonders.

What Marina and her roommate are experiencing is a difference in perception or the interpretation of the sensory stimulation provided by the artwork. Perception and its sister area of psychology, sensation, are the foci of this unit.

For many years, it was popular for psychologists to consider sensation and perception as two distinct processes. Sensation was defined in passive terms as the simple event of some stimulus energy (i.e., a sound wave) impinging on the body or on a specific sense organ that then reflexively transmitted appropriate information to the central nervous system. Both passivity and simple reflexes were stressed in this concept. Perception, on the other hand, was defined as an integrative and interpretive process that the higher centers of the brain supposedly accomplish based on sensory information and on available memories for similar events.

The Gestalt psychologists, early German researchers, were convinced that perception was a higher order function compared to sensation. The Gestalt psychologists believed that the whole stimulus was more than the sum of its individual sensory parts; Gestalt psychologists believed this statement was made true by the process of perception.

For example, when you listen to a song, you hear the words, the loudness, and the harmony as well as the main melody. However, you do not really hear each of these units separately; what you hear is a whole song. If the song is pleasant to you, you may say that you like the song. If the song is raucous to you, you may say that you do not like it. However, even the songs you do not like on first hearing may become likeable after repeated exposure. Hence perception, according to these early Gestalt psychologists, was a more advanced and complicated process than sensation.

This dichotomy of sensation and perception is no longer widely accepted. The revolution came in the mid-1960s when a psychologist published a then-radical treatise in which he reasoned that perceptual processes included all sensory events that he believed were directed by an actively searching central nervous system. Also, this view provided that certain perceptual patterns, such as recognition of a piece of artwork, may be species-specific. That is, all humans, independent of learning history, should share some of the same perceptual repertoires. This unit on perceptual processes is designed to further your understanding of these complex and interesting processes.

In the first article, "The Senses," one of the main topics of this unit is introduced to you. The author reviews many of the dominant senses in the human being and concludes that when we understand the senses, we also understand the brain.

The second article in this unit, "Sight Unseen," explores one of the most important senses in humans—vision. Michael Abrams guides us through the journey of a man, blind from childhood, in a quest to restore his vision. Even after surgery that should have assured good vision, the man still cannot see. Abrams explains why.

One of the other dominant senses in humans is audition or hearing. In the next article, "It's a Noisy, Noisy World Out There!," Richard Carmen discloses information about just how much noise Americans are exposed to and why certain noises can be detrimental. With enough exposure to certain sounds, individuals can become deaf. The article also reveals what we can do to avoid hearing loss.

In the fourth article in this section, an interesting ability—synesthesia—is explored. The article reveals information about this unusual phenomenon by which people combine sensations in unique ways so that pain may actually be perceived as a color, or a sound may conjure up a vision.

Another curious sensory/perceptual phenomenon is a phantom limb. Some individuals lose a limb—a leg or an arm—in an accident or in war. Even though the limb is gone, the amputee's brain still perceives that the limb is there. This phenomenon is known as phantom limbs. A fifth brief article provides several exercises the reader can try, to experience sensations similar to that of phantom limbs.

In the next article, "Pain and Its Mysteries," Marni Jackson describes what scientists are studying about pain—how and why it is experienced and how to reduce it.

The final selection of this unit, "Brains in Dreamland," relates to an altered state of perception or altered state of consciousness (something outside of normal sensation and perception). This last article is about dreaming, something we all do and something that fascinates most individuals. By studying sleep, especially dream or REM sleep, researchers are beginning to understand why we dream and what dreams may mean. Freud's was the first theory to address these issues, but newer theories are making headway on the nature and causes of dreaming. Author Bruce Bower explores both Freud's theory and other theories in a search for a better understanding of the function of dreams.

THE SENSES

They delight, heal, define the boundaries of our world. And they are helping unlock the brain's secrets

To the 19th-century French poet Charles Baudelaire, there was no such thing as a bad smell. What a squeamish, oversensitive bunch he would have deemed the denizens of 20th-century America, where body odors are taboo, strong aromas are immediately suppressed with air freshener, and perfume—long celebrated for its seductive and healing powers—is banned in some places to protect those with multiple chemical sensitivities.

Indeed, in the years since Baudelaire set pen to paper, civilization has played havoc with the natural state of all the human senses, technology providing the ability not only to tame and to mute but also to tease and overstimulate. Artificial fragrances and flavors trick the nose and tongue. Advertisers dazzle the eyes with rapid-fire images. Wailing sirens vie with the beeping of pagers to challenge the ears' ability to cope.

Yet even as we fiddle with the texture and scope of our sensibilities, science is indicating it might behoove us to show them a bit more respect. Growing evidence documents the surprising consequences of depriving or overwhelming the senses. And failing to nurture our natural capabilities, researchers are discovering, can affect health, emotions, even intelligence. Hear-

ing, for example, is intimately connected to emotional circuits: When a nursing infant looks up from the breast, muscles in the middle ear reflexively tighten, readying the child for the pitch of a human voice. The touch of massage can relieve pain and improve concentration. And no matter how we spritz or scrub, every human body produces a natural odor as distinctive as the whorls on the fingertips—an aroma that research is showing to be a critical factor in choosing a sexual partner.

Beyond their capacity to heal and delight, the senses have also opened a window on the workings of the human brain. A flood of studies on smell, sight, hearing, touch and taste in the last two decades have upended most of the theories about how the brain functions. Scientists once believed, for example, that the brain was hard-wired at birth, the trillions of connections that made up its neural circuits genetically predetermined. But a huge proportion of neurons in a newborn infant's brain, it turns out, require input from the senses in order to hook up to one another properly.

Similarly, scientific theory until recently held that the sense organs did the lion's share of processing information about the world: The eye detected move-

ment; the nose recognized smells. But researchers now know that ears, eyes and fingers are only way stations, transmitting signals that are then processed centrally. "The nose doesn't smell—the brain does," says Richard Axel, a molecular biologist at Columbia University. Each of our senses shatters experience into fragments, parsing the world like so many nouns and verbs, then leaving the brain to put the pieces back together and make sense of it all.

In labs across the country, researchers are drafting a picture of the senses that promises not only to unravel the mysterious tangle of nerves in the brain but also to offer reasons to revel in sensuous experience. Cradling a baby not only feels marvelous, scientists are finding, but is absolutely vital to a newborn's emotional and cognitive development. And the results of this research are beginning to translate into practical help for people whose senses are impaired: Researchers in Boston last year unveiled a tiny electronic device called a retinal chip that one day may restore sight to people blinded after childhood. Gradually, this new science of the senses is redefining what it means to be a feeling and thinking human being. One day it may lead to an understanding of consciousness itself.

SIGHT

Seeing is believing, because vision is the body's top intelligence gatherer, at least by the brain's reckoning. A full quarter of the cerebral cortex, the brain's crinkled top layer, is devoted to sight, according to a new estimate by neuroscientist David Van Essen of Washington University in St. Louis—almost certainly more than is devoted to any other sense.

SIGHT
Cells in the retina of the eye are so sensitive they can respond to a single photon, or particle of light.

It seems fitting, then, that vision has offered scientists their most powerful insights on the brain's structure and operations. Research on sight "has been absolutely fundamental" for understanding the brain, says neurobiologist Semir Zeki of University College in London, in part because the visual system is easier to study than the other senses. The first clues to the workings of the visual system emerged in the 1950s, when Johns Hopkins neurobiologists David Hubel and Torsten Wiesel conducted a series of Nobel Prize–winning experiments. Using hair-thin electrodes implanted in a cat's brain, they recorded the firing of single neurons in the area where vision is processed. When the animal was looking at a diagonal bar of light, one neuron fired. When the bar was at a slightly different angle, a different nerve cell responded.

Hubel and Wiesel's discovery led to a revolutionary idea: While we are perceiving a unified scene, the brain is dissecting the view into many parts, each of which triggers a different set of neurons, called a visual map. One map responds to color and form, another only to motion. There are at least five such maps in the visual system alone, and recent work is showing that other senses are similarly encoded in the brain. In an auditory map, for example, the two sets of neurons that respond to two similar sounds, such as "go" and "ko," are located near each other, while those resonating with the sound "mo" lie at a distance.

Though we think of sensory abilities as independent, researchers are finding that each sense receives help from the others in apprehending the world. In 1995, psycholinguist Michael Tanenhaus of the University of Rochester videotaped people as they listened to sentences about nearby objects. As they listened, the subjects' eyes flicked to the objects. Those movements—so fast the subjects did not realize they'd shifted their gaze—helped them understand the grammar of the sentences, Tanenhaus found. Obviously, vision isn't required to comprehend grammar. But given the chance, the brain integrates visual cues while processing language.

The brain also does much of the heavy lifting for color vision, so much so that some people with brain damage see the world in shades of gray. But the ability to see colors begins with cells in the back of the eyeball called cones. For decades, scientists thought everyone with normal color vision had the same three types of cone cell—for red, green and blue light—and saw the same hues. New research shows, however, that everybody sees a different palette. Last year, Medical College of Wisconsin researchers Maureen Neitz and her husband, Jay, discovered that people have up to nine genes for cones, indicating there may be many kinds of cones. Already, two red cone subtypes have been found. People with one type see red differently from those with the second. Says Maureen Neitz: "That's why people argue about adjusting the color on the TV set."

HEARING

Hearing is the gateway to language, a uniquely human skill. In a normal child, the ears tune themselves to human sounds soon after birth, cementing the neural connections between language, emotions and intelligence. Even a tiny glitch in the way a child processes sound can unhinge development.

About 7 million American children who have normal hearing and intelligence develop intractable problems with language, reading and writing because they cannot decipher certain parcels of language. Research by Paula Tallal, a Rutgers University neurobiologist, has shown that children with language learning disabilities (LLD) fail to distinguish between the "plosive" consonants, such as *b, t* and *p*. To them, "bug" sounds like "tug" sounds like "pug." The problem, Tallal has long argued, is that for such kids the sounds come too fast. Vowels resonate for 100 milliseconds or more, but plosive consonants last for a mere 40 milliseconds—not long enough for some children to process them. "These children hear the sound. It just isn't transmitted to the brain normally," she says.

Two years ago, Tallal teamed up with Michael Merzenich, a neurobiologist at the University of California–San Francisco, to create a set of computer games that have produced stunning gains in 29 children with LLD. With William Jenkins and Steve Miller, the neurobiologists wrote computer programs that elongated the plosive consonants, making them louder— "like making a yellow highlighter for the brain," says Tallal. After a month of daily three-hour sessions, children who were one to three years behind their peers in language and reading had leaped forward a full two years. The researchers have formed a company, Scientific Learning Corp., that could make their system available to teachers and professionals within a few years. (See their Web site: *http://www.scilearn.com* or call 415-296-1470.)

An inability to hear the sounds of human speech properly also may contribute to autism, a disorder that leaves children unable to relate emotionally to other people. According to University of Maryland psychophysiologist Stephen Porges, many autistic children are listening not to the sounds of human speech but instead to frightening noises. He blames the children's fear on a section of the nervous system that controls facial expressions, speech, visceral feelings and the muscles in the middle ear.

HEARING
At six months, a baby's brain tunes in to the sounds of its native tongue and tunes out other languages.

These muscles, the tiniest in the body, allow the ear to filter sounds, much the way muscles in the eye focus the eyeball on near or distant objects. In autistic children, the neural system that includes the middle ear is lazy. As a result, these children attend not to the pitch of the human voice but instead to sounds that are much lower: the rumble of traffic, the growl of a vacuum cleaner. In the deep evolutionary past, such noises signaled danger. Porges contends that autistic children feel too anxious to interact emotionally, and the neural system controlling many emotional responses fails to develop.

Porges says that exercising the neural system may help autistic kids gain language and emotional skills. He and his colleagues have begun an experimental treatment consisting of tones and songs altered by computer to filter out low sounds, forcing the middle ear to focus on the pitches of human speech. After five 90-minute sessions, most of the 16 children have made strides that surprised even Porges. Third grader Tomlin Clark, for example, who once spoke only rarely, recently delighted his parents by getting in trouble for talking out of turn in school. And for the first time, he shows a sense of humor. "Listening to sounds seems so simple, doesn't it?" says Porges. "But so does jogging."

TOUCH

The skin, writes pathologist Marc Lappé, "is both literally and metaphorically 'the body's edge'… a boundary against an inimical world." Yet the skin also is the organ that speaks the language of love most clearly—and not just in the erogenous zones. The caress of another person releases hormones that can ease pain and clear the mind. Deprive a child of touch, and his brain and body will stop growing.

This new view of the most intimate sense was sparked a decade ago, when child psychologist Tiffany Field showed that premature infants who were massaged for 15 minutes three times a day gained weight 47 percent faster than preemies given standard intensive care nursery treatment: as little touching as possible. The preemies who were massaged weren't eating more; they just processed food more efficiently, says Field, now director of the University of Miami's Touch Research Institute. Field found that massaged preemies were more alert and aware of their surroundings when awake, while their sleep was deeper and more restorative. Eight months later, the massaged infants scored better on mental and motor tests.

Being touched has healing powers throughout life. Massage, researchers have found, can ease the pain of severely burned children and boost the immune systems of AIDS patients. Field recently showed that office workers who received a 15-minute massage began emitting higher levels of brain waves associated with alertness. Af-

---

Wish you had that nose?

Folklore abounds with tales of animals possessing exceptional sensory powers, from pigs predicting earthquakes to pets telepathically anticipating their owners' arrival home. In some cases, myth and reality are not so far apart. Nature is full of creatures with superhuman senses: built-in compasses, highly accurate sonar, infrared vision. "Our worldview is limited by our senses," says Dartmouth College psychologist Howard Hughes, "so we are both reluctant to believe that animals can have capabilities beyond ours, and we attribute to them supernatural powers. The truth is somewhere between the two."

In the case of Watson, a Labrador retriever, reality is more impressive than any fiction. For over a year, Watson has reliably pawed his owner, Emily Ramsey, 45 minutes before her epileptic seizures begin, giving her time to move to a safe place. Placed by Canine Partners for Life, Watson has a 97 percent success rate, according to the Ramsey family. No one has formally studied how such dogs can predict seizure onset consistently. But they may smell the chemical changes known to precede epileptic attacks. "Whatever it is," says Harvard University neurologist Steven Schachter, "I think there's something to it."

Scientists have scrutinized other animals for decades, trying to decipher their sensory secrets. Birds, bees, moles and some 80 other creatures are known to sense magnetic fields. But new studies indicate birds have two magnetic detection systems: One seems to translate polarized light into visual patterns that act as a compass; the other is an internal magnet birds use to further orient themselves.

Dolphin sonar so intrigued government researchers that they launched the U.S. Navy Marine Mammal Program in 1960, hoping it would lead to more-sophisticated tracking equipment. But the animals still beat the machines, says spokesman Tom LaPuzza. In a murky sea, dolphins can pinpoint a softball two football fields away. A lobe in their forehead focuses their biosonar as a flashlight channels light, beaming 200-decibel clicks.

It took night-vision goggles for humans to replicate the infrared vision snakes come by naturally: A cameralike device in organs lining their lips lets them see heat patterns made by mammals. And humans can only envy the ability of sharks, skates and rays to feel electric fields through pores in their snouts—perhaps a primordial skill used by Earth's earliest creatures to scout out the new world.

BY ANNA MULRINE

---

ter their massage, the workers executed a math test in half their previous time with half the errors.

TOUCH
People with "synesthesia" feel colors, see sounds and taste shapes.

While such findings may sound touchy-feely, an increasing volume of physiological evidence backs them up. In a recent series of experiments, Swedish physiologist Kerstin Uvnas-Moberg found that gentle stroking can stimulate the body to release oxytocin, sometimes called the love hormone because it helps cement the bond between mothers and their young in many species. "There are deep, deep, physiological connections between touching and love," Uvnas-Moberg says. Oxytocin also blunts pain and dampens the hormones release when a person feels anxious or stressed.

For the babies of any species, touch signals that mother—the source of food, warmth and safety—is near. When she is gone, many young animals show physiological signs of stress and shut down their metabolism—an innate response designed to conserve energy until she returns. Without mother, rat pups do not grow, says Saul Schanberg, a Duke University pharmacologist, even when they are fed and kept warm. Stroking them with a brush in a manner that mimics their mother licking them restores the pups to robust health. "You need the right kind of touch in order to grow," says Schanberg, "even more than vitamins."

SMELL

Long ago in human evolution, smell played a prominent role, signaling who was ready to mate and who was ready to fight. But after a while, smell fell into disrepute. Aristotle disparaged it as the most animalistic of the senses, and Immanuel Kant dreamed of losing it. Recent research has restored the nose to some of its former glory. "Odor plays a far more important role in human behavior and physiology than we realize," says Gary Beauchamp, director of Philadelphia's Monell Chemical Senses Center.

SMELL
A woman's sense of smell is keener than a man's. And smell plays a larger role in sexual attraction for women.

A baby recognizes its mother by her odor soon after birth, and studies show that adults can identify clothing worn by their children or spouses by smell alone. In 1995, Beauchamp and colleagues at Monell reported that a woman's scent—genetically determined—changes in pregnancy to reflect a combination of her odor and that of her fetus.

The sense of smell's most celebrated capacity is its power to stir memory. "Hit a tripwire of smell, and memories explode all at once," writes poet Diane Ackerman. The reason, says Monell psychologist Rachel Herz, is that "smells carry an emotional quality." In her latest experiment, Herz showed people a series of evocative paintings. At the same time, the subjects were exposed to another sensory cue—an orange, for example—in different ways. Some saw an orange. Others were given an orange to touch, heard the word "orange" or smelled the fruit. Two days later, when subjects were given the same cue and were asked to recall the painting that matched it, those exposed to the smell of the orange recalled the painting and produced a flood of emotional responses to it.

Herz and others suspect that an aroma's capacity to spark such vivid remembrances arises out of anatomy. An odor's first way station in the brain is the olfactory bulb, two blueberry-sized lumps of cortex from which neurons extend through the skull into the nose. Smell molecules, those wafting off a cinnamon bun, for example, bind to these olfactory neurons, which fire off their signals first to the olfactory bulb and then to the limbic system—the seat of sexual drive, emotions and memory. Connections between the olfactory bulb and the neocortex, or thinking part of the brain, are secondary roads compared to the highways leading to emotional centers.

Scientists once thought all smells were made up of combinations of seven basic odors. But in an elegant series of experiments, research teams led by Columbia's Axel and Linda Buck of Harvard have shown the mechanics of smell to be much more complicated. In 1991, the scientists discovered a family of at least 1,000 genes

corresponding to about 1,000 types of olfactory neurons in the nose. Each of these neuronal types responds to one—and only one—type of odor molecule.

ARE YOU A SUPERTASTER?

All tongues are not created equal. How intense flavors seem is determined by heredity. In this test, devised by Yale University taste experts Linda Bartoshuk and Laurie Lucchina, find out if you are a **nontaster**, an **average taster** or a **supertaster**. Answers on next page.

TASTE BUDS. Punch a hole with a standard hole punch in a square of wax paper. Paint the front of your tongue with a cotton swab dipped in blue food coloring. Put wax paper on the tip of your tongue, just to the right of center. With a flashlight and magnifying glass, count the number of pink, unstained circles. They contain taste buds.

SWEET. Rinse your mouth with water before tasting each sample. Put ½ cup of sugar in a measuring cup, and then add enough water to make 1 cup. Mix. Coat front half of your tongue, including the tip, with a cotton swab dipped in the solution. Wait a few moments. Rate the sweetness according to the scale shown below.

SALT. Put 2 teaspoons of salt in a measuring cup and add enough water to make 1 cup. Repeat the steps listed above, rating how salty the solution is.

SPICY. Add 1 teaspoon of Tabasco sauce to 1 cup of water. Apply with a cotton swab to first half inch of the tongue, including the tip. Keep your tongue out of your mouth until the burn reaches a peak, then rate the pain according to the scale.

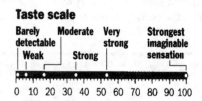

Taste scale

Barely detectable | Moderate | Very strong | Strongest imaginable sensation
Weak | Strong

0 10 20 30 40 50 60 70 80 90 100

The average person, of course, can detect far more than 1,000 odors. That's because a single scent is made up of more than one type of molecule, perhaps even dozens. A rose might stimulate neurons A,

B and C, while jasmine sets off neurons B, C and F. "Theoretically, we can detect an astronomical number of smells." says Axel—the equivalent of 10 to the 23rd power. The brain, however, doesn't have the space to keep track of all those possible combinations of molecules, and so it focuses on smells that were relevant in evolution, like the scent of ripe fruit or a sexually receptive mate—about 10,000 odors in all.

Axel and Buck have now discovered that the olfactory bulb contains a "map," similar to those the brain employs for vision and hearing. By implanting a gene into mice, the researchers dyed blue the nerves leading from the animals' olfactory bulbs to their noses. Tracing the path of these neurons, the researchers discovered that those responsible for detecting a single type of odor molecule all led back to a single point in the olfactory bulb. In other words, the jumble of neurons that exists in the nose is reduced to regimental order in the brain.

Smell maps may one day help anosmics, people who cannot smell. Susan Killorn of Richmond, Va., lost her sense of smell three years ago when she landed on her head while in-line skating and damaged the nerves leading from her nose to her brain. A gourmet cook, Killorn was devastated. "I can remember sitting at the dinner table and begging my husband to describe the meal I'd just cooked," she says. Killorn's ability to detect odors has gradually returned, but nothing smells quite right. One possibility, says Richard Costanzo, a neurophysiologist at Virginia Commonwealth University, is that some of the nerves from her nose have recovered or regenerated but now are hooked up to the wrong spot in her smell map.

Though imperfect, recoveries like Killorn's give researchers hope they may one day be able to stimulate other neurons to regenerate—after a spinal cord injury, for example. Costanzo and others are searching for chemicals made by the body that can act as traffic cops, telling neurons exactly where to grow. In the meantime, Killorn is grateful for every morsel of odor. "I dream at night about onions and garlic," she says, "and they smell like they are supposed to."

TASTE

Human beings will put almost anything into their mouths and consider it food, from stinging nettles to grubs. Fortunately, evolution armed the human tongue with a set of sensors to keep venturesome members of the species from dying of malnutrition or poison. The four simple flavors—sweet, salty, bitter and sour—tell human beings what's healthy and what's harmful. But as researchers are finding, the sense of taste does far more than keep us from killing ourselves. Each person tastes food differently, a genetically determined sensitivity that can affect diet, weight and health.

TASTE
Human beings are genetically hard-wired to crave sweetness; sugar on the lips of a newborn baby will bring a smile.

In a quest for novelty, people around the world have developed an affinity for foods that cause a modicum of pain. "Humans have the ability to say, 'Oh, that didn't really hurt me—let me try it again,'" says Barry Green, a psychologist at the John B. Pierce Laboratory in New Haven, Conn. Spicy food, Green has found, gives the impression of being painfully hot by stimulating the nerves in the mouth that sense temperature extremes. The bubbles in soda and champagne feel as if they are popping inside the mouth; in reality, carbon dioxide inside the bubbles irritates nerves that sense pain.

One person's spicy meatball, however, is another's bland and tasteless meal. Researchers have long known that certain people have an inherited inability to taste a mildly bitter substance with a tongue-twisting name: propylthiouracil, or PROP, for short. About a quarter of Caucasians are "nontasters," utterly insensitive to PROP, while the vast majority of Asians and Africans can taste it. Now, researchers

at Yale University led by psychologist Linda Bartoshuk have discovered a third group of people called "supertasters." So sensitive are supertasters' tongues that they gag on PROP and can detect the merest hint of other bitter compounds in a host of foods, from chocolate and saccharin to vegetables such as broccoli, "which could explain why George Bush hates it," Bartoshuk says. She has recently discovered that supertasters have twice as many taste buds as nontasters and more of the nerve endings that detect the feel of foods. As a consequence, sweets taste sweeter to supertasters, and cream feels creamier. A spicy dish can send a supertaster through the roof.

RESULTS OF TASTE TEST ON PREVIOUS PAGE		
	SUPER-TASTERS	NON-TASTERS
No. of taste buds	25 on average	10
Sweet rating	56 on average	32
Tabasco rating	64 on average	31
Average tasters lie in between. Bartoshuk and Lucchina lack the data to rate salt.		

In an ongoing study, Bartoshuk's group has found that older women who are nontasters tend to prefer sweets and fatty foods—dishes that some of the supertasters find cloying. Not surprisingly, supertasters also tend to be thinner and have lower cholesterol. In their study, the researchers ask subjects to taste cream mixed with oil, a combination Bartoshuk confesses she finds delicious. "I'm a nontaster, and I'm heavy," she says. "I gobble up the test." But tasting ability is not only a matter of cuisine preference and body weight. Monell's Marcia Pelchat and a graduate student recently completed a study indicat-

ing that nontasters also may be predisposed to alcoholism.

The human senses detect only a fraction of reality: We can't see the ultraviolet markers that guide a honeybee to nectar; we can't hear most of the noises emitted by a dolphin. In this way, the senses define the boundaries of mental awareness. But the brain also defines the limits of what we perceive. Human beings see, feel, taste, touch and smell not the world around them but a version of the world, one their brains have concocted. "People imagine that they're seeing what's really there, but they're not," says neuroscientist John Maunsell of Baylor College of Medicine in Houston. The eyes take in the light reflecting off objects around us, but the brain only pays attention to part of the scene. Looking for a pen on a messy desk, for example, you can scan the surface without noticing the papers scattered across it.

The word "sentience" derives from the Latin verb *sentire*, meaning "to feel." And research on the senses, especially the discovery of sensory mapping, has taken scientists one step further in understanding the state we call consciousness. Yet even this dramatic advance is only a beginning. "In a way, these sexy maps have seduced us," says Michael Shipley, director of neurosciences at the University of Maryland–Baltimore. "We still haven't answered the question of how do you go from visual maps to recognizing faces, or from an auditory map to recognizing a Mozart sonata played by two different pianists." The challenge for the 21st century will be figuring out how the brain, once it has broken the sensory landscape into pieces, puts them together again.

BY SHANNON BROWNLEE
WITH TRACI WATSON

From *U.S. News & World Report*, January 13, 1997, pp. 51-56, 58-59. © 1997 by U.S. News & World Report. Reprinted by permission.

Sight Unseen

Mike May was blind most of his life until surgery gave him his sight back.
But two years later he still can't recognize his own wife.
By learning why, psychologists are revealing the very origins of vision

BY MICHAEL ABRAMS

MIKE MAY HOLDS THE WORLD SPEED RECORD FOR downhill skiing by a blind person. In his competitive days he would slalom down the steepest black-diamond slopes at 65 miles an hour, with a guide 10 feet ahead to shout "left" and "right." The directions were just obvious cues. The rest came from the feel of the wind racing against his cheeks and the sound of the guide's skis snicking over the snow. But May's days as a world-class blind athlete are behind him. He's no longer blind.

May lost his vision at the age of 3, when a jar of fuel for a miner's lantern exploded in his face. It destroyed his left eye and scarred the cornea of his right, but over the next 43 years he never let those disabilities slow him down. He played flag football in elementary school, soccer in college, and nearly any activity that didn't involve projectiles as an adult. He earned a master's degree in international affairs from Johns Hopkins, took a job with the CIA, and became the president and CEO of the Sendero Group, a company that makes talking Global Positioning Systems for the blind. Along the way, he found time to help develop the first laser turntable, marry, have two children, and buy a house in Davis, California. "Someone once asked me if I could have vision or fly to the moon, what would I choose," he once wrote. "No question—I would fly to the moon. Lots of people have sight, few have gone to the moon."

Then one November day in 1999, he came back to his senses. At St. Mary's Hospital in San Francisco, surgeon Daniel Goodman dropped a doughnut of corneal stem cells onto May's right eye (his left was too severely damaged to be repaired). The cells replaced scar tissue and rebuilt the ocular surface, preparing the eye for a corneal transplant. On March 7, 2000, when the wraps were removed, May got his first look at his wife, his children, and for the first time since he was a toddler, himself.

Sight restoration is a periodic miracle both for its recipients and for the scientists who have the privilege of studying them. As early as the fifth century B.C., Egyptian surgeons used a needle to push their patients' cataract-covered lenses away from their pupils, affording them some degree of sight. More recently, in the late 1960s, surgeons learned to remove cataracts with ultrasound. The stem-cell surgery performed on May was developed in Japan and introduced in 1999. Since then hundreds of people have benefited from it. But of all those who have had their sight restored throughout history, only about 20 recorded cases were blind since childhood, and of those, most had less-than-perfect corneas after surgery. When Goodman peered into May's eye after the surgery, he saw a lens that ought to provide crystal-clear vision.

It doesn't—far from it. Pristine as his optical hardware is, May's brain has never been programmed to process the visual information it receives. May still travels with his dog, Josh, or taps the sidewalk with a cane, and refers to himself as "a blind man with vision." And that paradox fascinates Don MacLeod and Ione Fine, experimental psychologists at the University of California at San Diego. The speed with which babies learn to understand the world suggests that they're born with the ability to process some aspects of vision. But which aspects, exactly? What is learned and what is hardwired? During the past year and a half, Fine and MacLeod have put May through a battery of physical and psychological tests, including functional magnetic resonance imaging, or fMRI, which tracks blood flow in the brain. The results are opening the first clear view into how we learn to see.

MACLEOD'S LABORATORY AT THE UNIVERSITY IS A LABYRINTH of filing cabinets, optical equipment, and oddly placed desks. "It's well booby-trapped," he says, steering May toward the first of many tests one afternoon. "But May has an uncanny ability to navigate complicated arrangements." Tall and athletic, with features that look boyishly handsome despite his graying black hair, May would make a good James Bond if not for a few sic effects of his blindness. Unlike the rest of his body, his eyelids haven't had a lifelong workout. Perpetually half closed, they lend a stoic blankness to his face that's relieved only by the occasional smile. He has yet to learn facial expressions.

A blind man who is suddenly given vision, Molyneux suggested wouldn't be able to tell the difference between a cube and a sphere

Sitting obligingly in front of an ancient computer monitor, May watches as thick black-and-orange bars appear on the screen. MacLeod and Fine are testing his ability to see detail. His job is to adjust the contrast with a trackball until he can just see the bars. A click on a mouse brings up another set of bars, thinner than the last, and he plays around with those until he can see them too. Although his right eye ought to provide 20/20 vision, in reality it's closer to 20/500. Instead of discerning the letter *E* on an eye chart from 25 feet, May can see it only from two. In the past the blurred vision of people with restored sight was blamed on scar tissue from surgery. But stem-cell surgery leaves no scars. The signals are reaching May's brain, but they are not being interpreted very well.

More than 300 years ago, in a famous letter to the philosopher John Locke, the Irish thinker William Molyneux anticipated what May sees. A blind man who is suddenly given vision, Molyneux suggested, wouldn't be able to tell the difference between a cube and a sphere. Sight is one kind of perception and touch another; they can be linked only through experience.

The most dramatic proof of this theory came in an experiment published in 1963 by Richard Held and Alan Hein, who

were then professors at Brandeis University in Waltham, Massachusetts. Held and Hein raised two kittens in total darkness. But every so often they would place the kittens in separate baskets, suspend the baskets from a single circular track, and turn on the lights. Both baskets hung just above the floor, but one had holes for the kitten's legs to poke through; the other did not. The free-limbed cat ran in circles on the floor, pulling the other basket along behind it; the other kitten had no choice but to sit and watch. While the active kitten learned to see normally, the passive kitten stayed effectively blind: Its eyes could see, but its brain never learned to interpret the sensory input.

Held and Hein's experiment has never been duplicated. But in the past half century, studies of sight restoration, most notably by Oliver Sacks and Richard Gregory, have verified that some things can't be understood without experience. Objects, faces, depth—just about everything that helps us function in the world—are meaningless when a person who has never seen before gets sight. "Babies are born into a bright, buzzing confusion, but we can't ask them what it's like," Fine says. "In some ways talking to Mike May is like getting to talk to a 7-month-old."

IN THE FIRST MONTHS AFTER HIS SURGERY, MAY FULFILLED molyneux's prediction: He couldn't distinguish a sphere from a cube. Since then his sight has improved, but only slightly. He has a better grasp of spheres and squares ("We've shown him an awful lot of them," Fine says), and with practice he can understand things he's seen again and again. But this is only a workaround: He's past the critical period for learning to recognize objects instantly.

"Two of the major clues I have are color and context," May says. "When I see an orange thing on a basketball court, I assume it's round. But I may not be really seeing the roundness of it." Faces give him even more trouble. Although he has seen faces everywhere since the first day his vision was restored, they simply don't coalesce into recognizable people. Their expressions—their moods and personalities—elude him entirely. Even his wife is familiar to him only by the quality of her gait, the length of her hair, and the clothes she wears. "If a face has no hair and a fake moustache, we can still tell the gender," Fine says. "But he can't deal with it. The bit of the brain that does that isn't working."

The best proof of this can be seen in the basement, where MacLeod's interferometer sits. Designed to test the brain's ability to process visual information, the machine works by shining a split laser beam into a subject's eye. As the beams travel, their light waves interfere with each other, bypassing the optics of the cornea and projecting a pattern onto the retina. Most subjects who sit in front of the interferometer will see light and dark stripes, regardless of the quality of their optics. But when May opens his eyes to receive the beams, he sees nothing at all.

The interferometer results are backed by fMRI scans, which track May's brain activity as it's occurring. The scans show that when May sees faces and objects, the part of his brain that should be used to recognize them is inactive. But there's a catch. When he sees an object in motion, the motion-detection part of his brain lights up like a disco ball. He can interpret

Do You See What I See?

May ought to have 20/20 vision since his right eye was restored by stem-cell surgery and a corneal transplant. Instead, his vision is closer to 20/500—or about as blurry as the example to the right. "Basically, the results say that you can only get precise vision early in life at the critical period, " Don Macload says. "We don't really know where Mat will end up, but he isn't approaching normal vision at a quick rate."

Above: A lifetime of blindness has left May insusceptible to visual illusions. Most people would say that the top of the dark cube is darker than the front of the light cube. To May they're the same exact shade. It's only when MacLeod explains the illusion that May can even see that squares are supposed to look three-dimensional.

movement on a computer screen as well as any normal-sighted adult and seems to have the same skill in real life. "We were driving along, and a minivan came up to us pretty fast on his side," Fine remembers. "It whizzed by him, and he mentioned that it was going fast. That's a complicated calculation. The motion on the retina depends on how big the car is, how close, and how fast it's going."

It's hard to escape the conclusion that motion detection, unlike every other visual experience aside from color, is largely hardwired. The best illustration of this may be offered, once again, by cats. "If you roll a ball along a floor, the cat will chase it as long as it's moving," Fine says. "As soon as its stationary, the cat will have a hard time seeing it and will ignore it." That's why mice freeze when they're afraid. It may also explain why May, who can barely recognize a stationary ball, is pretty good at catching a moving one. It's his favorite use of his new sense. "I don't know who has more fun," he says, "my 8-year-old or me."

BLIND PEOPLE SPEND THEIR ENTIRE LIVES UNDERSTANDING THE world through their hands. Their memories, their mental maps of the places they know, their understanding of Labradors, doorknobs, and the moguls on a ski slope are all tactile. The sudden introduction of a new sense can't alter that fundamental way of experiencing the universe. Instead, any new information gleaned from light is simply graphed onto the original, tactile map. "The old idea that there is one picture of the world on the surface of the cortex is way too simple," MacLeod says. "In fact, we have a couple dozen complete maps." For someone just learning how to merge all that information, this can make for a great deal of confusion. But it might also offer a richer, truer sense of the world than the one perceived by those of us who have never been blind.

Sitting in the lab one day, MacLeod, smirking like a schoolboy who's hatching a prank, slides a drawing across the table to May. On the paper are four cubes. The top right cube and the bottom left cube are dark; the other two are light. The drawing is shaded as if light were coming from above, so the tops of the squares are lighter than their fronts. This makes the top of the dark square the same shade as the front of the light square. Experience tells us that the top of the dark cube has been brightened by a hidden light, but it still seems darker than the front of a light cube. It's an illusion based on knowledge. Naturally, May doesn't fall for it.

"He's actually closer to reality," Fine says. "We once showed him two circles—a small one close to him and a larger one farther away. To you or me they would have appeared to be the same size. But when we asked, 'What's the apparent size?' he couldn't understand. He kept saying, 'I know it's bigger because it's far away.'" Similarly, May's tactile experience with hallways and highways tells him that their sides are parallel, so he simply can't perceive converging lines of perspective. "A hallway doesn't look like it closes in at all," he says. "I see the lines on either side of the path, but I don't really think of them as coming closer in the distance." He pauses to mull this over. "Or maybe my mind doesn't believe what my mind is perceiving. When I see an object, it doesn't look different to me as I circle around it. I know orange cones around vehicles are cones because of context, not because I'm seeing the shape. If I picture looking down on a cone, it still looks like a cone."

Only a handful of adults have ever seen the world through the eyes of a newborn, and many who did came away wishing they were still blind

Learning to see, for May, is really about learning to fall for the same illusions we all do, to call a certain mass of colors and lines his son, to call another group of them a ball.

ONE APRIL MORNING, ONLY WEEKS AFTER HIS EYE SURGERY, may took his skis and his family up to the Kirkwood Mountain Resort in the Sierra Nevadas—a place he knew like the texture on the back of his hand. This was where he had first learned to ski and where he had later met his wife. The sun was out, the trees were green (greener than he'd imagined), and the slopes were surrounded by gorgeous cliffs (were they miles away or just a few hundred yards?). As the lift churned above, skiers in puffy parkas flitted by, popping into his field of vision. His wife, acting as a guide, had to remind him to stop gawking and ski.

With only one working eye, May already lacked depth perception. But he also had little experience reading the shades and contours of a landscape. Heading down the mountain, he could hardly distinguish shadows from people, poles, or rocks. At first, he tried to compute the lay of the land consciously: If a certain slope was being lit from the side and a shadow fell in such a way, then the slope must be convex. But once he hit his first bump, he was tempted to close his eyes and ski the way he knew and loved.

Only a handful of adults have ever seen the world through the eyes of a newborn, and many who did came away wishing they were still blind. Their family and friends had convinced them that vision would offer a miraculous new appreciation and understanding of the world. Instead, even the simplest actions—walking down stairs, crossing the street—became terrifyingly difficult. Dispirited and depressed, about a third of them reverted back to the world of the blind, preferring dark rooms and walking with their eyes shut.

If May feels differently, it may be because his expectations were so low. For a man who used to enjoy windsurfing blind and alone, able more often than not to return to the pier from which he'd started, sight is just another adventure in a life of invigorating obstacles. Two years after his return to Kirkwood

Mountain, May has learned to match what he sees on a ski slope with his repeated physical experience of it. "He has jury-rigged himself quite a functional little system," Fine says. "He knows that this kind of shadow makes this bump, this kind makes another." Instead of closing his eyes on even the easiest slopes, he can now negotiate moguls without a guide.

"People have this idea that it's so overwhelmingly practical to have sight," May says. "I say it's great from an entertainment point of view. I'm constantly looking for things that are unique to vision. Running and catching a ball is one of them—I've been chasing balls my whole life. Seeing the difference between the blue of my two sons' eyes is another. Or if you drop something, you can find it."

The gift of sight may seem most miraculous, in the end, to those who have never been blind. But May still finds things in the world to entrance him. Sitting in the passenger seat of Fine's car one day, with his dog, Josh, panting at his feet, he ignores the blue Pacific to the left, the towering, top-heavy eucalyptus trees lining the road like something out of Dr. Seuss. Instead, he gazes at the beam of sunlight filtering through the window onto his lap. "I can't believe the dust is just floating in the air like this," he says. Oceans and trees, Seussean or otherwise, he has known all his life through touch. But this glitter of dust, suspended in the bright La Jolla sun, is an entirely new awareness. He waves his hand through the sparkling beam. "It's like having little stars all around you."

From *Discover*, June 2002, pp. 54-59. © 2002. Reprinted with permission of the author, Michael Abrams.

IT'S A NOISY, NOISY WORLD OUT THERE!

From the acoustic trauma of airbag deployment to the blast of personal stereos, we must stop turning a deaf ear to the daily menace of noise in our environment.

by Dr. Richard Carmen

The 80-decibel (dB) alarm clock (two feet from my head) shatters the silence at 6:45 a.m. and does bad things to nice dreams. Anything less noisy risks not waking me up.

Moments later, the electric shaver mows precariously near my ears at 85 dB. After the shower, it's time for the hair-blower endurance test of 112 dB. If decibels were converted to wind velocity, the hair dryer could self-propel. This new dryer—a "Turbo-Rocket Torque-357"—should require special handling and be reclassified as a leaf blower. On days when I'm short on time, I move it closer to my hair and therefore nearer to my ears. Not a good idea.

This racket signals my four-year-old daughter that my day has begun. She bolts into the bathroom shouting louder than the dryer, sometimes toting her toy megaphone to amplify her morning song, "Fe Fi Fo Fum!" (135 dB one foot away) If this cacophony were to occur outside, my neighbors could have me fined and, in some cities, even arrested!

By the time I make it to my quiet morning coffee, a short but heartfelt reprieve, the doorbell is intermittently emitting sounds that remind me of an Alfred Hitchcock movie. Each 115 dB buzz (just below my auditory discomfort but exceeding my annoyance level) reminds me I have to get rid of it.

It's my daughter's ride to school. She dashes out the door, and I'm right behind her. We're greeted with a blare of the horn. It feels like dual five-inch cannons against our foreheads. Reflexively, I raise my arms and drop her lunchbox. Ears slightly ringing, I accept the driver's wave of apology and hobble back to my tepid coffee. I would normally use the microwave to reheat it, but the "Ready" alarm is just more than I can handle this morning. And the day has just begun.

I escape momentarily into the TV room, when my wife walks in. "How can you stand it that loud?" she queries. "You better check your hearing, honey!" she adds as she leaves.

I follow her into the kitchen where a high-speed blender prepares her morning nutritional drink. Military assault weapons make less noise.

"How can you stand it that loud?" I shout, wondering if the noise does as much mixing as the blades.

"What?" she asks. At least I think that's what she says; it was the right lip movement. I don't answer her because she can't read lips, and besides, she's turned on the disposal (94 dB)—loud, but inconsequential, considering the blender. I blow her a kiss, and I'm off to work.

The slam of the door on my old truck, metal to metal, surely has acoustic peaks exceeding 120 dB. It hurts, but if I don't slam it, the door remains ajar. I've noticed ringing in that left ear lately.

On the highway, I wave to a physician friend riding his motorcycle without a helmet, and wonder if he knows that riding at 80 mph for just one hour puts him at risk for hearing loss.

And so it goes for families all across America.

Despite the Occupational, Safety, and Health Administration's (OSHA) decree stating that workers should not be exposed to more than 90 dB for an eight-hour period, these limits

How's Your Hearing?

The following questions can help you determine if you have a hearing loss and need to have your hearing evaluated.

❑ Do you have a problem hearing over the telephone?

❑ Do you hear better with one ear than the other when you are on the telephone?

❑ Do you have trouble following the conversation when two or more people are talking at the same time?

❑ Do people complain that you turn the TV volume up too high?

❑ Do you have to strain to understand conversation?

❑ Do you have trouble hearing in a noisy background?

❑ Do you have trouble hearing in restaurants?

❑ Do you have dizziness, pain, or ringing in your ears?

❑ Do you find yourself asking people to repeat themselves?

❑ Do family members or coworkers remark about your missing what has been said?

❑ Do many people you talk to seem to mumble (or not speak clearly)?

❑ Do you misunderstand what others are saying and respond inappropriately?

❑ Do you have trouble understanding the speech of women and children?

❑ Do people get annoyed because you misunderstand what they say?

If you answer yes to more than two of these questions, you should have your hearing tested by a licensed audiologist.

are exceeded every day throughout U.S. industry. I've been in paper mills and factories where hard hats and earplugs are required upon entry.

The workers' biggest complaint about hearing protection is that they can't hear one another or potentially lifesaving warnings, like backup signals of heavy equipment. With good ear protection, you're not supposed to hear well. The solution is to provide ear defenders that incorporate telecommunication ability, like the kind pit crews wear at auto races so coworkers can share essential information. Although this technology works, it's expensive. Nevertheless, corporations should realize that protection is in their best interest; the average annual cost of medical management for hearing loss is $56 billion.

Unfortunately, government-approved noise levels for an eight-hour day are not proven to be safe. Furthermore, for many of us, dangerously loud noise levels may not even end at work. And if you happen to work around certain chemicals (e.g., lacquer or varnish containing toluene) while exposed to high-level noise, you have a significantly increased risk for hearing loss.

Noise holds a certain "prestige" for some. "Manly" men who model themselves after the character Tim Allen played on his TV show are proud to show off their latest power mowers (105 dB), sandblasters (110 dB), power drills (115 dB), or chain saws that can V-cut right into the hardest knot of an oak tree (135 dB)!

Recreational "boy toys" (yes, and "girl toys," too) range from snowmobiles (110 dB) to rifles and guns (120 to 140 dB). Then there are those kids with boom boxes (better identified as "bomb boxes") in their cars. The average continuous output of these devices exceeds 120 dB; these kids' window-rattling "music" will surely come back to haunt them one day.

Because women aren't typically exposed to as much noise as men, they may think they're safe from noise hazards. Not so. That sweet bundle of joy sleeping peacefully in your arms is capable of hurling cries at 120-plus dB. The toys that accompany such bundles can put not only children but also caretakers at risk.

Every year, children's toys are removed from the market because of their intolerably dangerous noise levels. Some peaks reach 150 dB. Despite the watchful eye of OSHA,

Noise Levels

dBA*	NOISE SOURCE
190 ...	105mm howitzer
170 ...	deployed auto airbag
163 ...	bazooka at one foot
155 ...	assault rifles 13 feet from the muzzle
150 ...	child's toy mimicking an assault rifle
145 ...	U.S. Army Sergeant missile at 100 feet
140 ...	threshold of pain; military assault rifle; toy cap gun; siren at 100 feet
135 ...	U.S. Army tactical launcher at 400 feet; jet taking off; child's voice-amplified toy; amplified music
130 ...	miniature rifles; air-raid siren
125 ...	child's toy phone
120 ...	threshold of discomfort; auto horn; chain saw; jackhammer; snowmobile (driver's seat); child's musical instruments
110 ...	MRI (at head location in the isocenter); inboard motorboat; sandblaster; baby rattle; films in movie theaters
105 ...	power saw; helicopter
100 ...	subway train; tractor; farm equipment
95 ...	ride in a convertible car on freeway
90 ...	industrial noise
80 ...	live piano music
70 ...	dog bark
60 ...	vacuum cleaner
50 ...	conversation; some vowels in conversation
40 ...	soft music
30 ...	some high-frequency consonants
20 ...	dripping water
10 ...	soft whisper
5 ...	soft rustling leaves
0 ...	the best hearing threshold

Sound pressure levels as measured on the A scale.

This table was compiled by the author from a variety of scientific sources.

some toys sneak through, even by brand-name companies we've come to trust.

A couple of years ago, one toy manufacturer's trendy slogan flashed through our industry like a thunderbolt: "Play It Loud." After much opposition from the hearing industry, this company backed down and eliminated the banner line. Yet, toy cellular telephones and walkie-talkies at clearly hazardous levels are still marketed to our children.

Although the polls say that women continue to shoulder the load when it comes to housework, heavy cleaning can be an equal-opportunity noise hazard. A manufacturer once put a quiet vacuum cleaner on the market, a product that was proven to be as effective as its competition. It died quietly in stores throughout the country. Consumers didn't believe it; noise is equated with power and effectiveness. We like it loud!

A front-row seat at a rock concert or in a bar with a live band can easily carry acoustic peaks exceeding 130 dB. This sound level can wreak the same results as excessive drinking: nausea and vomiting.

With the advent of CD-quality TVs, stereos, telephones, and the like, the tremendous enhancement in fidelity requires less volume. Improved signal-to-noise ratios produce less internal noise; however, we still demand louder volume levels. The problem is that we've grown accustomed to it, and the misperception that "louder is better" persists.

Current statistics suggest that about a third of all hearing loss is attributable to noise. From health club fitness classes, where bombardment

of music is maintained at 110 dB for 30 minutes or more, to movie theaters that exceed 130 dB (actually replicating the sound pressure level of a gun!), you as a willing participant are at risk. In a sure sign of progress, the associations for both these groups, The International Association of Fitness Professionals and the National Association of Theater Owners, are at long last recommending sound-level reductions, indicating that maybe "softer is better."

We all differ in our sensitivities. Some people have a more highly developed sense of smell, taste, vision, touch, or hearing. While there may be established norms, individual variability can be great. Some people with more acute hearing have an increased susceptibility to noise-induced hearing loss. Research data have shown that people with light-colored eyes (vs. dark eyes) run an increased risk of hearing loss when around high-level noise.

Furthermore, *The Lancet* (Jan. 2, 1999) reported on a French study among 1,208 men aged 18 to 24. They found that those who had regularly used personal stereo headsets for at least an hour daily and who also had a history of ear infections had significantly greater incidence of hearing loss.

Permanent, irreversible, instantaneous hearing loss occurs every day. Acoustic trauma is inflicted upon people in seemingly innocuous situations such as air-bag deployment, where sound-pressure levels can reach 170 dB. An estimated 30 million construction workers are at risk. Many airport workers are losing their hearing. And data now impli-

cate MRIs as a factor in hearing loss, a situation that can be solved by wearing earplugs during the test. Dentists and dental hygienists are at risk due to daily exposure to dental equipment such as blasters, drills, ultrasonic scalers, and so forth.

This is to name but a few of the culprits.

What are we doing to ourselves? While we don't have to buy products that emit toxic noise, sometimes we cannot escape, it, particularly when the noise is part of the work environment. Most of us can't just quit our jobs, but we can influence change.

Writing letters to manufacturers can make a difference. Professionals who use equipment with high noise levels (like dentists) must exert pressure on their suppliers. If we simply stopped purchasing their goods, manufacturers would respond accordingly. Nearly all products have noise reduction capability.

As parents, we must not support toy manufacturers that place our kids at risk. Stop buying their toys.

It has been said that one letter of complaint represents a hundred voices. Write one. When enough of us do, manufacturers will listen. Complain to theater managers and workout instructors. Noise will come down.

One person can make a difference. But in today's world, you may need to shout to be heard.

Richard Carmen, Au.D., FAAA, is a clinical audiologist and editor of the book *The Consumer Handbook on Hearing Loss & Hearing Aids: A Bridge to Healing*. His article appeared originally in *Hearing Health* magazine.

From *The Saturday Evening Post*, March/April 2002, pp. 52-53, 78, 80, 82. © 2002 by The Saturday Evening Post.

An Ear For Color

Exploring the Curious World of Synesthesia, Where Senses Merge in Mysterious Ways

Allison Hoover Bartlett

I'm told that the letters of my first name form the color of iced tea or pale plums or eucalyptus leaves (with silvery undersides). I'm a believer in the power of metaphor and all that, but the people who described how they saw the colors of a, l, l, i, s, o and n—and the hues they create as a single word—were being literal. They have a neurological condition known as synesthesia, which is often described as a sensory cross-wiring in the brain. In its most common manifestation, people see letters in color. Some also see numbers in color, hear music and speech in color, taste shapes, smell sounds—the list goes on. To hear their descriptions of the world is to feel half-blind, half-deaf or at least very simple.

A few years ago, after describing for my parents an article I'd read about synesthesia (which none of us had heard of), my father confessed that he had always seen numbers in color. Green 4's, red 3's, orange 7's. My mother was stunned. I was envious. He dismissed it as an association he must have learned as a child from building blocks. I filed it away as a question to return to. Such questions tend to linger.

I began to see language less as a bridge between people than as a threadbare rope tossed from one edge of a precipice to open hands at another.

I must have been 7 or 8, squatting on the summer-hot pavement with my sister, scrawling disappearing messages on the concrete with snapped leaves of an ice plant, when it occurred to me that people could agree on the name of a thing, in this case, a color—the green of the translucent fluid that oozed from the leaf, which we determined was chartreuse—while seeing it very differently. I understood that when my sister agreed on the name chartreuse, she might, in fact, be seeing what I call red or yellow or blue. I began to see language less as a bridge between people than as a threadbare rope tossed from one edge of a precipice to open hands at another.

I remember this moment on the pavement because it raised one of those Big Questions, a fundamental mystery: Do you see what I see? It stuck with me and eventually led me down a path that, unlike most fundamental mysteries, actually has an answer, albeit one I never anticipated.

Last spring, after doing preliminary research, I attended the first meeting of the American Synesthesia Association. While my official reason for attending was a journalist's quest for an unusual story, the equally compelling motivation was personal curiosity—what is this thing residing within my father? Roughly half of the 50 attendees of the meeting were "synesthetes," the other half scientists and physicians researching the phenomenon.

There I was, taking notes in a paneled meeting room at Princeton University, but I might as well have been on another planet, or at least in another country, one where I could grasp the words spoken but not the images conjured—images that these synesthetes, giddy with discovery of others like themselves, recognized as clearly as the spellings and colors of their own names.

… while synesthesia itself is fascinating, the real thrill… is how discoveries about it may improve the understanding of how thought and perception happen in general.

I had already read about the centuries-long documented history of synesthesia, beginning with John Locke, who wrote about it in 1690; famous synesthetes (Vladimir Nabokov, Franz Liszt, physicist Richard Feynman, etc.); and brain imaging technologies (positron emission tomography and functional magnetic resonance imaging) that validate this as a bona fide neurological happening. But here now were the faces of synesthesia, those who have it, describing how it affects their lives, and those who research it, presenting studies that were surprisingly simple and convincing.

V.S. Ramachandran, director of the Center for Brain and Cognition at the University of California, San Diego, described a study conducted last year where subjects were asked to find a pattern in a field of similarly shaped numbers (a triangle of 2's in a field of 5's, for example). Non-synesthetes took significantly longer than their sensorially gifted counterparts to identify the triangle. For those synesthetes (who see numbers in color and for whom 5 and 2 appear as different colors), the triangle popped out. According to Ramachandran, this and similar tests prove synesthesia is a genuine perceptual phenomenon.

Edward Hubbard, a psychology graduate student and colleague of Ramachandran's, described another study based on "crowding." Subjects were shown quickly a group of similarly shaped numbers crowded together (say, 252) in their peripheral vision. Since it's difficult to process the middle number in this situation, most subjects reported seeing only the 2's. Yet synesthetes who associate colors with numbers, while reporting seeing the 2's, also described a flash of color (whatever color they see 5 as) between the 2's, and were thus able to report the entire group: 252. The reason for their comprehension of 5's color but not form is something called "blindsight," in which certain visual information (in this case, color) gains access to conscious awareness while other information (form) does not.

Such explanations lead toward hot territory, for while synesthesia itself is fascinating, the real thrill among many researchers is how discoveries about it may improve the understanding of how thought and perception happen in general.

"Basically, we know a good deal about the early stages of neural processing of objects," says Eric Odgaard, a research associate at John B. Pierce Laboratory in New Haven, Conn. "What we have is a lot of information about how the brain breaks down the various components of an object—shape, motion, color—with very little information on where and how it puts them back together to create the seamless perception of an object we actually experience." This reconstructive process, or "binding," is what cognitive neuroscientists want to understand better.

They also hope that studying synesthetes will shed some light on the bridges between emotion and reason. Just how connected, Robert Root-Bernstein, professor of psychology at Michigan State University, asked, are physical sensations, intellectual activity and emotional feelings? He cited two mathematicians, Bertrand Russell and the late Harvard professor Norbert Wiener, both of whom described feeling physical discomfort when faced with unresolved equations and needing to resolve them before being able to release them from their bodies.

During a coffee break shortly before Root-Bernstein's presentation, Ramachandran had asked one of the synesthetes, Page Getz of Los Angeles, how she feels when she sees something incongruous—for example, if the letter A is yellow to her, what happens when she sees it printed in red? She said that, depending on the situation, it causes her varying degrees of discomfort.

"Is it mildly annoying or do you feel physically disturbed?" he asked. "What is the extent of your discomfort?"

"It's like I'm pedaling a bike," said Getz, "but the wheels are going in the wrong direction."

One of the problems with researching synesthesia is that since it has been found to be most common among artists, poets and drug users, historically scientists and doctors have dismissed their testimonies as metaphorical or just plain weird. It was also ignored, Ramachandran says, because it didn't make sense in neurological terms.

In many ways, it still doesn't. Brain imaging technologies may prove synesthesia is real, but no one knows why or how it happens—and there's little consensus. Ramachandran's explanation is that hyper-connectivity between areas in the brain that process color and for graphemes (letters, numbers) may be caused by a genetic mutation that causes defective "pruning," or trimming of connections. (In the immature brain, there are far more connections than in the adult brain, so the "pruning" process of trimming connections is normal. The less gardening, you could say, the more entangled the foliage.)

Researchers agree about synesthesia's hereditary nature— how DNA links between parent and child can shimmer with this ability to see, hear, taste, touch and smell what the rest of us cannot.

Richard Cytowic, a neurologist and author of "The Man Who Tasted Shapes" (MIT Press, 1998) has another theory. At a dinner party in 1980, he overheard his host, who was in the kitchen tasting the chicken, say, "There aren't enough points" on it, a sign for him that it wasn't done yet. After testing this person extensively, Cytowic proposed that synesthesia is a "cognitive fossil," a primitive limbic brain function left over from a time before the separation of sensory pathways evolved.

According to psychology professor Peter Grossenbacher of Naropa University in Boulder, Colo., synesthetic experiences may stem from "disinhibited cortical feedback." In other words, the neural pathways that normally suppress excess or irrelevant sensory input and allow focused perception in a single sensory mode may become disinhibited, resulting in simultaneous perception in other modes (color and speech, taste and shape, etc.). In this model, the condition is an anomaly in the brain's function.

Speculation about the number of people who have synesthesia is, to use a common metaphor, all over the map. While Cytowic estimates that it occurs in 1 in 20,000 people, Grossenbacher suggests that it may be closer to 1 in 300. Ramachrandan proposes 1 in 200.

One thing is clear. Researchers agree about synesthesia's hereditary nature—how DNA links between parent and child can shimmer with this ability to see, hear, taste, touch and smell what the rest of us cannot. Hearing this, I thought of my father and regretted what had not been passed to me.

During coffee breaks at the symposium at Princeton, I observed a community to which I was an outsider. Drifting from one conversation to another, I was transfixed by what I heard and anxious about what I might be missing across the room. Keir Allum, of St. Albans, England, told me how the content of a word can affect its color: When he sees the word "grass," for example, he sees white (g), maroon (r), sandy/beachy beige (a) and yellow (s), but because this is grass he's talking about, green is below the surface, "fighting to get through."

Carrie Schultz of Los Angeles described how she sees electric guitar riffs in purple swirls that envelop her. (For some, synesthetic perceptions are internal, in their "mind's eye"; for others, like this woman, they seem to exist outside the body.) Page Getz told me about how she quit her job as a journalist because her editors' word changes often disrupted what she saw as a sentence's natural chromatic progression. She told me, by the way, that the writer she enjoys

reading most, color-wise, is Adrienne Rich, whose poetry slides seamlessly from violets to blues.

Pad in hand, I moved from one synesthete to another and continued to ask questions, even as I felt envy growing (without any green). I was a peasant asking a room full of nobles to describe their jewels and castles. I coveted the riches of their sensory lives. I sidled up to a group where Getz, the ex-journalist, was stating that God is blue.

"Ah, so God is blue for you," commented Ramachandran, standing to her left.

"No," she said, "God is blue." Then she laughed. We non-synethetes were slow to comprehend, and she was enjoying herself. She described headache pain as a kind of greenish-orange, music by the rock group Nirvana as having the taste or sensation of Dr Pepper, and the color after sex as static silver.

While every synesthete I spoke with saw the letter "A" as a different color, all say that A's color has remained constant throughout their lives. In a study conducted in 1989 by Simon Baron-Cohen, synesthetes showed a 92 percent consistency in their color-sound associations after one year. Control subjects showed only 37 percent consistency after just one week.

In addition to their kaleidoscopically rich sensory minglings (which can include not just the color of objects, but their temperature, texture, taste and even personality), the synesthetes I spoke with shared a fondness for their experiences. "Imagine living without sight or hearing or touch," more than one person said to me when describing how they would feel about losing their synesthesia.

There are exceptions. Cameron LaFollette of Eugene, Ore., while treasuring her unique perceptions, says she sometimes suffers from sensory overload. While we spoke, the woman next to her poured tea that LaFollette described as cedar-colored, which for her makes the sound of middle C. When living in New Jersey, she tried to avoid taking New Jersey transit trains because their interiors are pale blue and pink, colors that made her feel cold.

As with most synesthetes, it's a family thing. Her mother is synesthetic, and

her grandmother remembers her own mother (LaFollette's great-grandmother) commanding her to "stop making that horrible green sound."

After coffee, Pat Duffy, one of the synesthetic speakers at the conference, described how as a preliterate child, she drew "word designs," colored pictures of words as she heard them. She then explained how in her mind the calendar year is shaped like an oval, the months of the year appearing in various colors and taking up different amounts of space.

At this point I experienced a kind of mental stutter, or a partial sensory shutdown: I stopped hearing what she was saying, focusing instead on the image she'd just described.

The image of her calendar year was very odd—because to me, it is normal. My year is a horseshoe, with January at one end, December at the other, and a large gap up around the bend between May and June. The fall months are elastic; October, for example, becomes bigger once September has passed, making it impossible to diagram on paper with any precision.

Then one of the researchers… mentioned spatial organization of time as a common trait. I felt as though someone had handed me a document indicating lineage connecting me to an eccentric monarch. I was in.

Like most revelatory moments, the realization that I might be synesthetic unfolded haltingly. Mentally darting between their words and my internal calendar, I heard only half of what people were saying. Back and forth, my thoughts raced between doubt and possibility. I tried to temper my excitement. I wanted to know more but was reluctant to ask questions, feeling like someone about to profess she's been visited by Jesus Christ at her first religious revival.

Then one of the researchers, while discussing "weak synesthesia," mentioned spatial organization of time as a common trait. I felt as though someone had handed me a document indicating lineage connecting me to an eccentric monarch. I was in.

My horseshoe year has always been as stable in my mind as the floor plan of my childhood home, the features of my mother's face. If someone mentions a party in December, I instantly see it near the right end of the horseshoe; a meeting in the middle of February, I skip to the other side.

I think again of my father and the hereditary nature of synesthesia, those twisting threads of DNA smuggling a secret from him to me. And like my father, who kept silent about his colored numbers, I had never considered mentioning my horseshoe to anyone.

After the conference, I quizzed my father and found that on rare occasions he experiences colored taste. I also realized that other forms of time are mapped in my head: The hours of the day hover in a vertical ring, with morning at the base, rising into evening, then looping back through the dark hours of the night. Still, nothing approaching purple swirls.

I've heard that synesthesia can grow stronger with time. It can also vanish.

I'm hoping that after a few more trips around the horseshoe, the months might begin take on quiet shades, and maybe a, l, l, i, s, o and n will reveal themselves to be more than the slate-gray forms my number 2 pencil scratches onto the page. Whether or not inter-sensory bridges will be built in my brain is one more mystery.

If they do, I imagine they'll be as tenuous and rich as language—and probably as evanescent as words scrawled onto hot pavement with ice plant pens.

Allison Hoover Bartlett is a San Francisco-based writer.

From the *Washington Post*, January 22, 2002. © 2002 by The Washington Post Writers Group. Reprinted by permission.

neuro quest EXPLORE YOUR BRAIN'S INNER WORKINGS

PHANTOM SENSATIONS

Understanding the pain felt by an amputee

BY ERIC HASELTINE

THE BRAIN HAS A REMARKABLE CAPACITY TO RE-wire itself. For instance, stroke patients can eventually regain speech by training nonspeech centers to process language. On the other hand, the brain's efforts to compensate for damage are not always beneficial. Mounting evidence suggests that re-routing of nerve fibers is also responsible for pathological conditions such as intractable pain in phantom limbs of amputees.

Until recently, brain researchers generally assumed that both "good" and "bad" rewiring took several weeks, allowing time for nerve cells to sprout fibers and make new connections. During the next few minutes, you may find cause to question this assumption as you grow your own phantom hand.

EXPERIMENT 1 Find a partner, a hardcover book, and a wire coat hanger. Bend the hanger into a crude, two-pronged fork as shown (on next page). Sit at a desk or table, lay the book directly in front of you, and open the cover. Place this article on the open book with the photographed palm adjacent to the up-turned cover. Then place your left hand palm-up next to the book so that the cover hides it from your view (the experiment won't work if you can see any part of your hand).

Ask your partner to tap the two ends of the hanger at pre-cisely the same time on your palm and the corresponding part of the photographed palm. The tapping should be random, like Morse code.

After watching the tapping on the photographed hand for a few minutes, you'll probably sense your hand shifting toward the photograph. Keep up the synchronous tapping for a few more minutes, and you may actually feel the hanger's touch on the photograph.

Psychiatrist Matthew Botvinick, who developed this proce-dure at the University of Pittsburgh, theorizes that awareness of body parts is not hardwired into the brain but learned from sen-sory experience. In his view, we learn that our hands are part of our bodies because whenever our hands are touched, the tactile sensations exactly correlate in time and place with visual and

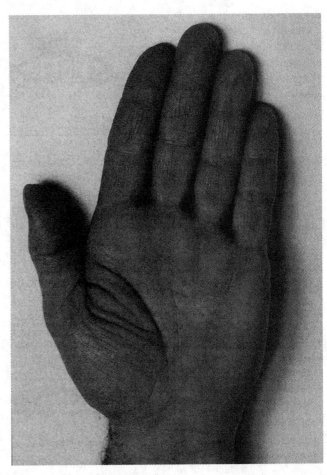

Photograph by Zeke Berman

proprioceptive (muscle and joint position) cues from the expe-rience. Repeated agreement of these three independent sensory channels ultimately convinces the brain that our hands belong to us and not someone (or something) else.

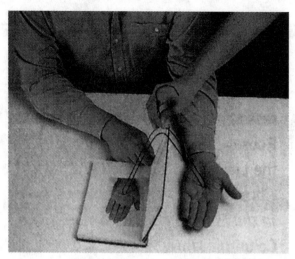

Photograph by Zeke Berman

However, what is learned can be unlearned when the three senses strongly disagree with one another. In this experiment, the tactile and proprioceptive cues were in sync but in violent discord with the visual feedback. Your brain gives the greatest weight to visual cues, so your eyes outvoted your other senses, making you believe the photograph was your hand.

EXPERIMENT 2 Reverse roles and try Experiment 1 on your partner. Meanwhile, as you tap away with the forked hanger, have a sharp pencil ready in your free hand. A few moments after your partner reports that she feels the photograph, stab the photograph with the pencil. Chances are you'll get your partner's heart racing, because emotional attachment to body parts closely follows on the heels of sensory attachment.

EXPERIMENT 3 Switch places with your partner again and have her repeat Experiment 1 on you. This time, after you've regained "feeling" in the photograph, ask your friend—without warning you—to continue tapping the photo only. You may actually feel a couple of phantom taps in the photograph, even though your real hand was not touched.

These experiments provide insights into how the brain can rewire itself to recover from damage. For example, Vilayanur S. Ramachandran, a neuroscientist at the University of California at San Diego, is using similar techniques to help stroke patients reclaim sensory awareness of numbed arms or legs that they've come to regard as foreign objects.

TRY MORE OF THESE TRICKS (STRETCH YOUR NOSE A COUPLE OF FEET AND WARP YOUR BODY) AT WWW.DISCOVER.COM/NEUROQUEST.

From *Discover*, May 2002, p. 88. © 2002. Reprinted with permission of the author, Eric Haseltine.

PAIN AND ITS MYSTERIES

Genetic and psychological factors help determine how well we withstand it

BY MARNI JACKSON

I was riding a bike in the Rockies, near Banff, when a bee flew into my mouth, and I felt a slim, unambiguous lance of pain, like a splinter of glass. Right away, I noticed, this sensation began to sprout a narrative. It wasn't just bad luck that the bee had stumbled into me; I saw the sting as punishment for biking "the wrong way"—distracted, churning along too fast, panting with open mouth. I had not been paying attention. Then pain had come along and rinsed the morning clear of small deceptions.

The next day, apart from having fabulous Angelina Jolie lips, I was back to normal. Unlike the chronic ache of arthritis or the lightning stab of trigeminal neuralgia, a bee sting is a wonderfully minor, finite form of pain. But the experience had nevertheless raised a swarm of questions about the mysterious nature of pain, and our relationship to it. For instance, why do we still talk about mental pain versus physical pain, when pain is always an emotional experience? How has it come about that something so universal remains so poorly understood, especially in an age of relentless self-scrutiny? And why hasn't anyone noticed the embarrassing fact that science is about to clone a human being, but it still can't cure the pain of a bad back?

The U.S. National Pain Foundation says more than four out of 10

American adults experience pain every day. The situation is likely much the same in Canada. North Americans consume four tons of ASA, a year, while chronic pain is on the rise. It's almost as if pain flourishes on our diet of analgesics. And it seems the more science learns how pain behaves (a quantum leap in the last 50 years), the less doctors want to do to treat it. To try to understand how we got ourselves in this pickle, I embarked on a four-year inquiry that zigzagged between art and science, doctor and patient. I talked to pain experts, and people who have learned to live with chronic pain. I tried to integrate the migrainish portrait of pain in Emily Dickinson's poetry or Virginia Woolf's novels with the latest MRI images of pain in the brain. I went back into the history of ideas about pain, where I encountered eccentric thinkers and unsung heroes, and forward into the genetic research into pain—where, once again, I ran into bees.

The inability to feel any pain at all is something that is inherited. Imagine: no hangovers, no sore pitching arm, no tremors in the dentist's chair. But congenital analgesia (as it's known) turns out to be both a nuisance and a life-threatening peril. Dr. Ron Melzack of McGill Univer-

sity and his British colleague, Dr. Patrick Wall—the two researchers whose "gate-control theory" revolutionized the way science now views pain—describe the consequences of a pain free life in their classic study, *The Challenge of Pain*. One girl with this condition suffered third-degree burns on her knees after climbing up on a hot radiator. And because there was no discomfort to let her know when she should shift her weight or posture, she eventually developed an inflammation in her joints and died at the age of 29.

Be glad it hurts when you stub your toe, because pain plays a vital role in our lives

Another woman with congenital analgesia felt nothing but a "funny, feathery feeling" when she delivered the first of her two children. But one of the best known examples of this rare inherited disorder was an American vaudeville performer in the 1920s, Edward H. Gibson, known as the Human Pincushion. His act involved sticking 50 to 60 pins into his body and then slowly removing them. It seems that for those born incapable of feeling pain, the career options are narrow, and life is short. Be glad it hurts when you stub your toe, because pain plays a vital, protective role in our lives.

Congenital analgesia is at the far end of a wide spectrum of inherited pain disorders. Genetic factors are involved in 39 to 55 per cent of migraines, 55 per cent of menstrual pain, and half of the back-pain population. Gender also has an influence, which will come as a surprise to no one. Men appear to suffer less pain, but require more pain relievers. There's no proof that women tolerate pain better than men, but they are three times more likely to suffer migraines, and six times more vulnerable to fibromyalgia. In a 1999 Gallup survey, 46 per cent of American women said they felt daily pain, compared to 37 per cent of men. And whether it's gene-related or stiletto-induced, one in four women also reported that their feet hurt.

"For a long time, people have accepted that there are wide variations in the way people respond to pain or to analgesics, but no one ever seriously considered attributing it to genetics, until now."

I was talking to Jeff Mogil, the first person in the world to put together training in psychology, genetics and pain. Mogil studied under psychologist and pain science pioneer John Liebeskind in California. After postdoctoral training in genetics, he joined the faculty at the University of Illinois in 1996. In 2001, Melzack lured him up to McGill University, where Mogil has succeeded him as the E. P. Taylor professor of pain research in psychology. This suggests that the pendulum is swinging back: science has moved away from seeing pain as a slippery psychological interpretation of something that only happens to the body, to approaching it as an experience that is at once neural, emotional and deeply rooted in our cells and genes.

"Pain genetics is where all the action is now, but it was a totally empty field when I moved into it," says Mogil, who is 35. "Nobody thought that pain had anything to do with genes. But then other people started working with knock-out mice, figuring out what happens when you remove this or that protein from a gene, and now knock-out mice are everywhere."

"Knock-out mice" always sounded to me like something you could order by the dozen at 3 a.m., from an infomercial. The sea monkeys of science. These mice are bred to lack a particular gene, and the protein it produces. "Then you look for what's wrong with the knock-out mouse when it doesn't have this or that protein any more," said Mogil. "It's the hottest technique in biology right now, and in pain research, too." It used to be that scientists didn't concern themselves with whatever strain of mouse they used in their studies, he added. But with knock-out mice "they discovered that the genetic background of the mouse was affecting their outcomes. It turned out that I was the only person paying attention to this sort of information."

When it comes to pain, he found, there is no such thing as a "universal rat." Pain sensitivity varies widely from strain to strain of rats and mice. Mogil also discovered that some mice are born either "doubly unlucky"—both over-sensitive to pain and under-responsive to analgesics—or vice versa, the lucky ones who feel less pain and require less painkiller.

"What the study of knock-out mice means for humans," Mogil said, "is that it helps explain individual sensitivities to pain and to drugs, as well as the fact that while most people will recover from an injury, some five per cent won't. They'll go on to develop chronic pain. Obviously, the factors that determine this are both environmental and genetic, and it's very tricky to sort these out. But if we know that some people have a propensity to chronic pain, then we might be able to find ways to keep it from developing in the first place. And as we learn more about pharmacogenetics, we can target their treatment with more precision. It also means that people who complain more about pain aren't necessarily whiners—they may actually feel more than other people. If humans really are like mice, then roughly half of that variability in pain response is due to their inherited genes."

Mogil has also studied the variety of ways people respond to painkillers. Indeed, the world seems to be divided into "responders" and "nonresponders," since morphine is only successful with about 65 per cent of the population. This explains why pain doctors have to fiddle with a variety of pain medications before they get it right. Among Caucasians, about seven to 10 per cent are known as "poor metabolizers" who won't respond to codeine. They end up getting all the side effects, but none of the pain relief.

I asked Mogil whether this news would encourage more magic-bullet thinking—the notion that we can simply zero in on these "pain genes," knock them out, and throw away the Tylenol.

Genes don't work like that, he replied. "Just as there is no pain centre, there is no single pain gene that controls it. But it doesn't look like there's a hundred of them either. We're looking for a particular type of gene that exists in different forms that can be inherited—and of those genes, there are five to 10, maybe 20 tops."

But people are so eager to blame their genes for everything now, I said. Doesn't this new focus on the genetic aspect downplay the way cultural, political and social forces shape our perception of pain?

"But that's the thing about pain—the cortical stuff is really, really important," he said. Mogil automatically translates the word "culture" as "cortical activity," but I got his drift. He was referring to the emotions, ideas and attitudes that are the result of our memory, learning, and experience. And in Melzack and Wall's gate-control theory of pain, it is the "cortical stuff" that descends to the spinal cord, amplifying or muting the pain signals coming in from the periphery of the body. In other words sensory data travels up; "culture" moves down. And for both Mogil and Melzack, "everything is equally biological."

Melding neuroscience and psychology, Mogil (like Melzack before him) seems to be describing culture not as something "out there" but embodied in the way the brain shapes our experience of pain. It's interesting, I said to Mogil, that he and Melzack are both psychologists, sometimes seen as low men on the totem pole when the hard-science boys get together.

"Pain *is* psychological," Mogil emphasized. "There's all this neural activity going on, but it can always be trumped by culture, attitudes and behaviour. Being a psychologist lets me do work with a high level of variability in my tests. Most scientists don't want to see variability in their results. They're looking for consistency. But I get happy when I see messy data."

Then the bee came back into the picture. It turns out that pain researchers will sometimes use bee venom to induce what Ron Melzack calls a "good, classic pain, the type we can learn a lot from." Although bee venom has a long list of active ingredients, the main toxin is a peptide called melittin. This can produce chemicals known as cytokines that play an important role in painkilling.

(Tests on beekeepers who have been stung repeatedly have revealed elevated levels of cytokines.) In fact, bee venom has been popular in treating the pain of arthritis for centuries, especially in Europe. Now it's also being touted as helpful therapy for autoimmune conditions like multiple sclerosis, and a protective agent against X-irradiation in cancer patients. The alternative-network literature for BVT (bee venom therapy) is vast, and that's only one aspect of apitherapy, which uses everything from bee pollen, royal jelly and honey to the wax and venom to treat an array of disorders.

So my original suspicion that a bee sting is a complicated thing was not entirely off-base. It turns out that everything involved in the orchestration of the event we call pain—the swelling, inflammation, redness, heat and stinging sensation—may, under different, controlled circumstances, also offer pain relief. In other words, better pain treatment may not lie in our efforts to suppress it or surgically excise it, but in a deeper understanding of how the body can use aspects of the pain process to promote healing and recovery. The answer to pain may lie inside pain itself.

As science looks beyond the role of pain as symptom, its hidden narrative will continue to unfold. If Jeff

Mogil is right, 50 years from now we will look at pain quite differently. Tylenol tablets will seem as quaint to us as sarsaparilla tonic. Instead, we'll take our ID bracelet to the local pharmacologist to order some bespoke analgesics, tailored to gender and genotype. Some of us may rise at 4 a.m. to meditate, and feel the struggle against pain lighten. We'll carry geno-cards that list our inherited predispositions: photosensitivity, osteoporosis and poor response to codeine.

Addiction might be redefined not as a character flaw but as "biochemical deficit management." Medical schools will actually teach doctors about the way pain behaves, and how to treat it. Our emotional habits will become an accepted factor of good health, and we'll know whether we're at risk for depression or rheumatoid arthritis in the same way we know that we're Scottish, or hazel-eyed. How we live with this new information, of course, will still be our choice. But we will understand that pain is sometimes history, in the body.

Adapted from Pain: The Fifth Vital Sign *by Marni Jackson. Copyright 2002 Marni Jackson. Reproduced by permission of the publisher, Random House Canada.*

From *Maclean's*, May 27, 2002, pp. 38-40. © 2002 by Maclean Hunter Ltd.

Brains in Dreamland

Scientists hope to raise the neural curtain on sleep's virtual theater

By BRUCE BOWER

After his father's death in 1896, Viennese neurologist Sigmund Freud made a momentous career change. He decided to study the mind instead of the brain. Freud began by probing his own mind. Intrigued by his conflicted feelings toward his late father, the scientist analyzed his own dreams, slips of the tongue, childhood memories, and episodes of forgetfulness.

Freud's efforts culminated in the 1900 publication of *The Interpretation of Dreams*. In that book, he depicted dreams as symbolic stories in which sleepers' unconscious sexual and aggressive desires play out in disguised forms.

Later in his life, Freud acknowledged that dreams don't always gratify wishes. For instance, he noted that some dreams represent attempts to master a past traumatic experience. Yet the father of psychoanalysis always held that dreams contain both surface events and subterranean themes of great personal importance. For that reason, he wrote, "the interpretation of dreams is the royal road to a knowledge of the unconscious activities of the mind."

Freud's theory of how dreams work has had a huge cultural impact over the past century, even as it attracted intense criticism. Now, brain scientists—members of the discipline that Freud left behind—have stepped to the forefront of this passionate dream dispute.

One prominent group of scientists asserts that Freud profoundly misunderstood dreams. In their view, the act of dreaming yields a guileless collage of strange but heartfelt images that carry no hidden meanings.

These scientists say that dreaming occurs when a primitive structure called the brain stem stirs up strong emotions, especially anxiety, elation, and anger. At the same time, neural gateways to the external world shut down, as do centers of memory and rational thought. The brain then creates bizarre, internal visions that strongly resonate for the dreamer.

An opposing view corresponds in many ways to Freud's ideas. Its supporters portray dreams as products of a complex frontal-brain system that seeks out objects of intense interest or desire. When provoked during sleep, this brain system depicts deep-seated goals in veiled ways so as not to rouse the dreamer.

A third group of investigators regards the brain data as intriguing but inconclusive. Dreams may serve any of a variety of functions, they argue. Depending on the society, these uses include simulating potential threats, grappling with personal and community problems, sparking artistic creativity, and diagnosing and healing physical illnesses.

"It is striking that 100 years after Freud [published *The Interpretation of Dreams*], there is absolutely no agreement as to the nature of, function of, or brain mechanism underlying dreaming," says neuroscientist Robert Stickgold of Harvard Medical School in Boston.

A broad consensus exists on one point, though. If neuroscientists hope to understand the vexing relationship of brain and mind, they need to get a handle on dreams.

Freud's royal road to the unconscious looks like a scientific dead-end to psychiatrist J. Allan Hobson. Neuroscientific evidence indicates that the sleeping brain churns out dreams as an afterthought to its other duties, argue Hobson, Stickgold, and Edward F. Pace-Schott, also of Harvard Medical School.

"Unconscious wishes play little or no part in dream instigation, dream emotion is uncensored and undisguised, sleep is not protected by dreaming, and dream interpretation has no scientific status," Hobson says.

Hobson's assault on Freudian dream theory began more than a decade ago. At that time, he proposed that dreams result from random bursts of activity in a brain stem area that regulates breathing and other basic bodily functions. These brain stem blasts zip to the frontal brain during periods of rapid eye movement (REM) sleep, when the entire brain becomes nearly as active as when a person is awake.

Dreams most often occur during REM sleep. A slumbering individual enters REM sleep about every 90 minutes.

Hobson's group published a revision of this theory in the December 2000 BEHAVIORAL AND BRAIN SCIENCES. Their new approach grants that dreams harbor emotional significance, but not in the way Freud posited.

Brain imaging and sleep-laboratory data clearly delineate among wakefulness, REM sleep, and non-REM sleep, the Harvard scientists note.

Three essential processes during REM sleep make it the prime time for dreaming, they say. First, brain stem activity surges and sets off responses in emotional and visual parts of the brain. Second, brain regions that handle sensations from the outside world, control movement, and carry out logical analysis shut down. Third, brain stem cells pump out acetylcholine, a chemical messenger that jacks up activity in emotional centers.

At the same time, two neurotransmitters essential for waking activity—noradrenaline and serotonin—take a snooze.

The result, in Hobson's view: a vivid hallucination, informed by strong emotions, that takes bizarre twists and turns. REM sleep's biological makeup fosters the mistaken belief that one is awake while dreaming, saps the ability to reflect on the weirdness of dreams as they occur, and makes it difficult to recall dreams after waking up.

REM sleep conducts far more important business than dreaming, Hobson argues. Its central functions may include supporting brain development, regulating body temperature, fortifying the immune system, and fostering memories of recently learned information. The last possibility evokes heated scientific debate (SN: 7/22/00, p. 55).

Hobson's theoretical focus on brain stems and REMs doesn't do dreams justice, argues neuropsychologist Mark Solms of St. Bartholomew's and Royal London (England) School of Medicine.

"Dreaming is generated under the direction of a highly motivated, wishful state of mind," Solms holds. "I won't be at all surprised if we find that Freud's understanding of [dream] mechanisms was basically on the right track."

To dream, the brain—both in and out of REM sleep—stimulates a frontal-lobe system that orchestrates motivation and the pursuit of goals and cravings, the British scientist proposes. A neurotransmitter called dopamine ferries messages in the brain's motivation system.

The crux of Solms' argument rests on studies of brain-damaged patients. In rare instances where people incur injuries only to their brain stem, dreaming continues despite severe disruptions of REM sleep. In contrast, people who suffer damage to frontal-brain regions involved in motivation report that they no longer dream but still have nightly REM sleep. These individuals also become apathetic and lose much of their initiative, imagination, and ability to plan. This group includes several hundred mental patients who decades ago, as a therapy, had some of their frontal-brain nerve fibers surgically cut.

Additional support for Solms' view comes from brain-imaging studies indicating that frontal areas involved in motivation, emotion, and memory exhibit elevated activity during REM sleep.

Various forms of cerebral activation can trigger the motivation system and lead to dreaming, Solms suggests. This explains why vivid dreams occur shortly after falling asleep and in the morning, not just in the depths of REM sleep, he says.

Brain data can't yet confirm or disprove Freud's idea that dreams play a symbolic game of hide-and-seek with unconscious desires, Solms adds.

For now, something of a standoff exists between the dreaming-brain theories of Hobson and Solms.

Hobson and his coworkers welcome the possibility, raised by neuroscientist Tore A. Nielsen of the University of Montreal, that crucial elements of REM sleep operate in non-REM states as well. For instance, as people fall asleep they display slow eye movements and electrical activity in the brain and muscles that may constitute a kind of "covert REM activity," Nielsen says.

If the REM state in one form or another saturates much of sleep, then the brain stem and related emotional centers create dreams throughout the night, Hobson asserts.

Solms regards "covert REM" as a hazy concept. REM sleep consists of diverse physiological changes in the brain and body. This sleep stage can't be equated with a few of its biological components that may appear at other times during the night, he contends.

Haziness also afflicts attempts to decipher dreams with recordings of brain activity, remarks neuroscientist Allen Braun of the National Institutes of Health in Bethesda, Md. These images of neural tissue show where the brain is stirring during specific sleep stages, Braun says, but not how those areas operate or whether they play a direct role in dreaming.

Brain-imaging reports generally support Solms' theory that dreams derive from a frontal-brain motivation system, Braun notes (SN: 1/17/98, p. 44). However, a frontal-brain area considered pivotal for self-monitoring and abstract thought naps throughout sleep. Braun considers this finding to clash with the Freudian notion of dreams as hotbeds of disguised meaning.

Freud's emphasis on wish fulfillment in dreams needs revision too, according to neuroscientist Antti Revonsuo of the University of Turku in Finland. Dreaming instead enables people to simulate

threatening events so that they can rehearse ways to either deal with or avoid them, Revonsuo theorizes.

Threatening incidents of various kinds and degrees frequently appear in the dream reports of adults and children around the world, the Finnish scientist says. They also show up in descriptions of recurrent dreams, nightmares, and post-traumatic dreams.

Hunter-gatherer populations, such as the Mehinaku Indians in Brazil, report many dreams about threatening events, he adds. Mehinaku men's dreams range from fending off an attacking jaguar to dealing with an angry wife.

Revensuo's theory faces threats of its own, though. Evidence from contemporary hunter-gatherers indicates that dreaming functions in a variety of ways, argues psychologist Harry T. Hunt of Brock University in St. Catharines, Ontario. Members of these groups generally view dreams as real events in which a person's soul carries out activities while the person sleeps.

Hunter-gatherers' dreams sometimes depict encounters with supernatural beings who provide guidance in pressing community matters, aid in healing physical illnesses, or give information about the future, Hunt says. Individuals who are adept at manipulating their own conscious states may engage in lucid dreaming, in which the dreamer reasons clearly, remembers the conditions of waking life, and acts according to a predetermined plan.

Dreaming represents a basic orienting response of the brain to novel information, ideas, and situations, Hunt proposes. It occurs at varying intensities in different conscious states, including REM sleep, bouts of reverie or daydreaming, and episodes of spirit possession that individuals in some cultures enter while awake (SN: 2/17/01, p. 104).

Scientists, musicians, inventors, artists, and writers often use dreaming of one kind or another to solve problems and spark creativity, Hunt notes.

Whatever purposes dreaming serves, Hobson's group and many other researchers underestimate the extent to which the brain tunes in to the external world during sleep, says neuroscientist Chiara M. Portas of University College London. Several studies indicate that sensory areas of the brain respond to relevant sounds and other sensations during REM and non-REM sleep.

No conclusive results support any theory of dreaming or sleep, in her view.

Ironically, dreams are attracting growing scientific interest as they fade into the background of modern life. Artificial lighting and society's focus on daytime achievements have fueled this trend (SN: 9/25/99, p. 205).

Sleep now typically occurs in single chunks of 7 hours or less. Yet as recently as 200 years ago in Europe, people slept in two nightly phases of 4 to 5 hours each. Shortly after midnight, individuals awoke for 1 to 2 hours and frequently reflected on their dreams or talked about them with others.

Well before Freud's time, Europeans prized dreams for their personal insights, and particularly for what they revealed about a dreamer's relationship with God, says historian A. Roger Ekirch of Virginia Polytechnic Institute and State University in Blacksburg.

Organizing sleep into two segments encouraged people to remember dreams and to use them as paths to self-discovery, Ekirch contended in the April AMERICAN HISTORICAL REVIEW.

Dreams have lost their allure even for the psychoanalytic theorists and clinicians who are the heirs to Freud's ideas, remarks Paul Lippmann of the William Alanson White Psychoanalytic Institute in Stockbridge, Mass. These days, psychoanalysts show far more interest in dissecting the emotional nature of their dealings with patients than in eliciting and interpreting dreams, according to Lippmann, himself a psychoanalytic clinician.

Like Ekirch, Lippmann suspects that modern culture has eroded interest in dreaming. "The American Dream has little room for the nighttime variety," he said in the Fall 2000 PSYCHOANALYTIC PSYCHOLOGY.

Yet many neuroscientists seem determined to swim against that cultural tide. Even the researchers who see little psychological significance in sleep's visions want to explain how and why the brain produces them.

They can dream, can't they?

From *Science News,* August 11, 2001, pp. 90-92. © 2001 by Science News. Reprinted by permission.

UNIT 4

Learning and Remembering

Unit Selections

Key Points to Consider

- What is learning? What is memory? How are the two linked? Are they necessarily always linked to each other? Why is memory so bad sometimes? How can we improve memory and learning?

- What is intelligence? Give examples of the multiple forms of intelligence. Should teachers try to match each child's dominant intellectual ability to educational materials or to a particular teaching method?

- What is a reward? What is punishment? Why is it better to reward than punish behaviors? Do many American parents use spanking to alter their child's behavior? Do you think spanking a child is the best recourse? What are some of the side effects of using spanking to modify children's behaviors?

- Why is memory important? What is forgetting? Why do psychologists want to know about the various mechanisms that underlie learning and remembering? To what use can we put this information? Why do we forget? Are there methods we can use to improve memory? What are they; can you give an example of each? What types of memory lapses are normal? What memory lapses signal problems? What are the seven sins of memory? Can you provide an example of each? What role does biology play in remembering, if any?

 **Links: www.dushkin.com/online/**
These sites are annotated in the World Wide Web pages.

Mind Tools
  http://www.psychwww.com/mtsite/
The Opportunity of Adolescence
  http://www.winternet.com/~webpage/adolescencepaper.html
Project Zero
  http://pzweb.harvard.edu

Do you remember your first week of classes at college? There were so many new buildings and so many people's names to remember. And you had to recall accurately where all your classes were as well as your professors' names. Just remembering your class schedule was problematic enough. For those of you who lived in residence halls, the difficulties multiplied. You had to remember where your residence was, recall the names of individuals living on your floor, and learn how to navigate from your room to other places on campus, such as the dining halls and library. Then came examination time. Did you ever think you would survive college exams? The material, in terms of difficulty level and amount, was perhaps more than you thought you could manage.

What a stressful time you experienced when you first came to campus! Much of what created the stress was the strain on your learning and memory systems, two complicated processes. Indeed, most of you survived just fine and with your memories, learning strategies, and mental health intact.

The processes you depended on when you first came to college are the processes of learning and memorizing, two of the oldest processes studied by psychologists. Today, with their sophisticated experimental techniques, psychologists have distinguished several types of memory processes and have discovered what makes learning more complete so that subsequent memory is more accurate. We also have discovered that humans aren't the only organisms capable of these processes. All types of animals can learn, even if the organism is as simple as an earthworm or an amoeba.

Psychologists know, too, that rote learning and practice are not the only forms of learning. For instance, at this point in time in your introductory psychology class, you might be studying operant and classical conditioning, two very simple but nonetheless important forms of learning of which both humans and simple organisms are capable. Both types of conditioning can occur without our awareness or active participation in them. The articles in this unit examine the processes of learning and remembering (or its reciprocal, forgetting) in some detail.

In "Memory and Learning," Ruth Weiss reviews both processes and demonstrates their relationship to each other. She provides a good overview as background for the next articles as well as tips for improving both memory and learning.

The second article examines learning styles and multiple forms of intelligence. Learning styles have long interested psychologists. Teachers today are often told that they should discover a child's learning style and then match teaching methods to it. Similarly, many psychologists now believe that intelligence is not one monolithic cerebral ability, but rather that multiple types of intelligence exist. In "Understanding Our Differences," Susan Reese discusses various kinds of intelligence and learning styles. She also explains how teachers can shape their educational strategies and assessment techniques to tap different styles and forms of intelligence.

In "New Evidence for the Benefit of Never Spanking," learning is again examined. However, one specific form of learning, childhood behavior change, is emphasized. Murray Straus discusses the ramifications of the use of spanking (punishment) by parents and concludes that this might not always be the best tactic for developing cooperative, well-behaved children.

We next turn our attention to memory, because once something is learned, it needs to be remembered to be useful. In "The Seven Sins of Memory: How the Mind Forgets and Remembers," Daniel Schacter discusses common memory problems and what causes them. He also elucidates several memory techniques from which we can all benefit, even if we don't have serious memory disorders such as Alzheimer's disease.

In the last article in unit 4, Sharon Begley examines "Memory's Mind Games," and points out the reasons why people forget.

Memory and Learning

So much learning, so little memory.

By Ruth Palombo Weiss

We take our memory for granted—until we can't recall someone's name, a word, or where we put our keys. Then we have a moment of panic: Are we losing our memory, or our mind?

Memory is essential for going about the daily business of our lives. We need memory for everything we do: perceiving the world, synethesizing and analyzing information, and applying knowledge to new situations. In fact, learning is the making of memory, which is laid down in our brains in chemical form. Chemical changes are created at the neuron level; without them, there's no substance for our minds to work with.

According to the current model of memory, input from our senses via the environment is processed through our perceptual memory in fractions of a second. If deemed important enough, either by one's unconscious or conscious mind, the input is put into the short-term memory. From there, it's either discarded or planted in the long-term memory.

Eric Jensen, educator and author of *Teaching With the Brain in Mind*, notes that "learning and memory are two sides of a coin. You can't talk about one without the other." He calls learning that lasts (information stored in our long-term memory) "long-term potentiation." When LTP occurs, "a cell is electrically stimulated over and over so that it excites a nearby cell. If a weaker stimulus is then applied to the neighboring cell a short time later, the cell's ability to get excited is enhanced."

Ken Kosik, professor of neurology at the Harvard Medical School and a co-founder of the Brigham and Women's Hospital Memory and Disorders Clinic, explains that our brain changes with learning in functional ways. When we learn something that stays with us for any length of time, it goes from the short-term into our medium- or long-term memory. When that occurs, certain genes in the brain turn on. When they turn on, new proteins are made and the connections between the axons and dendrites increase in complexity. In other words, new memories create new interconnecting pathways between neurons.

As we learn something new, each chemical message is laid down as a chain of neurons called a neural network. Those connections become stronger the more often our brains access the network. Synapses, or spaces between the neurons, also become stronger, says educator Marilee Sprenger in her book, *The Brain in Action*. She compares the process to creating a path in the woods: "The first time you create a path, it is rough and overgrown. The next time you use it, it's easier to travel because you have previously walked over the weeds and moved the obstacles. Each time thereafter, it gets smoother and smoother. In a similar fashion, the neural networks get more efficient, and messages travel more swiftly."

Neuroscientist Joseph LeDoux, author of *The Emotional Brain,* says that what we are conscious of at any given moment is what's in our short-term memory—especially our working memory, a special kind of short-term memory. Furthermore, only information that's registered in a person's short-term memory can eventually go into the long-term memory.

Jeb Schenck compares the short-term memory to a desktop: Once it's filled, if an additional item finds its way in, a pre-existing item will have to be pushed out.

Scientists agree that short-term memory capacity is limited to five to nine items, although it's capable of holding more information if packaged into chunks. Educator Jeb Schenck compares the short-term memory to a desktop: Once it's filled, if an additional item finds its way in, a pre-existing item will have to be pushed out. Moreover, with short-term memory, the more time that elapses between learning details and recalling them, the harder it is to access those details.

The hippocampus, a region deep within the brain, is the memory-staging area that connects stimuli and responses. It's vital for consolidation of memories. If we look at the cells in the hippocampus, we find a massive number of axons that move from deep within the brain as a two-way street. Hippocampal cells connect widely to many other regions in the brain, stopping at many way stations. Kosik explains that massive parallel processing takes place when we lay down or recall a memory, thus ensuring more flexibility in our ability to think in the sense that we can synthesize information from different sensory modalities.

Because new information builds on prior existing information, making new linkages and new insights is crucial to building up useful long-term memory. Each of us has thousands of feedback loops throughout our brains, all of which are cross-communicating and engaging the entire organ. In fact, the brain may discard unnecessary or useless information before we even known we've received it.

Kosik explains further that learning and experience can modify the number of neurons. The human brain has approximately 100 billion neurons, each with as many as 5,000 synaptic connections to other neurons. It's those synaptic connections that are forged and reinforced by experience. Therefore, as a broad generalization, one can say that the more experience we have, the more connections are forged.

In her book *The Human Brain: A Guided Tour,* Susan A. Greenfield ponders how memories become consolidated in the cortex. No one knows exactly how the hippocampus and medial thalamus (vital for relaying incoming sensory information into the cortex) lay down memories.

Says Greenfield: "One attractive idea draws on memory being composed of otherwise arbitrary elements, brought together for the first time in the event or the fact to be remembered. The role of the hippocampus and medial thalamus would be to ensure that disparate, previously unassociated elements are now associated and thus somehow bound into a cohesive memory. One metaphor might be that of scaffolding: While a building is being established, the removal of the scaffolding would lead to collapse of the edifice. However, once the building is completed, the scaffolding is redundant."

Greenfield continues: "Memory can be subdivided into different processes, and each process will be served by different combinations of brain regions. But common to all these memory processes is perhaps the most mysterious issue of all: We know that some people can remember what happened to them 90 years ago, but by then every molecule in their bodies will have been turned over many times. If long-term changes mediating memories are occurring continuously in the brain, how are they sustained? How do neurons register more or less permanent change as a result of experience?"

Kosik admits that any answers to those questions are at the moment speculative. "The way in which we access long-term memory isn't well understood at all," he says.

Schenck says that teaching directs the making of memory. "As an instructor, you select different forms of memory and then teach to the creation of those memories. For example, if I'm teaching something that's in the form of visual recall, I'm aware that when I go to assess the learning, I'm going to have to ask for performances related to something visual. It's crucial to match the assessment with the types of memory used in instruction and practice. In short, you're teaching the student how to find the memory."

Jensen echoes that thought when he says, "The variety of ways that we store and retrieve information tells us that we have to start thinking less of our memory in general and more of which kind of memory and how it can be retrieved."

Making a memory

One continual challenge to instructors is making sure participants perceive incoming information as important. A technique Schenck uses in the classroom to help that process is to make learners aware of how they are making a memory. He thinks it's necessary to bring to a conscious level how a person is learning, where he or she is storing the memory, and how to find it.

"In developing learners' skills in how to retrieve a specific memory when it's needed, it's crucial for them to become aware of how they are processing and accessing memory stores," says Schenck.

As each person learns in a unique way, it's vital for him or her to ask, "How do I learn?" That requires knowing how your own brain works. It means not only knowing conceptually how memory is built, but also being aware of when you are getting tired or when you're starting to loose track and drift away from the subject. To enhance one's focus, Schenck suggests having participants stand up and do some physical activity for several minutes to rev up their blood and circulation. Another tack is to change tasks for 15 to 20 minutes. "I tell my students to be alert to when they are learning," says Schenck, "but also to when they are not learning."

In order to create long-term memories, it's vital to be verbally explicit and to elaborate on any details. Creating personal linkages is an approach Schenck uses. He has participants make concept maps to show relationships between ideas. For those maps, he writes down a single key word or phrase. Then, participants provide everything that can be linked to the word or phrase. Each time a word is added, participants draw a line to the next word or concept. Some linkages may need an action verb to explain them.

For example, if the instructor gives the concept "Cells——>mitosis," then the line drawn by the learner would have "reproduce by" on top. As a concept map becomes progressively more intricate, it provides a visual map for learners of how the items or issues are related. Schenck says that technique improves memory for detail and the ability to make linkages to other topics.

> # The classic example is when we ask ourselves, "Where did I leave my keys? Mentally, we go through all the information we can recall before we blanked.

Using multiple forms of review also enhances long-term memory. Rather than doing just a written review, educators who are using brain-based learning theory suggest also using drawings, pantomime, and role play to access memory stores through multiple modalities.

Another strategy to enhance the recall of stored information is to provide a framework of retrieval cues. By teaching key words, a procedure, or a sequence, learners have another tool to retrieve information. Say that a learner has a concept and understands it well, but in asking him or her to explain that idea, the instructor uses words differently from those the learner has been taught and has practiced. In such cases, the instructor is giving the wrong cues.

Says Schenck, "The learner won't be able to find the correct memory file be-cause the wrong word has been typed in on the search mode. It's important to get students to expand those cues while they're learning a concept or information."

Yet another idea for helping learners enhance memory is to give them external retrieval cues. The classic example is when we ask ourselves, "Where did I leave my keys?"

Mentally, we go through all of the information we can recall before we blanked. We often find that it helps to go to the room where we suspect the loss occurred so that the environment provides cues.

> # As you would imagine, the more active a students is in the learning process, the greater the long-term memory is.

If you plan to test or assess a group in a particular type of room or facility, it will help if participants are taught or re-hearsed in that facility at the same time of day and with the same noise and temperature range—just as basic military training replicates a combat environment as closely as possible.

Past perfection

Schenck talks about reviewing past perfection: "If students have successfully learned something, then make them rehearse it five to 10 times. They can further solidify the memory by reviewing again the next day. Often when learners get something correct, the instructor stops, though the procedure or concept isn't yet stable in their minds. That's why it's necessary to practice it past perfection."

Schenck notes that after two to three weeks, memory decay stabilizes. "The greater the initial amount of information put into the long-term memory, the greater the final amount retained. As you would imagine, the more active a students is in the learning process, the greater the long-term memory is."

Research on the brain has proven to be a powerful factor in guiding learning specialists as they approach the complicated subject of learning and memory. Sprenger says, "Although nothing appears to remain constant in this field, I want teachers to know two things. One, the brain has everything to do with learning. Two, the more we know about brain science, the easier it will be to make the hundreds of decisions each day that affect students."

Says Kosik, "Ultimately the goal is not to give people photographic memories, but to learn how to improve intelligence, creativity, and imagination."

This is the third Training & Development article in a series by Weiss on learning and the brain. See "Brain-Based Learning" (July) and "Howard Gardner Talks About Technology" (September).

Ruth Palombo Weiss *is a freelance writer based in Potomac, Maryland; pivotal@erols.com. Many of the ideas in the article are from a paper by Kenneth S. Kosik, "Etching Memories in the Brain: The Reflection of Experience," given at the Brain-Based Learning Conference last April in Boston.*

From *Training & Development,* October 2000, pp. 46-50. © 2000 by ASTD, www.astd.org. Reprinted by permission. All rights reserved.

Understanding Our Differences

There are many things that set us apart as individuals—fingerprints, DNA, and the ways in which we think and learn.

Susan Reese

For years now, in traditional career and technical education classrooms, teachers have been instructing their students with a combination of written material, lectures and hands-on training. There is now a great deal of modern research to show that these educators were effectively addressing the issue of their students' varied learning styles and "intelligences."

Multiple Intelligences

Harvard psychologist Howard Gardner formulated a theory of multiple intelligences that revolutionized our way of thinking about learning and teaching. His theories are considered so relevant to career and technical education that he was invited to speak at our 75th Anniversary Convention.

Gardner identifies eight different intelligences:

- linguistic
- logical-mathematical
- spatial
- musical
- bodily-kinesthetic
- naturalistic
- intrapersonal (intelligence about ourselves)
- interpersonal (intelligence about others)

Gardner also considers a possible ninth human intelligence to be existential intelligence, which he defines as the proclivity to pose and ponder questions about life, death and ultimate realities.

According to Gardner, this set of intelligences defines us as a species, and while all human beings possess all of the intelligences he identifies, no two of us possess them in the exact same combination of strengths. He also believes that the configurations and relationships of these intelligences change in response to our acquired life experiences and our analysis of those experiences.

From 1972 until July 2000, Howard Gardner served as co-director (along with David Perkins) of Project Zero, a research group at the Harvard Graduate School of Education that investigates the development of learning processes in children, adults and organizations. Steve Seidel, an expert in alternative assessment became director in 2000, but Gardner remains active with the project through research and as a member of its steering committee. Work done by Project Zero includes the Adult Multiple Intelligences Study, which was initiated to develop and explore the use of the multiple intelligences theory in adult literacy, adult basic education and in English for Speakers of Other Languages. Project Zero has partnered with Walt Disney Company's Disney Learning Partnership on The Creative Classrooms Project to support creative teaching strategies for engaging children in learning. The Active Learning Practices for Schools (ALPS) Web site makes

Project Zero's "Teaching for Understanding and Thinking" resources available to schools. The site encompasses several approaches to teaching and assessing and is intended to encourage dialogue among teachers.

Learning Styles

Acknowledging that we have multiple intelligences that exist in strengths and configurations that vary widely among individuals leads us to the consideration that there must also be a variety of learning styles. While educators may not be able to address each and every style in their classrooms, awareness of these different ways of learning might enable them to assist students in finding their best ways of learning.

> ## "If students cannot learn the way we teach them, then we must teach them the way they learn."
>
> *Dr. Lenneth Dunn,*
> Professor at Queens College

Visual/Verbal Learners learn best from written language—textbooks, blackboards and class notes. Writing out technical information, mathematical information or information from diagrams and charts in sentences or phrases will benefit the visual/verbal learner.

For Visual/Nonverbal Learners, visual aids such as pictures, videos, maps, charts and diagrams work best. The visual/nonverbal or spatial learner may be an artistic type who will translate classroom information into drawings and diagrams to "get the picture."

Auditory/Verbal Learners ideally learn through oral language—classroom lectures, group discussions and audiotapes—and may benefit from taping lectures. These students might talk things through with a study partner, or talk out loud to themselves to learn technical and mathematical information. Musical intelligence might mean speaking rhythmically or turning lessons into lyrics to enable learning.

Physical activity and movement aid the Tactile/Kinesthetic Learners. Field trips, role-playing, hands-on training, using tools and working in laboratory settings provide the physical engagement that works best for the tactile/kinesthetic learner. Because they have a need for touching things and making things, these students may want to build a tangible representation of a lesson, such as a model.

Assessment and Testing

A number of schools assess learning styles by using the Dunn and Dunn Model, which was developed in 1967 by

Dr. Rita Dunn, who is the director of the Center for the Study of Learning and Teaching Styles at St. John's University, and her husband, Dr. Kenneth Dunn, a professor at Queens College. As Dr. Kenneth Dunn explains, "If students cannot learn the way we teach them, then we must teach them the way they learn."

The Dunn and Dunn model is based on cognitive style theory (the idea that individuals process information differently based on either learned or inherent traits) and brain lateralization theory (the idea that the left and right hemispheres of the brain have different functions). The model includes five strands (environmental, emotional, sociological, physiological and psychological), and within those five strands are 20 variables for adults. For children there are 22 variables, since teacher motivation and parent motivation are factored in.

> ## "Fads and theories fascinate us, but we're dealing with real kids and real adults. I want things that I know work."
>
> *Dr. Sue Ellen Reed,*
> Professor at Northeastern State University

Research has been conducted on the Dunns' learning style model at more than 115 universities worldwide, and studies have been done on students who are considered as gifted and talented, learning disabled, emotionally disabled, at risk, low achieving or average. The research has included Caucasian, African American, Asian American, Native American and Hispanic students. According to this research, using an individual's learning style can help increase concentration, processing and retention of new and difficult material.

Testing with the Dunn and Dunn Model utilizes a learning styles assessment consisting of 100 questions. There are different versions of the 30-minute assessment for children and adults—one for grades three and four, one for grades five through 12, and one for adults.

Dr. Sue Ellen Read of Northeastern State University is the director of the Oklahoma Institute for Learning Styles (OIL) and a member of the International Learning Styles Network Board of Directors. She is also a strong proponent of the Dunn and Dunn Model because of the body of research behind it. As Read explains, "Fads and theories fascinate us, but we're dealing with real kids and real adults. I want things that I know work."

Using the Dunn and Dunn Model, OIL did 30,000 tests last year for individuals from all over the world, charging only one dollar per person—and that includes providing them with a profile.

According to Read, the majority of those trained by the OIL program are adults, including teachers, administrators, principals and supervisors. "Every administrator who goes through our master's program takes our learning styles training," says Read.

Dr. Read was recently awarded a $1.2 million grant from the U.S. Department of Education for the RESULTS (Responsive Educators Supporting Unique Learning & Teaching Styles) Program. She will spend the next three years converting Locust Grove School District, which is 62 percent Native American, to a learning styles school district.

Technology

One of the many benefits of today's technology is that students and teachers now have a wider array of resources to assist in the learning process. The printed word is still alive and well but is now joined by new tools of technology for teaching and learning—and many of these are ideally suited to specific learning styles or intelligences. Those with strong visual/spatial intelligence may be drawn to programs such as computer-aided design and 3-D modeling. Interactive CD-ROMs and multimedia might engage the tactile/kinesthetic learner. Word processing can enhance writing for the linguistic, visual/verbal learner. There is even e-mail for the strong interpersonal intelligence.

> ... whether the student reads it, draws it, builds it, claps it or even sings it, the point is to learn it. A student who has found the style of learning that best suits his or her own intelligence has found the "right" way to learn.

Computer-based programs such as Fast ForWord and Earobics that use video-game formats are being introduced in some schools to help children learn to read, and while these programs may be expensive and controversial, there have also been reports of success.

The Interactive Metronome was originally developed to numerically test and improve the natural timing of musicians and athletes, but it is now being used to help children with attention problems such as attention-deficit disorder (ADD) and attention-deficit hyperactivity disorder (ADHD). According to a study published in March 2001 in the American Journal of Occupational Therapy, the Interactive Metronome was able to improve attention, learning, motor planning and sequencing capabilities, and even help control aggression in some children with attention-deficit problems. The Interactive Metronome includes a software program, two sets of headphones and two contact sensing triggers—one is a special glove to sense when hands are clapping and one is a pad on the floor to sense when a toe or heel is tapping on it. This product is no magic bullet and won't work for all children with attention-deficit disorders. Even the company that makes the Interactive Metronome advises that it should be considered as a possible component of a comprehensive program for children and adults with these types of problems. In fact, some experts claim there is no real evidence that the program even works, but others—along with the parents of some of these children—say that they have seen positive results from its use.

Finding What Works

Is there one "right" way to learn? Most educators and researchers who have studied different learning styles say that there is no "right" or "wrong" way to learn, and there are no "good" learning styles or "bad" learning styles. A good learning style is what works for an individual student. So, whether the student reads it, draws it, builds it, claps it or even sings it, the point is to learn it. A student who has found the style of learning that best suits his or her own intelligence has found the "right" way to learn.

Career Tech's Intelligences

In the summer Harvard Educational Review, high school English teacher Mary Ellen Dakin wrote a thoughtful essay called "The Poet, the CEO and the First-Grade Teacher." (The poet is Walt Whitman, the CEO is Hewlett-Packard's Carleton Fiorina and the first-grade teacher was a fellow student in the program—an older woman who had recently completed college and her first year of teaching.) During a program of study called "Research for Better Teaching," Dakin found some of her previous beliefs about intelligence and achievement changing and expanding, and within this essay is a revelation she had after a conversation with her hairdresser. Both of the young woman's parents were accountants, she told Dakin, but she and her four siblings have instead become "artists." Dakin was surprised at her use of the term, and even more surprised to learn that the other artists are a painter, two chefs and a landscape designer. But, as Dakin now says, "I did suddenly look at her work with different eyes."

Cosmetology, landscape design, culinary arts—these are all career and technical fields, and they can all be considered arts. It takes an artistic intelligence to excel in these fields.

Take the opportunity to explore your own interpretations, but here are two more to consider: Agriculture may require naturalistic and kinesthetic intelligence; family and consumer sciences may require artistic and interpersonal intelligence. Career and technical educators have probably been seeing these intelligences in students and helping them to find ways to best utilize these intelligences in a course of study and a career. Researchers like Howard Gardner and Rita and Kenneth Dunn have given them names and created models that recognize our differences. By understanding, accepting and respecting these differences, we acknowledge the importance of our individual strengths and talents. Those strengths and talents make us all valuable parts of the machinery and beautiful threads in the tapestry that make up our society.

Here are some resources for further exploration of learning styles and multiple intelligences.

International Learning Styles Network
The Learning Styles Network began in 1979 through an agreement between St. John's University and the National Association of Secondary School Principals. Today there are learning styles centers throughout the United States as well as abroad. For more information, visit www.learningstyles.net.

Dunn and Dunn Model Tests
Tests using the Dunn and Dunn Model for grades three through 12 and for adults are available from Price Systems at www.learningstyle.com. For children grades one to three, tests may be ordered through the Center for the Study of Learning and Teaching Styles, St. John's University, 8000 Utopia Parkway, Jamaica, NY 11439.

The Oklahoma Institute for Learning Styles
The Oklahoma Institute for Learning Styles based at Northeastern State University College of Education has seminars and training workshops and provides individual learning style testing and counseling. For more information, visit http://arapaho.nsuok.edu/~oil.

Learning Styles Assessments
Some schools have developed their own tests for assessing learning styles. To see the learning styles survey at Diablo Valley College in California, visit www.metamath.com//Isweb/dvclearn.htm. Middlesex Community College in Middletown, Conn., has a learning styles inventory at www.mxctc.commnet.edu/clc/survey.htm.

Project Zero
Originally founded to study and improve education in the arts, Project Zero at the Harvard Graduate School of Education researches the development of learning processes and human cognitive development. For more information, visit http://pzweb.harvard.edu.

The Interactive Metronome
For more research and information regarding the Interactive Metronome, visit www.interactivemetronome.com.

The Poet, the CEO and the First-Grade Teacher
To read the full article by Mary Ellen Dakin, visit http://gseweb.harvard.edu/~hepg/dakin.htm.

SUSAN REESE, TECHNIQUES CONTRIBUTING EDITOR

From *Techniques* magazine, January 2002, pp. 20-23. © 2002 by The Association for Career and Technical Education, www.acteonline.org.

Social Science and Public Policy

NEW EVIDENCE FOR THE BENEFITS OF NEVER SPANKING

Murray A. Straus

Virtually a revolution has occurred in the last four years in the state of scientific knowledge about the long-term effects of corporal punishment. This article summarizes the results of that research and explains why the new research shows, more clearly than ever before, the benefits of avoiding corporal punishment.

Somewhat ironically, at the same time as these new studies were appearing, voices arose in state legislatures, the mass media, and in social science journals to defend corporal punishment. Consequently, a second purpose is to put these recent defenses of corporal punishment in perspective.

This is followed by a section explaining a paradox concerning trends in corporal punishment. Public belief in the necessity of corporal punishment and the percentage of parents who hit teenagers is about half of what it was only 30 years ago. Despite these dramatic changes, 94 percent of parents of toddlers in a recent national survey reported spanking, which is about the same as it was in 1975 (Straus and Stewart, 1999).

The article concludes with an estimate of the benefits to children, to parents, and to society as a whole that could occur if corporal punishment were to cease.

Defenders of corporal punishment say or imply that no-corporal punishment is the same as no-discipline or "permissiveness." Consequently, before discussing the new research, it is important to emphasize that no-corporal punishment does not mean no-discipline. Writers and organizations leading the movement away from corporal punishment believe that rules and discipline are necessary, but that they will be *more* effective without corporal punishment. Their goal is to inform parents about these more effective disciplinary strategies, as exemplified in the very name of one such organization—the Center for Effective Discipline (see their web site: *http://www.stophitting.com;* see also the web site of Positive Parenting program *http://parenting.umn.edu*).

Previous Research on Corporal Punishment

In order to grasp the importance of the new research, the limitations of the previous 45 years of research need to be understood. These 45 years saw the publication of more than 80 studies linking corporal punishment to child behavior problems such as physical violence. A meta-analysis of these studies by Gershoff (in press) found that almost all showed that the more corporal punishment a child had experienced, the worse the behavior of the child. Gershoff's review reveals a consistency of findings that is rare in social science research. Thompson concluded that "Although... corporal punishment does secure children's immediate compliance, it also increases the likelihood of eleven [types of] negative outcomes [such as increased physical aggression by the child and depression later in life]. Moreover, even studies conducted by defenders of corporal punishment show that, even when the criterion is immediate compliance, non-corporal discipline strategies work just as well as corporal punishment.

The studies in my book *Beating the Devil Out of Them* are examples of the type of negative outcome reviewed by Thompson. For example, the more corporal punishment experienced, the greater the probability of hitting a wife or husband later in life. Another study of kindergarten children used data on corporal punishment obtained by interviews with the mothers of the children. Six months later the children were observed in school. Instances of physical aggression were tallied for each child. The children of mothers who used corporal punishment attacked other children twice as often as the children whose mothers did not. The children of mothers who went beyond ordinary corporal punishment had four times the rate of attacking other children. This illustrates another principle: that the psychologically harmful effects of corporal punishment are parallel to the harmful effects of physical abuse, except that the magnitude of the effect is less.

Despite the unusually high constancy in the findings of research on corporal punishment, there is a serious problem with all the previous research, these studies do not indicate which is cause and which is effect. That is, they do not take into account the fact that aggression and other behavior problems of the child lead parents to spank. Consequently, although there is clear evidence that the more corporal punishment, the greater the probability of hitting a spouse later in life, that finding could simply indicate that the parents were responding to a high level of aggression by the child at Time 1. For example, they might have spanked because the child repeatedly grabbed toys from or hit a brother or sister. Since aggression is a relatively stable trait, it is not surprising that the most aggressive children at Time 1 are still the most aggressive at Time 2 and are now hitting their wives or husbands. To deal with that problem, the research needs to take into account the child's aggression or other antisocial behavior at Time 1 (the time of the spanking). Studies using that design can examine whether, in the months or years following, the behavior of children who were spanked improves (as most people in the USA think will be the case) or gets worse. There are finally new studies that use this design and provide information on long term change in the child's behavior.

Five New Landmark Studies

In the three-year period 1997–1999 five studies became available that can be considered "landmark" studies because they overcame this serious defect in 45 years of previous research on the long-term effects of corporal punishment. All five of the new studies took into account the child's behavior at Time 1, and all five were based on large and nationally representative samples of American children. None of them depended on adults recalling what happened when they were children.

Study 1: Corporal Punishment and Subsequent Antisocial Behavior

This research studied over 3,000 children in the National Longitudinal Survey of Youth (Straus, et al., 1997). The children were in three age groups: 3–5, 6–9, and 10–14. The mothers of all three groups of children were interviewed at the start of the study in 1988, and then again in 1990 and 1992. The findings were very similar for all three age groups and for change after two years and four years. To avoid excess detail only the results for the 6–9 year old children and for the change in antisocial behavior two years after the first interview will be described here.

Measure of corporal punishment. To measure corporal punishment, the mothers were told "Sometimes kids mind pretty well and sometimes they don't," and asked "About how many times, if any, have you had to spank your child in the past week?"

Measure of Antisocial Behavior. To measure Antisocial Behavior the mothers were asked whether, in the past three months, the child frequently "cheats or tells lies," "bullies or is cruel/mean to others," "does not feel sorry after misbehaving," "breaks things deliberately," "is disobedient at school," "has trouble getting along with teachers." This was used to create a measure of the number of antisocial behaviors frequently engaged in by the child.

Other Variables. We also took into account several other variables that could affect antisocial behavior by the child. These include the sex of child, cognitive stimulation provided by the parents, emotional support by the mother, ethnic group of the mother, and socioeconomic status of the family.

Findings. The more corporal punishment used during the first year of the study, the greater the tendency for Antisocial Behavior to *increase* subsequent to the corporal punishment. It also shows that this effect applied to both Euro American children and children of other ethnic groups. Of course, other things also influence Antisocial Behavior. For example, girls have lower rates of Antisocial Behavior than boys, and children whose mothers are warm and supportive are less likely to behave in antisocial ways. Although these other variables do lessen the effect of corporal punishment, we found that the tendency for corporal punishment to make things worse over the long run applies regardless of race, socioeconomic status, gender of the child, and regardless of the extent to which the mother provides cognitive stimulation and emotional support.

Study 2: A Second Study of Corporal Punishment and Antisocial Behavior

Sample and Measures. Gunnoe and Mariner (1997) analyzed data from another large and representative sample of American children—the National Survey of Families and Households. They studied 1,112 children in two age groups: 4–7 and 8–11. In half of the cases the mother was interviewed and in the other half the father provided the information. The parents were first interviewed in 1987–88, and then five years later. Gunnoe and Mariner's measure of corporal punishment was the same as in the Straus et al. study just described; that is, how often the parent spanked in the previous week.

Gunnoe and Mariner examined the effect of corporal punishment on two aspects of the child's behavior: fighting at school and antisocial behavior. Their Antisocial Behavior measure was also the same as in the Straus et al. study.

Findings on Fighting. Gunnoe and Mariner found that the more corporal punishment in 1987–88, the greater the amount of fighting at school five years later. This is consistent with the theory that in the long run corporal punishment is counter-productive. However, for toddlers and for African-American children, they found the opposite, i.e. that corporal punishment is associated with *less* fighting 5 years later. Gunnoe and Mariner suggest that this occurs because younger children and African-American children tend to regard corporal punishment as a legitimate parental behavior rather than as an aggressive act. However, corporal punishment by parents of young children and by African-American parents is so nearly universal (for example, 94 percent of parents of toddlers) that it suggests an alternative explanation: that no-corporal punishment means no-discipline. If that is the case, it is no wonder that children whose parents exercise no-discipline are less well behaved. Corporal punishment may not be good for children, but failure to properly supervise and control is even worse.

Findings on Antisocial Behavior. The findings on the relation of corporal punishment to Antisocial Behavior show that the more corporal punishment experienced by the children in Year 1, the *higher* the level of Antisocial Behavior five years later. Moreover, they found that the harmful effect of corporal punishment applies to all the categories of children they studied—that is, to children in each age group, to all races, and to both boys and girls. Thus, both of these major long-term prospective studies resulted in evidence that, although corporal punishment may work in the short run, in the long run it tends to boomerang and make things worse.

An important sidelight of the Gunnoe and Mariner study is that it illustrates the way inconvenient findings can be ignored to give a desired "spin." The findings section includes one brief sentence acknowledging that their study "replicates the Straus et al. findings." This crucial finding is never again mentioned. The extensive discussion and conclusion sections omit mentioning the results showing that corporal punishment at Time 1 was associated with more antisocial behavior subsequently for children of all ages and all ethnic groups. Marjorie Gunnoe told me that she is opposed to spanking and has never spanked her own children. So the spin she put on the findings is not a reflection of personal values or behavior.

Perhaps it reflects teaching at a college affiliated with a church which teaches that God expects parents to spank.

Study 3: Corporal Punishment and Child-to-Parent Violence

Timothy Brezina (1999) analyzed data on a nationally representative sample of 1,519 adolescent boys who participated in the Youth in Transition study. This is a three-wave panel study that was begun in 1966. Although the data refer to a previous generation of high school students, there is no reason to think that the relationship between corporal punishment and children hitting parents is different now that it was then, except that the rate may have decreased because fewer parents now slap teen-agers.

Measure of Corporal Punishment. Corporal punishment was measured by asking the boys "How often do your parents actually slap you?" The response categories ranged from 1 (never) to 5 (always). Twenty eight percent of the boys reported being slapped by their parents during the year of the first wave of the study when their average age was 15, and 19 percent were slapped during the wave 2 year (a year and half later).

Measure of Child Aggression. The boys were asked similar questions about how often they hit their father and their mother. Eleven percent reported hitting a parent the first year, and 7 percent reported hitting a parent at Time 2 of the study.

Findings. Brezina found that corporal punishment at Time 1 was associated with an *increased* probability of a child assaulting the parent a year and a half later. Thus, while it is true that corporal punishment teaches the child a lesson, it is certainly not the lesson intended by the parents.

As with the other four studies, the data analysis took into account some of the many other factors that affect the probability of child-to-parent violence. These include the socioeconomic status and race of the family, the age of the parents, the child's attachment to the parent, child's attitude toward aggression, and child's physical size.

Study 4: Corporal Punishment and Dating Violence

Simons, Lin, and Gordon (1998) tested the theory that corporal punishment by the parents increases the probability of later hitting a partner in a dating relationship. They studied 113 boys in a rural area of the state of Iowa, beginning when they were in the 7th grade or about age 13.

Measure of Corporal Punishment. The mothers and the fathers of these boys were asked how often they spanked or slapped the child when he did something wrong, and how often they used a belt or paddle for corporal punishment. These questions were repeated in waves 2 and 3 of this 5-year study. The scores for the mother and the father for each of the three years were combined to create an overall measure of corporal punishment. More than half of the boys experienced corporal punishment during those years. Consequently, the findings about corporal punishment apply to the majority of boys in that community, not just to the children of a small group of violent parents.

Measure of Dating Violence. The information on dating violence came from the boys, so it is not influenced by whether the parents viewed the boy as aggressive. The boys were asked whether, in the last year, "When you had a disagreement with your girlfriend, how often did you hit, push, shove her?"

Measure of Delinquency at Time 1. As explained earlier, it is critical to take into account the misbehavior that leads parents to use corporal punishment. In this study, that was done by asking the boys at Time 1 how often they had engaged in each of 24 delinquent acts such as skipping school, stealing, and physically attacking someone with a weapon; and also how often they had used drugs and alcohol.

Parental involvement and support. Finally the study also took into account the extent to which the parents showed warmth and affection, were consistent in their discipline, monitored and supervised the child, and explained rules and expectations. In addition, it also controlled for witnessing parental violence.

Findings. Simons and his colleagues found that the more corporal punishment experienced by these boys, the greater the probability of their physically assaulting a girlfriend. Moreover, like the other prospective studies, the analysis took into account the misbehavior that led parents to use corporal punishment, and also the quality of parenting. This means that the relation of corporal punishment to violence against a girlfriend is very unlikely to be due to poor parenting. Rather, it is another study showing that the long run effect of corporal punishment is to engender more rather than less misbehavior. In short, spanking boomerangs.

Study 5: Corporal Punishment and Child's Cognitive Development

The last of these five studies (Straus and Paschall, 1999) was prompted by studies showing that talking to children (including pre-speech infants) is associated with an increase in neural connections in the brain and in cognitive performance. Those findings led us to theorize that if parents avoid corporal punishment, they are more likely to engage in verbal methods of behavior control such as explaining to the child, and that the increased verbal interaction with the child will in turn enhance the child's cognitive ability.

This theory was tested on 806 children of mothers in the National Longitudinal Study of Youth who were age 2 to 4 in the first year of our analysis, and the tests were repeated for an additional 704 children who were age 5 to 9 in the first year. Corporal punishment was measured by whether the mother was observed hitting the child during the interview and by a question on frequency of spanking in the past week. A corporal punishment scale was created by adding the number of times the parent spanked in two sample weeks. Cognitive ability was measured in Year 1 and two years later by tests appropriate for the age of the child at the time of testing such as the Peabody Picture Vocabulary Test.

The study took into account the mother's age and education, whether the father was present in the household, number of children in the family, mother's supportiveness and cognitive stimulation, ethnic group, and the child's age, gender, and child's birth weight.

The less corporal punishment parents use on toddlers, the greater the probability that the child will have an above average cognitive growth. The greater benefit of avoiding corporal punishment for the younger children is consistent with the research showing the most rapid growth of neural connections in the brain of early ages. It is also consistent with the theory that what the child learns as an infant and toddler is crucial because it provides the necessary basis for subsequent cognitive development. The greater adverse effect on cognitive development for toddlers has an extremely important practical implication because the defenders of corporal punishment have now retreated to limiting their advocacy to toddlers. Their recommendation is not based on empirical evidence. The evidence from this study suggests that, at least in so far as cognitive development is concerned, supporters of corporal punishment have unwittingly advised parents to use corporal punishment at the ages when it will have the most adverse effect.

The Message Of The Five Studies: "Don't Spank"

Each of the five studies I briefly summarized is far from perfect. They can be picked apart one by one, as can just about every epidemiological study. This is what the tobacco industry did for many years. The Surgeon General's committee on smoking did the opposite. Their review of the research acknowledged the limitations of the studies when taken one-by-one. But they concluded that despite the defects of the individual studies, the cumulative evidence indicated that smoking does cause lung cancer and other diseases, and they called for an end to smoking. With respect to spanking, I believe that the cumulative weight of the evidence, and especially the five prospective studies provides sufficient evidence for a new Surgeon General's warning. A start in that direction was made by the American Academy of Pediatrics, which in 1998 published "Guidelines for Effective Discipline" (*Pediatrics* 101: 723–728) that advises parents to avoid spanking.

Is There a Backlash?

It is ironic that during the same period as the new and more definitive research was appearing, there were hostile or ridiculing articles in newspapers and magazines on the idea of never spanking a child. In 1999, Arizona and Arkansas passed laws to remind parents and teachers that they have the right to use corporal punishment and to urge them to do so. There has also been a contentious debate in scientific journals on the appropriateness of corporal punishment. These developments made some advocates for children concerned that there is a backlash against the idea of no-spanking. However, there are several reasons for doubting the existence of a backlash in the sense of a reversal in the trend of decreasing public support for corporal punishment, or in the sense of non-spanking parents reverting to using corporal punishment.

One reason for doubting the existence of a backlash is that, each year, a larger and larger proportion of the American population opposes corporal punishment. In 1968, which was only a generation ago, almost everyone (94 percent) believed that corporal punishment is sometimes necessary. But in the last 30 years public support for corporal punishment has been decreasing. By 1999, almost half of US adults rejected the idea that spanking is necessary.

The Advocates Are Long-Time Supporters

In 1968, those who favored corporal punishment did not need to speak out to defend their view because, as just indicated, almost everyone believed it was necessary. The dramatic decrease in support for corporal punishment means that long time advocates of corporal punishment now have reason to be worried, and they are speaking out. Consequently, their recent publications do not indicate a backlash in the sense of a change from being opposed to corporal punishment to favoring it. I suggest that it is more like dying gasps of support for an ancient mode of bringing up children that is heading towards extinction.

The efforts of those who favor corporal punishment have also been spurred on by the increase in crime in many countries. The rise in youth crime in the United States, although recently reversed, is a very disturbing trend, and it has prompted a search for causes and corrective steps. It should be no surprise that people who have always believed in the use of corporal punishment believe that a return to their favored mode of bringing up children will help cure the crime problem. They argue that children need "discipline," which is correct. However, they equate discipline with corporal punishment, which is not correct. No-corporal punishment does not mean no-discipline. Delinquency prevention does require, among other things, discipline in the sense of clear rules and standards for behavior and parental supervision and monitoring and enforcement. To the extent that part of the explanation for crime, especially crime by youth, is the lack of discipline, the appropriate step is not a return to corporal punishment but parental standards, monitoring, and enforcement by non-violent methods. In fact, as the studies reviewed here indicate, if discipline takes the form of more corporal punishment, the problem will be exacerbated because, while corporal punishment does work with some children, more typically it boomer-

angs and increases the level of juvenile delinquency and other behavior problems.

The criticism in scientific journals of research on corporal punishment is also not a backlash. It has to be viewed in the light of the norms of science. A standard aspect of science is to examine research critically, to raise questions, and to suggest alternative interpretations of findings. This results in a somewhat paradoxical tendency for criticism to increase as the amount of research goes up. There has recently been an increase in research showing long-term harmful effects of corporal punishment. Given the critical ethos of science, it is only to be expected that the increased research has elicited more commentary and criticism, especially on the part of those who believed in corporal punishment in the first place.

Three Paradoxes About Corporal Punishment

Three paradoxical aspects of the movement away from corporal punishment are worth noting. The first is that, although approval of corporal punishment had declined precipitously in the last generation, almost all parents continue to spank toddlers. The second paradox is that professionals advising parents, including those who are opposed to spanking, generally fail to tell parents not to spank. They call this avoiding a "negative approach." Finally, and most paradoxically of all, focusing almost exclusively on a so-called "positive approach," unwittingly contributes to perpetuating corporal punishment and helps explain the first paradox.

Paradox 1: Contradictory Trends. Some aspects of corporal punishment have changed in major ways. A smaller and smaller percent of the public favors spanking (Straus and Mathur, 1996). Fewer parents now use belts, hairbrushes and paddles. The percent of parents who hit adolescents has dropped by half since 1975. Nevertheless, other aspects of corporal punishment continue to be prevalent, chronic, and severe. The 1995 Gallup national survey of parents (Straus and Stewart, 1999) found that:

- Almost all parents of toddlers (94 percent) used corporal punishment that year
- Parents who spanked a toddler, did it an average of about three times a week
- 28 percent of parents of children age 5–12 used an object such as a belt or hairbrush
- Over a third of parents of 13-year-old children hit them that year

The myths about corporal punishment in *Beating The Devil Out Of Them* provide important clues to understanding why parents who "don't believe in spanking" continue to do so. These myths also undermine the ability of professionals who advise parents to do what is needed to end corporal punishment.

Paradox 2: Opposing Spanking but Failing to Say Don't Spank. Many pediatricians, developmental psychologists, and parent educators are now opposed to corporal punishment, at least in principle. But most also continue to believe that there may be a situation where spanking by parents is necessary or acceptable (Schenck, 2000). This is based on cultural myths. One myth is that spanking works when other things do not. Another is that "mild" corporal punishment is harmless. All but a small minority of parents and professionals continue to believe these myths despite the experimental and other evidence showing that other disciplinary strategies work just as well as spanking, even in the short run and are more effective in the long run as shown by the first four of the studies described earlier in this article.

Consequently, when I suggest to pediatricians, parent educators, or social scientists that it is essential to tell parents that they should never spank or use any other type of corporal punishment, with rare exception, that idea has been rejected. Some, like one of America's leading developmental psychologists, object because of the unproven belief that it would turn off parents. Some object on the false belief that it could be harmful because parents do not know what else to do. They argue for a "positive approach" by which they mean teaching parents alternative disciplinary strategies, as compared to what they call the "negative approach" of advising to never spank. As a result, the typical pattern is to say nothing about spanking. Fortunately, that is slowly changing. Although they are still the exception, an increasing number of books for parents, parent education programs, and guidelines for professionals advise never-spanking.

Both the movement away from spanking, and an important limitation of that movement are illustrated by publication of the "Guidelines For Effective Discipline" of the American Academy of Pediatrics. This was an important step forward, but it also reflects the same problem. It recommends that parents avoid corporal punishment. However, it also carefully avoids saying that parents should *never* spank. This may seem like splitting hairs, but because of the typical sequence of parent-child interaction that eventuates in corporal punishment described in the next paragraph, it is a major obstacle to ending corporal punishment. Omitting a never-spank message is a serious obstacle because, in the absence of a commitment to never-spank, even parents who are against spanking continue to spank. It is important to understand what underlies the paradox of parents who are opposed to spanking, nonetheless spanking.

Paradox 3: Failing To Be Explicit Against Spanking Results in More Spanking. The paradox that fewer and fewer parents are in favor of spanking, but almost all spank toddlers reflects a combination of needing to cope with the typical behavior of toddlers and perceiving those behaviors through the lens of the myth that spanking works when other things do not.

When toddlers are corrected for misbehavior (such as hitting another child or disobeying), the "recidivism" rate is about 80 percent within the same day and about 50 percent within two hours. For some children it is within two

minutes. One researcher (who is a defender of corporal punishment) found that these "time to failure" rates apply equally to corporal punishment and to other disciplinary strategies (Larzelere, et al., 1996). Consequently, on any given day, a parent is almost certain to find that so-called alternative disciplinary strategies such as explaining, deprivation of privileges and time out, "do not work." When that happens, they turn to spanking. So, as pointed out previously, just about everyone (at least 94 percent) spanks toddlers.

The difference between spanking and other disciplinary strategies is that, when spanking does not work, parents do not question its effectiveness. The idea that spanking works when other methods do not is so ingrained in American culture that, when the child repeats the misbehavior an hour or two later (or sometimes a few minutes later) parents fail to perceive that spanking has the same high failure rate as other modes of discipline. So they spank again, and for as many times as it takes to ultimately secure compliance. That is the correct strategy because, with consistency and perseverance, the child will eventually learn. What so many parents miss is that it is also the correct strategy for non-spanking methods. Thus, unless there is an absolute prohibition on spanking, parents will "see with their own eyes" that alternatives do not work and continue to find it is necessary to spank.

"Never-Spank" Must Be The Message

Because of the typical behavior of toddlers and the almost inevitable information processing errors just described, teaching alternative disciplinary techniques by itself is not sufficient. There must also be an unambiguous "never-spank" message, which is needed to increase the chances that parents who disapprove of spanking will act on their beliefs. Consequently, it is essential for pediatricians and others who advise parents to abandon their reluctance to say "never-spank." To achieve this, parent-educators must themselves be educated. They need to understand why, what they now consider a "negative approach," is such an important part of ending the use of corporal punishment. Moreover, because they believe that a "negative approach" does not work, they also need to know about the experience of Sweden. The Swedish experience shows that, contrary to the currently prevailing opinion, a never-spank approach has worked (Durrant, 1999).

In short, the first priority step to end or reduce spanking may be to educate professionals who advise parents. Once professionals are ready to move, the key steps are relatively easy to implement and inexpensive.

> Parent-education programs, such as STEP, which are now silent on spanking, can be revised to include the evidence that spanking does *not* work better than other disciplinary tactics, even in the short run; and to specifically say "*never* spank."

The Public Health Service can follow the Swedish model and sponsor no-spanking public service announcements on TV and on milk cartons.

There can be a "No-Spanking" poster and pamphlets in every pediatrician's office and every maternity ward.

There could be a notice on birth certificates such as:

WARNING: SPANKING HAS BEEN DETERMINED TO BE DANGEROUS TO THE HEALTH AND WELL BEING OF YOUR CHILD—**DO NOT EVER, UNDER ANY CIRCUMSTANCES, SPANK OR HIT YOUR CHILD**

Until professionals who advise parents start advising parents to *never* spank, the paradox of parents becoming less and less favorable to spanking while at the same continuing to spank toddlers will continue. Fortunately, that is starting to happen.

The benefits of avoiding corporal punishment are many, but they are virtually impossible for parents to perceive by observing their children. The situation with spanking is parallel to that of smoking. Smokers could perceive the short run satisfaction from a cigarette, but had no way to see the adverse health consequences down the road. Similarly, parents can perceive the beneficial effects of a slap (and, for the reasons explained in the previous section, fail to see the equal effectiveness of alternatives), they have no way of looking a year or more into the future to see if there is a harmful side effect of having hit their child to correct misbehavior. The only way parents can know this would be if there were a public policy to publicize the results of research such as the studies summarized in this article.

Another reason the benefits of avoiding spanking are difficult to see is that they are not dramatic in any one case. This is illustrated by the average increase of 3 or 4 points in mental ability associated with no-corporal punishment. An increase of that size would hardly be noticed in an individual case. However, it is a well established principle in public health and epidemiology that a widely prevalent risk factor with small effect size, for example spanking, can have a much greater impact on public health than a risk factor with a large effect size, but low prevalence, for example physical abuse. For example, assume that: (1) 50 million US children experienced CP and 1 million experienced physical abuse. (2) The probability of being depressed as an adult is increased by 2 percent for children who experienced CP and by 25 percent for children who experienced physical abuse. Given these assumptions, the additional cases of depression caused by CP is 1.02 times 50 million, or 1 million. The additional cases of depression caused by physical abuse is 1.25 time 1 million or 250,000. Thus CP is associated with a four times greater increase in depression than is physical abuse.

Another example of a major benefit resulting from reducing a risk factor that has a small effect, but for a large proportion of the population, might be the increase in scores on intelligence tests that has been occurring worldwide. Corporal punishment has also been decreasing worldwide. The decrease in use of corporal punishment and the increase in scores in IQ tests could be just a coincidence. However, the results of the study described earlier in this article which showed that less spanking is associated with faster cognitive development suggest that the trend away from corporal punishment may be one of a number of social changes (especially, better educated parents) that explain the increase in IQ scores in so many nations.

The other four prospective studies reviewed in this article and the studies in *Beating the Devil Out of Them* show that ending corporal punishment is likely to also reduce juvenile violence, wife-beating, and masochistic sex, and increase the probability of completing higher education, holding a high income job, and lower rates of depression and alcohol abuse. Those are not only humanitarian benefits, they can also result in huge monetary savings in public and private costs for dealing with mental health problems, and crime.

I concluded the first edition of *Beating the Devil Out of Them* in 1994 by suggesting that ending corporal punishment by parents "portends profound and far reaching benefits for humanity." The new research summarized in this article makes those words even more appropriate. We can look forward to the day when children in almost all countries have the benefit of being brought up without being hit by their parents; and just as important, to the day when many nations have the benefit of the healthier, wealthier, and wiser citizens who were brought up free from the violence that is now a part of their earliest and most influential life experiences.

Suggested Further Readings

Brezina, Timothy. 1999. "Teenage violence toward parents as an adaptation to family strain: Evidence from a national survey of male adolescents." *Youth & Society* 30: 416–444.

Durrant, Joan E. 1999. "Evaluating the success of Sweden's corporal punishment ban." *Child Abuse & Neglect* 23: 435–448.

Gershoff, Elizabeth Thompson. In press. "Corporal punishment by parents and associated child behaviors and experiences: A meta-analytic and theoretical review." *Psychological Bulletin.*

Gunnoe, Marjorie L., and Carrie L. Mariner. 1997. "Toward a developmental-contextual model of the effects of parental spanking on children's aggression." *Archives of Pediatric and Adolescent Medicine* 151: 768–775.

Larzelere, Robert E., William N. Schneider, David B. Larson, and Patricia L. Pike. 1996. "The effects of discipline responses in delaying toddler misbehavior recurrences." *Child and Family Therapy* 18: 35–37.

Neisser, Ulric. 1997. "Rising scores on intelligence tests: Test scores are certainly going up all over the world, but whether intelligence itself has risen remains controversial." *American Scientist* 85: 440–447.

Schenck, Eliza R., Robert D. Lyman, and S. Douglas Bodin. 2000. "Ethical beliefs, attitudes, and professional practices of psychologists regarding parental use of corporal punishment: A survey." *Children's Services: Social Policy, Research, and Practice* 3: 23–38.

Simons, Ronald L., Kuei-Hsiu Lin, and Leslie C. Gordon. 1998. "Socialization in the Family of origin and male dating violence: A prospective study." *Journal of Marriage and the Family* 60: 467–478.

Straus, Murray A., and Anitia K. Mathur. 1996. "Social change and change in approval of corporal punishment by parents from 1968 to 1994." Pp. 91–105 in *Family violence against children: A challenge for society.*, edited by D. Frehsee, W. Horn, and K-D Bussmann, New York: Walter deGruyter.

Straus, Murray A., and Mallie J. Paschall. 1999. "Corporal punishment by mothers and children's cognitive development: A longitudinal study of two age cohorts." in *6th International Family Violence Research Conference.* Durham, NH: Family Research Laboratory, University of New Hampshire.

Straus, Murray A., and Julie H. Stewart. 1999. "Corporal punishment by American parents: National data on prevalence, chronicity, severity, and duration, in relation to child, and family characteristics." *Clinical Child and Family Psychology Review* 2: 55–70.

Straus, Murray A., David B. Sugarman, and Jean Giles-Sims. 1997. "Spanking by parents and subsequent antisocial behavior of children." *Archives of pediatric and adolescent medicine* 151: 761–767.

Murray A. Straus is professor of sociology and co-director of the Family Research Laboratory at the University of New Hampshire. He is the author or co-author or editor of 18 books including Stress, Culture, and Aggression. *This article is adapted from Chapter 12 of* Beating the Devil Out of Them: Corporal Punishment in American Families and Its Effects on Children, *2nd edition, published by Transaction.*

From *Society*, September/October 2001, pp. 52-60. © 2001 by Transaction Publishers. Reprinted by permission.

The Seven Sins of Memory:
How the Mind Forgets and Remembers

Memory's errors are as fascinating as they are important

By Daniel Schacter, Ph.D.

In Yasunari Kawabata's unsettling short story, "Yumiura," a novelist receives an unexpected visit from a woman who says she knew him 30 years earlier. They met when he visited the town of Yumiura during a harbor festival, the woman explains. But the novelist cannot remember her. Plagued recently by other troublesome memory lapses, he sees this latest incident as a further sign of mental decline. His discomfort turns to alarm when the woman offers more revelations about what happened on a day when he visited her room. "You asked me to marry you," she recalls wistfully. The novelist reels while contemplating the magnitude of what he had forgotten. The woman explains that she had never forgotten their time together and felt continually burdened by her memories of him.

After she finally leaves, the shaken novelist searches maps for the town of Yumiura with the hope of triggering recall of the place and the reasons why he had gone there. But no maps or books list a town called Yumiura. The novelist then realizes that he could not have been in the part of the country the woman described at the time she remembered. Her detailed, heart-felt and convincing memories were entirely false.

Kawabata's story dramatically illustrates different ways in which memory can get us into trouble. Sometimes we forget the past and at other times we distort it; some disturbing memories haunt us for years. Yet we also rely on memory to perform an astonishing variety of tasks in our everyday lives. Recalling conversations with friends or recollecting family vacations; remembering appointments and errands we need to run; calling up words that allow us to speak and understand others; remembering foods we like and dislike; acquiring the knowledge needed for a new job—all depend, in one way or another, on memory. Memory plays such a pervasive role in our daily lives that we often take it for granted until an incident of forgetting or distortion demands our attention.

Memory's errors have long fascinated scientists, and during the past decade they have come to occupy a prominent place in our society. Forgotten encounters, misplaced eyeglasses and failures to recall the names of familiar faces are becoming common occurrences for many adults who are busily trying to juggle the demands of work and family, and cope with the bewildering array of new communications technologies. How many passwords and "PINs" do you have to remember just to manage your affairs on the Internet, not to mention your voice mail at the office or on your cell phone?

In addition to dealing with the frustration of memory failures in daily life, the awful specter of Alzheimer's disease looms large on the horizon. As the general public becomes ever more aware of its horrors through such high-profile cases as Ronald Reagan's battle with the disorder, the prospects of a life dominated by catastrophic forgetting further increase our preoccupations with memory.

Although the magnitude of the woman's memory distortion in Yumiura seems to stretch the bounds of credulity, it has been equaled and even exceeded in everyday life. Consider the story of Binjimin Wikomirski, whose 1996 Holocaust memoir, *Fragments,* won worldwide acclaim for portraying life in a concentration camp from the perspective of a child. Wilkomirski presented readers with raw, vivid recollections of the unspeakable terrors he witnessed as a young boy. Even more remarkable, Wilkomirski had spent much of his adult life unaware of these traumatic childhood memories, only becoming aware of them in therapy. Because his story and memories inspired countless others, Wilkomirski became a sought-after international figure and a hero to Holocaust survivors.

The story began to unravel, however, in late August 1998, when Daniel Ganzfried, a Swiss journalist and himself the son of a Holocaust survivor, published a stunning article in a Zurich newspaper. Ganzfried revealed that Wilkomirski is actually Bruno Dossekker, a Swiss native born in 1941 to a young woman named Yvone Berthe Grosjean, who later gave him up for adoption to an orphanage. His foster parents, the Dossekkers, found him there. Young Bruno spent all of the war years in the safe confines of his native Switzerland. Whatever the basis for his traumatic "memories" of Nazi horrors, they did not come from childhood experiences in a concentration camp. Is Dossekker/Wilkomirski simply a liar? Probably not: he still strongly believes his recollections are real.

Memory's errors are as fascinating as they are important. They can be divided into seven fundamental transgressions or "sins," which I call transience, absentmindedness, blocking, misattribution, suggestibility, bias and persistence. Just like the ancient seven deadly sins—pride, anger, envy, greed, gluttony, lust and sloth—the memory sins occur frequently in everyday life and can have serious consequences for all of us.

Transience, absentmindedness and blocking are sins of omission: we fail to bring to mind a desired fact, event or idea. Transience refers to a weakening or loss of memory over time. It is a basic feature of memory, and the culprit in many memory problems. Absentmindedness involves a breakdown at the interface between attention and memory. Absentminded memory errors—misplacing your keys or eyeglasses, or forgetting a lunch appointment—typically occur because we are preoccupied with distracting issues or concerns, and don't focus attention on what we need to remember.

The third sin, blocking, entails a thwarted search for information we may be desperately trying to retrieve. We've all had the experience of failing to produce a name to a familiar face. This frustrating experience happens even though we are attending carefully to the task at hand, and even though the desired name has not faded from our minds—as we become acutely aware when we unexpectedly retrieve the blocked name hours or days later.

The next four sins of misattribution, suggestibility, bias and persistence are all sins of commission: some form of memory is present, but it is either incorrect or unwanted. The sin of misattribution involves assigning a memory to the wrong source: mistaking fantasy for reality, or incorrectly remembering that a friend told you a bit of trivia that you actually read about in a newspaper. Misattribution is far more common than most people realize, and has potentially profound implications in legal settings. The related sin of suggestibility refers to memories that are implanted as a result of leading questions, comments or suggestions when a person is trying to call up a past experience. Like misattribution, suggestibility is especially relevant to—and sometimes can wreak havoc within—the legal system.

The sin of bias reflects the powerful influences of our current knowledge and beliefs on how we remember our pasts. We often edit or entirely rewrite our previous experiences—unknowingly and unconsciously—in light of what we now know or believe. The result can be a skewed rendering of a specific incident, or even of an extended period in our lives, that says more about how we feel now than about what happened then.

The seventh sin—persistence—entails repeated recall of disturbing information or events that we would prefer to banish from our minds altogether: remembering what we cannot forget, even though we wish that we could. Everyone is familiar with persistence to some degree: Recall the last time you suddenly awoke at 3 a.m., unable to keep out of your mind a painful blunder on the job or a disappointing result on an important exam. In more extreme cases of serious depression or traumatic experience, persistence can be disabling and even life-threatening.

"Two regions of the brain showed greater activity when people made abstract/concrete judgments about words they later remembered compared with those they later forgot."

New discoveries, some based on recent breakthroughs in neuroscience that allow us to see the brain in action as it learns and remembers, are beginning to illuminate the basis of the seven sins. These studies allow us to see in a new light what's going on inside our heads during the frustrating incidents of memory failure or error that can have a significant impact on our everyday lives. But to understand the seven sins more deeply, we also need to ask why our memory systems have come to exhibit these bothersome and sometimes dangerous properties: Do the seven sins represent mistakes made by Mother Nature during the course of evolution? Is memory flawed in a way that has placed our species at unnecessary risk? I don't think so. To the contrary, I contend that each of the seven sins is a byproduct of otherwise desirable and adaptive features of the human mind. Let's consider two of the most common memory sins: transience and absentmindedness.

TRANSIENCE

On October 3, 1995 the most sensational criminal trial of our time reached a stunning conclusion: a jury acquitted O. J. Simpson of murder. Word of the verdict spread quickly, nearly everyone reacted with either outrage or jubilation, and many people could talk about little else for days and weeks afterward. The Simpson verdict seemed like just the sort of momentous event that most of us would always remember vividly: how we reacted to it, and where we were when we heard the news.

Now, can you recall how you found out that Simpson had been acquitted? Chances are that you don't remember, or that what you remember is wrong. Several days after the verdict, a group of California undergraduates provided researchers with detailed accounts of how they learned about the jury's decision. When the researchers probed students' memories again 15 months later, only half recalled accurately how they found out about the decision. When asked again nearly three years after the verdict, less than 30% of students' recollections were accurate; nearly half were dotted with major errors.

The culprit in this incident is the sin of transience: forgetting that occurs with the passage of time. Research has shown that minutes, hours or days after an experience, memory preserves a relatively detailed record, allowing us to reproduce the past with reasonable if not perfect accuracy. But with the passing of time, the particulars fade and opportunities multiply for interference—generated by later, similar experiences—to blur our recollections.

Consider the following question: If I measure activity in your brain while you are learning a list of words, can I tell from this activity which words you will later remember having studied, and which words you will later forget? In other words, do measurements of brain activity at the moment when a perception is being transformed into a memory allow scientists to predict future remembering and forgetting of that particular event? If so, exactly which regions allow us to do the predicting?

In 1997, our group at the imaging center of Massachusetts General Hospital came up with an experiment to answer the question. Holding still in this cacophonous tunnel [the magnetic resonance imaging or MRI scanner], participants in our experiment saw several hundred words, one every few seconds, flashed to them from a computer by specially arranged mirrors. To make sure that they paid attention to every word, we asked our volunteers to indicate whether each word refers to something abstract, such as "thought," or concrete, such as "garden." Twenty minutes after the scan, we showed subjects the words they had seen in the scanner, intermixed with an equal number of words they hadn't seen, and asked them to indicate which ones they did and did not remember seeing in the scanner. We knew, based on preliminary work, that people would remember some words and forget others. Could we tell from the strength of the signal when participants were making abstract/concrete judgments which words they would later remember and which ones they would later forget?

We could. Two regions of the brain showed greater activity when people made abstract/concrete judgments about words they later remembered compared with those they later forgot. One was in the inner part of the temporal lobe, a part of the brain that, when damaged, can result in severe memory loss. The other region whose activity predicted subsequent memory was located further forward, in the lower left part of the vast territory known as the frontal lobes.

This finding was not entirely unexpected, because previous neuroimaging studies indicated that the lower left part of the frontal lobe works especially hard when people elaborate on incoming information by associating it to what they already know.

These results were exciting because there is something fascinating, almost science fiction-like, about peering into a person's brain in the present and foretelling what she will likely remember and forget in the future. But beyond an exercise in scientific fortune-telling, these studies managed to trace some of the roots of transience to the split-second encoding operations that take place during the birth of a memory. What happens in frontal and temporal regions during those critical moments determines, at least in part, whether an experience will be remembered for a lifetime, or drop off into the oblivion of the forgotten.

ABSENTMINDEDNESS

On a brutally cold day in February 1999, 17 people gathered in the 19th floor office of a Manhattan skyscraper to compete for a title known to few others outside that room: National Memory Champion. The winner of the U.S. competition would go on to challenge for the world memory championship several months later in London.

The participants were asked to memorize thousands of numbers and words, pages of faces and names, lengthy poems and decks of cards. The victor in this battle of mnemonic virtuosos, a 27-year-old administrative assistant named Tatiana Cooley, relied on classic encoding techniques: generating visual images, stories and associations that link incoming information to what she already knows. Given her proven ability to commit vast amounts of information to memory, one might also expect that Cooley's everyday life would be free from the kinds of memory problems that plague others. Yet this memory champion considers herself dangerously forgetful. "I'm incredibly absentminded," Cooley told a reporter. Fearful that she will forget to carry out everyday tasks. Cooley depends on to-do lists and notes scribbled on sticky pads. "I live by Post-its," she admitted ruefully.

The image of a National Memory Champion dependent on Post-its in her everyday life has a paradoxical, even surreal quality: Why does someone with a capacity for prodigious recall need to write down anything at all? Can't Tatiana Cooley call on the same memory abilities and strategies that she uses to memorize hundreds of words or thousands of numbers to help remember that she needs to pick up a jug of milk at the store? Apparently not: The gulf that separates Cooley's championship memory performance from her forgetful everyday life illustrates the distinction between transience and absentmindedness.

The kinds of everyday memory failures that Cooley seeks to remedy with Post-it notes—errands to run, appointments to keep and the like—have little to do with transience. These kinds of memory failures instead reflect the sin of absentmindedness: lapses of attention that result in failing to remember information that was either never encoded property (if at all) or is available in memory but is overlooked at the time we need to retrieve it.

To appreciate the distinction between transience and absentmindedness, consider the following three examples:

A man tees up a golf ball and hits it straight down the fairway. After waiting a few moments for his partner to hit, the man tees up his ball again, having forgotten that he hit the first drive.

A man puts his glasses down on the edge of a couch. Several minutes later, he realizes he can't find the glasses, and spends a half-hour searching his home before locating them.

"Memory's errors have long fascinated scientists, and during the past decade they have come to occupy a prominent place in our society."

A man temporarily places a violin on the top of his car. Forgetting that he has done so, he drives off with the violin still perched on the roof.

Superficially, all three examples appear to reflect a similar type of rapid forgetting. To the contrary, it is likely that each occurred for very different reasons.

The first incident took place back in the early 1980s, when I played golf with a patient who had been taking part in memory research conducted in my laboratory. The patient was in the early stage of Alzheimer's disease, and he had severe difficulties remembering recent events. Immediately after hitting his tee shot, the patient was excited because he had knocked it straight down the middle; he realized he would now have an easy approach shot to the green. In other words, he had encoded this event in a relatively elaborate manner that would ordinarily yield excellent memory. But when he started teeing up again and I asked him about his first shot, he expressed no recollection of it whatsoever. This patient was victimized by transience: he was incapable of retaining the information he had encoded, and no amount of cueing or prodding could bring it forth.

In the second incident, involving misplaced glasses, entirely different processes are at work. Sad to say, this example comes from my own experience—and happens more often than I would care to admit. Without attending to what I was doing, I placed my glasses in a spot where I usually do not put them. Because I hadn't fully encoded

this action to begin with—my mind was preoccupied with a scientific article I had been reading—I was at a loss when I realized that my glasses were missing. When I finally found them on the couch, I had no particular recollection of having put them there. But unlike the golfing Alzheimer's patient, transience was not the culprit: I never adequately encoded the information about where I put my glasses and so had no chance to retrieve it later.

The third example, featuring the misplaced violin, turned into far more than just a momentary frustration. In August 1967, David Margetts played second violin in the Roth String Quartet at UCLA. He had been entrusted with the care of a vintage Stradivarius that was owned by the department of music. After Margetts put the violin on his car's roof and drove off without removing it, UCLA made massive efforts to recover the instrument. Nonetheless, it went missing for 27 years before resurfacing in 1994 when the Stradivarius was brought in for repair and a dealer recognized the instrument. After a lengthy court battle, the violin was returned to UCLA in 1998.

There is, of course, no way to know exactly what Margetts was thinking about when he put the violin on his car's roof. Perhaps he was preoccupied with other things, just as I was when I misplaced my glasses. But because one probably does not set down a priceless Stradivarius without attending carefully to one's actions, I suspect that had Margetts been reminded before driving off, he would have remembered perfectly well where he had just placed the violin. In other words, Margetts was probably not sabotaged by transience, or even by failure to encode the event initially. Rather, forgetting in Margett's case was likely attributable to an absent-minded failure to notice the violin at the moment he needed to recall where he had put it. He missed a retrieval cue—the violin on the car's roof—which surely would have reminded him that he needed to remove the instrument.

Even though they often seem like our enemies, the seven sins are an integral part of the mind's heritage because they are so closely connected to features of memory that make it work well. The seven sins are not merely nuisances to minimize or avoid. They illuminate how memory draws on the past to inform the present, preserves elements of present experience for future reference, and allows us to revisit the past at will. Memory's vices are also its virtues, elements of a bridge across time that allows us to link the mind with the world.

Adapted from Daniel Schacter, Ph.D.'s *The Seven Sins of Memory: How the Mind Forgets and Remembers* (Houghton-Mifflin, 2001)

Daniel L. Schacter, Ph.D., is chairman of the psychology department at Harvard University and also author of "Searching for Memory" (HarperCollins, 1997).

From *Psychology Today*, May/June 2001, pp. 62-87. Excerpted from *The Seven Sins of Memory: How the Mind Forgets and Remembers,* by Daniel Schacter. © 1990 by Soko Publications Ltd. Reprinted by permission of Houghton Mifflin Company. All rights reserved.

Memory's Mind Games

Absent-mindedness is just the start of memory problems. When the brain distorts the past, our view of who we are suffers.

By Sharon Begley

As slide shows go, it wasn't even in the same league as your aunt's vacation snapshots, but the audience was paying close attention: there was going to be a quiz. In one sequence a student sitting in a packed lecture hall topples onto the floor. In others, a hand retrieves oranges that have rolled all over a supermarket, and a woman picks up groceries scattered across a floor. Between 15 minutes and 48 hours later, the Boston University under-grads—volunteers in this psychology experiment—scrutinize more photos and, for each one, decide whether they ever saw it before. Yup, saw the student carelessly leaning back in his chair. Yeah, also saw the guy stupidly take an orange from the bottom of the pile. Uh-huh, saw the grocery bag rip. In all, 68 percent of the time the students remembered seeing the "cause" picture (a ripping bag) whose effect (spilled groceries) had been part of the show.

There was only one problem. The slides did not include a single such cause photo. "When people saw the effect photo but not the cause photo, they 'filled in the blank' by saying they *had* seen the cause with their own two eyes," says psychologist Mark Reinitz of the University of Puget Sound. Writing in the July issue of the Journal of Experimental Psychology, he and Sharon Hannigan of Bard College conclude that the mind's drive to infer causes can fool people into "remembering" something they never saw. In other words, says Reinitz, "memories can be illusions."

When it comes to memory problems, forgetting is only the tip of the iceberg. The failures and failings of memory run much deeper than an inability to recall your neighbor's name, the capital of Illinois or the location of your keys. Much recent memory research has focused on why we forget, shedding light on tragedies like Alzheimer's as well as puzzles like why we often know the first letter of a name or word we're trying to remember, but not the rest of it. But unlike absent-mindedness and other "sins of omission," as psychologist Daniel Schacter of Harvard University calls them in his new book, "The Seven Sins of Memory," memory's "sins of commission" shape—and often distort—our view of reality and relationships. Some of the sins:

Blocking. Somewhere between remembering and forgetting lies blocking. You *know* that the word for an oration at a funeral begins with a vowel, maybe even a "u"… but it just won't spring into consciousness. You *know* the name of the longtime neighbor who's approaching as you talk to the new people next door, but as the seconds tick down until you'll have to make the introduction, the best you can come up with is that his name begins with an "R." Proper names are blocked more than any other words, memory researchers find, and more in old people than young. The problem with names is that they are (in Western cultures, at least) completely arbitrary: that guy looks no more like a Richard than he does a Paul. Also, the sound of a word is encoded in the brain in a different place from its meaning. If the links from concept (the context in which you know a person) to visual representation (aha, that face belongs to my neighbor!) to the word itself (Paulie Walnuts) are weak, then we can't get to the word even though we may remember everything about it. You may tickle neurons here, but the reverberations never reach those deeper in the circuit.

Sometimes we get to the first sound in the word but no further: the phonemes of words are apparently encoded separately, too, and coming up with that "eu-" sound doesn't guarantee that you'll move on to "-lo." Words we use infrequently are especially subject to this tip-of-the-tongue phenomenon. If you need to remember which medicine to take for a common ailment, you'll probably come up easily with "aspirin" for a headache or "antacid" for a stomach upset. But you might well struggle before remembering what's needed to treat a sudden allergic reaction: "antihistamine."

Misattribution. The El Al cargo flight had smashed into an apartment building outside Amsterdam, killing 39 residents and all four crew members in a fiery explo-

BIAS:

YOUR BRAIN REWRITES THE PAST UNDER THE INFLUENCE OF CURRENT EVENTS… E.G., A DIVORCING COUPLE REMEMBER ONLY THE BAD TIMES TOGETHER, NOT THE GOOD

SUGGESTIBILITY:

LEADING QUESTIONS/REMARKS COLOR YOUR MEMORIES OR EVEN "CREATE" THEM… E.G., PARENT TO CHILD: REMEMBER WE TOOK YOU TO DISNEYLAND AND YOU TALKED TO MICKEY MOUSE? REMEMBER? AND CHILD "REMEMBERS."

MISATTRIBUTION:

YOU MISATTRIBUTE THE SOURCE OF YOUR MEMORY… E.G., JOE REMEMBERS SAYING SOMETHING TO SALLY WHEN IN FACT HE SAID IT TO SUE

BLOCKING:

YOU CAN'T REMEMBER A NAME OR WORD, BUT YOU CAN REMEMBER THE FIRST LETTER

PERSISTENCE:

YOU WANT TO FORGET TRAUMAS, TRAGEDIES, ETC., BUT CAN'T… THE UNWANTED MEMORIES PERSIST

sion. Ten months after the 1992 disaster, Dutch psychologists quizzed colleagues about how well they remembered television footage of the crash. Most remembered it so well that they could describe whether the fuselage was aflame before it hit, where the plane fell after impact and other details. But there was no such footage: people attributed to video what they had inferred from newspapers, discussions with friends and other sources.

In misattribution, people unconsciously transfer a memory from one mental category to another—from imagination to reality, from this time and place to that one, from hearsay to personal experience. The brain has made what psychologists call a "binding error," incorrectly linking the content of a memory with its context. The fault may lie in the hippocampus, a seahorse-shaped structure deep in the brain's temporal lobe, whose job includes binding together all facets of a memory. When the hippocampus is damaged, patients are more prone to binding errors. So next time you believe that you experienced something you only imagined, or that you mentioned your impending business trip to your wife when in

fact you told only your secretary, blame a hiccup in your hippocampus.

Suggestibility. In this memory error, people confuse personal recollection with outside sources of information. Suggestibility is therefore a form of misattribution, but an especially pernicious one. "Leading questions or even encouraging feedback can result in 'memories' of events that never happened," says Schacter. In one recent case, Korean War veteran Edward Daly became convinced that he participated in the horrific massacre of civilians at No Gun Ri. Military records show he was nowhere near the site at the time, suggesting that he had confused hearing rumors of the massacre with witnessing it. (Some reporters, though, believe he was outright lying.) But that wasn't the end of it. As Daly talked to vets who were present at the massacre, "reminding" them of his deeds that day, several became convinced, as one told The New York Times, that "Daly was there. I know that. I know that."

Suggestibility can lead to false eyewitness IDs because even seemingly innocuous feedback can distort recall. In one study, psychologist Gary Wells of Iowa State University and colleagues showed volunteers a security video of a man entering a Target store. Moments later, Wells told them, the man murdered a guard. He then showed them photos and asked them to identify the gunman (who actually appeared in none of the snapshots). Good, you identified the actual suspect, the scientists told some of the volunteers.

Those who received this encouragement later told Wells they were more confident in their recall and had had a better view of the man on the video than those who did not get a verbal pat on the back for their "correct" ID. Certainty and your assurance that you got a good look at the suspect are the kinds of details a jury uses when weighing eyewitness testimony. Positive feedback seems to cement memory and even erase any original uncertainty.

Persistence. Memories that refuse to fade tend to involve regret, trauma and other potent negative emotions. All emotions strengthen a memory, but negative ones seem to write on the brain in indelible ink, Schacter finds. That's especially true if the memory reinforces your self-image: if you think of yourself as a screw-up, you'll have a hard time erasing the memory of the time you spilled wine all over your boss. Blame your amygdala. When you experience a threatening event like the approach of a menacing stranger, the level of activity in this clutch of brain neurons predicts how well you will remember the experience. Stress hormones seem to strengthen the neuronal circuit that embodies a traumatic memory.

Bias. It is a cliché that couples in love recall their courtship as a time of bliss, while unhappy pairs recall that "I never really loved him [or her]." But the cliché is true. "We rewrite our memories of the past to fit our present views and needs," says Schacter. That may be an outgrowth of forgetting: we can't recall how we felt in the past, so we assume it must be how we feel today. But often bias arises when more powerful mental systems bully poor little memory. The left brain, driven to keep thoughts of yesterday and today from conflicting, reconciles past and present as boldly as the Ministry of Truth in Orwell's "1984."

Linda Levine of UC, Irvine, showed exactly this when she interviewed supporters of Ross Perot right after he unexpectedly dropped out of the 1992 presidential race that July. How did they feel about his decision? she asked. Soon after Perot re-entered in October, Levine revisited the same supporters, asking again how they had felt about the July drop-out. Those who'd never wavered in their support remembered feeling less sad about Perot's quitting than they had claimed in July: their happiness over his return had overwritten their unhappy memory. Disgruntled support-

ers who had initially switched to another candidate but had gone back to Perot recalled feeling less anger in October than they reported in July. Their relief over his return to the race trumped their ire at feeling abandoned.

Stereotyping can also bias memory. Researchers at Yale University led by Mahzarin Banaji asked students which names on a list they recalled as those of criminals recently in the news. The students were twice as likely to "remember" the stereotypically black names ("Tyrone Washington") as they were the stereotypically white ones ("Adam McCarthy"). None of the names had been in the news as criminal suspects or anything else, the scientists reported in 1999. When memory conflicts with what you're convinced is true, it often comes out on the losing end. And that can make forgetting where you put your keys seem trivial indeed.

From *Newsweek*, July 16, 2001, pp. 52-54. © 2001 by Newsweek, Inc. All rights reserved. Reprinted by permission.

UNIT 5
Cognitive Processes

Unit Selections

Key Points to Consider

- Why study cognition? Why study the development of cognitive abilities; why would this be of interest to psychologists? What role do you think culture plays in cognitive development? What aspects of culture most influence how we process incoming information about our world? Besides culture, can you think of other factors that influence our cognitive activity?

- What is brain mapping? How does it help us understand the human mind? Is the mind as complex as we think it is? What is morality? What is "self"? What is awareness? How does the brain play a role in each? How far advanced is the science of understanding the interrelationship between neurology and cognition?

- What are some of the myths that Americans believe about intelligence? Are these myths true? Why use science to investigate these myths if they seem so commonsensical? What does science say about intelligence and our commonly held beliefs?

- What is a savant? Are you a savant or do you know someone who might be classified as one? Are savants common in the general population? From where does this special cognitive functioning come? What are some examples of the kinds of abilities savants possess? What practical purposes could these abilities serve?

 **Links: www.dushkin.com/online/**
These sites are annotated in the World Wide Web pages.

Chess: Kasparov v. Deep Blue: The Rematch
http://www.chess.ibm.com/home/html/b.html

Introduction to Artificial Intelligence (AI)
http://www-formal.stanford.edu/jmc/aiintro/aiintro.html

As Rashad watches his 4-month old, he is convinced that the baby possesses a degree of understanding of the world around her. In fact, Rashad is sure he has one of the smartest babies in the neighborhood. Although he is indeed a proud father, he keeps these thoughts to himself so as not to alienate his neighbors whom he perceives as having less intelligent babies.

Gustav lives in the same neighborhood as Rashad. Gustav doesn't have any children, but he does own two fox terriers. Despite Gustav's most concerted efforts, the dogs never come to him when he calls them. In fact, the dogs have been known to run in the opposite direction on occasion. Instead of being furious, Gustav accepts his dogs' disobedience because he is sure the dogs are just dumb beasts and don't know any better.

Both of these vignettes illustrate important and interesting ideas about cognition or thought processes. In the first vignette, Rashad ascribes cognitive abilities and high intelligence to his child; in fact, Rashad perhaps ascribes too much cognitive ability to his 4-month old. On the other hand, Gustav assumes that his dogs are incapable of thought, more specifically incapable of premeditated disobedience, and he therefore forgives them.

Few adults would deny the existence of their cognitive abilities. Some adults, in fact, think about thinking, something which psychologists call metacognition. Cognition is critical to our survival as adults. But are there differences in mentation in adults? And what about other organisms? Can young children—infants for example—think? If they can, do they think like adults? And what about animals; can they think and solve problems? These and other questions are related to cognitive psychology and cognitive science, which is showcased in this unit.

Cognitive psychology has grown faster than most other specialties in psychology in the past 30 years. Much of this has occurred in response to new computer technology as well as to the growth of psycholinguistics. Computer technology has prompted an interest in artificial intelligence, the mimicking of human intelligence by machines. Similarly the study of psycholinguistics has prompted the examination of the influence of language on thought and vice versa.

While interest in these two developments has eclipsed interest in more traditional areas of cognition such as intelligence, we cannot ignore these traditional areas in this anthology. With regard to intelligence, one persistent problem has been the difficulty of defining just what intelligence is. David Wechsler, author of several of the most popular intelligence tests in current clinical use, defines intelligence as the global capacity of the individual to act purposefully, to think rationally, and to deal effectively with the environment. Other psychologists have proposed more complex definitions. The definitional problem arises when we try to develop tests that validly and reliably measure such abstract, intangible concepts. A valid test is one that measures what it purports to measure. A reliable test yields the same score for the same individual over and over again. Because defining and assessing intelligence has been so controversial and so difficult, historian Edward Boring once suggested that we define intelligence as whatever it is that an intelligence test measures!

The first article in this unit offers the reader a look into the world of cognitive development. Psychologist Mary Gauvain discusses how culture shapes cognitions and proclaims that psychologists have given the concept of culture short shrift in their theories and research on child development and cognition.

In "Mind in a Mirror" the role of the brain in cognition is examined. Specifically, the role that brain functioning plays in the development of morality, awareness, and the formation of self-concept is revealed. According to this article, however, the science is rudimentary because the research on brain and cognition is still in its preliminary stages.

We next continue with a discussion of intelligence—an important underpinning of cognitive ability. The article by psychologist Stephen Ceci reviews some of the myths about intelligence. Ceci shatters some commonly held misconceptions about what intelligence is and is not, using results of scientific investigations to do so.

"Savant" may be a new word to you. A savant is an individual who possesses extraordinary ability, usually in one aspect of cognitive functioning. What causes someone to be a savant and whether we all have this potential are thoughtfully explored in this article by Douglas Fox.

Cognitive Development in Social and Cultural Context

Abstract

The development of thinking is discussed from a sociocultural perspective. Three features of the social and cultural context that play important roles in organizing and directing cognitive development are presented and illustrated empirically: (a) activity goals and values of the culture, (b) material and symbolic tools for satisfying cultural goals and values, and (c) higher level structures that instantiate cultural goals and values in everyday practices. The article concludes with a discussion of the utility of this approach for advancing understanding of human intellectual growth.

Keywords

cognitive development; sociocultural influences; sociohistorical approach

Mary Gauvain[1]
Department of Psychology, University of California at Riverside, Riverside, California

In all societies throughout the world, most children grow up to be competent members of their communities. This impressive phenomenon—and indeed it is impressive—relies on some inherent human ability to develop intellectual and social skills adapted to the circumstances in which growth occurs. It also relies on social and cultural practices that support and maintain desired patterns of development. This article focuses on two questions pertaining to this process. First, how do children develop the skills and knowledge to become competent members of their community? Second, how are cultures uniquely suited to support and lead this development? To address these questions, I discuss culturally devised ways for supporting the development and maintenance of valued cultural skills. Several areas of research are foundational to the ideas presented here.

The first influence is a cultural-practice view of cognition (Chaiklin & Lave, 1996), which includes research on situated learning, everyday cognition and practical intelligence. This work takes as a starting point the idea that people learn to think in specific contexts in which human activity is directed toward practical goals. An important contribution of this work is attention to the coordination between the thinker and the actions performed. The main limitation for present purposes is that it concentrates on learning rather than development. A second influence is the sociohistorical tradition (Cole, 1996), which emphasizes the role of material, symbolic, and social resources in organizing and supporting mental growth. The primary contribution of this approach is attention to the opportunities and constraints for cognitive development provided by the cultural community in which growth occurs. A practical limitation is that this idea, to date, has been broad in conception, touching on many aspects of psychological development. An organizational framework that links this approach more systematically to contemporary domains of research is needed for further examination and incorporation into the field. A final influence is the concept of the *developmental niche* (Super & Harkness, 1986), which characterizes the psychological structure of the human ecosystem that guides children's development. The central idea is that it is not only the organism that provides structure and direction to development; rather, culture also possesses structure and direction, and it is through the conjoining of these two organized systems that human development unfolds. Super and Harkness proposed three subsystems of the developmental niche, physical and social settings, customs of child care, and psychology of the caregiver. These subsystems concentrate on social development. In this review, I extend this basic framework to the study of cognitive development.

THREE COGNITIVE SUBSYSTEMS OF THE DEVELOPMENTAL NICHE

Three subsystems of the developmental niche that connect cognitive development to culture are the activity goals and values of the culture and its members; historical means for satisfying cultural goals and values, especially the material and symbolic tools that support thinking and its development; and higher level structures that instantiate cultural goals and values in everyday practice and through which children become participants in the intellectual life of their community. These subsystems are hierarchically organized, from the microanalytic level (i.e., the level of individual psychological activity) to the broader social circumstances of development. A key point is the range of human experience represented: Culture penetrates human intellectual functioning and its development at many levels, and it does so through organized individual and social practices.

Activity Goals and Values of the Culture

Human behavior and thinking occur within meaningful contexts as people conduct purposeful, goal-directed activities (Vygotsky, 1978). The developmental implication is that children learn about and practice thinking in the course of participating in goal-directed activities—activities defined and organized by the cultural community in which development occurs. Much psychological research has focused on the organized, goal-directed nature of human activity (e.g., Duncker's classic studies of functional fixedness[2] and Bartlett's studies of memory), so this basic idea is not new. However, a cultural psychological approach offers two unique contributions: (a) an emphasis on the connection between activity structures (the means and goals that define human action) and the cultural practices from which they stem and (b) an examination of the relations among activity structures, cultural practices, and cognitive growth.

Research on children's everyday mathematics illustrates this linkage. Studies of the mathematical skills of Brazilian children who sell candy in the street (Carraher, Carraher, & Schliemann, 1985) indicate that mental activity reflects the practices that individuals engage in, that these practices are defined by cultural convention and routine, and that mathematical activities are handled differently, and more successfully, when the goal of the calculation is meaningful than when it is not. Another example

is found in how intelligent behavior changes following social reorganization. Inkeles and Smith (1974) observed industrialization in non-Western communities and found that one behavioral change was greater concern with time and planning activities in advance. The point is not that Westerners plan and non-Westerners do not. What occurred was a reorganization of cultural practices that, in turn, led to the reorganization of a cognitive behavior, planning.

The main point is that activities and the goals that guide them are expressions of culture. Focusing on the cultural context of human activity may advance understanding of how the human mind is organized over the course of development to fit with the requirements and opportunities of the culture. Incidentally, this point may offer insight into the issue of transfer or generalization of cognitive skills across different task contexts, a topic that has vexed psychologists for generations. Psychologists have often sought transfer by focusing on isomorphic tasks (i.e., tasks that are very similar in structure). However, the key psychological linkage supporting transfer may not be task properties per se, but may instead be the meaning and goals of an activity and how a culture has devised ways, such as problem-solving routines, to achieve these goals and connect human action over time and space.

Material and Symbolic Tools

Material and symbolic tools, or artifacts (Cole, 1996), are developed and used by cultural communities to support mental activity. Such tools not only enhance thinking but also transform it, and in so doing, they channel cognitive development in unique ways. Involvement with more experienced cultural members, who demonstrate and convey the use of these tools, is a critical part of this process. Through the use of such "tools for thinking," a person's mental functioning acquires an organized link to sociohistorically formulated means of thinking transmitted through these tools.

Research on the use of particular cultural tools and the development of mathematical thinking illustrates this point. Children who are skilled at using the abacus employ a "mental abacus" when calculating solutions in their heads (Hatano, Miyake, & Binks, 1977), and this skill enhances mental calculation. Historical examination lends further insight into this

process (Swetz, 1987). Late in the 12th century, a book by Leonardo of Pisa, who was also known as Fibonacci, introduced Hindu-Arabic notation and described the commercial applications of this system. This idea was picked up by Italian merchants in the next century and led to changes in conventions of calculating. At the time, Roman numerals were used, and large calculations were executed on the counting board, a form of abacus. These boards were very large, hard to transport, and difficult to use. Extensive training was needed to reach competence, and only a few people could do the calculations or check them for correctness. Hindu-Arabic numerals were entirely different. Far less equipment was needed to calculate with this system— ink and paper sufficed. This equipment was easy to transport, and, more important, it was easy to teach and learn. In a brief period of time, the long-established form of calculation was replaced. Although the Hindu-Arabic system limited the need for mental calculation, it helped lay the foundation for further developments in mathematics, especially in areas like number theory, in that calculations can be represented on paper and reexamined for patterns and structure (Swetz, 1987).

How does this historical case relate to the findings about skilled abacus users? Think again about mental calculation, a cognitive process that research indicates is aided by skill with the abacus. What this history tells us is that the shift from Roman to Hindu-Arabic numerals made mental calculation largely obsolete, as well as less valued, because calculating on paper allowed people to demonstrate their solution steps. It appears that differential skill of people who do and do not use the abacus may have origins in the notation shift introduced in the 13th and 14th centuries. The mathematical skills of experts are consistent with the requirements of the apparatus and the practice their notation systems afford.

The main point is that cultural tools and the thinking they support are not independent but merged. To describe thinking by concentrating on one and not the other is to ignore part of the problem-solving process. Too often in psychological research when tools of thinking are described, they are treated as entities outside the head, and therefore not part of, or at least not central to, the cognitive process being investigated. However, such thinking tools, both material and symbolic, are constituent elements of cognition and its development. The historical example suggests that many of the concepts considered fundamental to human cognition in the domains in which artifacts play important roles have not always been in place, at least not in the way they are conceptualized today. Certain tools of thought came into being at various points during human history, and these influenced thinking in extraordinary ways. These historical "changes of mind" may be illuminating for scholars interested in cognitive development. Although historical analysis is of limited use to psychologists for many reasons, such cases may be helpful for demonstrating an organized link among artifacts, social processes, and the mind that is often difficult to see in the more local, contemporary circumstances in which psychologists usually do their research.

Higher Level Structures and Practices

Organized social practices or conventions allow people to share their knowledge with one another. These structures help connect members of a community to each other and to a shared system of meaning. Examples of the connection between cognitive development and cultural ways of organizing and communicating knowledge exist in the developmental literature. Research on scripts, which are "outlines" of common, recurrent events (Nelson & Gruendel, 1981), treats the acquisition of culturally organized knowledge as a critical developmental achievement. Research on the development of other pragmatic conventions, such as skill at describing large-scale space (Gauvain & Rogoff, 1989) as if one is being taken on an imagined walk through it (a "mental tour"), also suggests that one important aspect of development is the increasing alignment of knowledge with the conventions of the community in which development occurs.

An intriguing question is whether these conventional forms influence the process of thinking and its development. There is far less data on this question. However, an interesting series of studies by Levinson (1996) in an Australian Aboriginal community, the Guugu Yimithirr, is relevant. To describe spatial location, the language used in this community does not rely on relativistic terms, like left and right, but on absolute or fixed directional terms, like north, south, windward, and upstream. How do these speakers encode spatial information? In one study, objects were positioned on a table in a windowless, nondescript room. Each participant studied these placements, was then taken to a similar room that was oriented differently, and asked to place the same set of objects on a table so as to duplicate the placements in the first room. Participants placed the items in ways that respected the cardinal directions of the original placements (i.e., an object placed on the north side of the table was placed on the north, even though this would mean that it would be on the "other side" of an object to an observer using relative position as a guide). Although these results do not specify the cognitive processes underlying this behavior, they suggest that performance on tasks involving spatial cognition involves the coordination of visual and linguistic encoding in ways related to practices of the cultural community.

Another set of higher level structures related to the development of thinking appears in practices of social interaction. In recent years, there has been extensive research on the influence of social interaction on cognitive development, with much of this work based on Vygotsky's (1978) notion of the zone of proximal development, which is defined as the distance between an individual's attained level of development and the individual's potential level of development that may be reached by guidance and support from others (see Rogoff, 1990). Results from this research support the claim that intelligence, especially in the early years, develops largely through social experiences. For example, when Tessler and Nelson (1994) tested the recall of 3- to 3-½-year-old children about a visit they took to a museum with their mothers, none of the children recalled any information that they had seen in the museum but not discussed with their mothers. Dyadic interaction with adults or peers is only one form of social exchange that may determine young children's opportunities for cognitive development in social context. Parents also influence children's learning via the practical routines they adopt to organize children's behaviors and by regulating the composition of children's social groups. Beyond the family and peer group, cognitive development is influenced by children's participation in more formal social institutions, especially school, and by opportunities to observe more competent cultural members as they engage in cognitive activities, a process Lave and Wenger (1991) call legitimate peripheral participation.

The point is that cognitive development occurs in and emerges from social situations. Conventions for organizing and conveying knowledge, as well as social practices within which knowledge is displayed and communicated, are an inherent aspect of thinking. For research to advance, these social systems need to be connected in a principled way to the developmental processes they help organize, as well as to the cultural system of meaning and practice they represent.

CONCLUSIONS

In summary, a sociocultural view of cognitive development enhances understanding of this psychological process. Dimensions of culture are realized in human action, and it is possible to specify and study these dimensions in relation to psychological development. They can bring the social and cultural character of intellectual development into relief. Understanding culture and cognitive development can be advanced via research designed for this purpose as well as by reexamining findings extant in the literature.

All this said, many hard questions remain. One concerns how to understand and describe individual skill that emerges in and is displayed in social situations. Psychologists have yet to devise a language for describing thinking that is not entirely in the head of the child or is only partially in place (i.e., evident only in some circumstances). Haith (1997) pointed out that many of the cognitive skills that children develop are defined in dichotomous terms. Consider mental representations. Representations are typically understood as something that a person either has or does not have (i.e., as states of understanding rather than as processes), and rarely as something that is partially or incompletely achieved. Such conceptualization may suffice in describing the mature thinker, though this is an open question. But it is surely inadequate for describing the development of knowledge that appears in the form of "partial understanding," such as that located in social performance. Thus, in order to incorporate the notion of partial or socially contextualized intellectual accomplishments into an understanding of cognitive development, we need a different conceptualization of many cognitive skills.

The analysis of culture in all aspects of psychological functioning is likely to increase dramatically in the next decade. How psychologists, especially those interested in intellectual development, will address this concern is unclear. Perhaps by developing conceptual frameworks, such as the one presented here, in which social and cultural systems of interacting and supporting psychological functions are an inextricable part of human behavior and development, this task may be eased.

Notes

1. Address correspondence to Mary Gauvain, Department of Psychology, University of California at Riverside, Riverside, CA 92521; e-mail: mary.gauvain@ucr.edu.
2. Functional fixedness is a problem-solving phenomenon in which people have difficulty seeing alternate uses for common objects.

Recommended Reading

Cole, M. (1996). (See References)

Gauvain, M. (1995). Thinking in niches: Sociocultural influences on cognitive development. *Human Development, 38*, 25–45.

Goodnow, J.J. (1990). The socialization of cognition. In J.W. Stigler, R.A. Schweder, & G. Herdt (Eds.), *Cultural psychology* (pp. 259–286). New York: Cambridge University Press.

Nelson, K. (1996). *Language in cognitive development: The emergence of the mediated mind.* Cambridge, England: Cambridge University Press.

Rogoff, B. (1998). Cognition as a collaborative process. In W. Damon (Series Ed.) & D. Kuhn & R.S. Siegler (Vol. Eds.), *Handbook of child psychology: Vol. 2. Cognition, perception, and language* (pp. 679–744). New York: John Wiley and Sons.

References

Carraher, T.N., Carraher, D.W., & Schliemann, A.D. (1985). Mathematics in the streets and in schools. *British Journal of Developmental Psychology, 3*, 21–29.

Chaiklin, S., & Lave, J. (1996). *Understanding practice: Perspectives on activity and context.* Cambridge, England: Cambridge University Press.

Cole, M. (1996). *Cultural psychology.* Cambridge, MA: Harvard University Press.

Gauvain, M., & Rogoff, B. (1989). Ways of speaking about space: The development of children's skill at communicating spatial knowledge. *Cognitive Development, 4*, 295–307.

Haith, M.M. (1997, April). *Who put the cog in infant cognition? Is rich interpretation too costly?* Paper presented at the biennial meeting of the Society for Research in Child Development, Washington, DC.

Hatano, G., Miyake, Y., & Binks, M. (1977). Performance of expert abacus operators. *Cognition, 9*, 47–55.

Inkeles, A., & Smith, D.H. (1974). *Becoming modern.* Cambridge, MA: Harvard University Press.

Lave, J., & Wenger, E. (1991). *Situated learning: Legitimate peripheral participation.* New York: Cambridge University Press.

Levinson, S.C. (1996). Frames of reference and Molyneux's question: Crosslinguistic evidence. In P. Bloom, M.A. Peterson, L. Nadel, & M.F. Garrett (Eds.), *Language and space* (pp. 109–169). Cambridge, MA: MIT Press.

Nelson, K., & Gruendel, J. (1981). Generalized event representations: Basic building blocks of cognitive development. In M.E. Lamb & A.L. Brown (Eds.), *Advances in developmental psychology* (Vol. 1, pp. 131–158). Hillsdale, NJ: Erlbaum.

Rogoff, B. (1990). *Apprenticeship in thinking.* New York: Oxford University Press.

Super, C.M., & Harkness, S. (1986). The developmental niche: A conceptualization at the interface of child and culture. *International Journal of Behavioral Development, 9*, 545–569.

Swetz, F.J. (1987). *Capitalism and arithmetic.* La Salle, IL: Open Court.

Tessler, M., & Nelson, K. (1994). Making memories: The influence of joint encoding on later recall. *Consciousness and Cognition, 3*, 307–326.

Vygotsky, L.S. (1978). *Mind in society.* Cambridge, MA: Harvard University Press.

From Current Directions in Psychological Science, December 1998, pp. 188-192. © 1998 by the American Psychological Society. Reprinted by permission of Blackwell Publishers.

Mind in a Mirror

Mapping morality, awareness, and 'self' in the brain

BY RACHEL K. SOBEL

So you're looking for your keys. You can't find them, but you keep looking and... all of a sudden, there they are, right where you already looked. Your eyes had rolled right over those keys. Then something happened and you *saw*. What explains that click, that sudden shift from looking to seeing?

Güven Güzeldere wants to find out. The Duke University researcher is a philosopher and a neuroscientist, and his work straddles both worlds. He has turned to functional magnetic resonance imaging (fMRI), an imaging tool that highlights regions of brain activity, to get a snapshot of the neural circuitry that supports this sudden flash of awareness. His work has just begun, but he hopes that what he learns about awareness will offer a peek into larger issues. "I'm ultimately interested in philosophical questions," he says. "Like what is the nature of consciousness? What is it for? And what makes us different than animals and machines?"

In the past, Güzeldere could have approached those questions only as a philosopher, not as a scientist. But after decades of refining their tools and techniques, brain imagers are trying to glimpse the seemingly unglimpseable. By challenging subjects with cleverly designed problems while using an fMRI scanner to map the ebb and flow of brain activity, these researchers are trying to learn how our 3-pound mass of gray flesh gives rise to the mind. So far, the data may resemble crude cartography. But neuroscientists think they will one day be able to unravel many of the intricate neural systems underlying our most elusive traits, including consciousness, morality, and empathy.

Until recently, brain mappers mostly charted more basic functions, such as memory, language, and vision. Even there, no one claims to have all the details. But neuroscientists believe they have enough of a blueprint to begin probing the biological underpinnings of more complex activities. Take a new study on the nature of moral decisions. Scientists asked subjects to contemplate a variety of moral dilemmas and imaged their brains while they were doing so. The researchers then used earlier data about where emotions are processed in the brain to interpret the scans. The results showed that even when people think they are making rational judgments, their emotions may actually be driving the outcome.

The findings, published in a September issue of *Science*, offer a glimpse of a process that philosophers have speculated about for centuries. "To start understanding the mechanisms of something as essentially human as the moral judgments we make," says Joshua Greene, a philosophy doctoral candidate at Princeton University and the lead author of the study, "we're really getting at the nuts and bolts of who we are."

You and me. Another trait thought to be at the core of who we are is our sense of "self." Marcus Raichle, a professor of radiology and neurology at Washington University in St. Louis, is trying to learn how the brain generates this sense that "you're you and I'm me and we know that." He and

his colleagues suspected that some of the brain's frenetic "resting" activity—it consumes about 20 percent of the body's entire energy budget even when not engaged in any particular task—might be supporting self-awareness. A hint of where this might be happening in the brain came from scans of people tackling challenges that seem to lie outside the self, such as math problems. Baseline resting activity dropped off in a portion of the brain's prefrontal cortex, a couple of inches behind the center of the forehead.

To investigate further, Raichle's team designed a new experiment that compared brain activity in situations that were identical except in the self-involvement they demanded. In one, the subjects had to say whether pictures of mundane objects, such as picnic scenes and kittens, belonged indoors or outdoors. This task—which required the subjects to step outside of themselves—caused activity in the prefrontal area to decrease. In the other, they were asked to consider whether the same pictures had pleasant or unpleasant associations. Activity in the supposed "self" networks surged as the viewers considered their own response to the pictures. The contrast, the researchers argued last March in *Proceedings of the National Academy of Sciences*, suggests that at least part of our sense of self depends on knots of neurons elaborately intertwined in the prefrontal cortex.

Other thoughts. At the other end of the spectrum, some researchers are looking for the underpinnings of "other"—our ability to put ourselves in other people's shoes and imagine their beliefs and desires. In one telling study, Chris Frith and his team at University College London asked subjects in the scanner to think about the following incident: A burglar robs a shop, walks down the street, and unknowingly drops his glove. A policeman coming from behind stops him to tell him about the glove. The burglar turns around and gives himself up. Why does he do this?

The answer—that the burglar thinks the policeman is about to arrest him—requires thinking about the "other": the thief and his mental state. Frith's team scanned subjects' brains at this moment of empathy. The data showed intriguing parallels between the neural circuits that lit up and the ones typically activated when thinking about one's self. "Thinking about yourself in a situation may be the way you think about other people," says Frith.

Researchers trying to image the mind are quick to hedge their claims. Dartmouth University's Michael Gazzaniga, the first scientist to secure an fMRI machine for a psychology department, admits that it is a somewhat crude tool. It traces brain activity by tracking blood flow, which rises wherever there's a surge in metabolism. It's possible, Gazzaniga says, that elements of certain tasks "may be so automatic that they require no increase in metabolism," which would allow active brain regions to slip past the technique undetected. Other sober scientists note that interpreting brain maps can get hairy. "If a number of areas show activation, we don't know whether they are causally involved or going along for the ride," says Eric Kandel, professor of neurobiology at Columbia University College of Physicians and Surgeons.

In the end, no one claims that the work will point to a single brain area for, say, morality or consciousness. Indeed, the brain mappers are careful to distance themselves from 19th-century phrenologists, who believed that every ability had its own brain compartment. "Everything that happens in the brain is based on the work of systems, like music in an orchestra performed from a score," says Antonio Damasio, professor of neurology at the University of Iowa. "It all sounds like one thing, but it's coming from 100 or more individual parts. What we're doing is finding out those little parts."

From *U.S. News & World Report,* November 12, 2001, pp. 64-65. © 2001 by U.S. News & World Report, L.P. Reprinted by permission.

INTELLIGENCE: THE SURPRISING TRUTH

Stephen Ceci, Ph.D., lays out 12 facts about intelligence that may astound even the experts.

By Stephen Ceci, Ph.D.

Every culture has a word for "smart," and for "stupid." And everyone feels entitled to have an opinion about intelligence. Unlike, say, brain surgery, intelligence is not an area of expertise that is considered off-limits. Because it's something that our society particularly values, just about everyone has taken a test that measures intelligence, whether it's billed as an IQ test or not. Will you be assigned to the radar corps or the mess tent?

OVER THE PAST TWO DECADES, A NATIONAL DEbate has raged about intelligence: what is it, who has it and how do we measure it? The argument is fueled by findings from two camps of research. There are the psychometricians, who look at the statistics and biology of IQ and try to determine how much of intelligence is innate. And then there are the cultural ecologists, who focus on environment and point out the mutability of intelligence and the unfairness of IQ tests. Unfortunately, the two lines of study seldom meet because their methods are so different. Rarely does one camp communicate with the other.

Birth order doesn't predict IQ, and there is no causal role for family size in determining a child's IQ.

That leaves most ordinary citizens on the outside of the debate, free to cling to their personal beliefs about intelligence. The only trouble is our theories of intelligence are too narrowly constructed. They tend to ignore real data, even though a voluminous literature exists on the topic.

At the very least, intelligence can be defined as the ability for complex thinking and reasoning. One thing the research shows for sure: much of the ability for complex reasoning depends on the situation. A person can be a genius at the racetrack but a dolt in the stock market, even though both pursuits require comparable mental activities. But the knowledge is organized in the mind differently in different domains, so what a person knows about the track can lie fallow on Wall Street.

I would like to present a dozen research-supported facts about intelligence that most people, including some IQ experts, might find surprising:

The truth is that smart people tend to have small families, but it is not small families per se that make people smart.

FACT 1: IQ correlates with some simple abilities

Glance at the two lines below in Figure 1 and decide which is longer; now decide whether the two letters in each pair of figure 1b have the same name or are physically identical. Finally, name the number in 1c. Simple, huh?

No one with a measurable IQ has difficulty answering that the line on the right is longer. But those with a higher IQ respond to the question faster.

Even individuals with an IQ below 70 can do this task at a high level of accuracy, but they need up to five times longer than subjects with a higher IQ. This may be because such tasks require a series of physiological processes, and the nervous systems of individuals with low

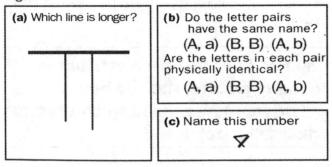

Figure 1.

(a) Which line is longer?

(b) Do the letter pairs have the same name?
(A, a) (B, B) (A, b)
Are the letters in each pair physically identical?
(A, a) (B, B) (A, b)

(c) Name this number
7

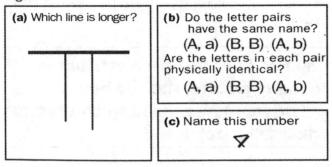

IQs are less efficient, requiring longer, visual displays. Whether you accept this explanation, studies show that IQ is modestly related to the speed at which you do some pretty simple things.

FACT 2: IQ is affected by school attendance

Although intelligence does influence the decision to stay in school, staying in school itself can elevate IQ. Or, more accurately, prevent it from slipping. Each additional month a student remains in school may increase his IQ above what would have been expected had he dropped out. The idea that schooling increases IQ may surprise anyone who views it as a measure of innate intelligence.

The earliest evidence comes from the turn of the last century, when the London Board of Education studied children who had very low IQ scores. The report revealed that the IQ of children in the same family decreased from the youngest to the oldest. The youngest group—ages 4 to 6—had an average IQ of 90, and the oldest children—12 to 22—had an average of only 60. This suggests that factors other than heredity are at work. The older children progressively missed more school, and their IQs plummeted as a result.

A few other facts about school attendance:

- IQ is affected by delayed schooling. Researchers in South Africa studied the intellectual functioning of children of Indian ancestry. For each year of delayed schooling, the children experienced a decrement of five IQ points. Similar data has been reported in the U.S.
- IQ is affected by remaining in school longer. Toward the end of the Vietnam War, a draft priority was established by lottery. Men born on July 9, 1951, were picked first so they tended to stay in school longer to avoid the draft; while men born July 7 had no incentive to stay in school longer because they were picked last in the lottery. As a result, men born on July 9 not only had higher IQs, they also earned more money—approximately 7% more.

- Dropping out of school can also diminish IQ. In a large-scale study, 10% of all males in the Swedish school population born in 1948 were randomly selected and given an IQ test at age 13. Upon reaching age 18 (in 1966), 4,616 of them were tested again. For each year of high school not completed, there was a loss of 1.8 IQ points.
- IQ is affected by summer vacations. Two independent studies have documented that there is a systematic decline in IQ scores over the summer months. With each passing month away from school, children lose ground from their end-of-year scores. The decline is pronounced for children whose summers are least academically oriented.

FACT 3: IQ is not influenced by birth order

The idea that birth order influences personality and intelligence is long-standing. First-borns are allegedly smarter and more likely to become leaders than are later-born siblings. Recently, however, this belief has come up against scrutiny. The idea that large families make low-IQ children may be unfounded because researchers have discovered that low-IQ parents actually make large families.

The truth is that smart people tend to have small families, but it is not small families per se that make people smart. Hence, birth order doesn't predict IQ, and there is no causal role for family size in determining a child's IQ.

Also, no structural aspects of family size influence a child's IQ. Otherwise two siblings closer in age would have more similar IQs than two siblings spaced far apart. But this is not the case.

FACT 4: IQ is related to breast-feeding

My colleagues and I were skeptical when we first heard claims that breast-fed infants grew into children with higher IQs than their siblings who were not breast-fed. There are factors that differ between breast-fed and non-breast-fed children, such as the amount of time mother and child spend together through nursing and the sense of closeness they gain from nursing.

It turns out, however, that even when researchers control for such factors, there still appears to be a gain of 3 to 8 IQ points for breast-fed children by age three. Exactly why is unclear. Perhaps the immune factors in mother's milk prevent children from getting diseases that deplete energy and impair early learning. Breast milk may also affect nervous system functioning. Mother's milk is an especially rich source of omega-3 fatty acids that are building blocks of nerve cell membranes and crucial to the efficient transmission of nerve impulses.

FACT 5: IQ varies by birth date

Most states have restrictions on the age of students entering schools, as well as policies mandating attendance until age 16 or 17. School attendance drops off for students born during the final three months of the year, as they are more likely to enter school a year later. When these individuals come of age, they have been in school one year less than their classmates.

For each year of school completed, there is an IQ gain of approximately 3.5 points.

Researchers have shown that for each year of schooling completed, there is an IQ gain of approximately 3.5 points. Students born late in the year, as a group, show a lower IQ score. Given the random processes involved in being born early versus late within a given year, we can assume that the genetic potential for intelligence is the same in both groups.

FACT 6: IQ evens out with age

Imagine interviewing two biological siblings, adopted by two different middle class families, at age five and again at 18. Will their IQs be more alike when they are younger and living in the homes of their adoptive parents, or when they are older and living on their own? Many people reason that IQs will be more alike when they're younger because they are under the influence of their respective middle class parents. Once they are on their own, they may diverge as they become exposed to different experiences that may influence their intelligence differently.

IQ has risen about 20 points with every generation.

But according to data, this isn't true. As these siblings go out on their own, their IQ scores become more similar. The apparent reason is that once they are away from the dictates of their adoptive parents, they are free to let their genotypes express themselves. Because they share approximately 50% of their segregating genes, they will become more alike because they are propelled to seek similar sorts of environments. Genes may be more potent in making siblings alike than similarities in home environments.

FACT 7: Intelligence is plural, not singular

Regardless of their views about the existence and the strength of so-called general intelligence, researchers agree that statistically independent mental abilities exist—such as spatial, verbal, analytical and practical intelligence.

The rise in IQ has been attributed to many factors, such as better nutrition, more schooling and better-educated parents.

In 1995, Yale psychologist Robert Sternberg and colleagues developed new evidence that practical and analytical intelligence are two different things. They demonstrated that the skills of practical intelligence, such as common sense, were important in predicting life outcomes, but were not associated with IQ-type analytic intelligence. There may even be at least seven or eight different kinds of intelligence, says researcher Howard Gardner of Harvard, including interpersonal, intrapersonal, linguistic, motoric and musical intelligence.

FACT 8: IQ is correlated with head size

The relationship between head size and IQ has long been a subject of controversy. Popular writers such as Stephen J. Gould have rightly objected to the crude and biased means 19th-century scholars used to establish this correlation, which were based on head size and contour. But modern neuroimaging techniques demonstrate that cranial volume is correlated with IQ. Evidence also comes from studies of the helmet sizes of members of the Armed Services, whose IQs were measured during basic training. The correlations, however, are quite small.

FACT 9: Intelligence scores are predictive of real-world outcomes

People who have completed more school tend to earn more—over a lifetime, college graduates earn $812,000 more than high school dropouts, and those with professional degrees earn nearly $1,600,000 more than the college grads. But more schooling can't be the only factor in earning differences, because at every level of schooling, there is a variety of intellectual ability.

Research appears to confirm our mothers' wisdom that diet influences brain functioning.

As Figure 2 shows, even among those with comparable levels of schooling, the greater a person's intellectual ability, the higher that person's weekly earnings. Workers with the lowest levels of intellectual ability earn only two-thirds the amount workers at the highest level earn. Because differences in schooling are statistically controlled, the rise in earning must be due to other factors, such as intelligence.

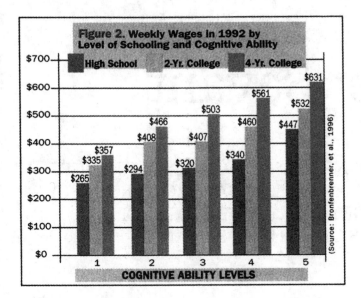

Figure 2. Weekly Wages in 1992 by Level of Schooling and Cognitive Ability

(Source: Bronfenbrenner, et al., 1996)

FACT 10: Intelligence is context-dependent

The setting in which we measure intelligence matters. In 1986, a colleague and I published a study of men who frequented the racetracks daily. Some were excellent handicappers, while others were not. What distinguished experts from non-experts was the use of a complex mental algorithm that converted racing data taken from the racing programs sold at the track. The use of the algorithm was unrelated to the men's IQ scores, however. Some experts were dockworkers with IQ scores in the low 80s, but they reasoned far more complexly at the track than all non-experts—even those with IQs in the upper 120s.

In fact, experts were always better at reasoning complexly than non-experts, regardless of their IQ scores. But the same experts who could reason so well at the track were often abysmal at reasoning outside the track—about, say, their retirement pensions or their social relationships.

FACT 11: IQ is on the rise

IQ has risen approximately 20 points with every generation, a steady increase called the "Flynn Effect," after New Zealand political scientist James Flynn. If people taking an IQ test today were scored with the norms of their grandparents' performances 50 years ago, more than 90% of them would be classified as "geniuses,"

while if our grandparents were scored today, most of them would be classed as "borderline mentally retarded." No one believes that real intelligence has risen as swiftly as IQ—if our grandparents were born today, they'd do just as well on IQ tests as they did a half century ago.

The rise in IQ has been attributed to many factors, such as better nutrition, more schooling, better-educated parents and more complex spatial environments thanks to smart toys and computers. The rise in IQ suggests that whatever it is that IQ tests test, it is not some inherent quality of the mind.

> Immune factors in mother's milk may prevent children from getting diseases that deplete energy and impair early learning.

FACT 12: IQ may be influenced by the school cafeteria menu

Recent research appears to confirm our mothers' wisdom that diet influences brain functioning. Eat your fish; it's brain food.

In one large-scale analysis of approximately 1 million students enrolled in the New York City school system, researchers examined IQ scores before and after preservatives, dyes, colorings and artificial flavors were removed from lunch offerings. They found a 14% improvement after the removal. And the improvement was greatest for the weakest students. Prior to the dietary changes, 120,000 of the students were performing two or more grade levels below average. Afterward, the figure dropped to 50,000.

Intelligence, IQ, heredity and ecology are intertwined in complex and intriguing ways. Technical journals are awash with data, and one should consider the facts before leaping to conclusions about what is and what is not intelligence. We should all challenge the implicit theories of intelligence; otherwise we are in danger of misinterpreting the truth.

READ MORE ABOUT IT:

On Intelligence: A Bio-ecological Treatise on Intellectual Development, Stephen J. Ceci, Ph.D. (*Harvard University Press, 1996*)

Resolving the debate of birth order, family size and intelligence, Rodgers, J.L., et al. (*American Psychologist, 2000*)

Stephen J. Ceci, Ph.D., is the Helen L. Carr Professor of Developmental Psychology at Cornell University.

From *Psychology Today*, July/August 2001, pp. 46-48, 50, 52-53. © 2001 by Sussex Publishers, Inc. Reprinted with permission of the author.

The Inner Savant

ARE YOU CAPABLE OF MULTIPLYING 147,631,789 BY 23,674 IN YOUR HEAD, INSTANTLY? PHYSICIST ALLAN SNYDER SAYS YOU PROBABLY CAN, BASED ON HIS NEW THEORY ABOUT THE ORIGIN OF THE EXTRAORDINARY SKILLS OF AUTISTIC SAVANTS

BY DOUGLAS S. FOX

DRAWINGS BY NORMAL 4-YEAR-OLDS
When 4-year-old children draw a horse, they typically choose to establish its contour and familiar features such as head, eyes, legs, and tail. Allan Snyder believes that these kids draw on a concept of the horse to re-create it rather than recalling the precise physical details, as savants do.

NADIA APPEARED HEALTHY AT BIRTH, BUT BY THE time she was 2, her parents knew something was amiss. She avoided eye contact and didn't respond when her mother smiled or cooed. She didn't even seem to recognize her mother. At 6 months she still had not spoken a word. She was unusually clumsy and spent hours in repetitive play, such as tearing paper into strips.

But at 3 1/2, she picked up a pen and began to draw—not scribble, *draw*. Without any training, she created from memory sketches of galloping horses that only a trained adult could equal. Unlike the way most people might draw a horse, beginning with its outline, Nadia began with random details. First a hoof, then the horse's mane, then its harness. Only later did she lay down firm lines connecting these floating features. And when she did connect them, they were always in the correct position relative to one another.

Nadia is an autistic savant, a rare condition marked by severe mental and social deficits but also by a mysterious talent that appears spontaneously—usually before age 6.

Sometimes the ability of a savant is so striking, it eventually makes news. The most famous savant was a man called Joseph, the individual Dustin Hoffman drew upon for his character in the 1988 movie *Rain Man*. Joseph could immediately answer this question: "What number times what number gives 1,234,567,890?" His answer was "Nine times 137,174,210." Another savant could double 8,388,628 up to 24 times within several seconds, yielding the sum 140,737,488,355,328. A 6-year-old savant named Trevor listened to his older brother play the piano one day, then climbed onto the piano stool himself and played it better. A savant named Eric could find what he called the "sweet spot" in a room full of speakers playing music, the spot where sound waves from the different sources hit his ears at exactly the same time.

Most researchers have offered a simple explanation for these extraordinary gifts: compulsive learning. But Allan Snyder, a vision researcher and award-winning physicist who is director of the Center for the Mind at the University of Sydney and the Australian National University, has advanced a new explanation of such talents. "Each of us has the innate capacity for savantlike skills," says Snyder, "but that mental machinery is unconscious in most people."

Savants, he believes, can tap into the human mind's remarkable processing abilities. Even something as simple as seeing, he explains, requires phenomenally complex information processing. When a person looks at an object, for example, the brain immediately estimates an object's distance by calculating the subtle differences between the two images on each retina (computers programmed to do this require extreme memory and speed). During the process of face recognition, the brain analyzes countless details, such as the texture of skin and the shape of the eyes, jawbone, and lips. Most people are not aware of these calculations. In savants, says Snyder, the top layer of mental processing—conceptual

thinking, making conclusions—is somehow stripped away. Without it, savants can access a startling capacity for recalling endless detail or for performing lightning-quick calculations. Snyder's theory has a radical conclusion of its own: He believes it may be possible someday to create technologies that will allow any nonautistic person to exploit these abilities.

THE ORIGINS OF AUTISM ARE THOUGHT TO LIE IN EARLY brain development. During the first three years of life, the brain grows at a tremendous rate. In autistic children, neurons seem to connect haphazardly, causing widespread abnormalities, especially in the cerebellum, which integrates thinking and movement, and the limbic region, which integrates experience with specific emotions. Abnormalities in these regions seem to stunt interest in the environment and in social interaction. Autistic children have narrowed fields of attention and a poor ability to recognize faces. They are more likely to view a face, for example, as individual components rather than as a whole. Imaging studies have shown that when autistic children see a familiar face, their pattern of brain activation is different from that of normal children.

That narrowed focus may explain the autistic child's ability to concentrate endlessly on a single repetitive activity, such as rocking in a chair or watching clothes tumble in a dryer. Only one out of 10 autistic children show special skills.

In a 1999 paper, Snyder and his colleague John Mitchell challenged the compulsive-practice explanation for savant abilities, arguing that the same skills are biologically latent in all of us. "Everyone in the world was skeptical," says Vilayanur Ramachandran, director of the Center for Brain and Cognition at the University of California at San Diego. "Snyder deserves credit for making it clear that savant abilities might be extremely important for understanding aspects of human nature and creativity."

SNYDER'S OFFICE AT THE UNIVERSITY OF SYDNEY IS IN A Gothic building, complete with pointed towers and notched battlements. Inside, Nadia's drawings of horses adorn the walls; artwork by other savants hangs in nearby rooms.

Snyder's interest in autism evolved from his studies of light and vision. Trained as a physicist, he spent several years studying fiber optics and how light beams can guide their own path. At one time he was interested in studying the natural fiber optics in insects' eyes. The question that carried him from vision research to autism had to do with what happens after light hits the human retina: How are the incoming signals transformed into data that is ultimately processed as images in the brain? Snyder was fascinated by the processing power required to accomplish such a feat.

During a sabbatical to Cambridge in 1987, Snyder devoured Ramachandran's careful studies of perception and optical illusions. One showed how the brain derives an object's three-dimensional shape: Falling light creates a shadow pattern on the object, and by interpreting the shading, the brain grasps the object's shape. "You're not aware how your mind comes to those conclusions," says Snyder. "When you look at a ball, you don't know why you see it as a ball and not a circle. The reason is your brain is extracting the shape from the subtle shading around the ball's surface." Every brain possesses that innate ability, yet only artists can do it backward, using shading to portray volume.

"Then," says Snyder, speaking slowly for emphasis, "I asked the question that put me on a 10-year quest"—how can we bypass the mind's conceptual thinking and gain conscious access to the raw, uninterpreted information of our basic perceptions? Can we shed the assumptions built into our visual processing system?

A few years later, he read about Nadia and other savant artists in Oliver Sacks's *The Man Who Mistook His Wife for a Hat and Other Clinical Tales*. As he sat in his Sydney apartment one afternoon with the book in hand, an idea surfaced. Perhaps someone like Nadia who lacked the ability to organize sensory input into concepts might provide a window into the fundamental features of perception.

IF SOMEONE CAN BECOME AN INSTANT SAVANT, SNYDER WONDERED, DOESN'T THAT SUGGEST WE ALL HAVE SAVANTLIKE POTENTIAL LOCKED AWAY IN OUR BRAINS?

Snyder's theory began with art, but he came to believe that all savant skills, whether in music, calculation, math, or spatial relationships, derive from a lightning-fast processor in the brain that divides things—time, space, or an object—into equal parts. Dividing time might allow a savant child to know the exact time when he's awakened, and it might help Eric find the sweet spot by allowing him to sense millisecond differences in the sounds hitting his right and left ears. Dividing space might allow Nadia to place a disembodied hoof and mane on a page precisely where they belong. It might also allow two savant twins to instantaneously count matches spilled on the floor (one said "111"; the other said "37, 37, 37"). Meanwhile, splitting numbers might allow math savants to factor 10-digit numbers or easily identify large prime numbers—which are impossible to split.

Compulsive practice might enhance these skills over time, but Snyder contends that practice alone cannot explain the phenomenon. As evidence, he cites rare cases of sudden-onset savantism. Orlando Serrell, for example, was hit on the head by a baseball at the age of 10. A few months later, he began recalling an endless barrage of license-plate numbers, song lyrics, and weather reports.

If someone can become an instant savant, Snyder thought, doesn't that suggest we all have the potential locked away in our brains? "Snyder's ideas sound very New Age. This is why people are skeptical," says Ramachandran. "But I have a more open mind than many of my colleagues simply because I've seen [sudden-onset cases] happen."

Bruce Miller, a neurologist at the University of California at San Francisco, has seen similar transformations in patients with frontotemporal dementia, a degenerative brain disease that strikes people in their fifties and sixties. Some of these patients, he says, spontaneously develop both interest and skill in art and music. Brain-imaging studies have shown that most patients with frontotemporal dementia who develop skills have abnormally low blood flow or low metabolic activity in their left temporal lobe. Because language abilities are concentrated in the left side of the brain, these people gradually lose the ability to speak, read, and write. They also lose face recognition. Meanwhile, the right side of the brain, which supports visual and spatial processing, is better preserved.

"They really do lose the linguistic meaning of things," says Miller, who believes Snyder's ideas about latent abilities complement his own observations about frontotemporal dementia. "There's a loss of higher-order processing that goes on in the anterior temporal lobe." In particular, frontotemporal dementia damages the ventral stream, a brain region that is associated with naming objects. Patients with damage in this area can't name what they're looking at, but they can often paint it beautifully. Miller has also seen physiological similarities in the brains of autistic savants and patients with frontotemporal dementia. When he performed brain-imaging studies on an autistic savant artist who started drawing horses at 18 months, he saw abnormalities similar to those of artists with frontotemporal dementia: decreased blood flow and slowed neuronal firing in the left temporal lobe.

ONE BLUSTERY, RAINY MORNING I DROVE TO MANSFIELD, a small farm town 180 miles northeast of Melbourne. I was heading to a day clinic for autistic adults, where I hoped to meet a savant. The three-hour drive pitched and rolled through hills, occasionally cutting through dense eucalyptus forests punctuated with yellow koala-crossing signs. From time to time, I saw large, white-crested

A DRAWING BY A 3-YEAR OLD SAVANT
A 3-year-old child named Nadia became famous for her ability to sketch spectacularly detailed horses and riders from memory. Savants like Nadia show the ability to perform unusual feats of illustration or calculation when they are younger than 6. Snyder wants to figure out how they do it.

then I saw the sheep. Viewed from the left, it was covered in wool. Viewed from the right, it was a skeleton, which I learned Guy had assembled without any help. Guy didn't say much about himself. He cannot read nor do arithmetic, but he has built an electric dog that barks, pants, wags its tail, and urinates.

During my visit, another Acorn participant, Tim, blew into the room like a surprise guest on *The Tonight Show*. He was in a hurry to leave again, but asked me my birthday—July 15, 1970.

"Born on a Wednesday, eh?" he responded nonchalantly—and correctly.

"How did you do that?" I asked.

"I did it well," he replied.

"But how?" I asked.

"*Very* well," he replied, with obvious pleasure. Then he was out the door and gone.

HOW DO CALENDAR SAVANTS DO IT? SEVERAL YEARS AGO Timothy Rickard, a cognitive psychologist at the University of California at San Diego, evaluated a 40-year-old man with a mental age of 5 who could assign a day of the week to a date with 70 percent accuracy. Because the man was blind from birth, he couldn't study calendars or even imagine calendars. He couldn't do simple arithmetic either, so he couldn't use a mathematical algorithm. But he could only do dates falling within his lifetime, which suggests that he used memory.

He could, however, do some arithmetic, such as answer this question: If today is Wednesday, what day is two days from now? Rickard suspects that memorizing 2,000 dates and using such arithmetic would allow 70 percent accuracy. "That doesn't reduce it to a trivial skill, but it's not inconceivable that someone could acquire this performance with a lot of effort," he says. It's especially plausible given the single-minded drive with which autistics pursue interests.

Yet Tim, the savant at Acorn, can calculate dates as far back as 1900, as well as into the future. And there are reports of twins who could calculate dates 40,000 years in the past or future. Still, practice may be part of it. Robyn Young, an autism researcher at Flinders University in Adelaide, Australia, says some calendar savants study perpetual calendars several days a week (there are only 14 different calendar configurations; perpetual calendars cross-reference them to years).

But even if savants practice, they may still tap into that universal ability Snyder has proposed. Here it helps to consider art savants. That Nadia began drawings with minor features rather than overall outlines suggests that she tended to perceive individual details more prominently than she did the whole—or the concept—of what she was drawing. Other savant artists draw the same way.

parrots; in one spot, a flock of a thousand or more in flight wheeled about like a galaxy.

I finally spotted my destination: Acorn Outdoor Ornaments. Within this one-story house, autistic adults learn how to live independently. They also create inexpensive lawn decorations, like the cement dwarf I see on the roof.

Joan Curtis, a physician who runs Acorn and a related follow-up program, explained that while true savants are rare, many people with autism have significant talents. Nurturing their gifts, she said, helps draw them into social interaction. Guy was one of the participants I met at Acorn. Although he was uncomfortable shaking my hand, all things electronic fascinated him, and he questioned me intently about my tape recorder.

Every horizontal surface in Guy's room was covered with his creations. One was an electric fan with a metal alligator mouth on the front that opened and closed as it rotated from side to side. On another fan a metal fisherman raised and lowered his pole with each revolution. And

DRAWING BY A SAVANT CHILD
As a child, Stephen Wiltshire did not communicate with the world except through drawing. At 10, he sketched London's Natural History Museum from memory. He is now, at 27, an accomplished artist.

PHOTOGRAPH FROM *NATURAL HISTORY MUSEUM*, J. M. DENT & SONS LTD., 1987, COPYRIGHT STEPHEN WILTSHIRE.

THERE ARE REPORTS OF TWINS WHO COULD CALCULATE DATES UP TO 40,000 YEARS IN THE PAST OR FUTURE

Autistic children differ from nonautistic children in another way. Normal kids find it frustrating to copy a picture containing a visual illusion, such as M. C. Escher's drawing in which water flows uphill. Autistic children don't. That fits with Snyder's idea that they're recording what they see without interpretation and reproducing it with ease in their own drawings.

Even accomplished artists sometimes employ strategies to shake up their preconceptions about what they're seeing. Guy Diehl is not a savant, but he is known for his series of crystal-clear still lifes of stacked books, drafting implements, and fruit. When Diehl finds that he's hit a sticking point on a painting, for example, he may actually view it in a mirror or upside down. "It reveals things you otherwise wouldn't see, because you're seeing it differ-

ently," he says. "You're almost seeing it for the first time again."

Diehl showed me how art students use this technique to learn to draw. He put a pair of scissors on a table and told me to draw the negative space around the scissors, not the scissors themselves. The result: I felt I was drawing individual lines, not an object, and my drawing wasn't half bad, either.

Drawing exercises are one way of coaxing conceptual machinery to take five, but Snyder is pursuing a more direct method. He has suggested that a technique called transcranial magnetic stimulation, which uses magnetic fields to disrupt neuronal firing, could knock out a normal person's conceptual brain machinery, temporarily rendering him savantlike.

Young and her colleague Michael Ridding of the University of Adelaide tried it. Using transcranial magnetic stimulation on 17 volunteers, they inhibited neural activity in the frontotemporal area. This language and concept-supporting brain region is affected in patients with frontotemporal dementia and in the art savant whom Miller studied. In this altered state, the volunteers performed savantlike tasks—horse drawing, calendar calculating, and multiplying.

Five of the 17 volunteers improved—not to savant levels, but no one expected that, because savants practice. Furthermore, transcranial magnetic stimulation isn't a precise tool for targeting brain regions. But the five volunteers who improved were those in whom separate neurological assessments indicated that the frontotemporal area was successfully targeted. "Obviously I don't think the idea is so outlandish anymore," says Young. "I think it is a plausible hypothesis. It always was, but I didn't expect we'd actually find the things we did."

Snyder himself is experimenting with grander ideas. "We want to enhance conceptual abilities," he says, "and on the other hand remove them and enhance objectivity."

He imagines a combination of training and hardware that might, for example, help an engineer get past a sticking point on a design project by offering a fresh angle on the problem. One method would involve learning to monitor one's own brain waves. By watching one's own brain waves during drawing exercises, Snyder imagines it may be possible to learn to control them in a way that shuts down their concept-making machinery—even the left temporal lobe itself.

Even if further research never fully reveals why savants have extraordinary skills, we may at least learn from their potential. Snyder is optimistic. "I envisage the day," he says, "when the way to get out of a [mental rut] is you pick up this thing—those of us with jobs that demand a certain type of creativity—and you stimulate your brain. I'm very serious about this."

From *Discover*, February 2002, pp. 42-49. © 2002. Reprinted with permission of the author, Douglas S. Fox.

UNIT 6
Emotion and Motivation

Unit Selections

Key Points to Consider

- What is motivation? What is an emotion? How are the two related to each other? Do you think they always affect one another?

- From where do emotions originate, nature or nurture? Why did you give the answer you did? Are various emotions controlled by different factors? For example, is one emotion controlled by the brain while other emotions are controlled by the situation? What role does the nervous system play in emotionality?

- What are some positive emotions? What are some examples of negative emotions? Do you think there is an "appropriate" emotion for every situation? Why are some people unemotional and others very expressive?

- Why are psychologists interested in deceit and lying? What has been used in the past to try to uncover deceit? Are there new methodologies now available? What technique do you think holds the most promise for detecting lying?

- What is emotional intelligence (EI)? Why are individuals with a high emotional quotient (EQ), the measurement of EI, successful? Can EI be cultivated? Emotional intelligence is important on the job. Where else might EI come in handy?

- Do you sometimes feel unmotivated or overwhelmed by too much to do? When you have to multitask, how do you usually respond to the challenge? Do you think you can improve your ability to juggle several tasks at the same time? If a friend asked you how she could improve her ability to multitask, what advice would you offer?

 **Links: www.dushkin.com/online/**
These sites are annotated in the World Wide Web pages.

CYFERNET-Youth Development
http://www.cyfernet.mes.umn.edu/youthdev.html

Emotional Intelligence Discovery
http://www.cwrl.utexas.edu/~bump/Hu305/3/3/3/

John Suler's Teaching Clinical Psychology Site
http://www.rider.edu/users/suler/tcp.html

Nature vs. Nature: Gergen Dialogue with Winifred Gallagher
http://www.pbs.org/newshour/gergen/gallagher_5-14.html

Jasmine's sister was a working mother and always reminded Jasmine about how exciting her life was. Jasmine stayed home because she loved her children, 2-year-old Min, 4-year-old Chi'Ming, and newborn Yuan. One day Jasmine was having a difficult time with the children. The baby, Yuan, had been crying all day from colic. The other two children had been bickering over their toys. Jasmine, realizing that it was already 5:15 and her husband would be home any minute, frantically started preparing dinner. She wanted to fix a nice dinner so that she and her husband could eat after the children went to bed, then relax and enjoy each other.

This was not to be. Jasmine sat waiting. When her husband finally walked in the door at 10:15, she was furious. His excuse that his boss had invited the whole office for dinner didn't reduce Jasmine's ire. She reasoned that her husband could have called to say that he wouldn't be home for dinner; he could have taken 5 minutes to do that. He said he did but that the phone was busy. Jasmine berated her husband. Her face was taut and red with rage and her voice wavered. Suddenly, bursting into tears, she ran into the living room. Her husband retreated to the safety of their bedroom.

Exhausted and disappointed, Jasmine sat alone and pondered why she was so angry with her husband. Was she just tired? Was she frustrated by negotiating with young children all day and simply wanted another adult around once in a while? Was she secretly worried and jealous that her husband was seeing another woman and had lied about his whereabouts? Was she combative because her husband's and her sister's lives seemed so much fuller than her own? Jasmine was unsure just how she felt and why she exploded in such rage at her husband, someone she loved dearly.

This story, while sad and gender-stereotypical, is not necessarily unrealistic when it comes to emotions. There are times when we are moved to deep emotion. On other occasions, when we expect waterfalls of tears, we find that our eyes are dry or simply a little misty. What are these strange things we call emotions? What motivates us to rage at someone we love?

These questions and others have inspired psychologists to study emotions and motivation. The above episode about Jasmine, besides introducing these topics to you, also illustrates why these two topics are usually interrelated in psychology. Some emotions, such as love, pride, and joy, are pleasant—so pleasant that we are motivated to keep them going. Other emotions, such as anger, grief, and jealousy, are terribly draining and oppressive—so negative that we hope they will be over as soon as possible. Emotions and motivation and their relationship to each other are the focus of this unit.

Four articles round out this unit. "Fundamental Feelings" is the first article and was written by noted scientist Antonio Damasio. Damasio is famous for his studies linking emotions to the nervous system. In this brief article he introduces us to his research and his ideas regarding emotionality.

A companion article, "Medical Detection of False Witness," also discusses emotions. The slant of the article, though, is not how we experience emotions but rather whether we can detect false emotions in others. The polygraph, used in the past to de-

tect guilt and lying, has received much criticism in the literature and from the courts. In the present article, new methods for uncovering deceit are discussed.

The final article on emotions regards emotional intelligence (EI) or emotional quotient (EQ), the measurement of EI. EI is the ability to recognize our own or another's emotional state. Those with a high EQ tend to be very successful regardless of intelligence level and other abilities. The article helps you discover just how high your EQ is.

One article on motivation is included at the end of this unit—"How to Multitask." Multitasking is a term frequently associated with computers, but it also is an apt description of what most of us are asked to do daily—undertake multiple tasks at the same time. Multitasking can divide our attention, demand more time than it ought, and make us complete each of our responsibilities less well than if we attempted them singly. How to be more successful at daily life—especially when confronted with the challenge of completing multiple jobs at the same time—is reviewed here by Catherine Bush.

Fundamental feelings

Antonio Damasio

The groundwork for the science of emotion was laid down most auspiciously over a century ago, but neuroscience has given the problem a resolute cold shoulder until recently. By the time that Charles Darwin had remarked on the continuity of emotional phenomena from non-human species to humans; William James had proposed an insightful mechanism for its production; Sigmund Freud had noted the central role of emotions in psychopathological states; and Charles Sherrington had begun the physiological investigation of the neural circuits involved in emotion, one might have expected neuroscience to be poised for an all-out attack on the problem. It is not usually appreciated that the probable cause of the neglect of the topic was the improper distinction between the concepts of emotion and feelings.

Some traits of feelings—their subjective nature, the fact that they are private, hidden from view, and often difficult to analyse—were projected onto emotions, so that they too were deemed subjective, private, hidden and elusive. Not surprisingly, neuroscientists were disinclined to give their best efforts to a problem that did not seem to be amenable to proper hypothesizing and measurement. Somewhat alarmingly, this conflation of the two concepts persists, as does the idea that the neurobiology of feelings is out of reach. A clarification is in order.

An emotion, be it happiness or sadness, embarrassment or pride, is a patterned collection of chemical and neural responses that is produced by the brain when it detects the presence of an emotionally competent stimulus—an object or situation, for example. The processing of the stimulus may be conscious but it need not be, as the responses are engendered automatically.

Emotional responses are a mode of reaction of brains that are prepared by evolution to respond to certain classes of objects and events with certain repertoires of action. Eventually, the brain associates other objects and events that occur in individual experience with those that are innately set to cause emotions, so that another set of emotionally competent stimuli arises.

The main target of the emotional responses is the body—the internal milieu, the viscera and the musculoskeletal system—but there are also targets within the brain itself, for example, monoaminergic nuclei in the brainstem tegmentum. The result of the body-targeting responses is the creation of an emotional state—involving adjustments in homeostatic balance—as well as the enactment of specific behaviours, such as freezing or fight-or-flight, and the production of particular facial expressions. The result of the brain-targeting responses is an alteration in the mode of brain operation during the emotional body adjustments, the consequence of which is, for example, a change in the attention accorded to stimuli.

Emotion

Emotion and feelings are closely related but separable phenomena; their elucidation, at long last, is now proceeding in earnest.

Emotions allow organisms to cope successfully with objects and situations that are potentially dangerous or advantageous. They are just the most visible part of a huge edifice of undeliberated biological regulation that includes the homeostatic reactions that maintain metabolism; pain signalling; and drives such as hunger and thirst. Most emotional responses are directly observable either with the naked eye or with scientific probes such as psychophysiological and neurophysiological measurements and endocrine assays. Thus, emotions are not subjective, private, elusive or undefinable. Their neurobiology can be investigated objectively, not just in humans but in laboratory species, from *Drosophila* and *Aplysia* to rodents and non-human primates.

A working definition of feelings is a different matter. Feelings are the mental representation of the physiological changes that characterize emotions. Unlike emotions, which are scientifically public, feelings are indeed private, although no more subjective than any other aspect of the mind, for example my planning of this sentence, or the mental solving of a mathematical problem. Feelings are as amenable to scientific analysis as any other cognitive phenomenon, provided that appropriate methods are used. Moreover, because feelings are the direct consequences of emotions, the elucidation of emotional neurobiology opens the way to elucidating the neurobiology of feelings.

If emotions provide an immediate response to certain challenges and opportunities faced by an organism, the feeling of those emotions provides it with a mental alert. Feelings amplify the impact of a given situation, enhance learning, and increase the probability that comparable situations can be anticipated.

The neural systems that are involved in the production of emotions are being identified through studies of humans and other animals. Various structures, such as the amygdala and the ventromedial prefrontal cortices, trigger emotions by functioning as interfaces between the processing of emotionally competent stimuli and the execution of emotions. But the real executors of emotions are structures in the hypothalamus, in the basal forebrain (for example, the nucleus accumbens) and in the brainstem (for example, the nuclei in the periaqueductal grey). These are the structures that directly signal, chemically and neurally, to the body and brain targets at which alterations constitute an emotional state.

No less importantly, recent functional imaging studies reveal that body-sensing areas, such as the cortices in the insula, the second somatosensory region (S2) and the cingulate region of the brain, show a statistically significant pattern of activation or deactivation when normal individuals experience the emotions of sadness, happiness, fear and anger. Moreover, these patterns vary between different emotions. Those body-related patterns are tangible neural correlates of feelings, meaning that we know where to look further to unravel the remaining neurophysiological mysteries behind one of the most critical aspects of human experience.

FURTHER READING

Damasio, A. R. *The Feeling of What Happens: Body and Emotion in the Making of Consciousness* (Harcourt Brace, New York, 1999).

Davidson, R. J. & Irwin, W. *Trends Cogn. Neurosci.* **3**, 11–22 (1999).

Panksepp, J. *Affective Neuroscience: The Foundations of Human and Animal Emotions* (Oxford Univ. Press, New York, 1998).

Vuillemier, P., Driver, J., Armony, J. & Dolan, R. J. *Neuron* **30**, 829–841 (2000).

Antonio Damasio is in the Department of Neurology, University of Iowa College of Medicine, 200 Hawkins Drive, Iowa City, Iowa 52242, USA.

From *Nature* magazine, October 25, 2001, p. 781. © 2001 by Nature. Reprinted by permission

Medical detection of false witness

High-tech lie detectors one day may be impossible to fool, but so far the only guarantee is that they will stir up as much controversy as the original polygraph.

By Brandon Spun

Try this scenario: Zacarias Moussaoui is led out of a dark cell into a silent room at an undisclosed location. An electrode headset is fitted to his skull while his lawyer watches disapprovingly. After nearly an hour of flicking switches and flashing lights, the procedure concludes. An investigator reviews the results and determines exactly what role Moussaoui played in the Sept. 11 terrorist attacks. You cannot hide your memories from the machine.

Some say this no longer is science fiction. In the months following Sept. 11, articles about techno-security have appeared in the popular press and in professional journals promising just such a result from high-tech lie detectors. One of these machines was featured in the *New York Times Magazine*'s "2001 Encyclopedia of Innovations, Conceptual Leaps and Harebrained Schemes." An INSIGHT review of new polygraph technologies suggests that most of them fit all three categories.

"When one uses any kind of lie detector, one is saying 'ask the body, not the person,'" says Mike Gazzaniga, director of the Center for Cognitive Neuroscience based at Dartmouth College. "One assumes with autonomic studies [polygraphs] that the body can't lie," Gazzaniga says. The assumption is that the body's autonomic reactions—such as blood pressure, breathing and heart rate—cannot be manipulated to support deception. "They assume that lies are mental constructs," Gazzaniga continues. "Among those things that separate man from animal is his capacity for deception. The question is how to make a science and not folk psychology out of this."

One investigative method established for autonomic research is the "guilty-knowledge test," which consists of confronting a suspect with a series of items, some relevant to a crime and others irrelevant. It is believed that a subject who has "guilty knowledge" will react most strongly to relevant or target items, while an innocent person will not.

Such tests have been disputed since the first polygraph was invented by William Marston in 1917. A polygraph can be an effective tool, but high-profile cases such as those of Aldrich Ames and Robert Hanssen, spies who beat the machine, frequently are cited to show its fallibility. Critics point out that data gathered from these tests are indicative of physiological response rather than veracity, with the latter being distinguished from the former. They say there is no necessary connection between a subject's verbal and physical report.

Polygraph expert Drew Richardson, a former FBI special agent at Quantico Laboratories, says "the test is generally not admissible in court because it is largely not accepted as a valid scientific technique."

But what if a better mousetrap were to become available? What if there were a machine that could not be fooled? What if an autonomic response to lying were to be identified that could not be suppressed? Recently, some have made such claims. Here is a look at those claims and what is being said about them.

Brain fingerprinting: According to Larry Farwell, an independent psychophysiologist at Human Brain Research Laboratory in Fairfield, Iowa, the fundamental difference between a guilty and innocent person is a record of the crime stored in the brain. "The difference between a terrorist who has been through a training camp and an Afghan student is the memory," Farwell says. Brain fingerprinting identifies memories, he claims.

This examination consists of a modified guilty-knowledge test that uses targets and irrelevants, but adds probes that are unique details of a crime that only the culprit could know. All subjects are familiarized with the targets in order actively to identify them during the test. A guilty subject is expected to have the same response to the probes as to the targets.

When one is exposed to something that already is stored in memory, the brain emits an electrical response called a p300 wave. This phenomenon occurs approximately 300 milliseconds after a meaningful stimulus. The "p" stands for positive electrical voltage (certain speech processes emit a negative 400). Electrodes on the parietal zero (the top of the back of the head) record this activity.

Brain fingerprinting has been tested on FBI agents and in field situations. Farwell reports a 99 percent success rate, though he estimates the process is applicable for only 70 percent of investigations. What has attracted attention is his claim that Sept. 11 may be a good fit. He proposes sorting suspects into three groups through his method for lie detecting: those involved in the planning of the attacks, terrorists from different cells and the innocent. "We were able to detect whether someone was an FBI agent by using information from their training manuals," Farwell says. "We could use the same method with al-Qaeda's manual for terrorists."

One of the first things other scientists familiar with Farwell's proposal for lie detection point out is that the last peer-reviewed paper he published on this was in 1991. Emanuel Donchin, a professor of psychology at the University of South Florida, contributed to the federal evaluation of Farwell's techniques. He also was Farwell's teacher and 1991 research partner. "Larry does a nice demonstration, but it needs much more research," Donchin says. "It is not ready as a practical tool." Donchin raises three major problems with the Farwell approach: stimuli, the oddball paradigm and interpretation.

The stimuli problem is that a probe is chosen by subjective analysis. "An investigator, not science, makes the decision," Donchin says.

The oddball paradigm involves the order of stimuli. Apparently probes change the environment of the brain. "A p300 is enormously sensitive to the order of events," Donchin says. It can occur because something is infrequent as well as meaningful. So detecting a p300 is equivalent to detecting that a memory has been distinguished by the brain. Thus, as Donchin succinctly puts it, "response to a probe ensures nothing."

Interpretation is a standard problem for lie detection. Donchin is not convinced that Farwell has overcome it. "Larry's interpretation of what must be remembered as significant is invalid and subjective," he says. "Larry is an entrepreneur, a businessman advertising a product. If you get people gullible enough to buy your product, that's all that is required."

A pre-eminent figure in psychophysiology had more to say on the subject. J.P. Rosenfeld, a professor at the University of Utah, says evaluators should look at the distribution of several p300s recorded from an individual subject while Farwell uses only one or two. "Farwell arbitrarily selected a wave," Rosenfeld says. "I am sure his data would be discounted by impartial psychophysiologists."

Rosenfeld also is concerned about Farwell's choice of subjects. "It turns out he has done extremely well using highly motivated, paid subjects from his labs," Rosenfeld says.

Conflict resolution: What first interested Daniel Langleben, assistant professor of psychiatry at the University of Pennsylvania, in lie detection was not terrorism but the behavior of drug addicts. "A substance abuser lies with no protective value," Langleben says. "For instance, you are practically suicidal if you don't tell an emergency doctor you take insulin," and yet they often don't.

Langleben, a psychiatrist as well as a self-taught anthropologist, says his mother, a linguistics professor, is an enthusiast for the works of St. Augustine and Immanuel Kant. He believes all this has been good preparation for studying the willful lie as opposed to philosophical truth. "That is, I am not interested in what philosophy would call objective truth," Langleben says. "My notion of a lie, what I explore, is remarkably similar to Augustine's."

Langleben has performed magnetic resonance imaging (MRI) on the brains of subjects as they underwent guilty-knowledge tests. While p300s provided information regarding quantity of activity, Langleben looked for blood flow and spatial resolution. He found what he says is the part of the brain active during a lie.

A normal or bold MRI is used to locate unusual activity, such as tumors, in the brain. It works by placing the body within a strong magnetic field while a weak, perpendicular magnetic field is turned on and off. This causes magnetic resonance, like flicking a car antenna. An fMRI, a bit less accurate, reads changes in blood flow up to 4 millimeters. However, by overlaying scans from fMRIs and bold MRIs, Langleben located blood flow at 6 to 8 millimeters even on the worst day.

When a person thinks, parts of the brain need more oxygen. Having performed fMRIs on people engaged in guilty-knowledge tests, Langleben claims to have isolated the location in the brain active during willful deception. He believes it is the anterior cingulate cortex, a part of the brain often associated with conflict. Though a subject might control supposed autonomic responses, this discovery is promising because we could pinpoint the very act of deception.

Langleben has not contacted the Department of Justice and was reluctant to comment on what should have been done to check the veracity of those arrested and interrogated for terrorism. However, he says, any tool to speed up the process of identifying lies in such circumstances is important. "Unlike most endless scientific questions, this one is solvable," he says.

But admittedly there are problems with this lie detector, says Langleben assistant Ruben Gur. "For one thing, you need a cooperative individual, as one must remain very still during these tests." Any movement invites error, and a subject also must remain relatively relaxed as emotional arousal can alter results.

Gur suggests the next step in research should be to perform fMRIs in conjunction with other bioindicators. And Langleben is aware of the need for more study. "If this is the Manhattan Project we are at 1941, not 1944," he says.

Other experts note problems. Rosenfeld suggests the theory may be flawed because it involves averaging multiple results, preventing case-by-case examination. He also points out that fMRIs are extremely expensive.

And, though the anterior cingulate cortex may be related to conflict and lying, not everyone is certain. This is a frontier subject. "Some say it is responsible for almost anything," says P.J. Casey, professor of psychology at Cornell University in New York. Others see it as a homunculus, or a little brain running the bigger show. "But most do say it has to do with conflict or conflict resolution," Casey says.

The foremost expert in this area, psychiatrist John Cohen of Princeton University, is of the opinion that activity in the anterior cingulate cortex is indicative of conflict but not resolution.

If so, Langleben's method may not always tell us what we want to know.

Casey explains this in a paper in which she says "paradigms of affective processing often require the subject to induce an affective state or think of emotional information that is contrary or in conflict with the subject's current state of affairs." This is crucial because, in other words, a person can consider an option without actually choosing that option, thereby inducing conflict but not producing it. This would leave investigators wondering whether a subject lied or merely considered lying.

The eye detector: Lying eyes are the latest addition to the list of science wizardry. Fox News and Science Daily are among those that have claimed that thermal-imaging lie detectors soon may be in place at airport-security checkpoints. They are referring to camera studies by James Levine, an endocrinologist at the Mayo Clinic's Honeywell Laboratories.

Levine and his collaborators theorized that subjects blush just before lying. They tested this theory using high-definition thermal-imaging cameras originally designed to see through heavy makeup and disguises.

Tests were conducted at Fort Jackson, S.C., as new recruits tried to fool the camera during an interrogation after some of them stole $20 from a mannequin they stabbed. Levine reported that in these tests the camera identified a lie with 80 percent accuracy. Advantages of the technology include quick investigations, real-time results, noninvasive screening and unskilled operation.

Levine says more testing is necessary and that the equipment must be refined for airport use, but he claims his lie detectors soon will be in commercial use. Other scientists tell INSIGHT that the "lying eye" needs more than refinement. In fact, some call the Levine system a mere blush detector. "Big Brother? More like special brother," commented one.

While Levine talks about his work as both "new" and "potentially accurate," critics say it is neither. Here are excerpts from a letter to the prestigious journal Nature that John Furedy, a professor of psychology at the University of Toronto, is preparing in response to Levine's lie-detector research:

"The procedure was only 'validated' against polygraph examination by experts (at the Department of Defense Polygraph Institute). There was no mention of a considerable body of scientific, psychophysiological literature that casts grave doubt on the scientific basis of this purported application of psychophysiology.

"The fundamental problem with the polygraph, even when administered by 'experts,' is that the measures it uses, such as electrodermal response, are virtually useless for differentiating the anxious but innocent person from the anxious and guilty one. Why should we think that thermal-imaging measures will be any more discriminating?

"It is disturbing not only for Americans, but also the world, that the national security of the world's only remaining superpower appears to depend on this modern flight of superstitious technological fancy, the only effect of which is to spread distrust within those organizations that employ it."

Or, as Rosenfeld says of the currently excited state of lie detection, "people were excited after 9/11, but that didn't advance knowledge at all, just funding."

BRANDON SPUN IS A REPORTER FOR Insight.

Reprinted with permission of Insight, February 4, 2002, pp. 24-25. © 2002 by News World Communications, Inc. All rights reserved.

What's your emotional IQ?

Emotional intelligence can affect your mental and physical health,
as well as those around you.

Melissa Abramovitz

On March 5, 2001, 15-year-old Andy Williams brought a 22-caliber pistol to school at Santana High School in Santee, California. With a smile on his face, he used the gun to kill two students and injure 13 other people. When later asked why he did it, Williams revealed that he'd had enough of his schoolmates' teasing, taunting, and ostracism because he was small and scrawny.

Some of Williams' friends reported that, prior to the shooting, the boy frequently drank alcohol and used illegal drugs. He also made repeated threats to shoot students at the school, but no one took these threats seriously. "I didn't think he was like that," said one boy who had laughed off Williams' promises to kill others.

Both Andy Williams' horrific act and his friends' lack of insight into his true intentions and feelings are frightening examples of how the lack of emotional intelligence can have disastrous consequences. Williams' inability to cope productively with his feelings of anger and rejection led him to endanger himself and others with drugs and violence. In a similar manner, his friends' unwillingness or inability to detect the desperation in his threats prevented them from stopping him from carrying out his deadly plans.

WHAT IS EI?

Emotional intelligence, or EI, is similar to cerebral intelligence, except that it involves awareness and insight into emotions rather than into other mental functions. Emotional IQ, also known as EQ (emotional quotient), refers to measurements of an individual's ability to understand and manage his or her emotions and interpersonal relationships.

Although many of the ideas related to EI and EQ were originally applied to business and leadership skills, these concepts are also relevant to everyday living and health. EI and EQ affect many aspects of an individual's mental and physical well-being, as well as the ability to get along with others, to make wise lifestyle choices, and to succeed in school, athletics, careers, and other areas.

Recent studies indicate that programs which seek to prevent violence, teen smoking, drug abuse, pregnancy, and dropping out of school are most effective when they address the elements of emotional intelligence. Indeed, according to the Center for the Advancement of Health in Washington, D.C., "Nearly half of the nation's premature deaths are attributable to controllable behavioral factors, such as using tobacco, alcohol, and illegal substances and engaging in risky sex." The center concludes that to be effective, a program must integrate behavioral and psychological perspectives with biomedical interventions.

Experts say that developing emotional intelligence can help you avoid both short-term injury risks and long-term illnesses such as heart disease, liver disease, and some cancers. These hazards are often a result of substance abuse and other dangerous lifestyle choices that go along with out-of-control emotional stress. Says Jan Wallender, Ph.D., "The way we feel and think and relate to others definitely has an impact on our biology, our health, and our disease experience."

THE ELEMENTS OF EI

Daniel Goleman, Ph.D., a well-known psychologist, has written extensively on the subject of EI and has identified five basic elements: self-awareness, managing emotions, motivating oneself, empathy, and social skills. Goleman and other EI experts point out that these elements are not automatically set in stone at birth, but instead can be learned and improved upon throughout a person's lifetime. Accordingly, many schools and businesses now offer EI training programs to help students and employees learn about and master these five aspects of dealing effectively with everyday challenges to emotional stability.

1. Self-awareness refers to the ability to recognize and identify your feelings. The EI experts emphasize that it's important to be able to recognize emotions such as anger or love in order to act appropriately. Bullies, for example, generally do not recognize their own feelings of insecurity or unhappiness and behave aggressively toward others as a result. One way that everyone can improve self-awareness is to verbalize emotions rather than ignore them. If you're angry, say "I'm angry" and explain why. If you're frightened, admit it, at least to yourself. Trying to appear tough and invincible at all times is OK only for legendary superheroes who don't have to live with their emotions the way real people do.

2. Managing your emotions involves using techniques for handling all sorts of feelings in a productive and appropriate manner. If your best friend suddenly informs you she has a new best friend, for example, most likely you will feel hurt, angry, and jealous. If you don't manage these emotions wisely, you might do something that you would probably regret. By effectively managing your emotions, though, hopefully you could take a deep breath, count to 10, control your desire to tell her off, and muster the strength to say something like, "I'm sorry you made that choice. I value our friendship and hope we can discuss this sometime."

3. Motivating oneself builds on managing your emotions to the extent that you can delay the immediate gratification of an impulse and can maintain a positive outlook. Studies show that individuals who are able to restrain themselves from immediately fulfilling a desire are more optimistic and successful in school, athletics, careers, and interpersonal relationships. This is due in part to using self-restraint, which is an important indicator of how someone responds to challenges. If you flunk a math test and say, "I'll never pass math, so I'm going to quit going to class," you will definitely not improve your math skills. If, however, you realize that going for tutoring can help you do better in the future, you have a good chance of passing the course and of applying these perseverance skills to other areas of your life.

4. Empathy is being sensitive to and understanding other people's feelings. Some individuals seem to have a natural ability to empathize, but this, like the other elements of EI, can be learned. To hone your empathy skills, try "putting yourself in someone else's shoes" and asking yourself how you would feel in his or her situation. Another useful technique is to focus on "reading" people's facial expressions and other body cues to gauge their true feelings. For example, observing the face and body language of a guy who says "I'm not scared"—yet exhibits wide-eyed terror and hunches his shoulders forward—will help you realize that this guy is definitely scared.

5. Social skills refers to an individuals's ability to interact with others in a positive and productive manner. Actually, if you do your homework on the other four elements of EI and master those concepts, you should be in pretty good shape in the social skills department. People who are self-aware, successfully manage their emotions, are motivated, and are able to empathize are generally quite adept in social situations.

TEST YOUR EMOTIONAL IQ

How would you deal with these emotional intelligence issues?

1. After a classmate dies in a car accident, you
   a. tell yourself it couldn't happen to you.
   b. realize you are feeling intense fear and sadness.
2. You've just been offered a beer at a party. Your friend Jamie says you're a wuss if you don't chug it. You don't want to be a wuss, so you
   a. drink the beer.
   b. politely refuse since you promised your parents there would be no alcohol at the party.
3. When you feel depressed, you
   a. cry and feel sorry for yourself.
   b. try to find a positive distraction like volunteering at a homeless shelter.
4. Your best friend just got dumped by his girlfriend. You
   a. tell him it doesn't matter.
   b. understand he's feeling depressed and encourage him to talk about it.
5. You hardly know anyone on your new hockey team. You
   a. request a transfer to a team where you know more people.
   b. look forward to getting to know the new people.

How did you do?
If you answered with a's, your emotional IQ needs some work. You are having trouble recognizing and managing your own emotions and recognizing other people's emotions. If you chose mostly b's, it means your emotional IQ is way up there! You are most likely successfully recognizing and managing your emotions and have good interpersonal relationships skills.

HOW EI AFFECTS THE WORLD

While emotional intelligence is certainly not a cure-all for the ills that exist in the world, it is an important factor in many global and personal issues. Road rage, child and spousal abuse, and school shootings are just a few of the serious problems in our society that raising people's EI can address. Experts point out that children and teens are especially vulnerable to the dangers of what psychologists call "emotional malaise." To combat this problem, many schools are including emotional-awareness training in their programs.

You alone have the power to improve your emotional intelligence with practice and effort. And becoming aware of your emotional intelligence can be beneficial not only to your own health and happiness, but it can also help make the world a more civilized and peaceful place.

FOR REVIEW

1. Define emotional intelligence. (It is similar to cerebral intelligence, except it involves awareness and insight into emotions rather than other mental functions. EQ is a measure of an individual's ability to understand and manage his or her emotions and interpersonal relationships.)

2. Summarize the five elements of emotional intelligence. (They include self-awareness—the ability to recognize and identify your feelings; managing emotions—using techniques for handling all sorts of feelings in a productive and appropriate manner; motivating oneself—ability to manage your emotions well enough to be able to delay immediate gratification of an impulse and to maintain a positive outlook; empathy—being sensitive to and understanding other people's feelings; and having social skills—the ability to interact with others in a positive, productive manner.)

ACTIVITY

Based on the five elements of emotional intelligence in the article, have students work in groups of three or four to write a skit in which a fellow student demonstrates a fairly low emotional intelligence. Have them act out the skits for the class and allow them to critique and make observations on the EI of the characters as they saw it. Then allow the authors of each skit to rewrite it to demonstrate improved EI skills.

From *Current Health 2,* December 2001, p. 1. © 2001 by Weekly Reader Corporation. Reprinted by permission.

How to Multitask

By Catherine Bush

Who can remember life before multitasking? These days we all do it: mothers, air-traffic controllers, ambidextrous athletes, high-flying executives who manage to eat, take conference calls, write e-mail and conduct board meetings all at the same time. We lionize those who appear to multitask effortlessly and despair at our own haphazard attempts to juggle even two tasks, secretly wondering if there exists a race of superior beings whose brains are hard-wired for multitasking feats. Only recently have neurologists begun to understand what our brains are up to when we do it. What they've learned offers hope to all multitasking delinquents out there.

1. Don't think you can actually do two things at once. Even when you think you're doing more than one thing simultaneously—say, driving and talking on a cell phone—you aren't. Unlike a computer, the brain isn't structured as a parallel processor. It performs actions, even very simple actions, in a strict linear sequence. You must complete the first task, or part of that task, before moving on to the next. What we call multitasking is actually task switching.

Hal Pashler, a professor of psychology at the University of California at San Diego, conducted an experiment in which he tested the brain's ability to respond to two different sounds in quick succession. What he found is that the brain stalls fractionally before responding to the second stimulus. The second sound is heard (the brain can take in information simultaneously), but it requires time, if only milliseconds, to organize a response. "When you really study precisely what people's brains are doing at any moment, there's less concurrent processing than you might think," Pashler explains. "The brain is more of a time-share operation." He adds, "When fractions of a second matter, we're better off not doing another task."

2. Prioritize. To know when to switch tasks, you must distinguish between the tasks you must perform and those you can afford to blow off.

Consider the experiment that Jordan Grafman developed at the National Institute of Neurological Disorders and Stroke (N.I.N.D.S.) in Bethesda, Md. It's a driving simulation in which you must avoid errant cars and jaywalkers, all while reciting sequences of numbers called out to you. Typically, your driving skills will grow more erratic as you pay attention to the numbers (although, frighteningly, you may not be aware of this). But when a virtual pedestrian dashes into the road, you'll most likely abandon the recitation. That's because in a driving simulation, avoiding killing people is the one challenge that outranks all others.

Before approaching multiple tasks, recommends Grafman, clearly establish which tasks are more important than others. "Mentally rehearsing," he says, "definitely improves performance."

3. Immerse yourself in your immediate task, but don't forget what remains to be done next. To switch tasks successfully, the brain must marshal the resources required to perform the new task while shutting off, or inhibiting, the demands of the previous one. At the same time, you must maintain the intention to break off at a certain point and switch to another activity. During such moments of mental juggling, a section of the brain called Brodmann's Area 10 comes alive. (Area 10 is located in the fronto-polar prefrontal cortex—at the very front of the brain.)

The crucial role played by Area 10 in multitasking was documented in a 1999 study that Grafman helped conduct; the results were published in the journal Nature. Functional magnetic resonance imaging scans (functional M.R.I.'s) were given to subjects at the Institute of Neurological Disorders while they performed simple multitasking experiments. Blood flow to Area 10 increased when people kept a principal goal in mind while temporarily engaged in secondary tasks. "This is presumably the last part of the brain to evolve, the most mysterious and exciting part," Grafman says. "It's what makes us most human."

Paul Burgess, who researches multitasking at University College, London, has also been focusing on the role of Area 10. "If you're missing it due to injury or a birth defect," he explains, "you keep forgetting to do things." He points out that successful multitasking requires that you not continuously think about switching tasks. That is, the activation of Area 10 does not require constant, conscious rehearsing of the need to switch tasks. For instance, if you have to make an important phone call at the end of the day, you don't tend to make an explicit mental note of this fact every five minutes. Rather, you engage in a less explicit act of remembrance—a kind of low-level arousal, Burgess speculates, in which blood flow increases to Area 10.

4. Depend on routines—and compare new tasks with old ones. Multitasking becomes easier, scientists believe, when you make parts of the process routine. For example, driving, a familiar activity for many of us, becomes largely automatic—the parts of the prefrontal cortex involved in cognition surrender to the regions deeper in the brain that govern visual and motor control. Once a task has been learned, the brain will try to shift the load for performance to its deeper structures, freeing up the cortex for other tasks requiring active cognition. That way, if something unexpected happens (like a pedestrian bolting into the road), you'll have the resources to deal with it.

When you are thrown into a new task, it's helpful to search for a comparison to something you've done before. The brain thrives on analogies. If you're suddenly forced to fly a crashing plane, you might want to draw on your PlayStation skills. "We solve task-switching dilemmas by trying to retrieve similar circum-

stances, similar situations being represented in similar regions of the prefrontal cortex," Grafman says. "If we don't, our experience will be totally chaotic, and we will clearly fail." He then laughs. "This cannot explain Art Tatum." The jazz pianist's wild two-handed improvising was pouring from his CD player when I entered his office. "With Tatum, nothing was routine. He must have had a great prefrontal cortex."

5. Make schedules, not to-do lists. And whatever you do, don't answer the phone. For those of us who find multitasking difficult, Burgess claims that the simplest aids—like timers and alarms—are the most effective. When the American astronaut Jerry Linenger was working aboard the space station Mir, he wore three or four watches with alarms set to notify him when to switch tasks.

"The alarm does not have to carry any information, just be a reminder that something has to be done," Burgess says. Studies have shown that neurologically impaired patients have been helped at multitasking by nothing more than someone clapping their hands at random intervals. An interruption breaks your train of thought and initiates a recall of what else needs to be done.

It's important, however, that the interruption itself not entail a task. For example, if the phone rings, don't answer it. Dealing with whatever the call is about will distract your brain from what you've already set out to do. Instead, use the in-

terruption to see if you're on track with other activities. "Make calling others one of the things that needs to be scheduled," Burgess advises. "And if you have to answer the call, don't go straight back to what you were doing before the call arrived. Very deliberately check the time, and ask yourself if there was something else you should have been doing."

By following such an approach, you can actually change your brain. Visualizing the circumstances in which you need to switch tasks will establish a mental pathway that will be available when you really need it. As functional brain scans suggest, just by thinking about what we need to do and when we need to do it, we can increase blood flow to Area 10, our multitasking hot spot.

Age also improves us. Children are easily distracted from tasks by competing signals, and younger adults, with their maturing prefrontal cortexes, are best at learning and combining new tasks. As we age (and our brains atrophy), learning new tasks becomes harder, but we get better at extracting themes and prioritizing tasks.

"For tasks performed in a short period of time, the younger tend to do better," Burgess says. "Older people learn from their mistakes and begin to compensate over time. This is very encouraging science for those of us not 20 years old."

Catherine Bush is the author of the novel "The Rules of Engagement."

From *The New York Times Magazine*, April 8, 2001. © 2001 by The New York Times Company. Reprinted by permission.

UNIT 7
Development

Unit Selections

Key Points to Consider

- What are the various milestones or developmental landmarks that signal stages in human development? What purpose do various developmental events serve? Can you give examples of some of these events?

- Why is embryonic and fetal life so important? How do the experiences of the fetus affect the child after it is born? What factors prevent the fetus from achieving its full potential?

- Do parents matter, or do you think that child development is mostly dictated by genes? Do you think that both nature and nurture affect development? Do you think one of these factors is more important than the other? Which one and why? Do you think it is important for both parents to be present during a child's formative years? Do you think fathers and mothers differ in their interactions with their children? How so? Why do some claim that parenting is a "lost art"? How and why are parents and schools at odds with each other?

- What is puberty? What is adolescence? How are today's teens different from teens in the past, for example, from their parents' generation? What societal factors influence teens today? If you had to rank these factors, which would be most influential, which would be least influential? Do you think teens actively search for identity? Is this the most important developmental task for adolescents? What can parents do to help guide their teens toward a healthy identity?

- Why do we age? Can we stay younger longer? What do you think Americans say is more important—a high-quality but shorter life or a poorer-quality and longer life? Why do you think they answer as they do? How would you answer and why? Would you want to live to 100? If so, what could you do to accomplish this?

- Why is death a stigmatized topic in America? Do you think people should discuss it more often and more openly? Do you think they ever will? How can we make dying easier for the dying person and for those close to the dying person? What can be done to help those with terminal illnesses?

 **Links: www.dushkin.com/online/**
These sites are annotated in the World Wide Web pages.

American Association for Child and Adolescent Psychiatry
http://www.aacap.org
Behavioral Genetics
http://www.ornl.gov/hgmis/elsi/behavior.html

The Garcias and the Szubas are parents of newborns. Both sets of parents wander down to the hospital's neonatal nursery where both babies, José Garcia and Kimberly Szuba, are cared for by pediatric nurses when the babies are not in their mothers' rooms. Kimberly is alert, active, and often crying and squirming when her parents watch her. On the other hand, José is quiet, often asleep, and less attentive to external stimuli when his parents monitor him in the nursery.

Why are these babies so different? Are the differences gender related? Will these differences disappear as the children develop or will the differences become exaggerated? What does the future hold for each child? Will Kimberly excel at sports and José excel at English? Can Kimberly overcome her parents' poverty and succeed in a professional career? Will José become a doctor like his mother or a pharmacist like his father? Will both of these children escape childhood disease, abuse, and the other misfortunes sometimes visited upon children?

Developmental psychologists are concerned with all of the Kimberlys and Josés of our world. Developmental psychologists study age-related changes in language, motoric and social skills, cognition, and physical health. They are interested in the common skills shared by all children as well as the differences between children and the events that create these differences.

In general, developmental psychologists are concerned with the forces that guide and direct development. Some developmental theorists argue that the forces that shape a child are found in the environment in such factors as social class, quality of available stimulation, parenting style, and so on. Other theorists insist that genetics and related physiological factors such as hormones underlie the development of humans. A third set of psychologists, in fact many psychologists, believe that some combination or interaction of all these factors, physiology and environment (or nature and nurture), are responsible for development.

In this unit, we are going to look at issues of development in a chronological fashion. In the first article, "The Biology of Aging," an overview of human development is given.

The very first stage is fetal development, which is crucial to the physical and psychological growth of the child after it is born. Various environmental factors can hinder development of or even damage the fetus. Janet Hopson reviews these in "Fetal Psychology."

In the next article, "Parenting: The Lost Art," Kay Hymowitz discusses children's misconduct and academic failure. She attempts to disentangle the blame that comes from schools and parents in order to discover the real cause. Part of the problem, she advises, is that today's parents want to be friends with rather than parents to their children.

The fourth article in this unit is about adulthood and aging. Some people want an extended adulthood or a long life. In fact, they hope they live to over 100 years of age. Such individuals are called centenarians; the secrets to making it that far are shared with the reader in "Living to 100: What's the Secret?"

The final article in this unit looks at the ultimate stage in development—death. Death is stigmatized in America; few people openly discuss it. The article claims that we ought to be more open, and is therefore designed to stimulate dialogue on this subject. There is much information contained in the article about issues surrounding death such as hospice care, how to be with a dying person, and so forth.

The Biology of Aging

Why, after being so exquisitely assembled, do we fall apart so predictably? Why do we outlive dogs, only to be outlived by turtles? Could we catch up with them? Living to 200 is not a realistic goal for this generation, but a clearer picture of how we grow old is already within our reach.

By Geoffrey Cowley

IF ONLY GOD HAD FOUND A more reliable messenger. Back around the beginning of time, according to east African legend, he dispatched a scavenging bird known as the halawaka to give us the instructions for endless self-renewal. The secret was simple. Whenever age or infirmity started creeping up on us, we were to shed our skins like tattered shirts. We would emerge with our youth and our health intact. Unfortunately, the halawaka got hungry during his journey, and happened upon a snake who was eating a freshly killed wildebeest. In the bartering that ensued, the bird got a satisfying meal, the snake learned to molt and humankind lost its shot at immortality. People have been growing old and dying ever since.

The mystery of aging runs almost as deep as the mystery of life. During the past century, life expectancy has nearly doubled in developed countries, thanks to improvements in nutrition, sanitation and medical science. Yet the potential life span of a human being has not changed significantly since the halawaka met the snake. By the age of 50 every one of us, no matter how fit, will begin a slow decline in organ function and sensory acuity. And though some will enjoy another half century of robust health, our odds of living past 120 are virtually zero. Why, after being so exquisitely assembled, do we fall apart so predictably? Why do we outlive dogs, only to be outlived by turtles? And what are our prospects for catching up with them?

Until recently, all we could do was guess. But as the developed world's population grows grayer, scientists are bearing down on the dynamics of aging, and they're amassing crucial insights. Much of the new understanding has come from the study of worms, flies, mice and monkeys—species whose life cycles can be manipulated and observed in a laboratory. How exactly the findings apply to people is still a matter of conjecture. Could calorie restriction extend our lives by half? It would take generations to find out for sure. But the big questions of why we age—and which parts of the experience we can change—are already coming into focus.

The starkest way to see how time changes us (aside from hauling out an old photo album) is to compare death rates for people of different ages. In Europe and North America the annual rate among 15-year-olds is roughly .05 percent, or one death for every 2,000 kids. Fifty-year-olds are far less likely to ride their skateboards down banisters, yet they die at 30 times that rate (1.5 percent annually). The yearly death rate among 105-year-olds is 50 percent, 1,000 times that of the adolescents. The rise in mortality is due mainly to heart disease, cancer and stroke—diseases that anyone over 50 is right to worry about. But here's the rub. Eradicating these scourges would add only 15 years to U.S. life expectancy (half the gain we achieved during the 20th century), for unlike children spared of smallpox, octogenarians without cancer soon die of something else. As the biologist Leonard Hayflick observes, what ultimately does us in is not disease per se, but our declining ability to resist it.

Biologists once regarded senescence as nature's way of pushing one generation aside to make way for the next. But under natural conditions, virtually no creature lives long enough to experience decrepitude. Our own ancestors typically starved, froze or got eaten long before they reached old age. As a result, the genes that leave us vulnerable to chronic illness in later life rarely had adverse consequences. As long as they didn't hinder reproduction, natural selection had no occasion to weed them out. Natural selection may even *favor* a gene that causes cancer late in life if it makes young adults more fertile.

But why should "later life" mean 50 instead of 150? Try thinking of the body as a vehicle, designed by a group of genes to transport them through time. You might expect durable bodies to have an inherent advantage. But if a mouse is sure to become a cat's dinner within five years, a body that could last twice that long is a waste of resources. A 5-year-old mouse that can produce eight litters annually will leave twice the legacy of a 10-year-old mouse that delivers only four each year. Under those conditions, mice will evolve to live roughly five years. A sudden disappearance of cats may improve their odds of completing that life cycle, but it won't change their basic genetic makeup.

That is the predicament we face. Our bodies are nicely adapted to the harsh conditions our Stone Age ancestors faced, but often poorly adapted to the cushy ones we've created. There is no question that we can age better by exercising, eating healthfully, avoiding cigarettes and staying socially and mentally active. But can we realistically expect to extend our maximum life spans?

The First Years of Growth

In childhood the body is wonderfully resilient, and **sound sleep** supports the growth of tissues and bones. During the teenage years, **hormonal changes** trigger the development of sexual organs. Boys add **muscle mass**. Even the muscles in their voice box lengthen, causing voices to deepen. In girls, fat is redistributed to hips and breasts.

Researchers have already accomplished that feat in lab experiments. In the species studied so far, the surest way to increase life span has been to cut back on calories—way back. In studies dating back to the 1930s, researchers have found that species as varied as rats, monkeys and baker's yeast age more slowly if they're given 30 to 60 percent fewer calories than they would normally consume. No one has attempted such a trial among humans, but some researchers have already embraced the regimen themselves. Dr. Roy Walford, a 77-year-old pathologist at the University of California, Los Angeles, has survived for years on 1,200 calories a day and expects to be doing the same when he's 120. That may be optimistic, but he looks as spry as any 60-year-old in the photo he posts on the Web, and the animal studies suggest at least a partial explanation. Besides delaying death, caloric restriction seems to preserve bone mass, skin thickness, brain function and immune function, while providing superior resistance to heat, toxic chemicals and traumatic injury.

How could something so perverse be so good for you? Scientists once theorized that caloric restriction extended life by delaying development, or by reducing body fat, or by slowing metabolic rate. None of these explanations survived scrutiny, but studies have identified several likely mechanisms. The first involves oxidation. As mitochondria (the power plants in our cells) release the energy in food, they generate corrosive, unpaired electrons known as free radicals. By reacting with nearby fats, proteins and nucleic acids, these tiny terrorists foster everything from cataracts to vascular disease. It appears that caloric restriction not only slows the production of free radicals but helps the body counter them more efficiently.

Food restriction may also shield tissues from the damaging effects of glucose, the sugar that enters our bloodstreams when we eat carbohydrates. Ideally, our bodies respond to any rise in blood glucose by releasing insulin, which shuttles the sugar into fat and muscle cells for storage. But age or obesity can make our

cells resistant to insulin. And when glucose molecules linger in the bloodstream, they link up with collagen and other proteins to wreak havoc on nerves, organs and blood vessels. When rats or monkeys are allowed to eat at will, their cells become less sensitive to insulin over time, just as ours do. But according to Dr. Mark Lane of the National Institute on Aging, older animals on calorie-restricted diets exhibit the high insulin sensitivity, low blood glucose and robust health of youngsters. No one knows whether people's bodies will respond the same way. But the finding suggests that life extension could prove as simple, or rather as complicated, as preserving the insulin response.

Another possible approach is to manipulate hormones. No one has shown conclusively that any of these substances can alter life span, but there are plenty of tantalizing hints. Consider human growth hormone, a pituitary protein that helps drive our physical development. Enthusiasts tout the prescription-only synthetic version as an antidote to all aspects of aging, but mounting evidence suggests that it could make the clock tick faster. The first indication came in the mid-1980s, when physiologist Andrzej Bartke outfitted lab mice with human or bovine genes for growth hormone. These mighty mice grew to twice the size of normal ones, but they aged early and died young. Bartke, now based at Southern Illinois University, witnessed something very different in 1996, when he began studying a strain of rodents called Ames dwarf mice. Due to a congenital lack of growth hormone, these creatures reach only a third the size of normal mice. But they live 50 to 60 percent longer.

As it happens, the mini-mice aren't the only ones carrying this auspicious gene. The island of Krk, a Croatian outpost in the eastern Adriatic, is home to a group of people who harbor essentially the same mutation. The "little people of Krk" reach an adult height of just 4 feet 5 inches. But like the mini-mice, they're exceptionally long-lived. Bartke's mouse studies suggest that besides stifling growth hormone, the gene that causes this stunting may also improve sensitivity to—you guessed it— insulin. If so, the mini-mice, the Croatian dwarfs and the half-starved rats and monkeys have more than their longevity in common. No one is suggesting that we stunt people's growth in the hope of extending their lives. But if you've been pestering your doctor for a vial of growth hormone, you may want to reconsider.

The Early Years of Adulthood

In many ways, the 20s are the prime of life. We're blessed with an efficient metabolism, **strong bones** and **good flexibility**. As early as the 30s, however, metabolism begins to slow and women's **hormone levels** start to dip. Bones may start to lose density in people who don't exercise or who don't get the vitamin D required for calcium absorption.

Growth hormone is just one of several that decline as we age. The sex hormones estrogen and testosterone follow the same pattern, and replacing them can rejuvenate skin, bone and muscle. But like growth hormone, these tonics can have costs as well as benefits. They evolved not to make us more durable but to make us more fertile. As the British biologist Roger Gosden observed in his 1996 book, "Cheating Time," "sex hormones are required for fertility and for making biological gender distinctions, but they do not prolong life. On the contrary, a price may have to be paid for living as a sexual being." Anyone suffering from breast or prostate cancer would surely agree.

The Joys of Middle Age

Around 40, people often start noticing gray hairs, mild **memory lapses** and difficulty focusing their eyes on small type. Around 51, most women will experience **menopause**. Estrogen levels plummet, making the skin thinner and bones less dense. Men suffer more **heart disease** than women at this age. Metabolism slows down in both sexes.

In most of the species biologists have studied, fertility and longevity have a seesaw relationship, each rising as the other declines. Bodies designed for maximum fertility have fewer resources for self-repair, some perishing as soon as they reproduce (think of spawning salmon). By contrast, those with extraordinary life spans are typically slow to bear offspring. Do these rules apply to people? The evidence is sketchy but provocative. In a 1998 study, researchers at the University of Manchester analyzed genealogical records of 32,000 British aristocrats born during the 1,135-year period between 740 and 1875 (long before modern contraceptives). Among men and women who made it to 60, the least fertile were the most likely to survive beyond that age. A whopping 50 percent of the women who reached 81 were childless.

Eunuchs seem to enjoy (if that's the word) a similar advantage in longevity. During the 1940s and '50s, anatomist James Hamilton studied a group of mentally handicapped men who had been castrated at a state institution in Kansas. Life expectancy was just 56 in this institution, but the neutered men lived to an average age of 69—a 23 percent advantage—and not one of them went bald. No one knows exactly how testosterone speeds aging, but athletes who abuse it are prone to ailments ranging from hypertension to kidney failure.

All of this research holds a fairly obvious lesson. Life itself is lethal, and the things that make it sweet make it *more* lethal. Chances are that by starving and castrating ourselves, we really could secure some extra years. But most of us would gladly trade a lonely decade of stubborn survival for a richer middle age. Our bodies are designed to last only so long. But with care and maintenance, they'll live out their warranties in style.

With RACHEL DAVIS

From *Newsweek*, Special Issue, Fall/Winter 2001, pp. 12-19. © 2001 by Newsweek, Inc. All rights reserved. Reprinted by permission.

FETAL PSYCHOLOGY

Behaviorally
speaking, there's little
difference between a newborn
baby and a 32-week-old fetus.
A new wave of research suggests
that the fetus can feel, dream, even
enjoy *The Cat in the Hat*. **The
abortion debate may never
be the same.**

By Janet L. Hopson

The scene never fails to give goose bumps: the baby, just seconds old and still dewy from the womb, is lifted into the arms of its exhausted but blissful parents. They gaze adoringly as their new child stretches and squirms, scrunches its mouth and opens its eyes. To anyone watching this tender vignette, the message is unmistakable. Birth is the beginning of it all, ground zero, the moment from which the clock starts ticking. Not so, declares Janet DiPietro. Birth may be a grand occasion, says the Johns Hopkins University psychologist, but "it is a trivial event in development. Nothing neurologically interesting happens."

Armed with highly sensitive and sophisticated monitoring gear, DiPietro and other researchers today are discovering that the real action starts weeks earlier. At 32 weeks of gestation—two months before a baby is considered fully prepared for the world, or "at term"—a fetus is behaving almost exactly as a newborn. And it continues to do so for the next 12 weeks.

A fetus spends hours in the rapid eye movement sleep of dreams.

As if overturning the common conception of infancy weren't enough, scientists are creating a startling new picture of intelligent life in the womb. Among the revelations:

- By nine weeks, a developing fetus can hiccup and react to loud noises. By the end of the second trimester it can hear.

- Just as adults do, the fetus experiences the rapid eye movement (REM) sleep of dreams.

- The fetus savors its mother's meals, first picking up the food tastes of a culture in the womb.

- Among other mental feats, the fetus can distinguish between the voice of Mom and that of a stranger, and respond to a familiar story read to it.

- Even a premature baby is aware, feels, responds, and adapts to its environment.

- Just because the fetus is responsive to certain stimuli doesn't mean that it should be the target of efforts to enhance development. Sensory stimulation of the fetus can in fact lead to bizarre patterns of adaptation later on.

The roots of human behavior, researchers now know, begin to develop early—just weeks after conception, in fact. Well before a woman typically knows she is pregnant, her embryo's brain has already begun to bulge. By five weeks, the organ that looks like a lumpy inchworm has already embarked on the most spectacular feat of human development: the creation of the deeply creased and convoluted cerebral cortex, the part of the brain that will eventually allow the growing person to move, think, speak, plan, and create in a human way.

At nine weeks, the embryo's ballooning brain allows it to bend its body, hiccup, and react to loud sounds. At week ten, it moves its arms, "breathes" amniotic fluid in and out, opens its jaw, and stretches. Before the first trimester is over, it yawns, sucks, and swallows as well as feels and smells. By the end of the second trimester, it can hear; toward the end of pregnancy, it can see.

117

FETAL ALERTNESS

Scientists who follow the fetus' daily life find that it spends most of its time not exercising these new abilities but sleeping. At 32 weeks, it drowses 90 to 95% of the day. Some of these hours are spent in deep sleep, some in REM sleep, and some in an indeterminate state, a product of the fetus' immature brain that is different from sleep in a baby, child, or adult. During REM sleep, the fetus' eyes move back and forth just as an adult's eyes do, and many researchers believe that it is dreaming. DiPietro speculates that fetuses dream about what they know—the sensations they feel in the womb.

Closer to birth, the fetus sleeps 85 to 90% of the time, the same as a newborn. Between its frequent naps, the fetus seems to have "something like an awake alert period," according to developmental psychologist William Fifer, Ph.D., who with his Columbia University colleagues is monitoring these sleep and wakefulness cycles in order to identify patterns of normal and abnormal brain development, including potential predictors of sudden infant death syndrome. Says Fifer, "We are, in effect, asking the fetus: 'Are you paying attention? Is your nervous system behaving in the appropriate way?' "

FETAL MOVEMENT

Awake or asleep, the human fetus moves 50 times or more each hour, flexing and extending its body, moving its head, face, and limbs and exploring its warm wet compartment by touch. Heidelise Als, Ph.D., a developmental psychologist at Harvard Medical School, is fascinated by the amount of tactile stimulation a fetus gives itself. "It touches a hand to the face, one hand to the other hand, clasps its feet, touches its foot to its leg, its hand to its umbilical cord," she reports.

Als believes there is a mismatch between the environment given to preemies in hospitals and the environment they would have had in the womb. She has been working for years to change the care given to preemies so that they can curl up, bring their knees together, and touch things with their hands as they would have for weeks in the womb.

By 15 weeks, a fetus has an adult's taste buds and may be able to savor its mother's meals.

Along with such common movements, DiPietro has also noted some odder fetal activities, including "licking the uterine wall and literally walking around the womb by pushing off with its feet." Laterborns may have more room in the womb for such maneuvers than first babies. After the initial pregnancy, a woman's uterus is bigger and the umbilical cord longer, allowing more freedom of movement. "Second and subsequent children may develop more motor experience in utero and so may become more active infants," DiPietro speculates.

Fetuses react sharply to their mother's actions. "When we're watching the fetus on ultrasound and the mother starts to laugh, we can see the fetus, floating upside down in the womb, bounce up and down on its head, bum-bum-bum, like it's bouncing on a trampoline," says DiPietro. "When mothers watch this on the screen, they laugh harder, and the fetus goes up and down even faster. We've wondered whether this is why people grow up liking roller coasters."

FETAL TASTE

Why people grow up liking hot chilies or spicy curries may also have something to do with the fetal environment. By 13 to 15 weeks a fetus' taste buds already look like a mature adult's, and doctors know that the amniotic fluid that surrounds it can smell strongly of curry, cumin, garlic, onion and other essences from a mother's diet. Whether fetuses can taste these flavors isn't yet known, but scientists have found that a 33-week-old preemie will suck harder on a sweetened nipple than on a plain rubber one.

"During the last trimester, the fetus is swallowing up to a liter a day" of amniotic fluid, notes Julie Mennella, Ph.D., a biopsychologist at the Monell Chemical Senses Center in Philadelphia. She thinks the fluid may act as a "flavor bridge" to breast milk, which also carries food flavors from the mother's diet.

FETAL HEARING

Whether or not a fetus can taste, there's little question that it can hear. A very premature baby entering the world at 24 to 25 weeks responds to the sounds around it, observes Als, so its auditory apparatus must already have been functioning in the womb. Many pregnant women report a fetal jerk or sudden kick just after a door slams or a car backfires.

Even without such intrusions, the womb is not a silent place. Researchers who have inserted a hydrophone into the uterus of a pregnant woman have picked up a noise level "akin to the background noise in an apartment," according to DiPietro. Sounds include the whooshing of blood in the mother's vessels, the gurgling and rumbling of her stomach and intestines, as well as the tones of her voice filtered through tissues, bones, and fluid, and the voices of other people coming through the amniotic wall. Fifer has found that fetal heart rate slows when the mother is speaking, suggesting that the fetus not only hears and recognizes the sound, but is calmed by it.

FETAL VISION

Vision is the last sense to develop. A very premature infant can see light and shape; researchers presume that a fetus has the same ability. Just as the womb isn't com-

What's the Impact on Abortion?

Though research in fetal psychology focuses on the last trimester, when most abortions are illegal, the thought of a fetus dreaming, listening and responding to its mother's voice is sure to add new complexity to the debate. The new findings undoubtedly will strengthen the convictions of right-to-lifers—and they may shake the certainty of pro-choice proponents who believe that mental life begins at birth.

Many of the scientists engaged in studying the fetus, however, remain detached from the abortion controversy, insisting that their work is completely irrelevant to the debate.

"I don't think that fetal research informs the issue at all," contends psychologist Janet DiPietro of Johns Hopkins University. "The essence of the abortion debate is: When does life begin? Some people believe it begins at conception, the other extreme believes that it begins after the baby is born, and there's a group in the middle that believes it begins at around 24 or 25 weeks, when a fetus can live outside of the womb, though it needs a lot of help to do so.

"Up to about 25 weeks, whether or not it's sucking its thumb or has personality or all that, the fetus cannot survive outside of its mother. So is that life, or not? That is a moral, ethical, and religious question, not one for science. Things can behave and not be alive. Right-to-lifers may say that this research proves that a fetus is alive, but it does not. It cannot."

"Fetal research only changes the abortion debate for people who think that life starts at some magical point," maintains Heidelise Als, a psychologist at Harvard University. "If you believe that life begins at conception, then you don't need the proof of fetal behavior." For others, however, abortion is a very complex issue and involves far more than whether research shows that a fetus hiccups. "Your circumstances and personal beliefs have much more impact on the decision," she observes.

Like DiPietro, Als realizes that "people may use this research as an emotional way to draw people to the pro-life side, but it should not be used by belligerent activists." Instead, she believes, it should be applied to helping mothers have the healthiest pregnancy possible and preparing them to best parent their child. Columbia University psychologist William Fifer, Ph.D., agrees. "The research is much more relevant for issues regarding viable fetuses—preemies."

Simply put, say the three, their work is intended to help the babies that live—not to decide whether fetuses should.—*Camille Chatterjee*

pletely quiet, it isn't utterly dark, either. Says Fifer: "There may be just enough visual stimulation filtered through the mother's tissues that a fetus can respond when the mother is in bright light," such as when she is sunbathing.

A fetus prefers hearing Mom's voice over a stranger's—speaking in her native, not a foreign tongue—and being read aloud familiar tales rather than new stories.

Japanese scientists have even reported a distinct fetal reaction to flashes of light shined on the mother's belly. However, other researchers warn that exposing fetuses (or premature infants) to bright light before they are ready can be dangerous. In fact, Harvard's Als believes that retinal damage in premature infants, which has long been ascribed to high concentrations of oxygen, may actually be due to overexposure to light at the wrong time in development.

A six-month fetus, born about 14 weeks too early, has a brain that is neither prepared for nor expecting signals from the eyes to be transmitted into the brain's visual cortex, and from there into the executive-branch frontal lobes, where information is integrated. When the fetus is forced to see too much too soon, says Als, the accelerated stimulation may lead to aberrations of brain development.

FETAL LEARNING

Along with the ability to feel, see, and hear comes the capacity to learn and remember. These activities can be rudimentary, automatic, even biochemical. For example, a fetus, after an initial reaction of alarm, eventually stops responding to a repeated loud noise. The fetus displays the same kind of primitive learning, known as habituation, in response to its mother's voice, Fifer has found.

But the fetus has shown itself capable of far more. In the 1980s, psychology professor Anthony James DeCasper, Ph.D., and colleagues at the University of North Carolina at Greensboro, devised a feeding contraption that allows a baby to suck faster to hear one set of sounds through headphones and to suck slower to hear a different set. With this technique, DeCasper discovered that within hours of birth, a baby already prefers its mother's voice to a stranger's, suggesting it must have learned and remembered the voice, albeit not necessarily consciously, from its last months in the womb. More recently, he's found that a newborn prefers a story read to it repeatedly in the womb—in this case, *The Cat in the Hat*—over a new story introduced soon after birth.

DeCasper and others have uncovered more mental feats. Newborns can not only distinguish their mother from a stranger speaking, but would rather hear Mom's voice, especially the way it sounds filtered through amniotic fluid rather than through air. They're xenophobes, too: they prefer to hear Mom speaking in her native language than to hear her or someone else speaking in a foreign tongue.

By monitoring changes in fetal heart rate, psychologist Jean-Pierre Lecanuet, Ph.D., and his colleagues in Paris have found that fetuses can even tell strangers' voices apart. They also seem to like certain stories more than others. The fetal heartbeat will slow down when a familiar French fairy tale such as *La Poulette* ("The Chick") or *Le Petit Crapaud* ("The Little Toad"), is read near the mother's belly. When the same reader delivers another unfamiliar story, the fetal heartbeat stays steady.

The fetus is likely responding to the cadence of voices and stories, not their actual words, observes Fifer, but the conclusion is the same: the fetus can listen, learn, and remember at some level, and, as with most babies and children, it likes the comfort and reassurance of the familiar.

FETAL PERSONALITY

It's no secret that babies are born with distinct differences and patterns of activity that suggest individual temperament. Just when and how the behavioral traits originate in the womb is now the subject of intense scrutiny.

In the first formal study of fetal temperament in 1996, DiPietro and her colleagues recorded the heart rate and movements of 31 fetuses six times before birth and compared them to readings taken twice after birth. (They've since extended their study to include 100 more fetuses.) Their findings: fetuses that are very active in the womb tend to be more irritable infants. Those with irregular sleep/wake patterns in the womb sleep more poorly as young infants. And fetuses with high heart rates become unpredictable, inactive babies.

"Behavior doesn't begin at birth," declares DiPietro. "It begins before and develops in predictable ways." One of the most important influences on development is the fetal environment. As Harvard's Als observes, "The fetus gets an enormous amount of 'hormonal bathing' through the mother, so its chronobiological rhythms are influenced by the mother's sleep/wake cycles, her eating patterns, her movements."

The hormones a mother puts out in response to stress also appear critical. DiPietro finds that highly pressured mothers-to-be tend to have more active fetuses—and more irritable infants. "The most stressed are working pregnant women," says DiPietro. "These days, women tend to work up to the day they deliver, even though the implications for pregnancy aren't entirely clear yet. That's our cultural norm, but I think it's insane."

Als agrees that working can be an enormous stress, but emphasizes that pregnancy hormones help to buffer both mother and fetus. Individual reactions to stress also mat-

ter. "The pregnant woman who chooses to work is a different woman already from the one who chooses not to work," she explains.

She's also different from the woman who has no choice but to work. DiPietro's studies show that the fetuses of poor women are distinct neurobehaviorally—less active, with a less variable heart rate—from the fetuses of middle-class women. Yet "poor women rate themselves as less stressed than do working middle-class women," she notes. DiPietro suspects that inadequate nutrition and exposure to pollutants may significantly affect the fetuses of poor women.

Stress, diet, and toxins may combine to have a harmful effect on intelligence. A recent study by biostatistician Bernie Devlin, Ph.D., of the University of Pittsburgh, suggests that genes may have less impact on IQ than previously thought and that the environment of the womb may account for much more. "Our old notion of nature influencing the fetus before birth and nurture after birth needs an update," DiPietro insists. "There is an antenatal environment, too, that is provided by the mother."

Parents-to-be who want to further their unborn child's mental development should start by assuring that the antenatal environment is well-nourished, low-stress, drug-free. Various authors and "experts" also have suggested poking the fetus at regular intervals, speaking to it through a paper tube or "pregaphone," piping in classical music, even flashing lights at the mother's abdomen.

Does such stimulation work? More importantly: Is it safe? Some who use these methods swear their children are smarter, more verbally and musically inclined, more physically coordinated and socially adept than average. Scientists, however, are skeptical.

"There has been no defended research anywhere that shows any enduring effect from these stimulations," asserts Fifer. "Since no one can even say for certain when a fetus is awake, poking them or sticking speakers on the mother's abdomen may be changing their natural sleep patterns. No one would consider poking or prodding a newborn baby in her bassinet or putting a speaker next to her ear, so why would you do such a thing with a fetus?"

Als is more emphatic: "My bet is that poking, shaking, or otherwise deliberately stimulating the fetus might alter its developmental sequence, and anything that affects the development of the brain comes at a cost."

Gently talking to the fetus, however, seems to pose little risk. Fifer suggests that this kind of activity may help parents as much as the fetus. "Thinking about your fetus, talking to it, having your spouse talk to it, will all help prepare you for this new creature that's going to jump into your life and turn it upside down," he says—once it finally makes its anti-climactic entrance.

Reprinted with permission from *Psychology Today*, September/October 1998, pp. 44-48, 76. © 1998 by Sussex Publishers, Inc.

PARENTING:
THE LOST ART

BY KAY S. HYMOWITZ

LAST FALL the Federal Trade Commission released a report showing what most parents already knew from every trip down the aisle of Toys R Us and every look at prime time television: Entertainment companies routinely market R-rated movies, computer games, and music to children. The highly publicized report detailed many of the abuses of these companies—one particularly egregious example was the use of focus groups of 9- and 10-year-olds to test market violent films—and it unleashed a frenzied week of headlines and political grandstanding, all of it speaking to Americans' alarm over their children's exposure to an increasingly foul-mouthed, vicious, and tawdry media.

But are parents really so alarmed? A more careful reading of the FTC report considerably complicates the fairy tale picture of big, bad wolves tempting unsuspecting, innocent children with ads for *Scream* and *Doom* and inevitably raises the question: "Where were the parents?" As it turns out, many youngsters saw the offending ads not when they were reading *Nickelodeon Magazine* or watching *Seventh Heaven* but when they were leafing through *Cosmo Girl*, a junior version of Helen Gurley Brown's sex manual *Cosmopolitan*, or lounging in front of *Smackdown!*—a production of the World Wrestling Federation where wrestlers saunter out, grab their crotches, and bellow "Suck It!" to their "ho's" standing by. Other kids came across the ads when they were watching the WB's infamous teen sex soap opera *Dawson's Creek* or MTV, whose most recent hit, "Undressed," includes plots involving whipped cream, silk teddies, and a tutor who agrees to strip every time her student gets an answer right. All of these venues, the report noted without irony, are "especially popular among 11- to 18-year-olds." Oh, and those focus groups of 9- and 10-year-olds? It turns out that all of the children who attended the meetings had permission from their parents. To muddy the picture even further, only a short time before the FTC report, the Kaiser Family Foundation released a study entitled *Kids and Media: The New Millennium*

showing that half of all parents have no rules about what their kids watch on television, a number that is probably low given that the survey also found that two-thirds of American children between the ages of eight and eighteen have televisions in their bedrooms; and even more shocking, one-third of all under the age of seven.

In other words, one conclusion you could draw from the FTC report is that entertainment companies are willing to tempt children with the raunchiest, bloodiest, crudest media imaginable if it means expanding their audience and their profits. An additional conclusion, especially when considered alongside *Kids and the Media*, would be that there are a lot of parents out there who don't mind enough to do much about it. After all, protesting that your 10-year-old son was subjected to a trailer for the R-rated *Scream* while watching *Smackdown!* is a little like complaining that he was bitten by a rat while scavenging at the local dump.

Neither the FTC report nor *Kids and the Media* makes a big point of it, but their findings do begin to bring into focus a troubling sense felt by many Americans—and no one more than teachers—that parenting is becoming a lost art. This is not to accuse adults of being neglectful or abusive in any conventional sense. Like always, today's boomer parents love their children; they know their responsibility to provide for them and in fact, as *Kids and the Media* suggests, they are doing so more lavishly than ever before in human history. But throughout that history adults have understood something that perplexes many of today's parents: That they are not only obliged to feed and shelter the young, but to teach them self-control, civility, and a meaningful way of understanding the world. Of course, most parents care a great deal about their children's social and moral development. Most are doing their best to hang on to their sense of what really matters while they attempt to steer their children through a dizzyingly stressful, temptation-filled, and in many ways unfamiliar world. Yet these parents know they often cannot count on the support of their peers. The parents of their 10-year-old's friend let the girls watch an R-rated movie until 2 a.m. during a sleepover; other parents are nowhere to be found when beer is passed around at a party attended by their 14-year-old. These AWOL parents have redefined the meaning of the term. As their children gobble down their own microwaved dinners, then go on to watch their own televisions or surf the Internet on their own computers in wired bedrooms where they set their own bedtimes, these parents and their children seem more like housemates and friends than experienced adults guiding and shaping the young. Such parent-peers may be warm companions and in the short run effective advocates for their children, but they remain deeply uncertain about how to teach them to lead meaningful lives.

If anyone is familiar with the fallout from the lost art of parenting, it is educators. About a year ago, while researching an article about school discipline, I spoke to teachers, administrators, and school lawyers around the country and asked what is making their job more difficult today. Their top answer was almost always the same: parents. Sometimes they describe overworked, overburdened parents who have simply checked out: "I work 10 hours a day, and I can't come home and deal with this stuff. He's *your* problem," they might say. But more often teachers find parents who rather than accepting their role as partners with educators in an effort to civilize the next generation come in with a "my-child-right-or-wrong" attitude. These are parent-advocates.

Everyone's heard about the growing number of suspensions in middle and high schools around the country. Now the state of Connecticut has released a report on an alarming increase in the number of young children—first-graders, kindergartners, and *preschoolers*—suspended for persistent biting, kicking, hitting, and cursing. Is it any wonder? Parent-advocates have little patience for the shared rules of behavior required to turn a school into a civil community, not to mention those who would teach their own children the necessary limits to self-expression. "'You and your stupid rules.' I've heard that a hundred times," sighs Cathy Collins, counsel to the School Administrators of Iowa, speaking not, as it might sound, of 16-year-olds, but of their parents. Even 10 years ago when a child got into trouble, parents assumed the teacher or principal was in the right. "Now we're always being second-guessed," says a 25-year veteran of suburban New Jersey elementary schools. "I know my child, and he wouldn't do this," or, proudly, "He has a mind of his own," are lines many educators repeat hearing.

In the most extreme cases, parent-advocates show (and teach their children) their contempt for school rules by going to court. Several years ago, a St. Charles, Mo., high schooler running for student council was suspended for distributing condoms on the day of the election as a way of soliciting votes. His family promptly turned around and sued on the grounds that the boy's free speech rights were being violated because other candidates had handed out candy during student council elections without any repercussions. Sometimes principals are surprised to see a lawyer trailing behind an angry parent arriving for a conference over a minor infraction. Parents threaten teachers with lawsuits, and kids repeat after them: "I'll sue you," or "My mother's

going to get a lawyer." Surveys may show a large number of parents in favor of school uniforms, but for parent-advocates, dress codes that limit their child's self-expression are a particular source of outrage. In Northumberland County, Pa., parents threatened to sue their children's *elementary* school over its new dress code. "I have a little girl who likes to express herself with how she dresses," one mother of a fourth-grader said. "They ruined my daughter's first day of school," another mother of a kindergartner whined.

Parent-advocates may make life difficult for teachers and soccer coaches. But the truth is things aren't so great at home either. Educators report parents of second- and third-graders saying things like: "I can't control what she wears to school," or "I can't make him read." It's not surprising. At home, parent-advocates aspire to be friends and equals, hoping to maintain the happy affection they think of as a "good relationship." It rarely seems to happen that way. Unable to balance warmth with discipline and affirmation with limit-setting, these parents are puzzled to find their 4-year-old ordering them around like he's Louis XIV or their 8-year-old screaming, "I hate you!" when they balk at letting her go to a sleepover party for the second night in a row. These buddy adults are not only incapable of helping their children resist the siren call of a sensational, glamorous media; in a desperate effort to confirm their "good relationship" with their kids, they actively reinforce it. They buy them their own televisions, they give them "guilt money," as market researchers call it, to go shopping, and they plan endless entertainments. A recent article in *Time* magazine on the Britney Spears fad began by describing a party that parents in Westchester, N.Y., gave their 9-year-old complete with a Britney impersonator boogying in silver hip-huggers and tube top. Doubtless such peer-parents tell themselves they are making their children happy and, anyway, what's the harm. They shouldn't count on it. "When one of our teenagers comes in looking like Britney Spears, they carry with them an attitude," one school principal was quoted as saying. There's a reason that some of the clothing lines that sell the Britney look adopt names such as "Brat" or "No Boundaries."

Of course, dressing like a Las Vegas chorus girl at 8 years old does not automatically mean a child is headed for juvenile hall when she turns 14. But it's reasonable to assume that parent-friends who don't know how to get their third-graders to stop calling them names, never mind covering their midriffs before going to school, are going to be pretty helpless when faced with the more serious challenges of adolescence. Some parents simply give up. They've done all they can, they say to themselves; the kids have to figure it out for themselves. "I feel if [my son] hasn't learned the proper values by 16, then we haven't done our job," announces the mother of a 16-year-old in a fascinating 1999 *Time* magazine series, "Diary of a High School." Others continue the charade of peer friendship by endorsing their adolescent's risk-taking as if they were one of the in-crowd. In a recent article in *Education Week*, Anne W. Weeks, the director of college guidance at a Maryland high school, tells how when police broke up a party on the field of a nearby college, they discovered that most of the kids were actually local high schoolers. High school officials called parents to express their concern, but they were having none of it; it seems parents were the ones providing the alcohol and dropping their kids off at what they knew to be a popular (and unchaperoned) party spot. So great is the need of some parents to keep up the pretense of their equality that they refuse to heed their own children's cry for adult help. A while back, the *New York Times* ran a story on Wesleyan University's "naked dorm" where, as one 19-year-old male student told the reporter: "If I feel the need to take my pants off, I take my pants off," something he evidently felt the need to do during the interview. More striking than the dorm itself—after all, when kids are in charge, as they are in many colleges, what would we expect?—was the phone call a worried female student made to her parents when she first realized she had been assigned to a "naked dorm." She may have been alarmed, but her father, she reports, simply "laughed."

Perhaps more common than parents who laugh at naked dorms or who supply booze for their kids' parties, are those who dimly realize the failure of their experiment in peer-parenting. These parents reduce their role to exercising damage control over kids they assume "are going to do it anyway." For them, there is only one value left they are comfortable fighting for: safety. One mother in *Time*'s "Diary of a High School" replenishes a pile of condoms for her own child and his friends once a month, doubtless congratulating herself that she is protecting the young. Safety also appears to be the logic behind the new fad of co-ed sleepover parties as it was described recently in the *Washington Post*. "I just feel it's definitely better than going to hotels, and this way you know all the kids who are coming over, you know who they are with," explains the mother of one high schooler. Kids know exactly how to reach a generation of parents who, though they waffled on whether their 8-year-old could call them "idiot," suddenly became tyrants when it came to seat belts and helmets. The article describes how one boy talked his parents into allowing him to give a co-ed sleepover party. "It's too dangerous for us to be out late at night with all the drunk drivers. Better that we are home. It's better than us lying about where we are and renting some sleazy motel room." The father found the "parental logic," as the reporter puts it, so irresistible that he allowed the boy to have not one, but two co-ed sleepover parties.

NOTHING GIVES a better picture of the anemic principles of peer-parenting—and their sorry impact on kids—than a 1999 PBS *Frontline* show entitled "The Lost Children of Rockdale County." The occasion for the show was an outbreak of syphilis in an affluent Atlanta suburb that ultimately led health officials to treat 200 teenagers. What was so remarkable was not that 200 teenagers in a large suburban area were having sex and that they have overlapping partners. It was the way they were having sex. This was teen sex as *Lord of the Flies* author William Golding might have imagined it—a heart of darkness tribal rite of such degradation that it makes a collegiate "hook up" look like splendor in the grass. Group sex was commonplace, as were 13-year-old participants. Kids would gather together after school and watch the Playboy cable TV channel, making a game of imitating everything they saw. They tried almost every permutation of

sexual activity imaginable—vaginal, oral, anal, girl-on-girl, several boys with a single girl, or several girls with a boy. During some drunken parties, one boy or girl might be "passed around" in a game. A number of the kids had upwards of 50 partners.

To be sure, the Rockdale teens are the extreme case. The same could not be said of their parents. As the *Frontline* producers show them, these are ordinary, suburban soccer moms and dads, more affluent than most, perhaps, and in some cases overly caught up in their work. But a good number were doing everything the books tell you to do: coaching their children's teams, cooking dinner with them, going on vacations together. It wasn't enough. Devoid of strong beliefs, seemingly bereft of meaningful experience to pass on to their young, these parents project a bland emptiness that seems the exact inverse of the meticulous opulence of their homes and that lets the kids know there are no values worth fighting for. "They have to make decisions, whether to take drugs, to have sex," the mother of one of the boys intones expressionlessly when asked for her view of her son's after-school activity. "I can give them my opinion, tell them how I feel. But they have to decide for themselves." These lost adults of Rockdale County have abdicated the age-old distinction between parents and children, and the kids know it. "We're pretty much like best friends or something," one girl said of her parents. "I mean I can pretty much tell 'em how I feel, what I wanna do and they'll let me do it." Another girl pretty well sums up the persona of many contemporary parents when she says of her own mother. "I don't really consider her a mom all that much. She takes care of me and such, but I consider her a friend more."

So what happened to the lost art of parenting? Why is it that so many adults have reinvented their traditional role and turned themselves into advocates, friends, and copious providers of entertainment?

For one thing, this generation of parents has grown up in a culture that devotedly worships youth. It's true that America, a nation of immigrants fleeing the old world, has always been a youthful country with its eye on the future. But for the "I-hope-I-die-before-I-get-old" generation, aging, with its threat of sexual irrelevance and being out of the loop, has been especially painful. Boomers are the eternal teenagers—hip, sexy, and aware—and when their children suggest otherwise, they're paralyzed with confusion. In an op-ed published in the *New York Times* entitled "Am I a Cool Mother?" Susan Borowitz, co-creator of *Fresh Prince of Bel-Air*, describes her struggle with her role as parent-adult that one suspects is all too common. On a shopping expedition, she is shocked when her 10-year-old daughter rolls her eyes at the outfits she has chosen for her. "There is nothing more withering and crushing," she writes. "I stood there stunned. 'This can't be happening to me. I'm a cool mom.'" Determined to hang on to her youthful identity, she buys a pair of bell-bottom pants to take her daughter to DJ Disco Night at her school where she spots other "cool moms… pumping their fist and doing the Arsenio woof." Finally Borowitz comes to her senses. "This was a party for the kids. I am not a kid. I am a mom." No one could quarrel with her there, but the telling point is that it took 10 years for her to notice.

The Parent as Career Coach

There is one exception to today's parents' overall vagueness about their job description: They *know* they want their children to develop impressive résumés. This is what William Doherty, professor of family science at the University of Minnesota, calls "parenting as product development."

As early as the preschool years, parent-product developers begin a demanding schedule of gymnastics, soccer, language, and music lessons. In New York City, parents take their children to "Language for Tots," beginning at six months—that is, before they can even speak. Doherty cites the example of one Minnesota town where, until some cooler—or more sleep-deprived—heads prevailed, a team of 4-year-olds was scheduled for hockey practice the only time the rink was available—at 5 A.M. By the time children are ready for Little League, some parents hire hitting and pitching coaches from companies like Grand Slam USA. So many kids are training like professionals in a single sport instead of the more casual three or four activities of childhood past that doctors report a high rate of debilitating and sometimes even permanent sports injuries.

Of course, there's nothing wrong with wanting to enrich your children's experience by introducing them to sports and the arts. But as children's list-worthy achievements take on disproportionate and even frenzied significance, parents often lose sight of some of the other things they want to pass down—such as kindness, moral clarity, and a family identity. One Manhattan nursery school director reports that if a child receives a high score on the ERB (the IQ test required to get into private kindergarten), parents often conclude that the child's brilliance excuses him or her from social niceties. "If he can't pass the juice or look you in the eye, it's 'Oh, he's bored.'" Douglas Goetsch, a teacher at Stuyvesant High School, the ultra-competitive school in New York City, recently wrote an article in the school newspaper about the prevalence of cheating; in every case, he says, cheating is related to an "excessively demanding parent." Other educators are seeing even young children complaining about stress-related headaches and stomachaches.

Katherine Tarbox, a Fairfield, Conn., teen, describes all this from the point of view of the child-product in her recently published memoir *Katie.com*. At 13, Katie was an "A" student, an accomplished pianist who also sang with the school choir, and a nationally ranked swimmer. Impressive as they were, Katie's achievements loomed too large. "I always felt like my self-worth was determined by how well I placed. And I think my parents felt the same way—their status among the team parents depended on how well their child placed." Like many middle-class children today, the combination of school, extracurricular activities, and her parents' work schedule reduced family time so much that, "Home was a place I always felt alone." Aching to be loved for herself rather than her swim times and grade point average, she develops an intense relationship with a man on the Internet who very nearly rapes her when they arrange to meet at an out-of-town swim meet.

Even after their daughter's isolation stands revealed, Katie's parents are so hooked on achievement they still don't really notice their daughter. Katie complains to her therapist that her mother is always either at the office or working on papers at home. The woman has a helpful suggestion that epitomizes the overly schematized, hyper-efficient lives that come with parenting as product development: She suggests that Katie schedule appointments with her mother.

Related to this youth worship is the boomer parents' intense ambivalence about authority. The current generation of parents came of age at a time when parents, teachers, the police, and the army represented an authority to be questioned and resisted. Authority was associated with *Father Knows Best*, the Vietnam War, Bull Connor, and their own distant fathers. These associations linger in boomer parents' subconscious minds and make them squirm uncomfortably when their own children beg for firm guidance. Evelyn Bassoff, a Colorado therapist, reports that when she asks the women in her mothers' groups what happens when they discipline their daughters, they give answers such as "I feel mean," "I feel guilty," and "I quake all over; it's almost like having dry heaves inside." A survey by Public Agenda confirms that parents feel "tentative and uncertain in matters of discipline and authority." And no wonder. Notice the way *Time* describes the dilemma faced by parents of Britney Spears wannabes; these parents, the writers explain, are "trying to walk the line between fashion and fascism." The message is clear; the opposite of letting your child do what she wants is, well, becoming Hitler.

It would be difficult to overstate how deep this queasiness over authority runs in the boomer mind. Running so hard from outmoded models of authority that stressed absolute obedience, today's parents have slipped past all recognition of the child's longing for a structure he can believe in. In some cases, their fear not only inhibits them from disciplining their children, it can actually make them view the rebellious child as a figure to be respected. (Oddly enough, this is true even when, as is almost always the case these days, that rebellion takes the form of piercings and heavy metal music vigorously marketed by entertainment companies.) It's as if parents believe children learn individuality and self-respect in the act of defiance, or at the very least through aggressive self-assertion. Some experts reinforce their thinking. Take Barbara Mackoff, author of *Growing a Girl* (with a chapter tellingly entitled "Make Her the Authority"). Mackoff approvingly cites a father who encourages a child "to be comfortable arguing or being mad at me. I figure if she has lots of practice getting mad at a six-foot-one male, she'll be able to say what she thinks to anyone." The author agrees; the parent who tells the angry child "calm down, we don't hit people," she writes, "is engaging in silencing." In other words, to engage in civilization's oldest parental task—teaching children self-control—is to risk turning your child into an automaton ripe for abuse.

But the biggest problem for boomer peer-parents is that many of them are not really sure whether there are values important enough to pursue with any real conviction. In his book *One Nation After All*, the sociologist Alan Wolfe argues that although Americans are concerned about moral decline, they are also opposed to people who get too excited about it. This inherent contradiction—people simultaneously judge and refuse to judge—explains how it is that parents can both dislike their children watching *Smackdown!* on TV, talking back to them, drinking, or for that matter, engaging in group sex, but also fail to protest very loudly. Having absorbed an ethos of nonjudgmentalism, the parents' beliefs on these matters have been drained of all feeling and force. The Rockdale mother who blandly repeats "her opinion" about drugs and sex to her son is a perfect example; perhaps she is concerned about moral decline, but because her concern lacks all gravity or passion, it can't possibly have much effect. All in all, Wolfe seems to find the combination of concern and nonjudgmentalism a fairly hopeful state of affairs—and surely he is right that tolerance is a key value in a pluralistic society—but refusing to judge is one thing when it comes to your neighbor's divorce and quite another when it comes to your 13-year-old child's attitudes toward, say, cheating on a test or cursing out his soccer coach.

WHEN PARENTS fail to firmly define a moral universe for their children, it leaves them vulnerable to the amoral world evoked by their peers and a sensational media. As the Rockdale story makes clear, the saddest consequences appear in the sex lives of today's teenagers. Recently in an iVillage chat room, a distraught mother wrote to ask for advice after she learned that her 15-year-old daughter had sex with a boy. The responses she got rehearsed many of the principles of peer-parenting. Several mothers stressed safety and told the woman to get her daughter on the pill. Others acted out the usual boomer uneasiness over the power they have with their children. "Let your daughter know you trust her to make the 'right' decision when the time comes," wrote one. "Tell her that you are not 'giving your permission,'" another suggested, "but that you are also very aware that she will not 'ask for permission' either when the time comes." But it was the one teenager who joined in that showed how little these apparently hip mothers understood about the pressures on kids today; when she lost her virginity at 14, the girl writes: "it was because of a yearning to be loved, to be accepted." Indeed, the same need for acceptance appears to be driving the trend among middle-schoolers as young as seventh grade engaging in oral sex. According to the December 2000 *Family Planning Perspectives*, some middle school girls view fellatio as the unpleasant price they have to pay to hang on to a boyfriend or to seem hip and sophisticated among their friends. The awful irony is that in their reluctance to evoke meaningful values, parent advocates and peers have produced not the free-thinking, self-expressive, confident children they had hoped, but kids so conforming and obedient they'll follow their friends almost anywhere.

And so in the end, it is children who pay the price of the refusal of parents to seriously engage their predicament in a media-saturated and shadowy adult world. And what a price it is. When parenting becomes a lost art, children are not only deprived of the clarity and sound judgment they crave. They are deprived of childhood.

Kay S. Hymowitz, a senior fellow at the Manhattan Institute and contributing editor at City Journal, *is the author of* Ready or Not: What Happens When We Treat Children as Small Adults *(Encounter Books, 2000).*

From *American Educator*, Spring 2001, pp. 4-9. © 2001 by American Educator, the quarterly journal of the American Federation of Teachers. Reprinted by permission.

Aging

Living to 100: What's the Secret?

Forget about Generation X and Generation Y. Today, the nation's most intriguing demographic is Generation Roman numeral C—folks age 100 and over. In the United States, the number of centenarians doubled in the 1980s and did so again in the 1990s. The total now exceeds 70,000. By 2050, according to midrange projections, there could be over 800,000 Americans who celebrate the century mark. Studies show the same trend in other industrialized countries and recently in China. Indeed, demographers are now counting the number of *supercentenarians,* people age 110 and over.

The swelling population of people age 100 and over has given researchers an opportunity to answer some of the most fundamental questions about human health and longevity: What does it take to live a long life? How much do diet, exercise, and other lifestyle factors matter compared with "good" genes? And, perhaps most importantly, what is the quality of life among the "old old"? Does getting older inevitably mean getting sicker, or can people remain productive, social, and independent on their 100th birthday and beyond?

Centenarian studies

There are a dozen or so centenarian studies. The Harvard-based New England Centenarian Study started with 46 people age 100 and over in the Boston area but is now recruiting people from throughout the United States. A health-advice book has been recently published based on findings from the centenarian study in Okinawa, where the average life expectancy, 81.2 years, is the highest in the world. There are active centenarian studies in Italy, Sweden, and Denmark. For the most part, results from these studies belie the myth that the oldest old are doddering and dependent. Some harsh demographic selection may come into play. Frail individuals die sooner, leaving only a relatively robust group still alive. In fact, one of the rewards of living a long life is that, for the most part, the "extra" years are healthy years.

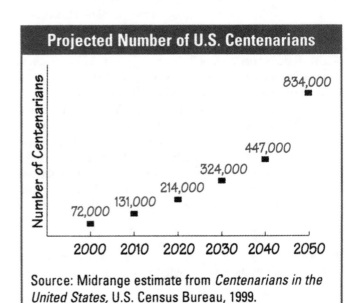

Projected Number of U.S. Centenarians

Number of Centenarians

72,000 (2000)
131,000 (2010)
214,000 (2020)
324,000 (2030)
447,000 (2040)
834,000 (2050)

Source: Midrange estimate from *Centenarians in the United States,* U.S. Census Bureau, 1999.

Physical activity is a recurring them: the people in these studies are walkers, bikers, and golfers. In Okinawa, centenarians do tai chi and karate. People who live to 100 and beyond exercise their brains, too, by reading, painting, and playing musical instruments. Some continue to work, an indication that our love affair with retirement may be a mixed blessing.

100 is still old

This isn't to say that centenarians escape unscathed. Although 75% of the people in the New England study were well enough to live at home and take care of themselves at age 95, this number dropped to 30% by age 102. About two-thirds of centenarians suffer from some form of dementia. Danish investigators, who have taken a decidedly less sunny view of extremely old age than their New England counterparts, published a study earlier this year reporting that many of the centenarians in their study had cardiovascular disease (72%), urinary incontinence (60%), osteoarthritis of a major joint (54%), and dementia (51%). And life expectancy is short at 100. On average, centenarians will only live another year or two, although that might change as the size of the age group increases.

It is notable, however, that the period of serious illness and disability for the exceptionally long-lived tends to be brief. Aging experts say that *compressing morbidity* in this way should be our goal. The Stanford researcher who coined the term, James F. Fries, has compared the ultimate in compressed morbidity to the "wonderful one-hoss shay" described in Oliver Wendell Holmes's poem "The Deacon's Masterpiece." The shay in the poem is a carriage built so carefully by the deacon that no single part breaks down for 100 years. Then it collapses "all at once, and nothing first/Just as bubbles do when they burst." Notwithstanding the Danish study, centenarians approach this ideal, as they tend to live well into their nineties free of serious diseases such as cancer and Alzheimer's.

Good genes

Traits that run in families are not necessarily genetic. After all, families often share the same eating habits, activity levels, and other so-called environmental factors that influence health. Still, similarities within families are often a good clue of a strong genetic influence, and longevity does seem to run in families. The New England Centenarian Study, for example, has found that its subjects were four times more likely to have a sibling who lived past age 90 than people with an average life span.

Now the search is on for genetic attributes. Researchers have previously identified some forms of a gene called apolipoprotein E that increase the risk for cardiovascular disease and Alzheimer's disease. Studies have shown that those dangerous variants are rare among centenarians. Scientists have had success building long life into some animals. They've genetically engineered a strain of fruit fly to live 35% longer than normal strains. Certain mice genes have been mutated so the animals live 30% longer than normal.

No one has found such a mutation in people. But last year, Thomas Perls, director of the New England study, and Louis Kunkel, a molecular geneticist at Children's Hospital in Boston, believe they got closer by identifying a section of chromosome 4 that may predispose people to long life. They made their discovery by scanning the genes of 137 sets of very old siblings—one person age 98 or older with a brother who was at least age 91 or a sister who was at least age 95. The siblings shared this distinctive section of chromosome 4.

Health conditions

But genes aren't the whole story. Public health advances like sanitation and routine vaccination have greatly improved the odds for long life. Indeed, it may be the intersection of genes with ever-changing health conditions that really determines how long we live. Today's centenarians may have survived so long partly because they had genes that protected them against infectious diseases prevalent in the early 20th century. Tomorrow's centenarians may need to have a different kind of genetic advantage attuned to 21st century circumstances.

The Gender Gap

Female centenarians outnumber males by a 9:1 ratio. The longest documented life was that of a French woman, Jeanne Calment, who died in 1997 at age 122. And throughout most of the world, women, on average, live longer than men. Some researchers say it is estrogen that gives women the longevity edge. Others theorize that menstruation and systems related to childbirth better equip women to rid their bodies of toxins. Women also tend to be more social than men, and social connections are believed to be critical to weathering old age.

Yet the men who reach their 100th birthday are, on the whole, healthier than the women. They are far less likely to have dementia or other serious medical problems. Thomas Perls, head of the New England Centenarian Study, calls these men "aging superstars."

Longevity statistics favoring women suggest that there may be some protective genes lurking on the X chromosome, the sex chromosome that women have two copies of and men only one. Another possibility: genetics are relatively neutral but social conditions favor long life for women. But healthy, odds-defying 100-year-old gentlemen hint of healthy aging genes somewhere else in the genome.

Medical interventions are starting to make a demographic difference, particularly with respect to mortality from cardiovascular disease. Most centenarians still die from heart disease, but they might have died much sooner without the medicines we now have to control cholesterol levels and hypertension.

Diet and other choices

Diet and other health habits play a role, too. Okinawans lose their actuarial edge when they move to Western countries and, presumably, adopt a more Western lifestyle. Italian researchers reported last year that healthy centenarians had exceptionally high blood levels of vitamins A and E compared with healthy younger adults. The study didn't address, however, what causes high levels. Still, the authors theorized that vitamin-rich blood may both strengthen the immune system of these centenarians and defend them against damage done by *oxygen free radicals,* the reactive molecules that some researchers believe is the principal cause of aging.

It's not a centenarian study, but a large, long-term study of Seventh-Day Adventists in California has produced some valuable information about longevity because the Adventists, on average, live several years longer than their fellow Californians. By some reckonings, they even outlive the Okinawans. There is no reason to believe the Adventists have any special genes, so other factors probably explain their longevity. Researchers broke down their health habits in a statistical analysis published in the July 9, 2001, *Archives of Internal Medicine.* A great deal of physical activity, frequent consumption of nuts, not eating meat, and medium body weight each was found to add about 1.5–2.5 years of life.

Centenarians may well have a genetic head start on most of us, but in his 1999 book *Living to 100,* Perls argues that we can make choices that may help us catch up. Of course, we don't have complete free will over these choices; behavior of almost all kinds has a genetic component. Still, there are some lessons to be learned from the do's and don'ts of centenarians:

- *They don't smoke or drink heavily.*
- *Those who had smoked didn't do so for long.*
- *They gained little or no weight during adulthood.* Being overweight makes people more vulnerable to many life-threatening illnesses, including heart disease, diabetes, cancer, and stroke.
- *They don't overeat.* Okinawan centenarians consume 10%–20% fewer calories per day than typical Americans. And in animal studies, calorie-restricted diets have consistently increased the life span. The old Okinawans consume less fat, too. About 26% of their energy intake comes from fat, compared with 30% or more for Americans. And more of that fat is beneficial—omega-3 fatty acids and the unsaturated fats found in vegetable oils.
- *They eat many fruits and vegetables.* The Okinawans have an average of seven servings a day.
- *They get regular physical activity for as long as they are able.* Strength-building activities, such as climbing stairs or lifting small weights, are especially beneficial because they help slow the age-related loss of muscle mass.
- *They challenge their minds.* Stimulating mental activity may help prevent age-related thinking and memory problems by stimulating communication between brain cells. Particularly among elderly men, decreased cognitive performance is strongly associated with mortality.
- *They have a positive outlook.* Perls says centenarians seem to have personalities that shed stress easily. An inability to control emotional stress has been linked to memory loss and heart disease.
- *They are friendly and maintain close ties with family and friends.* Not surprisingly, positive relationships are associated with lower rates of depression. And lower rates of depression may result in lower rates of heart disease.

Many researchers think that people could add up to a decade to their lives if they emulated the centenarians. And, from what we know so far, they aren't doing anything mysterious. They're simply following the standard health commandments: don't smoke, keep trim, get exercise, manage stress, and avoid social isolation.

All easier said than done, but after all, what are New Year's resolutions for?

From *Harvard Health Letter,* January 2002, pp. 1-3. © 2002 by President and Fellows of Harvard College. Reprinted by permission.

Start the Conversation

The MODERN MATURITY guide to end-of-life care

The Body Speaks

Physically, dying means that "the body's various physiological systems, such as the circulatory, respiratory, and digestive systems, are no longer able to support the demands required to stay alive," says Barney Spivack, M.D., director of Geriatric Medicine for the Stamford (Connecticut) Health System. "When there is no meaningful chance for recovery, the physician should discuss realistic goals of care with the patient and family, which may include letting nature take its course. Lacking that direction," he says, "physicians differ in their perception of when enough is enough. We use our best judgment, taking into account the situation, the information available at the time, consultation with another doctor, or guidance from an ethics committee."

Without instructions from the patient or family, a doctor's obligation to a terminally ill person is to provide life-sustaining treatment. When a decision to "let nature take its course" has been made, the doctor will remove the treatment, based on the patient's needs. Early on, the patient or surrogate may choose to stop interventions such as antibiotics, dialysis, resuscitation, and defibrillation. Caregivers may want to offer food and fluids, but those can cause choking and the pooling of dangerous fluids in the lungs. A dying patient does not desire or need nourishment; without it he or she goes into a deep sleep and dies in days to weeks. A breathing machine would be the last support: It is uncomfortable for the patient, and may be disconnected when the patient or family finds that it is merely prolonging the dying process.

The Best Defense Against Pain

Pain-management activists are fervently trying to reeducate physicians about the importance and safety of making patients comfortable. "In medical school 30 years ago, we worried a lot about creating addicts," says Philadelphia internist Nicholas Scharff. "Now we know that addiction is not a problem: People who are in pain take

pain medication as long as they need it, and then they stop." Spivack says, "We have new formulations and delivery systems, so a dying patient should never have unmet pain needs."

In Search of a Good Death

If we think about death at all, we say that we want to go quickly, in our sleep, or, perhaps, while fly-fishing. But in fact only 10 percent of us die suddenly. The more common process is a slow decline with episodes of organ or system failure. Most of us want to die at home; most of us won't. All of us hope to die without pain; many of us will be kept alive, in pain, beyond a time when we would choose to call a halt. Yet very few of us take steps ahead of time to spell out what kind of physical and emotional care we will want at the end.

The new movement to improve the end of life is pioneering ways to make available to each of us a good death—as we each define it. One goal of the movement is to bring death through the cultural process that childbirth has achieved; from an unconscious, solitary act in a cold hospital room to a situation in which one is buffered by pillows, pictures, music, loved ones, and the solaces of home. But as in the childbirth movement, the real goal is choice—here, to have the death you want. Much of death's sting can be averted by planning in advance, knowing the facts, and knowing what options we all have. Here, we have gathered new and relevant information to help us all make a difference for the people we are taking care of, and ultimately, for ourselves.

In 1999, the Joint Commission on Accreditation of Healthcare Organizations issued stern new guidelines about easing pain in both terminal and nonterminal patients. The movement intends to take pain seriously:

to measure and treat it as the fifth vital sign in hospitals, along with blood pressure, pulse, temperature, and respiration.

The best defense against pain, says Spivack, is a combination of education and assertiveness. "Don't be afraid to speak up," he says. "If your doctor isn't listening, talk to the nurses. They see more and usually have a good sense of what's happening." Hospice workers, too, are experts on physical comfort, and a good doctor will respond to a hospice worker's recommendations. "The best situation for pain management," says Scharff, "is at home with a family caregiver being guided by a hospice program."

The downsides to pain medication are, first, that narcotics given to a fragile body may have a double effect: The drug may ease the pain, but it may cause respiratory depression and possibly death. Second, pain medication may induce grogginess or unconsciousness when a patient wants to be alert. "Most people seem to be much more willing to tolerate pain than mental confusion," says senior research scientist M. Powell Lawton, Ph.D., of the Philadelphia Geriatric Center. Dying patients may choose to be alert one day for visitors, and asleep the next to cope with pain. Studies show that when patients control their own pain medication, they use less.

Final Symptoms

Depression This condition is not an inevitable part of dying but can and should be treated. In fact, untreated depression can prevent pain medications from working effectively, and antidepressant medication can help relieve pain. A dying patient should be kept in the best possible emotional state for the final stage of life. A combination of medications and psychotherapy works best to treat depression.

Anorexia In the last few days of life, anorexia—an unwillingness or inability to eat—often sets in. "It has a protective effect, releasing endorphins in the system and contributing to a greater feeling of well-being," says Spivack. "Force-feeding a dying patient could make him uncomfortable and cause choking."

Dehydration Most people want to drink little or nothing in their last days. Again, this is a protective mechanism, triggering a release of helpful endorphins.

Drowsiness and Unarousable Sleep In spite of a coma-like state, says Spivack, "presume that the patient hears everything that is being said in the room."

Agitation and Restlessness, Moaning and Groaning The features of "terminal delirium" occur when the patient's level of consciousness is markedly decreased; there is no significant likelihood that any pain sensation can reach consciousness. Family members and other caregivers may interpret what they see as "the patient is in pain" but as these signs arise at a point very close to death, terminal delirium should be suspected.

Hospice: The Comfort Team

Hospice is really a bundle of services. It organizes a team of people to help patients and their families, most often in the patient's home but also in hospice residences, nursing homes, and hospitals:

• Registered nurses who check medication and the patient's condition, communicate with the patient's doctor, and educate caregivers.
• Medical services by the patient's physician and a hospice's medical director, limited to pain medication and other comfort care.
• Medical supplies and equipment.
• Drugs for pain relief and symptom control.
• Home-care aides for personal care, homemakers for light housekeeping.
• Continuous care in the home as needed on a short-term basis.
• Trained volunteers for support services.
• Physical, occupational, and speech therapists to help patients adapt to new disabilities.
• Temporary hospitalization during a crisis.
• Counselors and social workers who provide emotional and spiritual support to the patient and family.
• Respite care—brief noncrisis hospitalization to provide relief for family caregivers for up to five days.
• Bereavement support for the family, including counseling, referral to support groups, and periodic check-ins during the first year after the death.

Hospice Residences Still rare, but a growing phenomenon. They provide all these services on-site. They're for patients without family caregivers; with frail, elderly spouses; and for families who cannot provide at-home care because of other commitments. At the moment, Medicare covers only hospice services; the patient must pay for room and board. In many states Medicaid also covers hospice services (see How Much Will It Cost?). Keep in mind that not all residences are certified, bonded, or licensed; and not all are covered by Medicare.

Getting In A physician can recommend hospice for a patient who is terminally ill and probably has less than six months to live. The aim of hospice is to help people cope with an illness, not to cure it. All patients entering hospice waive their rights to curative treatments, though only for conditions relating to their terminal illness. "If you break a leg, of course you'll be treated for that," says Karen Woods, executive director of the Hospice Association of America. No one is forced to accept a hospice referral, and patients may leave and opt for curative care at any time. Hospice programs are listed in the Yellow Pages. For more information, see Resources.

The Ultimate Emotional Challenge

A dying person is grieving the loss of control over life, of body image, of normal physical functions, mobility and strength, freedom and independence, security, and the illusion of immortality. He is also grieving the loss of an earthly future, and reorienting himself to an unknowable destiny.

At the same time, an emotionally healthy dying person will be trying to satisfy his survival drive by adapting to this new phase, making the most of life at the moment, calling in loved ones, examining and appreciating his own joys and accomplishments. Not all dying people are depressed; many embrace death easily.

Facing the Fact

Doctors are usually the ones to inform a patient that he or she is dying, and the end-of-life movement is training physicians to bring empathy to that conversation in place of medspeak and time estimates. The more sensitive doctor will first ask how the patient feels things are going. "The patient may say, 'Well, I don't think I'm getting better,' and I would say, 'I think you're right,' " says internist Nicholas Scharff.

At this point, a doctor might ask if the patient wants to hear more now or later, in broad strokes or in detail. Some people will need to first process the emotional blow with tears and anger before learning about the course of their disease in the future.

"Accept and understand whatever reaction the patient has," says Roni Lang, director of the Geriatric Assessment Program for the Stamford (Connecticut) Health System, and a social worker who is a longtime veteran of such conversations. "Don't be too quick with the tissue. That sends a message that it's not okay to be upset. It's okay for the patient to be however she is."

Getting to Acceptance

Some patients keep hoping that they will get better. Denial is one of the mind's miracles, a way to ward off painful realities until consciousness can deal with them. Denial may not be a problem for the dying person, but it can create difficulties for the family. The dying person could be leaving a lot of tough decisions, stress, and confusion behind. The classic stages of grief outlined by Elisabeth Kübler-Ross—denial, anger, bargaining, depression, and acceptance—are often used to describe post-death grieving, but were in fact delineated for the process of accepting impending loss. We now know that these states may not progress in order. "Most people oscillate between anger and sadness, embracing the prospect of death and unrealistic episodes of optimism," says Lang. Still, she says, "don't place demands on them

Survival Kit for Caregivers

A study published in the March 21, 2000, issue of **Annals of Internal Medicine** shows that caregivers of the dying are twice as likely to have depressive symptoms as the dying themselves.

No wonder. Caring for a dying parent, says social worker Roni Lang, "brings a fierce tangle of emotions. That part of us that is a child must grow up." Parallel struggles occur when caring for a spouse, a child, another relative, or a friend. Caregivers may also experience sibling rivalry, income loss, isolation, fatigue, burnout, and resentment.

To deal with these difficult stresses, Lang suggests that caregivers:

• Set limits in advance. How far am I willing to go? What level of care is needed? Who can I get to help? Resist the temptation to let the illness always take center stage, or to be drawn into guilt-inducing conversations with people who think you should be doing more.
• Join a caregiver support group, either disease-related like the Alzheimer's Association or Gilda's Club, or a more general support group like The Well Spouse Foundation. Ask the social services department at your hospital for advice. Telephone support and online chat rooms also exist (see Resources).
• Acknowledge anger and express it constructively by keeping a journal or talking to an understanding friend or family member. Anger is a normal reaction to powerlessness.
• When people offer to help, give them a specific assignment. And then, take time to do what energizes you and make a point of rewarding yourself.
• Remember that people who are critically ill are self-absorbed. If your empathy fails you and you lose patience, make amends and forgive yourself.

to accept their death. This is not a time to proselytize." It is enough for the family to accept the coming loss, and if necessary, introduce the idea of an advance directive and health-care proxy, approaching it as a "just in case" idea. When one member of the family cannot accept death, and insists that doctors do more, says Lang, "that's the worst nightmare. I would call a meeting, hear all views without interrupting, and get the conversation around to what the patient would want. You may need another person to come in, perhaps the doctor, to help 'hear' the voice of the patient."

What Are You Afraid Of?

The most important question for doctors and caregivers to ask a dying person is, What are you afraid of? "Fear aggravates pain," says Lang, "and pain aggravates fear." Fear of pain, says Spivack, is one of the most common problems, and can be dealt with rationally. Many people do not know, for example, that pain in dying is not inevitable. Other typical fears are of being separated from loved ones, from home, from work; fear of being a burden, losing control, being dependent, and leaving things undone. Voicing fear helps lessen it, and pinpointing fear helps a caregiver know how to respond.

How to Be With a Dying Person

Our usual instinct is to avoid everything about death, including the people moving most rapidly toward it. But, Spivack says, "In all my years of working with dying people, I've never heard one say 'I want to die alone.' " Dying people are greatly comforted by company; the benefit far outweighs the awkwardness of the visit. Lang offers these suggestions for visitors:

• Be close. Sit at eye level, and don't be afraid to touch. Let the dying person set the pace for the conversation. Allow for silence. Your presence alone is valuable.

• Don't contradict a patient who says he's going to die. Acceptance is okay. Allow for anger, guilt, and fear, without trying to "fix" it. Just listen and empathize.

• Give the patient as much decision-making power as possible, as long as possible. Allow for talk about unfinished business. Ask: "Who can I contact for you?"

• Encourage happy reminiscences. It's okay to laugh.

• Never pass up the chance to express love or say goodbye. But if you don't get the chance, remember that not everything is worked through. Do the best you can.

Taking Control Now

Sixty years ago, before the invention of dialysis, defibrillators, and ventilators, the failure of vital organs automatically meant death. There were few choices to be made to end suffering, and when there were—the fatal dose of morphine, for example—these decisions were made privately by family and doctors who knew each other well. Since the 1950s, medical technology has been capable of extending lives, but also of prolonging dying. In 1967, an organization called Choice in Dying (now the Partnership for Caring: America's Voices for the Dying; see Resources) designed the first advance directive—a document that allows you to designate under what conditions you would want life-sustaining treatment to be continued or terminated. But the idea did not gain popular understanding until 1976, when the parents of Karen Ann Quinlan won a long legal battle to disconnect her from respiratory support as she lay for months in a vegetative state. Some 75 percent of Americans are in favor of advance directives, although only 30–35 percent actually write them.

Designing the Care You Want

There are two kinds of advance directives, and you may use one or both. A Living Will details what kind of life-sustaining treatment you want or don't want, in the event of an illness when death is imminent. A durable power of attorney for health care appoints someone to be your decision-maker if you can't speak for yourself. This person is also called a surrogate, attorney-in-fact, or health-care proxy. An advance directive such as Five Wishes covers both.

Most experts agree that a Living Will alone is not sufficient. "You don't need to write specific instructions about different kinds of life support, as you don't yet know any of the facts of your situation, and they may change," says Charles Sabatino, assistant director of the American Bar Association's Commission on Legal Problems of the Elderly.

The proxy, Sabatino says, is far more important. "It means someone you trust will find out all the options and make a decision consistent with what you would want." In most states, you may write your own advance directive, though some states require a specific form, available at hospital admitting offices or at the state department of health.

When Should You Draw Up a Directive?

Without an advance directive, a hospital staff is legally bound to do everything to keep you alive as long as possible, until you or a family member decides otherwise. So advance directives are best written before emergency status or a terminal diagnosis. Some people write them at the same time they make a will. The process begins with discussions between you and your family and doctor. If anybody is reluctant to discuss the subject, Sabatino suggests starting the conversation with a story. "Remember what happened to Bob Jones and what his family went through? I want us to be different...." You can use existing tools—a booklet or questionnaire (see Resources)—to keep the conversation moving. Get your doctor's commitment to support your wishes. "If you're asking for something that is against your doctor's conscience" (such as prescribing a lethal dose of pain medication or removing life support at a time he considers premature), Sabatino says, "he may have an obligation to transfer you to another doctor." And make sure the person you name as surrogate agrees to act for you and understands your wishes.

Filing, Storing, Safekeeping...

An estimated 35 percent of advance directives cannot be found when needed.

• Give a copy to your surrogate, your doctor, your hospital, and other family members. Tell them where to find the original in the house—not in a safe deposit box where it might not be found until after death.

Five Wishes

Five Wishes is a questionnaire that guides people in making essential decisions about the care they want at the end of their life. About a million people have filled out the eight-page form in the past two years. This advance directive is legally valid in 34 states and the District of Columbia. (The other 16 require a specific state-mandated form.)

The document was designed by lawyer Jim Towey, founder of Aging With Dignity, a nonprofit organization that advocates for the needs of elders and their caregivers. Towey, who was legal counsel to Mother Teresa, visited her Home for the Dying in Calcutta in the 1980s. He was struck that in that haven in the Third World, "the dying people's hands were held, their pain was managed, and they weren't alone. In the First World, you see a lot of medical technology, but people die in pain, and alone." Towey talked to MODERN MATURITY about his directive and what it means.

What are the five wishes? Who do I want to make care decisions for me when I can't? What kind of medical treatment do I want toward the end? What would help me feel comfortable while I am dying? How do I want people to treat me? What do I want my loved ones to know about me and my feelings after I'm gone?

Why is it so vital to make advance decisions now? Medical technology has extended longevity, which is good, but it can prolong the dying process in ways that are almost cruel. Medical schools are still concentrating on curing, not caring for the dying. We can have a dignified season in our life, or die alone in pain with futile interventions. Most people only discover they have options when checking into the hospital, and often they no longer have the capacity to choose. This leaves the family members with a guessing game and, frequently, guilt.

What's the ideal way to use this document? First you do a little soul searching about what you want. Then discuss it with people you trust, in the livingroom instead of the waiting room—before a crisis. Just say, "I want a choice about how I spend my last days," talk about your choices, and pick someone to be your health-care surrogate.

What makes the Five Wishes directive unique? It's easy to use and understand, not written in the language of doctors or lawyers. It also allows people to discuss comfort dignity, and forgiveness, not just medical concerns. When my father filled it out, he said he wanted his favorite afghan blanket in his bed. It made a huge difference to me that, as he was dying, he had his wishes fulfilled.

For a copy of Five Wishes in English or Spanish, send a $5 check or money order to Aging With Dignity, PO Box 1661, Tallahassee, FL 32302. For more information, visit www.agingwithdignity.org.

• Some people carry a copy in their wallet or glove compartment of their car.

• Be aware that if you have more than one home and you split your time in several regions of the country, you should be registering your wishes with a hospital in each region, and consider naming more than one proxy.

• You may register your Living Will and health-care proxy online at uslivingwillregistry.com (or call 800-548-9455). The free, privately funded confidential service will instantly fax a copy to a hospital when the hospital requests one. It will also remind you to update it: You may want to choose a new surrogate, accommodate medical advances, or change your idea of when "enough is enough." M. Powell Lawton, who is doing a study on how people anticipate the terminal life stages, has discovered that "people adapt relatively well to states of poor health. The idea that life is still worth living continues to readjust itself."

Assisted Suicide: The Reality

While advance directives allow for the termination of life-sustaining treatment, assisted suicide means supplying the patient with a prescription for life-ending medication. A doctor writes the prescription for the medication; the patient takes the fatal dose him- or herself. Physician-assisted suicide is legal only in Oregon (and under consideration in Maine) but only with rigorous preconditions. Of the approximately 30,000 people who died in Oregon in 1999, only 33 received permission to have a lethal dose of medication and only 26 of those actually died of the medication. Surrogates may request an end to life support, but to assist in a suicide puts one at risk for charges of homicide.

Good Care: Can You Afford It?

T he ordinary person is only one serious illness away from poverty," says Joanne Lynn, M.D., director of the Arlington, Virginia, Center to Improve Care of the Dying. An ethicist, hospice physician, and health-services researcher, she is one of the founding members of the end-of-life-care movement. "On the whole, hospitalization and the cost of suppressing symptoms is very easy to afford," says Lynn. Medicare and Medicaid will help cover that kind of acute medical care. But what is harder to afford is at-home medication, monitoring, daily help with eating and walking, and all the care that will go on for the rest of the patient's life.

"When people are dying," Lynn says, "an increasing proportion of their overall care does not need to be done by doctors. But when policymakers say the care is nonmedical, then it's second class, it's not important, and nobody will pay for it."

Bottom line, Medicare pays for about 57 percent of the cost of medical care for Medicare beneficiaries.

Another 11 percent is paid by Medicaid, 20 percent by the patient, 10 percent from private insurance, and the rest from other sources, such as charitable organizations.

Medi-what?

This public-plus-private network of funding sources for end-of-life care is complex, and who pays for how much of what is determined by diagnosis, age, site of care, and income. Besides the private health insurance that many of us have from our employers, other sources of funding may enter the picture when patients are terminally ill.

•**Medicare** A federal insurance program that covers health-care services for people 65 and over, some disabled people, and those with end-stage kidney disease. Medicare Part A covers inpatient care in hospitals, nursing homes, hospice, and some home health care. For most people, the Part A premium is free. Part B covers doctor fees, tests, and other outpatient medical services. Although Part B is optional, most people choose to enroll through their local Social Security office and pay the monthly premium ($45.50). Medicare beneficiaries share in the cost of care through deductibles and co-insurance. What Medicare does not cover at all is outpatient medication, long-term nonacute care, and support services.

•**Medicaid** A state and federally funded program that covers health-care services for people with income or assets below certain levels, which vary from state to state.

•**Medigap** Private insurance policies covering the gaps in Medicare, such as deductibles and co-payments, and in some cases additional health-care services, medical supplies, and outpatient prescription drugs.

Many of the services not paid for by Medicare can be covered by private long-term-care insurance. About 50 percent of us over the age of 65 will need long-term care at home or in a nursing home, and this insurance is an extra bit of protection for people with major assets to protect. It pays for skilled nursing care as well as non-health services, such as help with dressing, eating, and bathing. You select a dollar amount of coverage per day (for example, $100 in a nursing home, or $50 for at-home care), and a coverage period (for example, three years—the average nursing-home stay is 2.7 years). Depending on your age and the benefits you choose, the insurance can cost anywhere from around $500 to more than $8,000 a year. People with pre-existing conditions such as Alzheimer's or MS are usually not eligible.

How Much Will It Cost?

Where you get end-of-life care will affect the cost and who pays for it.

•**Hospital** Dying in a hospital costs about $1,000 a day. After a $766 deductible (per benefit period), Medicare reimburses the hospital a fixed rate per day, which varies by region and diagnosis. After the first 60 days in a hospital, a patient will pay a daily deductible ($194) that goes up (to $388) after 90 days. The patient is responsible for all costs for each day beyond 150 days. Medicaid and some private insurance, either through an employer or a Medigap plan, often help cover these costs.

•**Nursing home** About $1,000 a week. Medicare covers up to 100 days of skilled nursing care after a three-day hospitalization, and most medication costs during that time. For days 21–100, your daily co-insurance of $97 is usually covered by private insurance—if you have it. For nursing-home care not covered by Medicare, you must use your private assets, or Medicaid if your assets run out, which happens to approximately one-third of nursing-home residents. Long-term-care insurance may also cover some of the costs.

•**Hospice care** About $100 a day for in-home care. Medicare covers hospice care to patients who have a life expectancy of less than six months. (See Hospice: The Comfort Team.) Such care may be provided at home, in a hospice facility, a hospital, or a nursing-home. Patients may be asked to pay up to $5 for each prescription and a 5 percent co-pay for in-patient respite care, which is a short hospital stay to relieve caregivers. Medicaid covers hospice care in all but six states, even for those without Medicare.

About 60 percent of full-time employees of medium and large firms also have coverage for hospice services, but the benefits vary widely.

•**Home care without hospice services** Medicare Part A pays the full cost of medical home health care for up to 100 visits following a hospital stay of at least three days. Medicare Part B covers home health-care visits beyond those 100 visits or without a hospital stay. To qualify, the patient must be homebound, require skilled nursing care or physical or speech therapy, be under a physician's care, and use services from a Medicare-participating home-health agency. Note that this coverage is for medical care only; hired help for personal nonmedical services, such as that often required by Alzheimer's patients, is not covered by Medicare. It is covered by Medicaid in some states.

A major financial disadvantage of dying at home without hospice is that Medicare does not cover out-patient prescription drugs, even those for pain. Medicaid does cover these drugs, but often with restrictions on their price and quantity. Private insurance can fill the gap to some extent. Long-term-care insurance may cover payments to family caregivers who have to stop work to care for a dying patient, but this type of coverage is very rare.

Resources

MEDICAL CARE

For information about pain relief and symptom management: **Supportive Care of the Dying** (503-215-5053; careofdying.org).

For a comprehensive guide to living with the medical, emotional, and spiritual aspects of dying:

Handbook for Mortals by Joanne Lynn and Joan Harrold, Oxford University Press.

For a 24-hour hotline offering counseling, pain management, downloadable advance directives, and more:

The Partnership for Caring (800-989-9455; www.partnershipforcaring.org).

EMOTIONAL CARE

To find mental-health counselors with an emphasis on lifespan human development and spiritual discussion:
American Counseling Association (800-347-6647; counseling.org).

For disease-related support groups and general resources for caregivers:
Caregiver Survival Resources (caregiver911.com).

For AARP's online caregiver support chatroom, access
America Online every Wednesday night, 8:30–9:30 EST (keyword: AARP).

Education and advocacy for family caregivers:
National Family Caregivers Association (800-896-3650; nfcacares.org).

For the booklet,
Understanding the Grief Process (D16832, EEO143C), e-mail order with title and numbers to member@aarp.org or send postcard to AARP Fulfillment, 601 E St NW, Washington DC 20049. Please allow two to four weeks for delivery.

To find a volunteer to help with supportive services to the frail and their caregivers:
National Federation of Interfaith Volunteer Caregivers (816-931-5442; nfivc.org).

For information on support to partners of the chronically ill and/or the disabled:
The Well Spouse Foundation (800-838-0879; www.wellspouse.org).

LEGAL HELP

AARP members are entitled to a free half-hour of legal advice with a lawyer from **AARP's Legal Services Network**. (800-424-3410; www.aarp.org/lsn).

For **Planning for Incapacity,** *a guide to advance directives in your state,* send $5 to Legal Counsel for the Elderly, Inc., PO Box 96474, Washington DC 20090-6474. Make out check to LCE Inc.

For a **Caring Conversations** *booklet on advance-directive discussion:*
Midwest Bioethics Center (816-221-1100; midbio.org).

For information on care at the end of life, online discussion groups, conferences:
Last Acts Campaign (800-844-7616; lastacts.org).

HOSPICE

To learn about end-of-life care options and grief issues through videotapes, books, newsletters, and brochures:
Hospice Foundation of America (800-854-3402; hospice-foundation.org).

For information on hospice programs, FAQs, and general facts about hospice:
National Hospice and Palliative Care Organization (800-658-8898; nhpco.org).

For **All About Hospice: A Consumer's Guide** (202-546-4759; www.hospice-america.org).

FINANCIAL HELP

For **Organizing Your Future,** *a simple guide to end-of-life financial decisions,* send $5 to Legal Counsel for the Elderly, Inc., PO Box 96474, Washington DC 20090-6474. Make out check to LCE Inc.

For **Medicare and You 2000** *and a* **2000 Guide to Health Insurance for People With Medicare** (800-MEDICARE [633-4227]; medicare.gov).

To find your State Agency on Aging: **Administration on Aging, U.S. Department of Health and Human Services** (800-677-1116; aoa.dhhs.gov).

GENERAL

For information on end-of-life planning and bereavement: (www.aarp.org/endoflife/).

For health professionals and others who want to start conversations on end-of-life issues in their community:
Discussion Guide: On Our Own Terms: Moyers on Dying, based on the PBS series, airing September 10–13. The guide provides essays, instructions, and contacts. From PBS, www.pbs.org/onourownterms Or send a postcard request to On Our Own Terms Discussion Guide, Thirteen/WNET New York, PO Box 245, Little Falls, NJ 07424-9766.

Funded with a grant from The Robert Wood Johnson Foundation, Princeton, N.J. *Editor* Amy Gross; *Writer* Louise Lague; *Designer* David Herbick

Reprinted from *AARP Modern Maturity,* September/October 2000. © 2000 by American Association for Retired Persons (AARP).

UNIT 8
Personality Processes

Unit Selections

Key Points to Consider

- What is the study of personality; what is the definition of personality? What are some of the major tenets of personality theories? Do you know any personality theories? Can you differentiate one theory from another?

- What do you think contributes most to our unique personalities, biology or environment? If you answered biology, what does this imply about the possibility of personality change? If you answered environment, do you think that biology plays any role in personality? Is personality stable or ever changing across a lifetime? What are the advantages of a stable personality? What would be the advantages of an ever-changing personality?

- In a nutshell, what is Freud's theory of personality? What are some of the criticisms of his theory? Do you think his theory is sound? based on logical thought? based on science? What contributions did Freud make to psychology? What did Freud contribute to the average person?

- What is positive psychology? What is optimism? Why is it important to the human condition? What other aspects of personality play a role in the theories and research endeavors of positive psychologists? How does the notion of positive psychology compare to psychoanalysis? Where should psychology head in the future according to positive psychologists?

- Do you believe that birth order influences personality traits? What birth position do you occupy? Do you have any of the traits consistent with that ordinal position? What else could explain birth order effects?

- Out of all the personality theories that you studied, which do you think is best and why? Was your answer based on science, anecdote, or some other factor?

 **Links: www.dushkin.com/online/**
These sites are annotated in the World Wide Web pages.

The Personality Project
http://personality-project.org/personality.html

Sabrina and Sadie are identical twins. When the girls were young children, their parents tried very hard to treat them equally. Whenever Sabrina received a present, Sadie received one. Both girls attended dance school and completed early classes in ballet and tap dance. In elementary school, the twins were both placed in the same class with the same teacher. The teacher also tried to treat them the same.

In junior high school, Sadie became a tomboy. She loved to play rough-and-tumble sports with the neighborhood boys. On the other hand, Sabrina remained indoors and practiced the piano. Sabrina was keenly interested in the domestic arts such as sewing, needlepoint, and crochet. Sadie was more

interested in reading novels, especially science fiction, and in watching adventure programs on television.

As the twins matured, they decided it would be best to attend different colleges. Sabrina went to a small, quiet college in a rural setting, and Sadie matriculated at a large public university. Sabrina majored in English, with a specialty in poetry; Sadie switched majors several times and finally decided on a communications major.

Why, when these twins were exposed to the same early childhood environment, did their interests and paths diverge later? What makes people, even identical twins, so unique, so different from one another?

The study of individual differences is the domain of personality. The psychological study of personality has included two major thrusts. The first has focused on the search for the commonalties of human life and development. Its major question is: How are humans, especially their personalities, affected by specific events or activities? Personality theories are based on the assumption that a given event, if it is important, will affect almost all people in a similar way, or that the processes by which events affect people are common across events and people. Most psychological research into personality variables has made this assumption. Failures to replicate a research project are often the first clues that differences in individual responses require further investigation.

While some psychologists have focused on personality-related effects that are presumed to be universal among humans, others have devoted their efforts to discovering the bases on which individuals differ in their responses to environmental events. In the beginning, this specialty was called genetic psychology, because most people assumed that individual differences resulted from differences in genetic inheritance. By the 1950s the term genetic psychology had given way to the more current term: the psychology of individual differences.

Does this mean that genetic variables are no longer the key to understanding individual differences? Not at all. For a time, psychologists took up the philosophical debate over whether

genetic or environmental factors were more important in determining behaviors. Even today, behavior geneticists compute the heritability coefficients for a number of personality and behavior traits, including intelligence. This is an expression of the degree to which differences in a given trait can be attributed to differences in inherited capacity or ability. Most psychologists, however, accept the principle that both genetic and environmental determinants are important in any area of behavior. These researchers devote more of their efforts to discovering how the two sources of influence interact to produce the unique individual. Given the above, the focus of this unit is on personality characteristics and the differences and similarities among individuals.

What is personality? Most researchers in the area define personality as patterns of thoughts, feelings, and behaviors that persist over time and over situations, are characteristic or typical of the individual, and usually distinguish one person from another.

We will examine several different theories of personality in this unit. Sigmund Freud developed one of the first personality theories—psychoanalysis. In "Psychoanalyst: Sigmund Freud," Peter Gay reviews Freud's theory and his contributions to psychology. Gay further reminds us of the way Freud contributed to our vocabularies and how he influenced other psychologists.

We next look at a second theory or strand of thought: positive psychology. While Freud often focused on the negative aspects of human nature, the humanists focus on humanity's positive aspects. Two prominent psychologists describe to us positive psychology that examines human contentment, optimism, and well-being.

In the last article, Margaret Renkl scrutinizes information on whether birth order affects our personalities. While much research suggests that the answer is "no," Renkl assumes that the answer is "yes." She covers differences in being the youngest, middle, or oldest child in a family and the consequent personality differences.

PSYCHOANALYST
SIGMUND FREUD

He opened a window on the unconscious—where, he said, lust, rage and repression battle for supremacy—and changed the way we view ourselves

By PETER GAY

There are no neutrals in the Freud wars. Admiration, even downright adulation, on one side; skepticism, even downright disdain, on the other. This is not hyperbole. A psychoanalyst who is currently trying to enshrine Freud in the pantheon of cultural heroes must contend with a relentless critic who devotes his days to exposing Freud as a charlatan. But on one thing the contending parties agree: for good or ill, Sigmund Freud, more than any other explorer of the psyche, has shaped the mind of the 20th century. The very fierceness and persistence of his detractors are a wry tribute to the staying power of Freud's ideas.

BORN May 6, 1856, Freiberg, Moravia

1881 Earns medical degree

1885 Receives appointment as lecturer in neuropathology, University of Vienna

1886 Begins private neurology practice in Vienna; marries Martha Bernays

1900 Publishes *The Interpretation of Dreams*

1910 Establishes International Psychoanalytic Association

1938 Emigrates from Vienna to London

1939 Dies Sept. 23 in London

There is nothing new about such embittered confrontations; they have dogged Freud's footsteps since he developed the cluster of theories he would give the name of psychoanalysis. His fundamental idea—that all humans are endowed with an unconscious in which potent sexual and aggressive drives, and defenses against them, struggle for supremacy, as it were, behind a person's back—has struck many as a romantic, scientifically unprovable notion. His contention that the catalog of neurotic ailments to which humans are susceptible is nearly always the work of sexual maladjustments, and that erotic desire starts not in puberty but in infancy, seemed to the respectable nothing less than obscene. His dramatic evocation of a universal Oedipus complex, in which (to put a complicated issue too simply) the little boy loves his mother and hates his father, seems more like a literary conceit than a thesis worthy of a scientifically minded psychologist.

Freud first used the term psychoanalysis in 1896, when he was already 40. He had been driven by ambition from his earliest days and encouraged by his doting parents to think highly of himself. Born in 1856 to an impecunious Jewish family in the Moravian hamlet of Freiberg (now Pribor in the Czech Republic), he moved with the rest of a rap-idly increasing brood to Vienna. He was his mother's firstborn, her "golden Siggie." In recognition of his brilliance, his parents privileged him over his siblings by giving him a room to himself, to study in peace. He did not disappoint them. After an impressive career in school, he matriculated in 1873 in the University of Vienna and drifted from one philosophical subject to another until he hit on medicine. His choice was less that of a dedicated healer than of an inquisitive explorer determined to solve some of nature's riddles.

As he pursued his medical researches, he came to the conclusion that the most intriguing mysteries lay concealed in the complex operations of the mind. By the early 1890s, he was specializing in "neur-asthenics" (mainly severe hysterics); they taught him much, including the art of patient listening. At the same time he was beginning to write down his dreams, increasingly convinced that they might offer clues to the workings of the unconscious, a notion he borrowed from the Romantics. He saw himself as a scientist taking material both from his patients and from himself, through introspection. By the mid-1890s, he was launched on a full-blown self-analysis, an enterprise for which he had no guidelines and no predecessors.

TODAY WE ALL SPEAK FREUD

*His ideas—or ideas that can be traced, sometimes circuitously,
back to him—have permeated the language*

PENIS ENVY Freud's famous theory—not favored by feminists—that women wish they had what men are born with

FREUDIAN SLIP A seemingly meaningless slip of the tongue that is really e-mail direct from the unconscious

UNCONSCIOUS Repressed feelings, desires, ideas and memories that are hidden from the conscious mind

REPRESSION Involuntary blocking of an unsettling feeling or memory from conscious thought

OEDIPUS COMPLEX In classic Freudian theory, children in their phallic phase (ages three to six) form an erotic attachment to the parent of the opposite sex, and a concomitant hatred (occasionally murderous) of the parent of the same sex

CASTRATION ANXIETY A boy's unconscious fear of losing his penis, and his fantasy that girls have already lost theirs

SUBLIMATION Unconscious shifting of an unacceptable drive (lust for your sister, say) into culturally acceptable behavior (lust for your friend's sister)

TRANSFERENCE Unconscious shifting of feelings about one person (e.g., a parent) to another (e.g., your analyst)

ID The part of the mind from which primal needs and drives (e.g., lust, rage) emerge

SUPEREGO The part of the mind where your parents' and society's rules reside; the original guilt trip

EGO The mind's mechanism for keeping in touch with reality, it referees the wrestling match between id and superego

PHALLIC SYMBOLS Almost anything can look like a penis, but sometimes, as Freud is supposed to have remarked, "a cigar is just a cigar"

The book that made his reputation in the profession—although it sold poorly—was *The Interpretation of Dreams* (1900), an indefinable masterpiece—part dream analysis, part autobiography, part theory of the mind, part history of contemporary Vienna. The principle that underlay this work was that mental experiences and entities, like physical ones, are part of nature. This meant that Freud could admit no mere accidents in mental procedures. The most nonsensical notion, the most casual slip of the tongue, the most fantastic dream, must have a meaning and can be used to unriddle the often incomprehensible maneuvers we call thinking.

Although the second pillar of Freud's psychoanalytic structure, *Three Essays on the Theory of Sexuality* (1905), further alienated him from the mainstream of contemporary psychiatry, he soon found loyal recruits. They met weekly to hash out interesting case histories, converting themselves into the Vienna Psychoanalytic Society in 1908. Working on the frontiers of mental science, these often eccentric pioneers had their quarrels. The two best known "defectors" were Alfred Adler and Carl Jung. Adler, a Viennese physician and socialist, developed his own psychology, which stressed the aggression with which those people lacking in some quality they desire—say manliness—express their discontent by acting out. "Inferiority com-

plex," a much abused term, is Adlerian. Freud did not regret losing Adler, but Jung was something else. Freud was aware that most of his acolytes were Jews, and he did not want to turn psycho-analysis into a "Jewish science." Jung, a Swiss from a pious Protestant background, struck Freud as his logical successor, his "crown prince." The two men were close for several years, but Jung's ambition, and his growing commitment to religion and mysticism—most unwelcome to Freud, an aggressive atheist—finally drove them apart.

Freud was intent not merely on originating a sweeping theory of mental functioning and malfunctioning. He also wanted to develop the rules of psychoanalytic therapy and expand his picture of human nature to encompass not just the couch but the whole culture. As to the first, he created the largely silent listener who encourages the analysand to say whatever comes to mind, no matter how foolish, repetitive or outrageous, and who intervenes occasionally to interpret what the patient on the couch is struggling to say. While some adventurous early psychoanalysts thought they could quantify just what proportion of their analysands went away cured, improved or untouched by analytic therapy, such confident enumerations have more recently shown themselves untenable. The efficacy of analysis remains a matter of controversy, though the possibil-

ity of mixing psychoanalysis and drug therapy is gaining support.

"If often he was wrong and, at times, absurd, to us he is no more a person now but a whole climate of opinion."

W. H. AUDEN,
after Freud's death
in 1939

Freud's ventures into culture—history, anthropology, literature, art, sociology, the study of religion—have proved little less controversial, though they retain their fascination and plausibility and continue to enjoy a widespread reputation. As a loyal follower of 19th century positivists, Freud drew a sharp distinction between religious

POST-FREUDIAN ANALYSIS

Other psychologists continued the work that Freud began, though not always in ways that he would have approved

CARL JUNG A former disciple of Freud's, Jung shared his mentor's enthusiasm for dreams but not his obsession with the sex drive. Jung said humans are endowed with a "collective unconscious" from which myths, fairy tales and other archetypes spring.

ALFRED KINSEY A biologist who knew little about sex and less about statistics, Kinsey nonetheless led the first large-scale empirical study of sexual behavior. The Kinsey reports shocked readers by documenting high rates of masturbation and extramarital and homosexual sex.

BENJAMIN SPOCK One of the first pediatricians to get psychoanalytic training, Dr. Spock formed commonsense principles of child rearing that helped shape the baby-boom generation. Since 1946 his book on baby care has sold 50 million copies.

B. F. SKINNER A strict behaviorist who avoided all reference to internal mental states, Skinner believed that behavior can best be shaped through positive reinforcement. Contrary to popular misconception, he did not raise his daughter in the "Skinner box" used to train pigeons.

faith (which is not checkable or correctable) and scientific inquiry (which is both). For himself, this meant the denial of truth-value to any religion whatever, including Judaism. As for politics, he left little doubt and said so plainly in his late—and still best known—essay, *Civilization and Its Discontents* (1930), noting that the human animal, with its insatiable needs, must always remain an enemy to organized society, which exists largely to tamp down sexual and aggressive desires. At best, civilized living is a compromise between wishes and repression—not a comfortable doctrine. It ensures that Freud, taken straight, will never become truly popular, even if today we all speak Freud.

In mid-March 1938, when Freud was 81, the Nazis took over Austria, and after some reluctance, he immigrated to England with his wife and his favorite daughter and colleague Anna "to die in freedom." He got his wish, dying not long after the Nazis unleashed World War II by invading Poland. Listening to an idealistic broadcaster proclaiming this to be the last war, Freud, his stoical humor intact, commented wryly, "*My* last war."

Yale historian Peter Gay's 22 books include Freud: A Life for Our Times

From *Time*, March 29, 1999, pp. 66-69. © 1999 by Time, Inc. Magazine Company. Reprinted by permission.

Positive Psychology

An Introduction

A science of positive subjective experience, positive individual traits, and positive institutions promises to improve quality of life and prevent the pathologies that arise when life is barren and meaningless. The exclusive focus on pathology that has dominated so much of our discipline results in a model of the human being lacking the positive features that make life worth living. Hope, wisdom, creativity, future mindedness, courage, spirituality, responsibility, and perseverance are ignored or explained as transformations of more authentic negative impulses....

Martin E.P. Seligman
University of Pensylvania

Mihaly Csikszentmihalyi
Claremont Graduate University

Entering a new millennium, we face an historical choice. Left alone on the pinnacle of economic and political leadership, the United States can continue to increase its material wealth while ignoring the human needs of its people and that of the rest of the planet. Such a course is likely to lead to increasing selfishness, alienation between the more and the less fortunate, and eventually to chaos and despair.

At this juncture the social and behavioral sciences can play an enormously important role. They can articulate a vision of the good life that is empirically sound while being understandable and attractive. They can show what actions lead to well being, to positive individuals, and to thriving communities. Psychology should be able to help document what kind of families result in children who flourish, what work settings support the greatest satisfaction among workers, what policies result in the strongest civic engagement, and how our lives can be most worth living.

Yet psychologists have scant knowledge of what makes life worth living. They have come to understand quite a bit about how people survive and endure under conditions of adversity. (For recent surveys of the history of psychology see, e.g. Koch & Leary, 1985; Benjamin, 1985; and Smith, 1997). But we know very little about how normal people flourish under more benign conditions. Psychology has, since World War II, become a science largely about healing. It concentrates on repairing damage within a disease model of human functioning. This almost exclusive attention to pathology neglects the fulfilled individual and the thriving community. The aim of Positive psychology is to begin to catalyze a change in the focus of psychology from preoccupation only with repairing the worst things in life to also building positive qualities.

The field of positive psychology at the subjective level is about valued subjective experience: well-being, contentment, and satisfaction (in the past), hope and optimism (for the future), and flow and happiness (in the present). At the individual level it is about positive individual traits—the capacity for love and vocation, courage, interpersonal skill, aesthetic sensibility, perseverance, forgiveness, originality, future-mindedness, spirituality, high talent, and wisdom. At the group level it is about the civic virtues and the institutions that move individuals toward better citizenship: responsibility, nurturance, altruism, civility, moderation, tolerance, and work ethic.

Two personal stories, one told by each author, explain how we arrived at the conviction that a movement toward positive psychology was needed and how [a] special issue* of the *American Psychologist* came about. For Martin E.P. Seligman, it began at a moment in time a few months after he had been elected president of the American Psychological Association:

The moment took place in my garden while I was weeding with my five-year old daughter, Nikki. I have to confess that even though I write books about children, I'm really not all that good with children. I am goal-oriented and time-urgent and when I'm weeding in the garden, I'm actually trying to get the weeding done. Nikki, however, was throwing weeds into the air, singing, and dancing around. I yelled at her. She walked away came back and said,

"Daddy, I want to talk to you."

"Yes, Nikki?"

"Daddy, do you remember before my fifth birthday? From the time I was three to the time I was five, I was a whiner. I whined every day. When I turned five, I decided not to whine anymore. That was the hardest thing I've ever done. And if I can stop whining, you can stop being such a grouch."

This was for me an epiphany, nothing less. I learned something about Nikki, about raising kids, about myself, and a great deal about my profession. First, I realized that raising Nikki was not about correcting whining. Nikki did that herself. Rather, I realized that raising Nikki is about taking this marvelous strength she has—I call it "seeing into the soul,"—amplifying it, nurturing it, helping her to lead her life around it to buffer against her weaknesses and the storms of life. Raising children, I realized, is vastly more than fixing what is wrong with them. It is about identifying and nurturing their strongest qualities, what they own and are best at, and helping them find niches in which they can best live out these strengths.

As for my own life, Nikki hit the nail right on the head. I was a grouch. I had spent 50 years mostly enduring wet weather in my soul, and the past 10 years being a nimbus cloud in a household full of sunshine. Any good fortune I had was probably not due to my grumpiness, but in spite of it. In that moment, I resolved to change.

However, the broadest implication of Nikki's teaching was about the science and profession of psychology: Before World War II, psychology had three distinct missions: curing mental illness, making the lives of all people more productive and fulfilling, and identifying and nurturing high talent. The early focus on positive psychology is exemplified by such work as Terman's studies of giftedness (Terman, 1939) and marital happiness (Terman, Buttenwieser, Ferguson, Johnson & Wilson, 1938), Watson's writings on effective parenting (Watson, 1928), and Jung's work concerning the search and discovery of meaning in life (Jung, 1933). Right after the war, two events—both economic—changed the face of psychology: In 1946 the Veteran's Administration (now Veterans Affairs) was founded, and thousands of psychologists

found out that they could make a living treating mental illness. In 1947, the National Institute of Mental Health (which, in spite of its charter, has always been based on the disease model, and should now more appropriately be renamed the National Institute of Mental Illness) was founded, and academics found out that they could get grants if their research was about pathology.

This arrangement brought many benefits. There have been huge strides in the understanding and therapy for mental illness: At least 14 disorders, previously intractable, have yielded their secrets to science and can now be either cured or considerably relieved (Seligman, 1994). But the downside, however, was that the other two fundamental missions of psychology—making the lives of all people better and nurturing genius—were all but forgotten. It wasn't only the subject matter that was altered by funding, but the currency of the theories underpinning how psychologists viewed themselves. They came to see themselves as a mere sub-field of the health professions, and we became a victimology. Psychologists saw human beings as passive foci: Stimuli came on and elicited responses (what an extraordinarily passive word!). External reinforcements weakened or strengthened responses. Drives, tissue needs, instincts, and conflicts from childhood pushed each of us around.

Psychology's empirical focus shifted to assessing and curing individual suffering. There has been an explosion in research on psychological disorders and the negative effects of environmental stressors such as parental divorce, the deaths of loved ones, and physical and sexual abuse. Practitioners went about treating the mental illness of patients within a disease framework by repairing damage: damaged habits, damaged drives, damaged childhoods, and damaged brains.

Mihaly Csikszentmilhalyi realized the need for a positive psychology in Europe during World War II: As a child, I witnessed the dissolution of the smug world in which I had been comfortably ensconced. I noticed with surprise how many of the adults I had known as successful and self-confident became helpless and dispirited once the war removed their social supports. Without jobs, money or status they were reduced to empty shells. Yet there were a few who kept their integrity and purpose despite the surrounding chaos. Their serenity was a beacon that kept others from losing hope. And these were not the men and women one would have expected to emerge unscathed: they were not necessarily the most respected, better educated, or more skilled individuals. This experience set me thinking: What sources of strength were these people drawing on?

Reading philosophy, dabbling in history and religion did not provide satisfying answers to that question. I found the ideas in these texts to be too subjective, dependent on faith, or dubious assumptions; they lacked the clear-eyed skepticism, the slow cumulative growth that I associated with science. Then, for the first time, I came across psychology: first the writings of Carl Jung, then

Freud, then a few of the psychologists who were writing in Europe in the 1950s. Here, I thought, was a possible solution to my quest—a discipline that dealt with the fundamental issues of life, and attempted to do so with the patient simplicity of the natural sciences.

However, at that time psychology was not yet a recognized discipline. In Italy, where I lived, one could take courses in it only as a minor while pursuing a degree in medicine or in philosophy. So I decided to come to the United States, where psychology had gained wider acceptance. The first courses I took were somewhat of a shock. It turned out that in the United States psychology had indeed became a science, if by science one meant only a skeptical attitude and a concern for measurement. What seemed to be lacking, however, was a vision that justified the attitude and the methodology. I was looking for a scientific approach to human behavior, but I never dreamed that this could yield a value-free understanding. In human behavior, what is most intriguing is not the average, but the improbable. Very few people kept their decency during the onslaught of World War II; yet it was these few who held the key to what humans could be like at their best. However, at the height of its behaviorist phase, psychology was being taught as if it were a branch of statistical mechanics. Ever since, I have struggled to reconcile the twin imperatives that a science of human beings should include: to understand what *is*, and what *could be*.

A decade later, the "third way" heralded by Abraham Maslow, Carl Rogers, and other "humanistic" psychologists promised to open a new perspective in addition to the entrenched clinical and behaviorist approaches. Their generous vision had a strong effect on the culture at large and held enormous promise. Unfortunately humanistic psychology did not attract much of a cumulative empirical base and it spawned myriad therapeutic self-help movements. In some of its incarnations it emphasized the self and encouraged a self-centeredness that played down concerns for collective well-being. We leave it to future debate to determine whether this came about because Maslow and Rogers were ahead of their times, or because these flaws were inherent in their original vision, or because of overly enthusiastic "followers." But one legacy of the 1960s is prominently displayed in any large bookstore: The "psychology" section will contain at least 10 shelves on crystal healing, aromatherapy, and reaching the inner child for every shelf of books that tries to uphold some scholarly standard.

Whatever the personal origins of our conviction that the time has arrived for a positive psychology, our message is to remind our field that psychology is not just the study of pathology, weakness, and damage; it is also the study of strength and virtue. Treatment is not just fixing what is broken; it is nurturing what is best. Psychology is not just a branch of medicine concerned with illness or health; it is much larger. It is about work, education, insight, love, growth, and play. And in this quest for what is best, positive psychology does not rely on wishful thinking, faith, self-deception, fads, or hand-waving; it tries to adapt what is best in the scientific method to the unique problems that human behavior presents to those who wish to understand it in all its complexity.

What foregrounds this approach is the issue of prevention. In the last decade psychologists have become concerned with prevention, and this was the presidential theme of the 1998 American Psychological Association meeting in San Francisco. How can we prevent problems like depression or substance abuse or schizophrenia in young people who are genetically vulnerable or who live in worlds that nurture these problems? How can we prevent murderous schoolyard violence in children who have access to weapons, poor parental supervision, and a mean streak? What we have learned over fifty years is that the disease model does not move us closer to the prevention of these serious problems. Indeed the major strides in prevention have largely come from a perspective focused on systematically building competency, not correcting weakness.

Prevention researchers have discovered that there are human strengths that act as buffers against mental illness: courage, future mindedness, optimism, interpersonal skill, faith, work ethic, hope, honesty, perseverance, the capacity for flow and insight, to name several. Much of the task of prevention in this new century will be to create a science of human strength whose mission will be to understand and learn how to foster these virtues in young people.

Working exclusively on personal weakness and on damaged brains, however, has rendered science poorly equipped to effectively prevent illness. Psychologists need now to call for massive research on human strength and virtue. Practitioners need to recognize that much of the best work they already do in the consulting room is to amplify strengths rather than repair the weaknesses of their clients. Psychologists working with families, schools, religious communities, and corporations, need to develop climates that foster these strengths. The major psychological theories have changed to undergird a new science of strength and resilience. No longer do the dominant theories view the individual as a passive vessel responding to stimuli; rather, individuals are now seen as decision makers, with choices, preferences, and the possibility of becoming masterful, efficacious, or, in malignant circumstances, helpless and hopeless (Bandura, 1986; Seligman, 1992). Science and practice that rely on this worldview may have the direct effect of preventing much of the major emotional disorders. It may also have two side effects: making the lives of our clients physically healthier, given all that psychologists are learning about the effects of mental well-being on the body. This science and practice will also reorient psychology back to its two neglected missions, making normal people stronger and more productive as well as making high human potential actual....

References

Allport, G. W. (1961). *Pattern and growth in personality*. New York: Holt, Rinehart, & Wilson.

Baltes, P. B. & Staudinger, U.M. (2000).Wisdom: A metaheuristic (pragmatic) to orchestrate mind and virtue toward excellence. *American Psychologist, 55*, 122–136.

Bandura, A. (1986). *Social foundations of thoughts and action*. Englewood Cliffs, New Jersey: Prentice-Hall.

Benjamin, L. T. Jr. (Ed.) (1992) The history of American psychology. [Special Issue], *American Psychologist, 47*(2).

Buss, D.M. (2000).The evolution of happiness. *American Psychologist, 47*(2).

Diener, E. (2000). Subjective well-being: The science of happiness, and a proposal for a national index. *American Psychologist, 55*, 34–43.

Hall, G.S. (1922). *Senescence: The last half of life*. New York: Appleton.

James, W. (1958). *Varieties of religious experience*. New York: Mentor. (Original work published 1902)

Jung, C. (1933). *Modern man in search of a soul*. New York, Harcourt.

Jung, C.G. (1969). *The archetypes of the collective unconscious. Vol. 9, The collective works of C.G. Jung*. Princeton, NJ: Princeton University Press. (Original work published 1936)

Kahneman, D. (1999). Objective happiness. In D. Kahneman, E. Diener, & N. Schwartz (Eds.) *Well-Being: The foundations of hedonic psychology* (pp. 3–25). New York: Russell Sage Foundation.

Koch, S. & Leary, D.E. (Eds.) (1985) (Eds) *A century of psychology as science*. New York: McGraw-Hill.

Larson, R. W. (2000). Toward a psychology of positive youth development. *American Psychologist, 55*, 170–183.

Ledoux, J. & Armony, J. (1999). Can neurobiology tell us anything about human feelings? In D. Kahneman, E. Diener, & N. Schwartz (Eds.) *Well-Being: The foundations of hedonic psychology* (pp.489–499). New York: Russell Sage Foundation.

Lubinski, D. & Benbow, C.P. (2000). States of excellence. *American Psychologist, 55*, 137–150.

Maslow, A. (1971). *The Farthest Reaches of Human Nature*. New York: Viking.

Massimini, F. & Delle Fave, A. (2000) Individual development in a bio-cultural perspective. *American Psychologist, 55*, 24–33.

Myers, D.G. (2000) The funds, friends, and faith of happy people. *American Psychologist, 55*, 56–67.

Peterson, C. (2000). The future of optimism. *American Psychologist, 55*, 68–78.

Ryan, R.M. & Deci, E.L. (2000). Self-determination theory and the facilitation of intrinsic motivation, social development, and well-being. *American Psychologist, 55*, 110–121.

Salovey, P., Rothman, A.J., Detweiler, J.B. & Steward, W.T. (2000). Emotional states and physical health. *American Psychologist, 55*, 110–121.

Schwartz, B. (2000). Self-determination: The tyranny of freedom. *American Psychologist, 55*, 79–88.

Seligman, M. (1992). *Helplessness: On depression, development, and death*. New York: Freeman.

Seligman, M. (1994). *What you can change & what you can't*. New York: Knopf.

Seligman, M. Schulman, P., DeRubeis, R., & Hollon, S. (1999). The prevention of depression and anxiety. *Prevention and Treatment, 2*, Article 8. Available on the World Wide Web: http://journals.apa.org/prevention/volume2/pre0020008a.html

Simonton, D.K. (2000). Creativity: Cognitive, personal, developmental, and social aspects. *American Psychologist, 55*, 151–158.

Smith, R. (1997). *The human sciences*. New York: Norton.

Taylor, S.E., Kemeny, M.E., Reed, G.M., Bower, J.E. & Gruenwald, T.L. (2000). Psychological resources, positive illusions, and health. *American Psychologist, 55*, 99–109.

Terman, L.M. (1939). The gifted student and his academic environment. *School and Society, 49*, 65–73.

Terman, L.M., Buttenweiser, P., Fergusun, L.W., Johnson, W.B., & Wilson, D.P. (1938). *Psychological factors in marital happiness*. New York: McGraw-Hill.

Vaillant, G.E. (2000). Adaptive mental mechanisms: Their role in a positive psychology. *American Psychologist, 55*, 89–98.

Watson, J. (1928). *Psychological care of infant and child*. New York: Norton.

Winner, E. (2000). The origins and ends of giftedness. *American Psychologist, 55*, 159–169.

Editor's note. Martin E.P. Seligman and Mihaly Csikszentmihalyi served as guest editors for the special issue of *American Psychologist*.

* See the special millennial issue of *American Psychologist*, January 2000, for 16 articles on the topic of Positive Psychology.

Author's note. Martin E.P. Seligman, Department of Psychology, University of Pennsylvania; Mihaly Csikszentmihalyi, Department of Psychology, Claremont Graduate University.

Correspondence concerning this article should be addressed to Martin E.P. Seligman, Department of Psychology, University of Pennsylvania, 3813 Walnut Street, Philadelphia, PA 19104–3604. Electronic mail may be sent to seligman@cattell.psych.upenn.edu.

From *American Psychologist*, January 2000, pp. 5-14. © 2000 by the American Psychological Association. Reprinted by permission.

Oldest, Youngest, or in Between

**How your child's birth order can affect her personality—
and what you can do to influence its impact**

By Margaret Renkl

MY TWO OLDER SONS are very different kinds of boys. Ten-year-old Sam, for example, hates birthday parties, preferring to ask just one other child to go to the movies rather than have 12 kids over to play games. Henry, 5, has adored every big birthday bash he's ever attended. Sam's a dynamo on the baseball field; Henry's opinion of sports can be summed up in a single word: boring.

Certainly, many individual traits and tendencies among brothers and sisters are the products of a unique arrangement of genes. But birth order also plays a key role in shaping a child's personality: Sam and Henry, as well as their 3-year-old brother, Joe, are all different from one another in part because of the order in which they were born.

We've all heard the stereotypes: Firstborns tend to be perfectionists; middle kids, peacemakers; babies, spoiled rotten. But the reality is much more nuanced. Though kids in the same birth position often do share certain character traits, the variables within each family determine the degree to which they fulfill or defy the propensities of birth rank. The youngest of any family may be more freewheeling than the firstborn but won't necessarily turn out to be a brat.

"A firstborn may not be a neat freak or reliable or conscientious," says Kevin Leman, Ph.D., author of *The New Birth Order Book: Why You Are the Way You Are*. But if you're aware of the potential advantages and disadvantages of a child's rank, you can help your kids resist any negative stereotypes. So here's what to expect:

Firstborns

Natural Leaders

ADVANTAGES: Before any siblings come along, oldest children get the lion's share of parents' attention, says Meri Wallace, author of *Birth Order Blues: How Parents Can Help Their Children Meet the Challenges of Birth Order*. Mom and Dad have the time to sing songs with them during baths or read them extra books before bed. As only children

for a while, they're the first to be the focus of their parents' love and affection and the first to wow the grown-ups by reaching major childhood milestones.

All that undivided attention can translate into a highly successful individual. "If a parent is there providing encouragement, a child can gain tremendous amounts of self-confidence," says Wallace. So the oldest kid in a family often does very well both in school and at work because she tends to be focused and detail-oriented and works hard to please authority. Nanette Kirsch, a mother of three in Wexford, PA, says that her firstborn child, Nathan, now 5, has always been very businesslike about what he needs to do. On his fourth birthday, for example, Nathan handed over to his mom the stuffed bear he'd slept with every night since infancy. "I think I'm ready to give up my bear now," he announced. And he's never looked back.

And once firstborns become older siblings, they have the opportunity to lead. "The younger child often adores the older one because she can do so many things," says Wallace. This chance to teach and nurture a younger sister or brother further boosts the firstborn's self-esteem.

Barb Waugh, a mom of two in Houston, says that she can already see her 4-year-old daughter leading her baby brother. "Now that Sean is two, Eleanor mothers him a lot. I hear her repeat everything that comes out of my mouth to him."

CHALLENGES: The greatest strengths of the firstborn can also become her biggest obstacles. For instance, a child who's a natural leader can have trouble making and keeping friends if she's always bossing them around.

Firstborns also risk becoming perfectionists because of the scrutiny they're subjected to by doting parents, who, though well-meaning, may focus on tiny flaws, making their child feel inadequate. Even when parents are supportive, firstborns can still put enormous pressure on themselves to succeed. Christine Ives, a mother of three in Morrison, Colorado, says of her oldest son, Jacob, 5: "We really have to help him stay positive when things don't go his way because he gets so frustrated."

HOW YOU CAN HELP: Don't be too domineering. Refrain from correcting minor imperfections. If your child's bedspread is crooked, don't straighten it; if her attempt to style her hair goes awry, leave it be. Brush off mistakes with a "Good try," then move on. And show how you can roll with the punches yourself—accept compliments gracefully, apologize when you've made a mistake, and let your child know when something didn't go as you'd planned.

Acknowledge her, not the products of her efforts, says Leman. Well-intentioned praise like "That's the most beautiful picture you've ever painted" may make a child think she has to create even more impressive art next time. More effective: open-ended encouragement—"I bet you're really happy with those bright colors"—that shows you're proud of how hard she's working.

Second-borns

Innovators

ADVANTAGES: Kids in the number-two spot have the luxury of more relaxed parents. In part, that's because Mom and Dad are too busy juggling the demands of a growing family to focus as much anxious energy on him as they did the firstborn, or perhaps because they feel more confident about their decisions. Either way, their calmer demeanor tends to transfer to a second child, who'll typically recover from setbacks more easily than his older sibling and be more creative and playful.

Waugh says of her children: "When she was a baby, Eleanor was nicknamed 'The Fussa'—she's very dramatic and demanding. But Sean has been laid-back since birth; he's content just to watch the scenery go by." She attributes much of their differences in personality to her attitude as a mother. "I can't give Sean as much attention as I gave Eleanor at the same age. I had time to sit with her while she fell asleep after her bedtime story. But Sean has learned to be perfectly happy taking his book to bed until he nods off."

Second-born kids also try to be different just to get noticed by their parents, which can make them real innovators. "The firstborn establishes the theme, and the younger child, to be an individual, develops a variation on the theme," says Wallace. Even if the kids share the same talent, they rarely express that gift in the same way. One child may play the piano, while the other sings in the chorus.

At the same time, second-borns tend to be more competent than firstborns of the same age because they've worked hard to emulate their older brother or sister and they're more independent—they've had an older sibling to show them the way.

CHALLENGES: A second child may feel inadequate when he compares himself to his older sister. If Mom and Dad are constantly applauding her accomplishments, he may worry that they love her more. To get attention, he may become a show-off or be extra competitive with other kids. And by the age of 3, he may also resent the fact that his older sister had Mom and Dad all to herself before he came along.

HOW YOU CAN HELP: Encourage him to talk about his feelings, giving him words to express himself. Show him pictures of his sister at the same age and remind him that he'll grow up and be able to do what she can do. Also explain that jealousy is normal. Say, "We know it's hard for you to share us, but we have enough love to go around." Let him know that you love him for who he is and that he doesn't need to outdo anyone to gain your attention.

Then be sure to praise him for his own strengths and abilities: It's fine for him to excel in baseball and for his sister to be a great figure skater. If you rejoice in each child's uniqueness, says Leman, you'll end up with kids who are very different, but each will feel that he's a cherished member of the family.

If you have a third baby, your second-born, of course, becomes a middle child, a birth position that comes with its own set of potential traits:

Middle Kids

Sharp Negotiators

ADVANTAGES: A child who has both an older and a younger sibling has someone to learn from and someone she can nurture—and she has two playmates instead of just one. Like her older sibling, she has the opportunity to be a leader—an experience that will help build her self-confidence. As one of three (or more) kids, she's able to learn how to relate to a group, how to share, listen to others, and join in activities—so she'll probably get along well with others. My own middle child, Henry, has learned to negotiate both the demands of an older brother who tends to be very bossy and a little brother who insists on doing everything he's doing. Middle kids are usually less pressured than firstborns but are taken more seriously and aren't as overprotected as the youngest.

CHALLENGES: When a third child is born, the second's status takes on a new variation: Middle kids may feel left out and overlooked and may be anxious and insecure as a result. If this pattern continues throughout childhood, it can make a child less likely to speak up for herself.

To get her parent's attention, a middle child may act out. She also has to struggle to maintain her identity; to define herself, she may become obsessed with a hobby or be overly competitive. Some middle children may become people pleasers to win affection, and others will withdraw, especially if their parents are always engaged in battles with the other two kids.

HOW YOU CAN HELP: Work hard to make a middle child feel special. Try to spend at least some time alone with her every day—and with each of your kids. A ten-minute cuddle at bedtime in a child's room goes a long way.

Ask her opinion, to help build her confidence. When you're dressing for work, for instance, hold up two outfits and let her choose, or remind her that Dad's birthday is coming up and have her help think of a great gift for him.

Whether it's your second, third, or later child, someone will be the baby, with the quirks that go along with that position:

Babies

Free Spirits

ADVANTAGES: Like the middle child, the youngest benefits from having more relaxed parents and having older siblings to follow. He's also exposed to more than other kids his age because he's watched his brothers and sisters develop and reach milestones, says Wallace. Since he wants to be like them, he'll insist on doing things by himself.

Jess Hill, a mother of three in Nashville, says her youngest child, 8-year-old Noni, has always been eager to catch up to her older brother and sister. "She set her own alarm clock and made her bed at a very early age to be like Becca and Morey."

Sometimes the baby is the most creative, since he has so much time to himself. And he often has fewer responsibilities than his siblings because others always lend him a hand. Babies often become fun-loving, affectionate, and outgoing people.

CHALLENGES: Because the family may be more lax with the youngest, he may have difficulty respecting authority later on. And since people often take over for him, he may become too dependent on others and struggle with handling his own problems. He may also feel less competent than his older siblings—though he learns from them, they can still do much more than he can. Older kids can become jealous of the little one, especially if they feel that he gets extra privileges, says Wallace. They'll say things like "You're just in baby school, but I have real homework."

HOW YOU CAN HELP: There will be sibling rivalry, but step in if your baby's being bullied—kids need help developing the skills to work it out. If your kindergartner's dominating the dinner conversation, ask your preschooler to share his day. Give him responsibilities—even a small task like helping to clear the dishes will be beneficial. Let him hear you remind older siblings that they also used to take longer to put their coats on and had a tough time learning to play Candy Land.

Birth-order traits often emphasize the differences between siblings, but it's important to remember that they have a lot in common too. My son Sam once heard me call his little brother "sugar pie," to which he replied, "Joe's not a 'sugar pie.' I'm the big boy, I'm the 'sugar pie'; Henry's the medium boy, he's the 'sugar cookie'; Joe's the littlest, he's the 'sugar lump.'"

What About Onlies?

Studies show that only children can turn out to be higher achievers and more motivated than kids with siblings. They tend to mature faster than other kids their age; since they're the center of their parents' universe, expectations can be high. And without a brother or sister to play with, they spend more time in the company of adults.

As much as an only child may enjoy being alone or with adults, it's a good idea to try to expand her network of other kids. Preschool, daycare, or any group setting is an important way to allow an only to develop friendships that can stand in for sibling bonds. And it's equally vital that you not inflate expectations. Give her a sense of privacy and her own identity, something she would automatically get if you were caring for more than one.

Defying the Stereotypes

Two factors that can affect how birth order shapes a child's personality and behavior:

SIBLING SPACING Houston mom Pia Byrd, whose three kids were all born about five years apart, says that each of them behaves like a firstborn. Even 4-year-old Dane, the baby, has had his mom entirely to himself during these early years while his older siblings, Brit, 9, and Isabella, 15, are in school. Likewise, a second-born child who's already, say, 4 when the third child is born will probably show both middle- and youngest-child tendencies because during infancy and early childhood she was the baby.

GENDER Many parents have specific assumptions about their sons that are different from those about their daughters, influencing the way they treat their kids. A girl who's born after an older brother will often show qualities of both a second- and a firstborn because she's the only daughter. If a youngest child is the only boy following several daughters, he can seem more like a firstborn than the baby for the same reason—he's the first child in the family to grow up influenced by his parents' notions of maleness.

Contributing editor MARGARET RENKL wrote about family rituals in the May issue.

From *Parenting*, June/July 2002, pp. 82–86. © 2002 by Parenting. Reprinted by permission.

UNIT 9
Social Processes

Unit Selections

Key Points to Consider

- What is friendship? Why are friends important? How do adult and childhood friendships differ? Why should adults salvage their friendships, especially today when life already seems so full?

- What types of events can be classified as terrorist? How does terrorism affect the general population? How does it affect you? What can we do as a nation to better cope with terrorism? What can you do as an individual? If the prospect of more terrorism causes the government to abridge certain individual rights, will you agree or disagree with the government? Why? Do you think it is fair to target "Arab-looking" individuals as possible future terrorists?

- What do you think are the effects of televised violence on our behavior? What other media (e.g., video games) influence us in violent ways? Do you think American media are too violent? Why is research on violence in the media so complicated? What can we do to reduce media violence? Is reducing media violence a government, media, or personal responsibility?

- What is culture? Do you think a culture can be feminine or masculine? Do you agree that the American culture is becoming feminized? If yes, what do you think will be the ultimate outcome of this trend? Is feminization of culture a good, bad, or neutral trend in your opinion? How does a culture become feminized or masculinized?

- What characterizes an individualistic culture? What typifies a collectivist culture? Can you give examples of each by describing a specific culture? On what other dimensions can cultures differ besides individualism/collectivism and femininity/masculinity? Do cultures regularly evolve or change? What recent changes have occurred in American culture? What do you think ultimately causes the demise of a great culture?

- What is bullying? What causes bullying? Why is bullying so deleterious to its victim? What can schools and parents do to reduce or prevent bullying? How is bullying related to violence? Is the violence done only to others?

 **Links: www.dushkin.com/online/**
These sites are annotated in the World Wide Web pages.

National Clearinghouse for Alcohol and Drug Information
http://www.health.org
Nonverbal Behavior and Nonverbal Communication
http://www3.usal.es/~nonverbal/

Everywhere we look there are groups of people. Your general psychology class is a group. It is what social psychologists would call a secondary group, a group that comes together for a particular, somewhat contractual reason and then disbands after its goals have been met. Other secondary groups include athletic teams, church associations, juries, committees, and so forth.

There are other types of groups, too. One other type is a primary group. A primary group has much face-to-face contact, and there is often a sense of "we-ness" in the group (cohesiveness as social psychologists would call it). Examples of primary groups include families, apartment mates, and teenage cliques.

Collectives are loosely knit, large groups of people. A bleacher full of football fans would be a collective. A long line of people waiting to get into a rock concert would also be a collective. A voting mob would

also be labeled a collective. As you might guess, collectives behave differently from primary and secondary groups.

Mainstream American society and any other large group that shares common rules and norms is also a group, albeit an extremely large group. While we might not always think about our society and how it shapes our behavior and our attitudes, society and culture nonetheless have a measureless influence on us. Psychologists, anthropologists, and sociologists alike are all interested in studying the effects of a culture on its members.

In this unit we will look at both positive and negative forms of social interaction. We will move from focused forms of social interaction to broader forms of social interaction, from interpersonal to group to societal processes.

In the first few articles, we concentrate on general social phenomena such as friendship and violence. In "Got Time for Friends?" Andy Steiner contemplates why friendship is so important. He reminds us that friends are valuable for a number of psychological reasons. Steiner then concludes that adult friendships often fall by the wayside, unlike childhood friendships. We need to renew adult friendships because they are just as valuable as our childhood ones.

We next move to a larger societal problem in the United States—terrorism and trauma. Erica Goode, writing for the *New York Times,* discusses recent terrorist events and how people

usually respond to them in an irrational way. Events that are unfamiliar and threatening often produce terror.

A second problem in our society is violence committed by Americans on other Americans. Is the wave of violence that is spewing out onto our streets caused by media violence? According to "Whodunit—The Media?" by Maggie Cutler, the answer is a resounding "yes." Cutler unfolds the results of complex research that attempts to unravel the effects of the media from other stimuli for violence.

In the next article in this unit on social behavior, we explore another issue affecting American society. Leonard Sax suggests that the prevailing American culture is becoming more feminine—even for men and boys. Why this is occurring and what the results are comprise the main points of Sax's essay.

We then move to a comparison among cultures. While American culture is largely individualistic, other cultures are collective. Elizabeth Nair contests this bipolarity and says that it is too simplistic. Cultures not only vary on other dimensions, she says, they also do not remain unchanged over time. Cross-cultural researchers need to investigate other aspects of cultures, too.

Finally, in "Disarming the Rage," Richard Jerome and his colleagues discuss the all-important and timely topic of bullying. How parents and schools can guard against bullying and therefore prevent violence are highlighted in this article.

Got time for Friends?

Sure, you're busy. But are you paying attention to what's really important?
Why finding—and keeping—friends is the key to a happy life.

BY ANDY STEINER

It's not the last time my daughter will make me look foolish, but it was one of the first. Maybe it was silly to take a toddler to an art opening, but there we were, the effervescent Astrid and her uptight mama. As I hovered near her, hoping to intercept toppling *objets d'art*, Astrid spotted Claire across the room.

Maybe their attraction was predestined, since Claire and Astrid, 18 and 16 months respectively, were the only under-three-footers in what to them must have looked like a sea of kneecaps. Still, Astrid's eyes lit up when she saw young Claire, and she turned on the charm, hopping and squealing and running in some strange kiddie ritual. Claire squealed back, Astrid flashed her tummy, and that was it: They were fast friends.

The culture-at-large tells us that once school is over or we hit 30, friendship ought to take a backseat to more pressing concerns.

It wasn't so easy for Claire's mother and me. When our kids started making nice, we smiled politely, and as the junior friendship heated up, we attempted shy (on my part at least) and distracted attempts at conversation. "How old is she?" I asked. "What's her name?" she countered. I'd like to say that today Claire's mommy is a good friend, but that's not the case. We continued to exchange pleasantries while our daughters pranced around together, but when our partners appeared, we picked up our squirmy squirts and said good-bye. We haven't seen each other since. Too bad, because I could have used a new friend. Who couldn't?

In college, and for several years after, I was immersed in a warm circle of friends, the kind of exciting and exotic people I'd spent my small-town youth dreaming about. These friends came to my college from around the world, and after graduation, many of them stayed. We had a great time. We went to movies—and for a bit created our own monthly film group. We gathered at each other's apartments to cook big dinners and stay up late, sharing our opinions on music, sex, and dreams. We even took a few trips together—to a friend's wedding in the mountains of Colorado and to a cabin on the edge of a loon-covered lake. But time passes, and as these friends moved on, got married, or found great jobs, my gang of compatriots began to dwindle.

"We cannot tell the precise moment when friendship is formed. As in filling a vessel drop by drop, there is at last a drop which makes it run over; so in a series of kindnesses there is at last one which makes the heart run over."

Samuel Johnson

Now many of them have moved to other states—other countries, even. Though a precious core group still lives within shouting distance, I worry that grown-up life will soon scatter them all and I'll be left, lonely and missing them.

So it goes for many of us as we leave our youth behind and face "real" life. While generations of young adults have probably felt the same way, the yearning for close friends takes on a greater sense of urgency now as modern life makes our lives busier and more fragmented. "It's not that it's so hard to make friends when you're older," says sociologist Jan Yager, author of *Friendshifts*, "but making friends—and finding time to maintain and nurture old friendships as well as new ones—is just one of the many concerns that occupy your time."

Astrid's encounter with Claire (and my parallel one with her mother) cast a spotlight on one reality: Kids see potential friends everywhere. Adults, on the other hand, have a harder time of it, especially as we (and our potential friends) enter the realm of romantic commitments, full-time jobs, motherhood and fatherhood. While we may wish to add to our collection of friends, we feel too busy, too consumed by other obligations, too caught up in everyday bustle to make time to help a friendship blossom and grow.

"Be a friend to thyself, and others will befriend thee."

English proverb

And we may be following subtle clues from the culture-at-large telling us that, once school is over or we near 30, friendship ought to take a back seat to more pressing concerns. Despite the central role that idealized gangs of pals play on sitcoms, our primary sources of information—self-help books, magazines, and personal interest TV shows—rarely talk about how to get—or keep—friends. Instead they barrage us with detailed advice on how to attract a lover, get ahead in a career, rekindle a marriage, or keep peace in the family. Friendships, unlike these other kinds of relationships, are supposed to just happen, with little effort on your part. But what if they don't?

"Friends can get relegated to secondary status," says Aurora Sherman, assistant professor of psychology at Brandeis University. "Even if you don't have children or a partner or aging parents, the pressures of adult responsibility can force people to place friendship in the background."

"All I can do is to urge you to put friendship ahead of all other human concerns, for there is nothing so suited to man's nature, nothing that can mean so much to him, whether in good times or in bad... I am inclined to think that with the exception of wisdom, the gods have given nothing finer to men than this."

Marcus Tullius Cicero

Children's full-scale focus on friendship may have to do with more than just their carefree attitude about life. Sherman cites the research theorizing that kids' interest in making friends serves a larger developmental purpose.

"A young person's primary motivation for social interaction is to get information and to learn about the world," Sherman explains. "When you're a kid, practically everybody that you meet has the potential to help you learn about something that you didn't know." Grown-ups already know most things (or at least they think they do), so as you get older, you may feel less of a drive to make new friends.

So, if you're someone who embraces the goal of lifelong learning, it's important not to write off friendship as a thing of the past. Meeting new people is a lot less work than going back to college for another degree, and more fun, too. Want to learn yoga or steep yourself in South American culture? How about sharpening your skills as an entrepreneur or activist? Think outside the classroom by finding someone eager to show what they know. An added benefit is that you, too, can share your passion about knitting or bocce ball or radical history. If the people you currently hang out with don't know much about the things you want to know, maybe it's time to break into some new circles.

"The proper office of a friend is to side with you when you are in the wrong. Nearly anybody will side with you when you are in the right."

Mark Twain

The tangible rewards of friendship go far beyond exchanges of information. In 1970 Lenny Dee left New York and moved across the country to Portland, Oregon, where he knew barely a soul. "The first week I was there I met probably half the people who became my lifelong friends," says Dee. "It was like I walked through this magic door and a whole world opened up for me." Within a day of his arrival, he had moved into a house that was an epicenter of the city's alternative culture. He could barely step out of the house without running into one of his new friends.

"At one point in my life all of the people I knew were footloose and fancy free," Dee says, "but over the years that changed. A certain segment of my friends in Portland became more settled while I remained less settled. People got families and jobs, and they started disappearing. Now you have to make an appointment to get together."

Still, Dee has been vigilant in nurturing old friendships; people all across the country can count on a birthday phone call from Portland. "I have always thought you could invest your energies in making money or making friends," Dee says, "and they achieve much the same ends—security, new experiences, personal options, travel, and so forth. I have always found it more fulfilling to make friends."

And Dee's life has been shaped in many ways by the enduring connections he's maintained, including a key position at the start-up of a now successful educational software company and a recent vacation in Corsica at the summer home of an old Portland friend who now lives in Paris.

A slew of recent research supports Dee's example that friends make life complete.

"As hard as it is with everyone so busy and consumed with the day-to-day workings of their lives, it's important to understand that making and maintaining friendships is really pivotal to social, emotional, and physical well-being," says Yager. She ticks off research that touts the value of building strong nonfamilial bonds, including: an in-depth study of thousands of Northern California residents that revealed that having ties to at least one close friend extends a person's life, and another study of 257 human resource managers that discovered adults who have friends at work report not only higher productivity but also higher workplace satisfaction.

When you know who his friend is, you know who he is.
Senegal proverb

For New York psychotherapist Kathlyn Conway, a three-time cancer survivor and author of the memoir *An Ordinary Life*, friends provided an anchor during times when she felt her life was drifting off course.

"I had friends I could talk to at any time," Conway says of her 1993 battle with breast cancer. "If I was upset, it was easy for me to call someone and expect them to listen—no matter what."

And when the busy mother of two needed physical help, friends came to her aid. "One friend went to the hospital after my mastectomy and helped me wash my hair," Conway recalled in an article she wrote for the women's cancer magazine *Mamm*. "Another, who herself had had breast cancer, visited and stealthily, humorously, kindly opened her blouse to show me her implanted breast in order to reassure me. Yet another left her very busy job in the middle of the week to go shopping with me for a wig."

One time when adults tend to make new friends is during major life changes, like a move, a new job, or the birth of a child. Ellen Goodman and Patricia O'Brien, authors of *I Know Just What You Mean*, a book chronicling their quarter-century friendship, met in 1973 when both were completing Neiman fellowships at Harvard. At the time, Goodman, now a nationally syndicated newspaper columnist, and O'Brien, a novelist and former editorial writer for the *Chicago Sun-Times*, were both newly divorced mothers in their 30s.

"We were both broke and busy and we were not at all alike—at least on the surface," Goodman recalls, "but we bonded, maybe out of some sense of great urgency, and during that year we spent an enormous amount of time in Harvard Square, drinking coffee and talking. We missed a lot of classes, but those times together were some of the best seminars either of us ever attended."

"Life shifts—like a divorce or an illness or another unexpected change—can occur at any time, and when that happens, there's always this powerful draw to another person who's going through the same thing," O'Brien says. "For Ellen and me there was this wonderful opportunity to talk to another woman who was hitting the same bumps in the road as we were. We could talk for hours and always understand what the other person was saying." After the short spell at Harvard, they never again lived in the same place but kept the friendship going with letters, phone calls, and frequent visits.

Three is the magic number

When it comes to making friends, there's much we can learn from kids about flashing a wide grin and harboring a playful spirit. But Stanford University psychology professor Laura Carstensen emphasizes that an important lesson also comes from the over-65 set. In studying senior citizens' social networks, she has found that "it is the *quality* of their relationships that matters—not the *quantity*. In our work we find that three is the critical friend number. If you have three people in your life that you can really count on, then you are doing as well as someone who has 10 friends. Or 20, for that matter. If you have fewer than three friends, then you could be a little precarious."

So sit down, get out a piece of paper, and start listing your friends. Got three folks you're always excited about seeing and feel certain you can trust? Then put down the pencil. Who says you can't put a number on success?

—Andy Steiner

A while back—inspired by my daughter's happy, open face and ready giggle—I resolved that making new friends might be just the cure for the post-baby blahs I was experiencing.

So I set my sights on one particular woman. Even though I have wonderful old friends, people I wouldn't trade for a billion dollars, this particular woman caught my eye. She seemed smart and funny. We were both writers. I'd heard that she lived in my neighborhood. Then, the kicker: Someone we both knew suggested that we would hit it off. So I called her—out of the blue—and invited her to coffee. Sure, she said. So we met.

Just the other day, this woman told me that at the time she wondered about my motivation, this strange, nervously enthusiastic young woman who peppered her with questions about writing and reading and her impressions of the university we'd both attended, she as an undergraduate, I as a master's student. Still, a few weeks later she took me up on my invitation to go for a walk, and our conversation soon became natural and fun. Suddenly, she became my new friend.

Astrid, riding in her stroller, witnessed it all. Besides babbling and napping, she was watching closely as my new friend and I laughed and told the stories of our lives. Taking a risk and extending yourself is one way to form a bond with someone. We weren't squealing or flashing our tummies, but it was close.

Andy Steiner, mother of gregarious Astrid, is a senior editor of Utne Reader.

Reprinted with permission from *Utne Reader*, September/October 2001, pp. 67–71. © 2001 by Utne Reader. To subscribe, call 800-736-UTNE or visit our website at www.utne.com.

Rational and Irrational Fears Combine in Terrorism's Wake

By ERICA GOODE

The familiar became strange, the ordinary perilous.

On Sept. 11, Americans entered a new and frightening geography, where the continents of safety and danger seemed forever shifted.

Is it safe to fly? Will terrorists wage germ warfare? Where is the line between reasonable precaution and panic?

Jittery, uncertain and assuming the worst, many people have answered these questions by forswearing air travel, purchasing gas masks and radiation detectors, placing frantic calls to pediatricians demanding vaccinations against exotic diseases or rushing out to fill prescriptions for Cipro, an antibiotic most experts consider an unnecessary defense against anthrax.

Psychologists who study how people perceive potential hazards say such responses are not surprising, given the intense emotions inspired by the terrorist attacks.

"People are particularly vulnerable to this sort of thing when they're in a state of high anxiety, fear for their own well-being and have a great deal of uncertainty about the future," said Dr. Daniel Gilbert, a professor of psychology at Harvard.

"We don't like that feeling," Dr. Gilbert said. "We want to do something about it. And, at the moment, there isn't anything particular we can do, so we buy a gas mask and put an American decal on our car and take trains instead of airplanes."

But, he added, "I'll be very surprised if five years from now even one life was saved by these efforts."

Still, many psychologists said avoiding flying might be perfectly reasonable if someone is going to spend the entire flight in white-knuckled terror. And though experts say gas masks will offer dubious protection in a chemical attack, if buying them helps calm people down, it can do no harm.

"The feelings may be irrational, but once you have the feelings, the behavior is perfectly rational," said Dr. George Lowenstein, a professor of economics and psychology at Carnegie Mellon University. "It doesn't make sense to take a risk just because it's rational if it's going to make you miserable. The rational thing is to do what makes you comfortable."

The public's fears may be heightened, he and other experts said, by the sense that the government failed to predict or prevent the Sept. 11 attacks, making people less trusting of the reassurances offered by the authorities, who have said that biological attacks are unlikely and, with vastly heightened security, air travel is safe.

The vivid, the involuntary and the unfamiliar seem to be more threatening.

Checkpoints on highways, closed parking structures at airports, flyovers by military aircraft and other security measures, they added, while reassuring many people, may for others increase anxiety by providing a constant reminder of danger.

In fact, the threats now uppermost in many people's minds, Dr. Lowenstein and other psychologists said, are examples of the kinds of risks that people find most frightening.

"All the buttons are being pushed here," said Dr. Paul Slovic, a professor of psychology at the University of Oregon and the author of "The Perception of Risk." Threats posed by terrorism, he said, "are horrific to contemplate, seem relatively uncontrollable and are catastrophic."

He and other researchers have found that risks that evoke vivid images, that are seen as involuntary, that are unfamiliar or that kill many people at once are often perceived as more threatening than risks that are voluntary, familiar and less extreme in their effects. For example, in studies, people rank threats like plane crashes and nuclear accidents higher than dangers like smoking or car accidents, which actually cause many more deaths each year.

This fact is a source of endless frustration to some scientists, who cannot understand why people panic over almost undetectable quantities of pesticides on vegetables but happily devour charcoal-broiled hamburgers and steaks, which contain known carcinogens formed in grilling. And, when asked to rank the relative dangers of a variety of potential hazards, scientific experts routinely give lower ratings to things like nuclear power and pesticides than do laypeople, researchers have found.

"Everything in some sense is dangerous, in some concentration and some place, and usually not in others," said Dr. James Collman, a chemistry professor at Stanford and the author of "Naturally Dangerous: Surprising Facts About Food, Health and the Environment."

He said his daughter called him after the terrorist attacks to ask if she should buy a gas mask.

"I told her not to panic," he said. "I thought it was sort of statistically a silly thing to do, and were there ever any toxic gases out there, whatever mask she had might or might not be effective anyway."

Yet psychologists say the average person's responses make sense if one realizes that human beings are not the cool, rational evaluators that economists and other social scientists once assumed them to be.

Rather, the human brain reacts to danger through the activation of two systems, one an instant, emotional response, the other a higher level, more deliberate reaction.

The emotional response to risk, Dr. Lowenstein said, is deeply rooted in evolution and shared with most other animals. But rationality—including the ability to base decisions about risk on statistical likelihood—is unique to humans.

Yet the two responses, he said, often come into conflict, "just as the experts clash with the laypeople."

"People often even within themselves don't believe that a risk is objectively that great, and yet they have feelings that contradict their cognitive evaluations," Dr. Lowenstein said.

For example, he said, "The objective risk of driving for four or five hours at high speeds still has got to be way higher than the risk of flying."

What You Don't Know . . .

Whether people fear something depends not only on how dangerous it actually is, but also on how much they know about it and how much control they believe they have over their exposure to it. Researchers use diagrams like this to chart perceptions of risk.

HORIZONTAL AXIS ▶
At left, things described as controllable. At right, things that seem beyond one's control.

VERTICAL AXIS
At bottom, risks that subjects view as known and observable; at top, those whose effects are hardest to observe.

UNKNOWN RISKS

Less risky, less frightening
- Marijuana
- Aspirin
- Sunbathing

Most frightening
- Terrorism
- Nuclear weapons
- Nuclear power
- Nerve gas

CONTROLLABLE RISKS · UNCONTROLLABLE RISKS

Least frightening
- Surfing
- Motorcycles
- Alcoholic beverages
- Hunting

More risky, more frightening
- Smoking
- Heroin
- Crime
- Open-heart surgery

KNOWN RISKS

Items are shown in no special order.

Source: "The Perception of Risk," by Paul Slovic

The New York Times

Yet Dr. Lowenstein added that a group of his colleagues, all academic experts on risk assessment, chose to drive rather than fly to a conference after the terrorist attacks.

"If you ask them which is objectively more dangerous, they would probably say that driving is," Dr. Lowenstein said. And though his colleagues cited potential airport delays, he said he suspected fear might also have played into their decision.

President Bush and other policy makers in Washington, Dr. Lowenstein said, must contend with a similar struggle between reason and emotion in shaping their response to the attacks.

"A lot of what's going on is this battle where the emotions are pushing us to respond in a way that would give us quick release but would have all sorts of long-term consequences," Dr. Lowenstein said.

In fact, studies show that once awakened, fear and other emotions heighten people's reactions to other potential hazards. In one study, for example, students shown sad films perceived a variety of risks as more threatening than students who saw emotionally neutral films.

Fear can also spread from person to person, resulting in wild rumors and panic.

One example often cited by sociologists who study collective behavior is the so-called Seattle windshield pitting epidemic, which occurred in 1954, a time when cold war fears ran high and the United States was testing the hydrogen bomb.

That year, tiny holes in car windshields were noticed in Bellingham, Wash., north of Seattle. A week later, similar pitting was seen by residents of towns south of Bellingham. Soon, people in Seattle and all over the state were reporting mysterious damage to their windshields. Many speculated that fallout from the H-bomb tests was the cause. Others blamed cosmic rays from the sun. At the height of the panic, the mayor of Seattle even called President Dwight D. Eisenhower for help.

But eventually, a more mundane explanation revealed itself: In the usual course of events, people did not examine their windshields that closely. The holes, pits and dings turned out to be a result of normal wear and tear, which few had noticed until it was drawn to their attention.

The antidote to such fears, psychologists say, is straightforward information from trustworthy sources.

"Trustworthiness has two elements," said Dr. Baruch Fischhoff, a psychologist in Carnegie Mellon's department of social and decision sciences. "One is honesty and the other is competence."

Attempts by the authorities to use persuasion often fall flat, Dr. Fischhoff said, because "if people feel they have to peel away the agenda of the communicator in order to understand the content of the message, that's debilitating."

"Give me the facts in a comprehensible way, and leave it to me to decide what's right for me," he said.

Yet what psychologists can say with some certainty is that, if no further attacks occur in the near future, people's fears are likely to fade quickly—even faster than the fearful themselves would predict.

Studies suggest, Dr. Gilbert said, that "people underestimate their resilience and adaptiveness."

We have remarkable both psychological and physiological mechanisms to adapt to change," he said. "I guarantee you that in six months whatever New Yorkers are feeling will seem pretty normal to them, even if it is not exactly what they were feeling before."

From the *New York Times*, October 2, 2001. © 2001 by The New York Times Company. Reprinted by permission.

Whodunit—the Media?

IT'S EASY TO BLAME CARTOONS FOR GUN-TOTING KIDS. BUT THE TRUTH ISN'T SO TIDY.

MAGGIE CUTLER

Will girls imitate the new, kickass heroines in the Japanese animé *Cardcaptors*? Will the impressionable 12-year-olds exposed to trailers for MGM's *Disturbing Behavior* forever after associate good teen behavior with lobotomies? Did Nine Inch Nails and the video game Doom inspire the Trenchcoat Mafia's bloodbath at Columbine? Thousands of studies have been done to try to answer variants of the question: Does media violence lead to real-life violence, making children more antisocial and aggressive?

Like most complex issues, discussions about the impact of media violence on children suffer from that commonest of media problems: fudge. Almost any simple statement on the subject obscures the complexity of the facts, half-facts and "results suggest" findings of the past forty years. The right-wing Parents Television Council, for example, announces that the per-hour rate in the United States of sexual and violent material and coarse language combined almost tripled from 1989 to 1999. But while PTC president Brent Bozell castigates the media for lowering standards of acceptable speech and behavior, he doesn't mention that in the final years of this avalanche of dreck the juvenile crime rate *dropped* more than 30 percent. Or, again, in August 1999 the Senate Judiciary Committee, headed by Orrin Hatch, reported confidently that "Television alone is responsible for 10 percent of youth violence." Given the overall juvenile crime count in 1997, the report implied, some 250 murders and 12,100 other violent crimes would not have been committed if it weren't for the likes of *Batman Beyond*.

But this, of course, is deeply misleading. One of the reasons so many media violence studies have been done is that the phenomenon may be too complex to study conclusively. There's no way, after all, to lock two clones in a black box, feed them dif-

ferent TV, movie and video-game diets and open the box years later to determine that, yes, it was definitely those Bruce Lee epics that turned clone A into Jesse Ventura, while clone B's exposure to the movie *Babe* produced a Pee Wee Herman.

It has been hard, in other words, for media violence studies to shake the ambiguity of correlations. Several studies have shown that violent boys tend to watch more TV, choose more violent content and get more enjoyment out of it. But the studies admittedly can't show exactly how or why that happens. Do temperamentally violent kids seek out shows that express feelings they already have, or are they in it for the adrenaline boost? Do the sort of parents who let kids pig out on gore tend to do more than their share of other hurtful things that encourage violent behavior? To what extent is violent media producing little Johnny's aggression—or inspiring it, making it appear glamorous, righteous, acceptably gratuitous, fun or "normal"—and to what extent is it merely satisfying little Johnny's greater-than-average longings for the mayhem, vengeance, superhuman power and sweet revenge that most people, at times, secretly crave?

According to James Garbarino, author of *Lost Boys: Why Our Sons Turn Violent and How We Can Save Them*, it makes no sense to talk about violent media as a direct cause of youth violence. Rather, he says, "it depends": Media violence is a risk factor that, working in concert with others, can exacerbate bad behavior.

Like Orrin Hatch's committee, Garbarino estimates the effect of violent media on juvenile violence at about 10 percent, but his ecology-of-violence formulation is far less tidy than the Hatch committee's pop-psych model. Garbarino himself reports in an e-mail that he would like to see media violence treated as a public health problem—dammed at its Hollywood source the way sewage treatment plants "reduce the problem of cholera." Nevertheless, his ecology model of how juvenile violence emerges from complex, interacting factors means that hyperaggressive, "asset poor" kids are likely to be harmed by graphic depictions of violence, while balanced, "asset rich" kids are likely to remain unscathed. A few studies have even found that a "cathartic effect" of media violence makes some kids *less* aggressive. This wide range of individual variance makes policy prescriptions a tricky matter.

The American Psychological Association's Commission on Violence and Youth (1994) mentions violent media as only one among many factors in juvenile violence. It stresses that inborn temperament, early parental abuse or neglect, poverty, cognitive impairment, plus a deficiency of corrective influences or role models in various combinations will put a child at greater risk for violence, both as perpetrator and as victim. The APA found that many damaged kids' lives can be salvaged with early intervention. By the age of 8, these at-risk kids can be identified. Once identified they can be taught skills that enable them to resolve conflicts peacefully. The APA adds that parental guidance along with reducing kids' exposure to graphic violence can help keep them out of the correctional system. But for the kids most at risk, reducing representational violence is obviously no cure. So this past fall, when Senators John McCain and Joseph Lieberman ordered the entertainment industry to stop advertising its nastier products to young children or else face (shudder) regulation, it was fair of media critics to castigate them for exploiting the media violence problem for its bipartisan glow rather than attempting to find the least coercive, most effective ways of keeping children safe and sane.

Perhaps the biggest problem in mitigating the effect of media violence on children is that it's hard to nail down just what "violent media" means to actual kids. As with adult pornography, we all think we know what it is until we have to define it. That's because kids not only process content differently depending on their temperament, background and circumstances, they seem to process it differently at different ages, too.

A series of often-cited studies known as Winick and Winick (1979) charted distinct stages in media processing abilities. Fairly early, from about 6 until about 10, most—but not all—kids are learning to deal with media much as adults do: interactively rather than passively. In her 1985 book, *Watching Dallas: Soap Opera and the Melodramatic Imagination*, Ien Ang of the University of Western Sydney in Australia showed that different adult viewers rewrote the "messages" of shows to suit their own views. So a wise little girl whose parents discuss media with her might enjoy *Wrestlemania* as an amusing guide to crazy-guys-to-avoid, while an angry, abandoned, slow-witted child is more likely to enter its world of insult and injury with uncritical awe.

At first blush, measures like content labeling would seem to make more sense for the 2-to-6 set because young kids do get confused about reality, fantasy, information and advertising.

But again, what constitutes "violent" content isn't always obvious. The Winicks found that young children whose parents fought a lot responded with more distress to representations of people yelling and screaming—because it seemed real—than to blatant violence for which they had no frame of reference. Should there be a label for "loud and emotional"? And if so, should we slap it on *La Bohème*?

Because representational violence is so hard to define, the recently reported Stanford media effects studies, which focused on third and fourth graders, ducked the problem. The study team, headed by Thomas Robinson, simply worked with teachers, parents and kids to help children lower their overall media use voluntarily. As a result of the six-month program, which involved classroom instruction, parental support and peer pressure, kids used media about 30 percent less than usual. And, they found, verbal and physical aggression levels subsequently dropped 25 percent on average. These numbers are being taken especially seriously because they were established "in the field" rather than in the lab, so that the verbal and physical aggression measured was actual, not simulated by, say, asking a child to kick or insult a doll. As media violence studies predicted, the more aggressive kids were to begin with, the more their behavior improved when they consumed less of whatever it was they normally consumed.

Although the Stanford study—perhaps to stay popular with granters—is being promoted as a study on media violence, it is really a study of media overuse, self-awareness and the rewards of self-discipline. Its clearest finding wasn't that media violence is always harmful but that too much mediated experience seems to impair children's ability to interact well with other people. Follow-up studies at Stanford will show whether the remarkable benefits of its media reduction program last over a longer period. If they do, such classes may be a helpful addition to school curriculums in conjunction, perhaps, with courses in conflict resolution. But in any case, its results demonstrate less the effects of specific content than what could be called "the rule of the real."

The rule of the real says that however strong media influences may be, real life is stronger. Real love, real money, real political events and real-life, unmediated interpersonal experience all shape kids' lives, minds and behavior more powerfully than any entertainment products. Even media seen or understood as real—news, documentaries, interviews—will have more impact than that which a kid knows is make-believe. As the Winicks found, kids understand early that cartoon violence is a joke, not a model. Even wrestling, once kids figure out that it's staged, gets processed differently from, say, a schoolyard beating.

It's more likely that the Santana High killer shot up his school after seeing coverage of Columbine than after watching The Mummy.

Without belittling the importance of media research, it's time that the rule of the real governed policy as well. After all, boys whose dads do hard time tend to end up in jail, while boys who see *Fight Club* tend to end up in film clubs; it's more likely that the Santana High killer decided to shoot up his school after seeing the anniversary coverage of Columbine than because he watched *The Mummy*. Abused young women don't kill their battering husbands because they grew up watching *Charlie's Angels*, and teens who hear no criticism of the Gulf War tend to want another. Given limited energies and resources, if our politicians really wanted to reduce youth violence, they would push to reform prison policies, provide supervised after-school activities for teens and get early, comprehensive help to high-risk children. As a community, we would do better to challenge the corporate conglomeration of news outlets than to legislate the jugs 'n' jugular quotient in *Tomb Raider*, its labeling or ad placements—and this is true even though the stuff kids like is often quite nasty, and even though the better part of the scientific establishment now agrees that such excitements are less than benign. But setting priorities like these is hard because, while the real may rule children's lives as it rules our own, it's much more fun to imagine controlling their dreams.

Maggie Cutler is the author, at nerve.com, of the biweekly satirical column "The Secret Life of Maggie Cutler," which demonstrates in a graphic and explicit manner the confusion between politics, media and sex in American culture.

From *The Nation*, March 26, 2001, pp. 18-20. © 2001 by The Nation. Reprinted by permission.

THE FEMINIZATION OF AMERICAN CULTURE

How Modern Chemicals May Be Changing Human Biology

Leonard Sax, M.D.

In ancient times—by which I mean, before 1950—most scholars agreed that women were, as a rule, not quite equal to men. Women were charming but mildly defective. Many (male) writers viewed women as perpetual teenagers, stuck in an awkward place between childhood and adulthood. German philosopher Arthur Schopenhauer, for example, wrote that women are "childish, silly and short-sighted, really nothing more than overgrown children, all their life long. Women are a kind of intermediate stage between the child and the man."[1]

Psychologists in that bygone era devoted considerable time and energy to the question of why women couldn't outgrow their childish ways. The Freudians said it was because they were trapped in the pre-Oedipal stage, tortured by penis envy. Followers of Abraham Maslow claimed that women were fearful of self-actualization. Jungians insisted that women were born with a deficiency of imprinted archetypes.

A mature adult nowadays is someone who is comfortable talking about her inner conflicts, someone who values personal relationships above abstract goals, someone who isn't afraid to cry. In other words: a mature adult is a woman.

Back then, of course, almost all the psychologists were men.

Things are different now. Male psychologists today are so rare that Ilene Philipson—author of *On the Shoulders of Women: The Feminization of Psychotherapy*—speaks of "the vanishing male therapist" as a species soon to be extinct.[2] As the gender of the modal psychotherapist has changed from male to female, the standard of mental health has changed along with it. Today, Dr. Philipson observes, the badge of emotional maturity is no longer the ability to control or sublimate your feelings but rather the ability to *express* them. A mature adult nowadays is someone who is comfortable talking about her inner conflicts, someone who values personal relationships above abstract goals, someone who isn't afraid to cry. In other words: a mature adult is a woman.

It is now the men who are thought to be stuck halfway between childhood and adulthood, incapable of articulating their inner selves. Whereas psychologists fifty years ago amused themselves by cataloging women's (supposed) deficiencies, psychologists today devote themselves to demonstrating "the natural superiority of women."[3] Psychologists report that women are better able to understand nonverbal communication and are more expressive of emotion.[4] Quantitative personality inventories reveal that the average woman is more trusting, nurturing, and outgoing than the average man.[5] The average eighth-grade girl has a command of language and writing skills equal to that of the average eleventh-grade boy.[6]

As the influence of the new psychology permeates our culture, women have understandably begun to wonder whether men are really, well, human. "What if these women are right?" wonders one writer in an article for *Marie Claire*, a national woman's magazine. "What if it's true that some men don't possess, or at least can't express, nuanced emotions?"[7] More than a few contemporary psychologists have come to regard the male of our species as a coarsened, more violent edition of the normal, female, human. Not surprisingly, they have begun to question whether having a man in the house is desirable or even safe.

Eleven years ago, scholar Sara Ruddick expressed her concern about "the extent and variety of the psychological, sexual, and physical battery suffered by women and children of all classes and social groups… at the hands of fathers, their mothers' male lovers, or male relatives. If putative fathers are absent or perpetually disappearing and actual fathers are controlling or abusive, *who needs a father*? What mother would want to live with one or wish one on her children?"[8] Nancy Polikoff, former counsel to the Women's Legal Defense Fund, said that "it is no tragedy, either on a national scale or in an individual family, for children to be raised without fathers."[9]

The feminization of psychology manifests itself in myriad ways. Consider child discipline. Seventy years ago, doctors agreed that the best way to discipline your child was to punish the little criminal. ("Spare the rod, spoil the child.") Today, spanking is considered child abuse.[10] You're supposed to *talk* with your kid. Spanking sends all the wrong messages, we are told, and may have stupendously horrible consequences. Psychoanalyst Alice Miller confidently informed us, in her book *For Your Own Good*, that Adolf Hitler's evil can be traced to the spankings his father inflicted on him in childhood.[11]

THE NEW MEN'S MAGAZINES

It isn't only psychology that has undergone a process of feminization over the past fifty years, and it isn't only women whose attitudes have changed. Take a stroll to your neighborhood bookstore or newsstand. You'll find magazines such as *Men's Health, MH-18, Men's Fitness, Gear*, and others devoted to men's pursuit of a better body, a better self-image. None of them existed fifteen years ago. The paid circulation of *Men's Health* has risen from 250,000 to more than 1.5 million in less than ten years.[12] Many of the articles in these magazines are reminiscent of those to be found in women's magazines such as *Glamour, Mademoiselle*, and *Cosmopolitan*: "The Ten Secrets of Better Sex," "The New Diet Pills—Can They Work For You?" or "Bigger Biceps in Five Minutes a Day." (The women's magazine equivalent might be something like "slimmer thighs in five minutes a day.")

Today, the best qualification for leadership may be the ability to listen. The feminine way of seeing the world and its problems is, arguably, becoming the mainstream way.

Men didn't use to care so much about their appearance. Psychiatrists Harrison Pope and Katharine Phillips report that in American culture today, "Men of all ages, in unprecedented numbers, are preoccupied with the appearance of their bodies."[13] They document that "men's dissatisfaction with body appearance has nearly tripled in less than thirty years—from 15 percent in 1972, to 34 percent in 1985, to 43 percent in 1997."[14] Cosmetic plastic surgery, once marketed exclusively to women, has found a rapidly growing male clientele. The number of men undergoing liposuction, for instance, quadrupled between 1990 and 2000.[15]

THE FEMINIZATION OF ENTERTAINMENT AND POLITICS

This process of femininization manifests itself, though somewhat differently, when you turn on the TV or watch a movie. Throughout the mid-twentieth century, leading men were, as a rule, infallible: think of Clark Gable in *Gone With the Wind*, Cary Grant in *North by Northwest*, or Fred McMurray in *My Three Sons*. But no longer. In family comedy, the father figure has metamorphosed from the all-knowing, all-wise Robert Young of *Father Knows Best* to the occasional bumbling of Bill Cosby and the consistent stupidity of Homer Simpson. Commercially successful movies now often feature women who are physically aggressive, who dominate or at least upstage the men. This description applies to movies as diverse as *Charlie's Angels* and *Crouching Tiger, Hidden Dragon*. In today's cinema, to paraphrase Garrison Keillor, all the leading women are strong and all the leading men are good-looking.

A transformation of comparable magnitude seems to be under way in the political arena. Military command used to be considered the best qualification for leadership—as it was with Ulysses Grant, Theodore Roosevelt, Charles de Gaulle, and Dwight Eisenhower, to name only a few. Today, the best qualification for leadership may be the ability to listen. The feminine way of seeing the world and its problems is, arguably, becoming the mainstream way.

In 1992, Bill Clinton ran against George Bush *père* for the presidency. Clinton was an acknowledged draft evader. Bush, the incumbent, was a World War II hero who had just led the United States to military success in Operation Desert Storm. Clinton won. In 1996, Clinton was challenged by Bob Dole, another decorated World War II veteran. Once again, the man who had evaded military service defeated the combat veteran. In 2000, Gov. George W. Bush and Sen. John McCain competed for the Republican presidential nomination. McCain was a genuine war hero whose courageous actions as a prisoner of war in Vietnam had won him well-deserved honors and praise. Bush, on the other hand, was alleged to have used family influence to obtain a position in the Texas National Guard, in order to avoid service in Vietnam. Once again, the man who had never experienced combat defeated the military veteran. Moral of the story: It's all very well to be a war hero, but in our modern, feminized society, being a war hero won't get you elected president. Conversely, being a draft dodger isn't as bad as it used to be.

A number of authors have recognized the increasing feminization of American society. With few exceptions, most of those acknowledging this process have welcomed it.[16] As Elinor Lenz and Barbara Myerhoff wrote in their 1985 book *The Feminization of America*, "The feminizing influence is moving [American society] away from many archaic ways of thinking and behaving, toward the promise of a saner and more humanistic future.... Feminine culture, with its commitment to creating and protecting life, is our best and brightest hope for overcoming the destructive, life-threatening forces of the nuclear age."[17]

> *The question is, what's causing this shift? Some might argue that the changes I've described are simply a matter of better education, progressive laws, and two generations of consciousness-raising.*

I think we can all agree on one point: there have been fundamental changes in American culture over the past fifty years, changes that indicate a shift from a male-dominated culture to a feminine or at least an androgynous society. The question is, what's causing this shift? Some might argue that the changes I've described are simply a matter of better education, progressive laws, and two generations of consciousness-raising: an evolution from a patriarchal Dark Ages to a unisex, or feminine, Enlightenment. I'm willing to consider that hypothesis. But before we accept that conclusion, we should ask whether there are any other possibilities.

FEMINIZED WILDLIFE

We have to make a big jump now, a journey that will begin at the Columbia River in Washington, near the Oregon border. James Nagler, assistant professor of zoology at the University of Idaho, recently noticed something funny about the salmon he observed in the Columbia. Almost all of them were—or appeared to be—female. But when he caught a few and analyzed their DNA, he found that many of the "female" fish actually were male: their chromosomes were XY instead of XX.[18]

> *Many of these chemicals, it turns out, mimic the action of female sex hormones called estrogens.*

Nagler's findings echo a recent report from England, where government scientists have found some pretty bizarre fish. In two polluted rivers, half the fish are female,

and the other half are... something else. Not female but not male either. The English scientists call these bizarre fish "intersex": their gonads are not quite ovaries, not quite testicles, but some weird thing in between, making neither eggs nor sperm. In both rivers, the intersex fish are found downstream of sites where treated sewage is discharged into the river. Upstream from the sewer effluent, the incidence of intersex is dramatically lower. The relationship between the concentration of sewer effluent and the incidence of intersex is so close that "the proportion of intersex fish in any sample of fish could perhaps be predicted, using a linear equation, from the average concentration of effluent constituents in the river."[19]

It's something in the water. Something in the water is causing feminization of male fish.

And it's not just fish. In Lake Apopka, in central Florida, Dr. Louis Guillette and his associates have found male alligators with abnormally small penises; in the blood of these alligators, female hormone levels are abnormally high and male hormone levels abnormally low.[20] Male Florida panthers have become infertile; the levels of male sex hormones in their blood are much lower (and the levels of female hormones higher) than those found in panthers in less-polluted environments.[21]

What's going on?

Our modern society generates a number of chemicals that never existed before about fifty years ago. Many of these chemicals, it turns out, mimic the action of female sex hormones called estrogens. Plastics—including a plasticizer called phthalate, used in making flexible plastic for bottles of Coke, Pepsi, Sprite, Evian water, and so forth—are known to have estrogenic effects.[22] Many commonly used pesticides have estrogenlike actions on human cells.[23] Estrogenic chemicals ooze out of the synthetic lacquer that lines the inside of soup cans.[24] These chemicals and others find their way into sewage and enter the rivers and lakes. Hence the effects on fish, alligators, and other wildlife.

EFFECTS ON HUMANS?

Modern chemicals may have a feminizing effect on wildlife. That's certainly cause for concern in its own right. But is there any evidence that a similar process of feminization is occurring in humans?

Answer: there may be. Just like the Florida panther, human males are experiencing a rapid decline in fertility and sperm count. The sperm count of the average American or European man has declined continuously over the past four decades, to the point where today it is less than 50 percent of what it was forty years ago.[25] This downward trend is seen only in industrialized regions of North America and western Europe. Lower sperm counts are being reported in urban Denmark but not in rural Finland, for example.[26] Of course, that's precisely the pattern one would expect, if the lower sperm counts are an effect of "modern" materials such as plastic water bottles.

Male infertility, one result of that lower count, is now the single most common cause of infertility in our species.[27] The rate of infertility itself has quadrupled in the past forty years, from 4 percent in 1965 to 10 percent in 1982 to at least 16 percent today.[28]

WHAT ABOUT GIRLS?

So far we've talked mainly about the effect of environmental estrogens on males. What about girls and women? What physiological effects might excess environmental estrogens have on them? Giving estrogens to young girls would, in theory, trigger the onset of puberty at an earlier than expected age. In fact, in the past few years doctors have noticed that girls *are* beginning puberty earlier than ever before. Just as the environmental-estrogen hypothesis would predict, this phenomenon is seen only in girls, not in boys. Dr. Marcia Herman-Giddens, studying over seventeen thousand American girls, found that this trend to earlier puberty is widespread. "Girls across the United States are developing pubertal characteristics at younger ages than currently used norms," she concluded.[29]

Rather than labeling all these pubescent eight-year-olds as "abnormal," Dr. Paul Kaplowitz and his associates recently recommended that the earliest age for "normal" onset of puberty simply be redefined as age seven in Caucasian girls and age six in African-American girls.[30] Dr. Kaplowitz is trying, valiantly, to define this problem out of existence. If you insist that normal puberty begins at age six or age seven, then all these eight-year-old girls with well-filled bras suddenly become "normal."

But saying so doesn't make it so. Last year, doctors in Puerto Rico reported that most young girls with premature breast development have toxic levels of phthalates in their blood; those phthalates appear to have seeped out of plastic food and beverage containers. The authors noted that Puerto Rico is a warm island. Plastic containers that become warm are more likely to ooze phthalate molecules into the food or beverages they contain.[31] These authors, led by Dr. Ivelisse Colón, reported their findings in *Environmental Health Perspectives*, the official journal of the National Institute of Environmental Health Sciences (a branch of the National Institutes of Health). On the cover of the issue in which the report appeared, the editors chose to feature the picture of a young woman drinking water from a plastic bottle.

Premature puberty in girls has become so widespread that it has begun to attract the attention of major media. This topic made the cover of *Time* magazine on October 30, 2000. Unfortunately, few of these high-profile articles show any understanding of the possible role of environmental estrogens. The *Time* article barely mentioned the *Environmental Health Perspectives* study, nor did it link the phenomenon of early puberty in girls with declining

sperm counts, intersex fish, or tiny penises in alligators. Instead, it featured a picture of a short boy staring at a taller girl's breasts.

What effect might extra estrogen have on adult women? Many scientists have expressed concern that exposure to excessive environmental estrogens may lead to breast cancer. The rate of breast cancer has risen dramatically over the past fifty years. Today, one in every nine American women can expect to develop breast cancer at some point in her life. But this increase is seen only in industrialized countries,[32] where plastics and other products of modern chemistry are widely used. Women born in Third World countries are at substantially lower risk. When they move from a Third World country to the United States, their risk soon increases to that seen in other women living here, clearly demonstrating that the increased risk is an environmental, not a genetic, factor.[33]

CONNECTION?

At this point, you may feel that you've been reading two completely disconnected essays: one about the feminization of American culture, and the second about the effects of environmental estrogens. Could there be any connection between the two?

If human physiology and endocrinology are being affected by environmental estrogens then there is no reason in principle why human psychology and sexulaity should be exempt.

There may be. If human physiology and endocrinology are being affected by environmental estrogens—as suggested by lower sperm counts, increasing infertility, earlier onset of puberty in girls, and rising rates of breast cancer—then there is no reason in principle why human psychology and sexuality should be exempt. If we accept the possibility that environmental estrogens are affecting human physiology and endocrinology, then we must also consider the possibility that the feminization of American culture may, conceivably, reflect the influence of environmental estrogens.

The phenomena we have considered show a remarkable synchrony. Many of the cultural trends discussed in the first half of the article began to take shape in the 1950s and '60s, just as plastics and other modern chemicals began to be widely introduced into American life. There are, of course, many difficulties in attempting to measure any correlation between an endocrine variable—such as a decline in sperm counts—and a cultural variable, such as cultural feminization. One of many problems is that no single quantitative variable accurately and reliably measures the degree to which a culture is becoming feminized. However, we can get some feeling for the synchrony of the cultural process with the endocrine process by considering the correlation of the decline in sperm counts with the decline in male college enrollment.

We've already mentioned how sperm counts have declined steadily and continuously in industrialized areas of North America and western Europe since about 1950. Let's use that decline as our endocrine variable. As the cultural variable, let's look at college graduation rates. Since 1950, the proportion of men among college graduates has been steadily declining. In 1950, 70 percent of college graduates were men; today, that number is about 43 percent and falling. Judy Mohraz, president of Goucher College, warned not long ago that if present trends continue, "the last man to graduate from college will receive his baccalaureate in the year 2067.... Daughters not only have leveled the playing field in most college classrooms, but they are exceeding their brothers in school success across the board."[34]

Plot these two phenomena on the same graph. Use no statistical tricks, no manipulation of the data—simply use best-fit trend lines, plotted on linear coordinates—and the two lines practically coincide. The graph of declining sperm density perfectly parallels the decline in male college graduation rates.

Of course, the correlation between these phenomena—one endocrine, one cultural—doesn't prove that they must derive from the same underlying source. But such a strong correlation certainly provides some evidence that the endocrine phenomenon of declining sperm counts may derive from the same source as the cultural phenomenon of declining male college enrollment (as a percentage of total enrollment).

If this hypothesis is ultimately shown to be at least partly correct, it would not be the first time that items of daily household life contributed to the transformation of a mighty civilization.

THE DECLINE AND FALL OF THE MALE AMERICAN EMPIRE?

I have suggested that the feminization of American culture and endocrine phenomena such as declining sperm counts are both manifestations of the effects of environmental estrogens. To the best of my knowledge, no other author has yet made such a suggestion. If this hypothesis is ultimately shown to be at least partly correct, it would not be the first time that items of daily household life con-

tributed to the transformation of a mighty civilization. A number of scientists, most notably toxicologist Jerome Nriagu, have suggested that one factor leading to the decline and fall of the Roman Empire was the lead glaze popular among the Roman aristocracy after about A.D. 100.[35] Bowls and dishes were glazed with lead, which was also widely used in household plumbing. (Our word *plumbing* comes from the Latin *plumbum*, which means lead.) The neurological symptoms of lead toxicity—mania, difficulty concentrating, and mood swings—were not recognized as manifestations of poisoning. No Roman scientist conducted the necessary controlled experiment: a comparison of families that used lead-glazed pottery with families that did not. The scientific worldview necessary for such an experiment did not exist at the time. It is thought-provoking to consider that something as insignificant as pottery glazing may have brought down the Roman Empire.

Could anything of comparable magnitude be happening right now, in our own culture? Testing the hypothesis I have proposed will be difficult. It is probably not possible to randomize humans to a "modern, plasticized" environment versus a "primitive, no-plastics, no-cans, no-pesticide" environment—and even it were possible, it would not be ethical to do so. (It should be noted, however, that one careful study has already been published demonstrating that men who consumed only organic produce had higher sperm counts than men eating regular, pesticide-treated produce.[36]) Measures of the degree to which a culture is "feminized" would be controversial, and only seldom would such measures be objectively quantifiable.

Nevertheless, the world around us is changing in ways that have never occurred in the history of our species. It is possible that some of these changes in our culture may reflect the influence of environmental estrogens, an influence whose effects are subtle and incremental. To the extent that human dignity means being in control of one's destiny, we should explore the possibility that our minds and bodies are being affected by environmental estrogens in ways that we do not, as yet, fully understand.

NOTES

1. "Dass sie selbst kindisch, läppisch und kurzsichtig, mit einem Worte: zeitlebens grosse Kinder sind—eine Art Mittelstufe zwischen dem Kinde und dem Manne." Arthur Schopenhauer, *Parerga und Paralipomena*, §364 (1851).

2. Ilene Philipson, *On the Shoulders of Women: The Feminization of Psychotherapy* (New York: Guilford Press, 1993), 145.

3. *The Natural Superiority of Women* is of course the title of one of Ashley Montagu's most famous books, initially published in 1953. Montagu issued a final revised edition in 1998, in which he eagerly documented the published research that supported what had been mere conjecture forty years before.

4. Judith Hall, *Nonverbal Sex Differences: Accuracy of Communication and Expressive Style* (Baltimore: Johns Hopkins Univ. Press, 1990). See also: Ann Kring and Albert Gordon, "Sex Differences in Emotion: Expression, Experience, and Physiology," *Journal of Personality and Social Psychology* 74 (1998): 686–703.

5. Alan Feingold, "Gender Differences in Personality: a Meta-Analysis," *Psychological Bulletin* 116, no. 3 (1994): 429–556.

6. U.S. Department of Education, *Educational Equity for Girls and Women* (Washington: U.S. Government Printing Office, 2000), 4. The report can be read online at nces.ed.gov/spider/webspider/2000030.html.

7. Marilyn Berlin Snell, "Wisdom of the Ages," *Marie Claire*, September 1999, 123.

8. Ruddick 1990, cited in Philipson, *On the Shoulders of Women*, 142–43. Emphasis added.

9. Quoted in Cathy Young, *Ceasefire!* (New York: Free Press, 1999), 60.

10. According to both the American Academy of Pediatrics and the American Academy of Family Physicians, there is no situation in which spanking is appropriate. Spanking is always child abuse. You can read the AAFP's statement at www.aafp.org/afp/990315ap/1577.html and the AAP's position at www.aap.org/advocacy/archives/aprspr2.html.

11. Alice Miller, *For Your Own Good: Hidden Cruelty in Child-Rearing and the Roots of Violence* (Noonday Press, 1990).

12. Harrison Pope, Katharine Phillips, and Roberto Olivardia, *The Adonis Complex: The Secret Crisis of Male Body Obsession* (New York: Free Press, 2000), 56.

13. Pope, Phillips, and Olivardia, *The Adonis Complex*, xiii.

14. Pope, Phillips, and Olivardia, *The Adonis Complex*, 27.

15. Pope, Phillips, and Olivardia, *The Adonis Complex*, 31.

16. One notable exception is Rich Zubaty's misogynistic diatribe, *Surviving the Feminization of America* (Tinley Park, Ill.: Panther Press, 1993).

17. Elinor Lenz and Barbara Myerhoff, *The Feminization of America: How Women's Values Are Changing Our Public and Private Lives* (New York: St. Martin's Press, 1985), 2.

18. James Nagler et al., "High Incidence of a Male-Specific Genetic Marker in Phenotypic Female Chinook Salmon From the Columbia River," *Environmental Health Perspectives* 109 (2001): 67–69.

19. Susan Jobling et al., "Widespread Sexual Disruption in Wild Fish," *Environmental Science and Technology* 32, no. 17 (1998): 2498–2506.

20. Louis Guillette et al., "Developmental Abnormalities of the Gonad and Abnormal Sex Hormone Concentrations in Juvenile Alligators from Contaminated and Control Lakes in Florida," *Environmental Health Perspectives* 102 (1994): 680–88.

21. C.F. Facemire et al., "Reproductive Impairment in the Florida Panther," *Environmental Health Perspectives* 103, supplement 4 (1995): 79–86.

22. Susan Jobling et al., "A Variety of Environmentally Persistent Chemicals, Including Some Phthalate Plasticizers, Are Weakly Estrogenic," *Environmental Health Perspectives* 103 (1995): 582–87.

23. Ana Soto, Kerrie Chung, and Carlos Sonnenschein, "The Pesticides Endosulfan, Toxaphene, and Dieldrin Have Estrogenic Effects on Human Estrogen-Sensitive Cells," *Environmental Health Perspectives* 102, no. 4 (1994): 380–83.

24. José Brotons et al., "Xenoestrogens Released From Lacquer Coatings in Food Cans," *Environmental Health Perspectives* 103, no. 6 (1995): 608–12.

25. Shanna Swan, Eric Elkin, and Laura Fenster, "The Question of Declining Sperm Density Revisited: Analysis of 101 Studies Published 1934–1996," *Environmental Health Perspectives* 108 (2000): 961–66.

26. Tina Jensen et al., "Semen Quality Among Danish and Finnish Men Attempting to Conceive," *European Journal of Endocrinology* 142 (2000): 47–52.

27. D. Stewart Irvine, "Epidemiology and Aetiology of Male Infertility," *Human Reproduction* 13 (1998): 33–44.

28. Schmidt, Münster, and Helm (*British Journal of Obstetrics and Gynaecology* 102 (December 1995): 978–84, found that 26.2 percent of couples attempting to have a child have experienced infertility. Most authorities regard this figure as too high, however. The rule of thumb currently popular among infertility specialists is "one couple in six" (i.e., a rate of 16.6 percent).

29. Marcia Herman-Giddens et al., "Secondary Sexual Characteristics and Menses in Young Girls Seen in Office Practice," *Pediatrics* 99, no. 4 (1997): 505–12.

30. Paul Kaplowitz et al., "Re-examination of the Age Limit for Defining When Puberty Is Precocious in Girls in the United States: Implications for Evaluation and Treatment," *Pediatrics* 104, no. 4 (1999): 936–41.

31. Ivelisse Colón et al., "Identification of Phthalate Esters in the Serum of Young Puerto Rican Girls with Premature Breast Development," *Environmental Health Perspectives* 108, no. 9 (2000): 895–900.

32. Pisani, Parkin, and Feraly, "Estimates of the Worldwide Mortality From Eighteen Major Cancers in 1985," *International Journal of Cancer* 55, no. 6 (1993): 891–903.

33. J.L. Standford et al., "Breast Cancer Incidence in Asian Migrants to the United States and Their Descendants," *Epidemiology* 6, no. 2 (1995): 181–83.

34. Judy Mohraz, "Missing Men on Campus," *Washington Post*, 16 January 2000.

35. See Jerome Nriagu's book, *Lead and Lead Poisoning in Antiquity* (Baltimore: Johns Hopkins University Press, 1983). See also Lionel and Diane Needleman, "Lead Poisoning and the Decline of the Roman Aristocracy," *Classical Views* 4, no. 1 (1985): 63–94.

36. T.K. Jensen et al., "Semen Quality Among Members of Organic Food Associations in Zealand, Denmark," *Lancet* 347 (1996): 1844.

Leonard Sax, M.D., Ph.D., is a physician and psychologist practicing in Montgomery County, Maryland.

From *The World & I*, October 2001, pp. 263-275. © 2001 by The World & I, a publication of The Washington Times Corporation. Reprinted by permission.

CROSS-CULTURAL PERSPECTIVES

The Emperor Has No Clothes, or, Do You See Individualist-Collectivist Societies?

Elizabeth Nair, PhD

This article will take a critical look at research that is conducted with the aim of drawing cross-cultural comparisons. Selected aspects of concern pertaining to the process of conceptualization and model-building, methodology, procedure of data-collection, the tools used, and the manner in which interpretations are made will be examined. The title draws attention in a rhetorical question to the paradigm of individualist and collectivist societies that has been flogged in various ways for a quarter of a century. The scope of this article will extend beyond this paradigm to various aspects of cross-country and ethnic studies, and the global platform.

Large scale cross-country studies

Large-scale cross-country studies using the same questionnaire tend to convey a false illusion of security in drawing conclusions based on a large total sample size. There are several problems often associated with such studies, three of which are highlighted.

Single strata of society as sample

Several studies use only one strata of the society, for example, students/teachers/IBM employees. Hofstede (1998) ably defended the need to provide only for equivalent matched samples in comparing groups across countries. There is, however, an obvious problem in using such cross-national studies to infer the prevailing characteristics of any single country that participated in the study. Each of these selected groups have peculiarities such as educational level and type of education and training, which is specific in nature, and which is not generally true for the rest of the population in their countries of origin. This narrow band of sample selection means that there should not be generalization to speak of the culture of the rest of the country. This sin is committed, many times over, when the original study is cited in other articles.

Small intra-country sample size

The total sample size may be impressively large, for example, 116,000 IBM employees from 40 countries in the original study (Hofstede, 1980). Singapore was one such country. When the intra-country sample size is examined, there may be little justification to extrapolate further. A case in point is a total sample size of 58 for the Singapore IBM sample, consisting of 53 men and 5 women. Yet, many ensuing learned journal articles confidently cite the relative positioning of Singapore society with regard to various cultural dimensions such as Masculinity-Femininity, Power Distance, Uncertainty Avoidance and Individualism-Collectivism on the basis of this deficient sample.

Forcing square peg conceptualizations

There would appear to be a clear case of entrapment in some lines of enquiry that persist in spite of clear evidence that calls for a final burial rather than a phoenix-like resurrection. One example is research looking for similarities or a common theme in Chinese values across different countries. Bond (1996) very correctly drew the conclusion that the study of values endorsed by ethnic Chinese in different countries has reflected more divergences than similarities. He found little statistical support to reliably group ethnic Chinese from Hong Kong. Singapore and Taiwan together as sharing distinctive Chinese values compared to other countries.

The Chinese culture studies could be better translated to an acknowledgment and celebration of the diversity found amongst ethnic Chinese in various parts of the globe, such as has been found in epidemiological studies of disease prevalence of ethnic Indians living in different countries. In the latter case, diet and lifestyle are held accountable. In the study of 'values', the diversity would best be explained by the differences in history, geography and sociopolitical environment as well as diet and lifestyle.

OB markers in international psychology research

The advances in information technology and instantaneous global communication via the Internet have meant that physical geographical boundaries no longer exist. Computerized data-collection will enable running simultaneous experiments across latitudes and longitudes if so desired. Are there OB (out-of-bound) markers that need to be respected in international psychology research, or should 'freedom' prevail over all other considerations? In the sports arena, there are always rules and regulations that one is obliged to follow. National psychology societies have their ethical codes and regulations for professional practice. There is no such equivalent for international psychology research.

I shall in the following paragraphs make out a case for why there is a need to establish such a code of professional conduct for international psychology research, by highlighting specific areas of concern.

Negative ethnic attributions

In studying differences across ethnic groups, there must be heightened sensitivity in making negative attributions purely on the basis of ethnicity, and thereby committing the fundamental attribution error (Nair, in press). The solution lies in being thorough in looking for explanations of observed differences, and not generalizing on the basis of simple correlations. Intelligence testing and drawing inferences and racial aspersions on the basis of such measures should have served as a learning experience. International psychology should not contribute to history repeating itself yet again, this time by associating ethnicity with various denigrated personality attributes such as dispositional anger or hostility.

While knowledge is best served by not suppressing negative information, professionalism demands thoroughness in the scientific enquiry.

Constructing conceptual frameworks

In studying the culture of a country, taking a leaf from anthropology, structural and conceptual frames of reference should be based on detailed work done within a country. For greater accuracy, psychologists within the country should do this initial work. Their advantage would be familiarity with the culture, language and nuances of meaning in the communication during data-collection. Hofstede (1998) had correctly drawn attention to the fact that both the key players involved in the study of cross-country values were of Anglo-Saxon origin, and this may have affected the development of the structural framework for comparison.

It is argued here that inter-country comparisons can only validly be inferred commending with this initial mapping of country-based conceptual frameworks. Similarities or differences between countries vis-à-vis these structural conceptual frameworks can then be examined.

Changing international norms for excellence in research

The continuing sin of resorting to the inappropriate use of undergraduate psychology students as research participants in social and cross-cultural research should be robustly challenged. The soundness of the study and the boundaries of its generalization should be the priority in place of expediency and availability of a ready subject pool. To bring about such a change would require a shared norm amongst peer-reviewers for journal publications. There is a need to target journal editors as a group in order to change this norm on an international platform.

One intervention would be to organize workshops with the specific objective of changing the international norms for publication in psychology journals of repute, and working towards the genesis of a code of acceptable practices in cross-cultural research. Such workshops would need to be repeated periodically so that new journal editors continue to be invited to participate. To encourage attendance, sponsorship could be sought, and the invitation to attend these should be seen as prestigious and important within the discipline. APA as a world leader in psychology is well positioned to initiate this norm changing activity for global psychology.

Avoiding tunnel vision

As one becomes a specialist, the research and reading tends to be circumscribed more and more within a very narrow band of research pursuits. This can lead to insularity and tunnel vision within sub-specialties of the discipline. The issue is applicable to all branches of the discipline, and a problem faced by psychologists everywhere.

The value of large international congresses like the International Congress of Psychology and the International Congress of Applied Psychology is the cross-fertilization of ideas theoretically possible with co-location of different specialties at the same congress. One possible solution would be to make it a Continuing Education requirement that there is attendance at a specified minimum number of cross-divisional papers/workshops—for the purpose of maintaining a broader perspective in psychology. For professional associations and academic staff that do not require certification, there could be provision for making the certification available as an additional credit. As forced compliance is unfailingly repulsive, this suggestion is offered to generate dialogue, which may lead to a generally acceptable modus operandi for the health of the discipline.

Conclusion

The scope of international psychology by definition would cover all the countries in the world, developed and developing. The latter are the majority world. To stimulate and nurture the growth of the discipline, colleagues in the developing world can be invited to present the issues that psychology can help with in their countries. There can be research initiatives, perhaps collaboratively, that can address these issues. This requires dialogue to establish research and training priorities, and can be set as an agenda to truly harness psychology theory, research and skills where it can be of help—psychology beyond national boundaries, on a global platform.

References

Bond, M. H. (1996). Chinese values. In M. H. Bond (Ed.) The handbook of Chinese psychology. Hong Kong: Oxford University Press.

Hofstede, G. (1980). Culture's consequences: International differences in work-related values. Newbury Park, CA: Sage.

Hofstede, G. (198). A case for comparing apples with oranges. In M. Sasaki (Ed.) Values and attitudes across nations and time (pp. 16–31). Leiden, Netherlands: Brill.

Nair, E. (in press). Dichotomous issues in psychology: Intransigency or developmental phase? Applied Psychology: An International Review.

Elizabeth Nair, PhD—National University of Singapore, Singapore

From *International Psychology Reporter*, Fall/Winter 2001, pp. 18-19. © 2001 by the American Psychological Association. Reprinted by permission.

DISARMING THE RAGE

Across the country, thousands of students stay home from school each day, terrified of humiliation or worse at the hands of bullies. In the wake of school shootings—most recently in California and Pennsylvania—parents, teachers and lawmakers are demanding quick action

Richard Jerome

In the rigid social system of Bethel Regional High School in Bethel, a remote town in the tundra of southwest Alaska, Evan Ramsey was an outcast, a status earned by his slight frame, shy manner, poor grades and broken family. "Everybody had given me a nickname: Screech, the nerdy character on *Saved by the Bell*," he recalls. "I got stuff thrown at me, I got spit on, I got beat up. Sometimes I fought back, but I wasn't that good at fighting." Taunted throughout his years in school, he reported the incidents to his teachers, and at first his tormentors were punished. "After a while [the principal] told me to just start ignoring everybody. But then you can't take it anymore."

On the morning of Feb. 19, 1997, Ramsey, then 16, went to school with a 12-gauge shotgun, walked to a crowded common area and opened fire. As schoolmates fled screaming, he roamed the halls shooting randomly—mostly into the air. Ramsey would finally surrender to police, but not before killing basketball star Josh Palacios, 16, with a blast to the stomach, and principal Ron Ed-

wards, 50, who was shot in the back. Tried as an adult for murder, Ramsey was sentenced to 210 years in prison after a jury rejected a defense contention that he had been attempting "suicide by cop," hoping to be gunned down but not intending to kill anyone. Still, Ramsey now admits in his cell at Spring Creek Correctional Center in Seward, Alaska, "I felt a sense of power with a gun. It was the only way to get rid of the anger."

Unfortunately Ramsey is not alone. Children all over the country are feeling fear, hopelessness and rage, emotions that turn some of them into bullies and others into their victims. Some say that is how it has always been and always will be—that bullying, like other adolescent ills, is something to be endured and to grow out of. But that view is changing. At a time when many parents are afraid to send their children to school, the wake-up call sounded by the 13 killings and 2 suicides at Columbine High School in Colorado two years ago still reverberates. It is now clear that Columbine shooters Dylan Klebold and

Eric Harris felt bullied and alienated, and in their minds it was payback time.

In recent months there have been two other horrifying shooting incidents resulting, at least in part, from bullying. On March 5, 15-year-old Charles "Andy" Williams brought a .22-cal. pistol to Santana High School in Santee, Calif., and shot 15 students and adults, killing 2. He was recently certified to stand trial for murder as an adult. His apparent motive? Lethal revenge for the torment he had known at the hands of local kids. "We abused him pretty much, I mean verbally," concedes one of them. "I called him a skinny faggot one time."

Two days after the Williams shooting, Elizabeth Bush, 14, an eighth grader from Williamsport, Pa., who said she was often called "idiot, stupid, fat, ugly," brought her father's .22-cal. pistol to school and shot 13-year-old Kimberly Marchese, wounding her in the shoulder. Kimberly, one of her few friends, had earned Elizabeth's ire by allegedly turning on her and joining in with the taunters. Bush admitted her guilt and offered apologies. A ward of the court until after she turns 21, she is now in a juvenile psychiatric facility. Kimberly, meanwhile, still has bullet fragments in her shoulder and is undergoing physical therapy.

As school enrollment rises and youths cope with the mounting pressures of today's competitive and status-conscious culture, the numbers of bullied children have grown as rapidly as the consequences. According to the National Education Association, 160,000 children skip school each day because of intimidation by their peers. The U.S. Department of Education reports that 77 percent of middle and high school students in small midwestern towns have been bullied. And a National Institutes of Health study newly released in the *Journal of the American Medical Association* reveals that almost a third of 6th to 10th graders—5.7 million children nationwide—have experienced some kind of bullying. "We are talking about a significant problem," says Deborah Prothrow-Stith, professor of public health practice at Harvard, who cites emotional alienation at home as another factor in creating bullies. "A lot of kids have grief, loss, pain, and it's unresolved."

Some experts see bullying as an inevitable consequence of a culture that rewards perceived strength and dominance. "The concept of power we admire is power over someone else," says Jackson Katz, 41, whose Long Beach, Calif., consulting firm counsels schools and the military on violence prevention. "In corporate culture, in sports culture, in the media, we honor those who win at all costs. The bully is a kind of hero in our society." Perhaps not surprisingly, most bullies are male. "Our culture defines masculinity as connected to power, control and dominance," notes Katz, whose work was inspired in part by the shame he felt in high school when he once stood idly by while a bully beat up a smaller student.

As for the targets of bullying, alienation runs like a stitch through most of their lives. A study last fall by the U.S. Secret Service found that in two-thirds of the 37 school shootings since 1974, the attackers felt "persecuted, bullied, threatened, attacked or injured." In more than three-quarters of the cases, the attacker told a peer of his violent intentions. William Pollack, a clinical psychologist and author of *Real Boys' Voices,* who contributed to the Secret Service study, said that several boys from Columbine described bullying as part of the school fabric. Two admitted to mocking Klebold and Harris. "Why don't people get it that it drives you over the edge?" they told Pollack. "It isn't just Columbine. It is everywhere."

That sad fact is beginning to sink in, as the spate of disturbing incidents in recent years has set off desperate searches for answers. In response, parents have begun crusades to warn and educate other families, courts have seen drawn-out legal battles that try to determine who is ultimately responsible, and lawmakers in several states—including Texas, New York and Massachusetts—have struggled to shape anti-bullying legislation that would offer remedies ranging from early intervention and counseling to the automatic expulsion of offenders.

One of the most shocking cases of victimization by bullies took place near Atlanta on March 28, 1994. That day, 15-year-old Brian Head, a heavyset sophomore at suburban Etowah High School, walked into his economics class, pulled out his father's 9-mm handgun and pressed it to his temple. "I can't take this anymore," he said. Then he squeezed the trigger. Brian had been teased for years about his weight. "A lot of times the more popular or athletic kids would make him a target," his mother, Rita, 43, says of her only child, a sensitive boy with a gift for poetry [see box, next page]. "They would slap Brian in the back of the head or push him into a locker. It just broke him." Not a single student was disciplined in connection with his death. After his suicide, Rita, a magazine copy editor, and her husband, Bill, 47, counseled other parents and produced a video for elementary school students titled *But Names Will Never Hurt Me* about an overweight girl who suffers relentless teasing.

Georgia residents were stunned by a second child's death on Nov. 2, 1998. After stepping off a school bus, 13-year-old Josh Belluardo was fatally punched by his neighbor Jonathan Miller, 15, who had been suspended in the past for bullying and other infractions. In that tragedy's wake Georgia Gov. Roy Barnes in 1999 signed an anti-bullying law that allows schools to expel any student three times disciplined for picking on others.

On the other side of the continent, Washington Gov. Gary Locke is pressing for anti-bullying training in schools, following two high-profile cases there. Jenny Wieland of Seattle still cannot talk of her only child, Amy Ragan, shot dead at age 17 more than eight years ago, without tearing up. A soccer player and equestrian in her senior year at Marysville-Pilchuck High School, Amy was heading to the mall on the night of Nov. 20, 1992, when she stopped at a friend's apartment. There, three schoolmates had gathered by the time Trevor Oscar Turner showed up. Then 19, Turner was showing off a .38-cal. revolver, holding it to kids' heads, and when he got to Amy, the weapon went off. Turner pleaded guilty to first-degree manslaughter and served 27 months of a 41-month sentence.

"I can't help but wonder what Amy's life would be like if she was still alive," says Wieland today. "I wonder about her career and if she'd be in love or have a baby." Wieland turned her grief into action. In 1994 she helped start Mothers Against Violence in America (MAVIA), an activist group patterned after Mothers Against Drunk Driving. She left her insurance job to become the program's director and speaks annually at 50 schools. In 1998 she became the first director of SAVE (Students Against Violence Everywhere), which continues to grow, now boasting 126 student chapters nationwide that offer schools anti-harassment and conflict-resolution programs. "People ask how I can stand to tell her story over and over," she says. "If I can save just one child, it's well worth the pain."

Not long after Amy Ragan's death, another bullying scenario unfolded 50 miles away in Stanwood, Wash. Confined to a wheelchair by cerebral palsy, Calcutta-born Taya Haugstad was a fifth grader in 1993, when a boy began calling her "bitch" and "retard." The daily verbal abuse led to terrible nightmares. By middle school, according to a lawsuit Taya later filed, her tormentor—a popular athlete—got physical, pushing her wheelchair into the wall and holding it while his friends kicked the wheels. Eventually Taya was diagnosed with posttraumatic stress disorder. "Imagine that you can't run away or scream," says her psychologist Judith McCarthy. "Not only was she traumatized, she's handicapped. She felt terribly unsafe in the world." Her adoptive parents, Karrie and Ken Haugstad, 48 and 55, complained to school authorities and went to court to get a restraining order against the bully, but it was never issued. Taya sued the school district and the boy in 1999. The judge awarded her $300,000 last year, ruling that the school was negligent in its supervision, thus inflicting emotional distress. (The ruling is under appeal.) Taya, now 19 and a high school junior, hopes to study writing in college. She says she holds no grudge against her nemesis, who received undisclosed punishment from the school. "I don't think about him," she says.

But Josh Sneed may never forgive the boys he refers to as the Skaters. It was in 1996, late in his freshman year at Powell High School in Powell, Tenn., when, he says, a group of skateboarders began to terrorize him. With chains clinking and baseball bats pounding the pavement, he claims, they chased him and threatened to beat him to death. Why Josh? He was small and "a country boy," says his homemaker mother, Karen Grady, 41. "They made fun of him for that. They told him he was poor and made fun of him for that."

Then on Oct. 17, 1996, "I just snapped," her son says. As Jason Pratt, known as one of the Skaters, passed him in the cafeteria, Sneed whacked him on the head with a tray. "I figured if I got lucky and took him out, all the other non-

Lost in the Shadows

BRIAN HEAD, 15

After years of being tormented at school, this Georgia teen who loved music and video games ended his life with a gunshot. Later, his parents found this poem among his belongings.

As I walk in the light, the shadow draws me closer,
with the ambition and curiosity of a small boy
and the determination of a man.
The shadow is sanctuary, a place to escape the light.
In the light they can see me,
in the light they can see all.
Although the light is wide in its spread,
they still cannot see the pain in my face.
The pain that their eyes bring to bear when
they look upon me.
They see me as an insignificant "thing,"
Something to be traded, mangled and mocked.
But in the shadows I know they would not,
nor could not, see such a lie.
In the shadows, their evil eyes cannot stare
my soul into oblivion.
In the dark, I am free to move without their
judgmental eyes on me.
In the shadows, I can sleep without dreams of
despair and deception.
In the shadows I am home.

sense would stop." But after a few punches, Josh slipped on a scrap of food, hit his head on the floor and lost consciousness as Pratt kneed him in the head several times. Finally a football player leapt over two tables and dragged Sneed away, likely saving his life. Four titanium plates were needed to secure his shattered skull, and he was so gravely injured that he had to relearn how to walk and talk. Homeschooled, Sneed eventually earned his GED, but he hasn't regained his short-term memory. Assault charges against both him and Pratt were dismissed, but Pratt (who declined to comment) was suspended from school for 133 days.

Grady sued the county, claiming that because the school knew Josh was being terrorized but never disciplined the tormentors, they effectively sanctioned the conditions that led to the fight. Her attorney James A. H. Bell hopes the suit will have national implications. "We tried to make a statement, holding the school system accountable for its failure to protect," he says. In February Sneed and Grady were awarded $49,807 by a judge who found the county partly at fault. A tractor buff who once aspired to own a John Deere shop, Josh now lives on his grandfather's farm, passing his days with cartoons, video games and light chores. "Everybody's hollering that they need to get rid of guns, but it's not that," he says. "You need to find out what's going on in school."

Around the country, officials are attempting to do precisely that, as many states now require a safe-school plan that specifically addresses bullying. Most experts agree that metal detectors and zero-tolerance expulsions ignore the root of the problem. Counseling and fostering teamwork seem most effective, as evidenced by successful programs in the Cherry Creek, Colo., school district and DeKalb County, Ga. "We create an atmosphere of caring—it's harder to be a bully when you care about someone," says John Monferdini, head counselor at the DeKalb Alternative School, which serves 400 county students, most of whom have been expelled for bullying and violent behavior. Apart from academics, the school offers conflict-resolution courses and team-oriented outdoor activities that demand cooperation. "Yeah, I'm a bully," says Chris Jones, 15. "If I'm with friends and we see someone coming along we can jump on, we do it. It's like, you know, an adrenaline rush." But a stint in DeKalb is having a transformative effect. "When I came here, it was because we beat up a kid so badly—sticking his head in the bleachers—and the only thing I wished was that we'd had a chance to hurt him worse before we got caught. That's not the way I am now."

One wonders if intervention might have restrained the bullies who tormented Evan Ramsey. Ineligible for parole until 2066, when he'll be 86, Ramsey, now 20, spends most days working out, playing cards, reading Stephen King novels and studying for his high school diploma. He also has plenty of time to reflect on the horrible error in judgment he made. "The worst thing is to resort to violence," he says. "I'd like to get letters from kids who are getting problems like I went through. I could write back and help them." His advice: "If they're being messed with, they have to tell someone. If nothing's done, then they have to go [to] higher and higher [authority] until it stops. If they don't get help, that's when they'll lose it and maybe do something bad—really bad. And the pain of doing that never really stops."

Ron Arias in Seward, **Mary Boone** in Seattle, **Lauren Comander** in Chicago, **Joanne Fowler** in New York City, **Maureen** Harrington in Stanwood, **Ellen Mazo** in Jersey Shore, Pa., **Jamie Reno** in Santee, **Don Sider** in West Palm Beach and **Gail Cameron Wescott** in Atlanta

BULLIES 101

How can parents tell when their child is being bullied—or bullying others?

In 1993 a panel of experts in the Cherry Creek School District in Englewood, Colo., published Bully-Proofing Your School, *a manifesto designed to stop bullying at an early age. One of its coauthors, Dr. William Porter, 55, a clinical psychologist, offers the following guidelines for parents.*

• **What is a bully?**
A bully is a child who takes repeated hostile actions against another child and has more power than the individual he targets. Bullies tend to be very glib and don't accept responsibility for their behavior.

• **How do I know if my child is being bullied?**
He or she may show an unwillingness to go to school and may have bruises or damage to belongings that can't be explained. Children who are being bullied tend to keep silent about it and may become withdrawn, depressed and feel no one can help.

• **What do I do if my child is being bullied?**
Listen to your child and express confidence that the problem can be solved. Keep trying until you find someone at the school to help. Practice with your child such protective skills as avoiding the confrontation or using humor to deflate a tense moment.

• **What if my child is a bully?**
Set clear and consistent expectations of behavior, and work with the school on follow-up. Don't let the child talk his or her way out of the behavior, and find positive ways for him or her to get attention.

From *People Weekly*, June 4, 2001, pp. 54-61. © 2001 by Richard Jerome. Reprinted by permission. All rights reserved.

UNIT 10
Psychological Disorders

Unit Selections

41. **Mental Health Gets Noticed**, David Satcher
42. **Up From Depression**, Peggy Eastman
43. **The Quest for a Cure**, Mark Nichols
44. **Post-Traumatic Stress Disorder**, *Harvard Health Letter*
45. **The Schizophrenic Mind**, Sharon Begley
46. **The Secrets of Autism**, J. Madeleine Nash

Key Points to Consider

- Do you believe that everyone has the potential for developing a mental disorder? Just how widespread is mental disorder in the United States? What circumstances lead an individual to mental illness? In general, what can be done to reduce the number of cases of mental disorder or to promote better mental health in the United States?

- Why did some individuals recover from the trauma of September 11, 2001, while others remain adversely affected? What is post–traumatic stress disorder? How does it differ from everyday stress? What can we do to assist people suffering from post-traumatic stress disorder? What can you do for yourself should another major terrorist event occur?

- What is schizophrenia? What are its symptoms? Can a person with schizophrenia appear "normal" at times? What are the suspected causes of schizophrenia? What are the currently available treatments for schizophrenia?

- Do you know anyone with a mental illness? If yes, can you describe the symptoms experienced by the individual? Do the symptoms appear to be consistent with several diagnostic categories or one particular disorder? What type of dilemmas do multiple symptoms produce for psychologists and psychiatrists? How, then, can they make an accurate diagnosis?

- In addition to asking what causes autism, scientists are also questioning the large increase in the number of children diagnosed with the disorder. Describe what the article "The Secrets of Autism" has revealed about the biology and psychology of the disorder. What elements do you think contribute to the growth of this population?

 **Links: www.dushkin.com/online/**
These sites are annotated in the World Wide Web pages.

American Association of Suicidology
http://www.suicidology.org/top.htm

Anxiety Disorders
http://www.adaa.org/mediaroom/index.cfm

Ask NOAH About: Mental Health
http://www.noah-health.org/english//illness/mentalhealth/mental.html

Mental Health Net Disorders and Treatments
http://www.mentalhelp.net/

Mental Health Net: Eating Disorder Resources
http://www.mentalhelp.net/poc/center_index.php/id/46

National Women's Health Resource Center (NWHRC)
http://www.healthywomen.org

Jay and Harry were two brothers who owned a service station. They were the middle children of four. The other two children were sisters, the oldest of whom had married and moved out of the family home. The service station was once owned by their father who retired and turned it over to his sons.

Harry and Jay had a good working relationship. Harry was the "up-front" man. Taking customer orders, accepting payments, and working with parts distributors, Harry was the individual who dealt most directly with the public, delivery personnel, and other people accessing the station. Jay worked behind the scenes. Jay was the one who did the diagnostic and corrective work. Some of his friends thought Jay was a mechanical genius.

Preferring to spend time by himself, Jay had always been a little odd and a bit of a loner. His emotions had been more inappropriate and intense than other people's emotional states. Harry was the stalwart in the family. He was the acknowledged leader and decision-maker when it came to family finances.

One day Jay did not show up for work on time. When he did, he was dressed in the most garish outfit and was laughing hysterically and talking to himself. Harry at first suspected that his brother had taken some illegal drugs. However, Jay's condition persisted. Out of concern, his family took him to their physician who immediately sent Jay and his family to a psychiatrist. After several visits, the diagnosis was schizophrenia. Jay's uncle had also been schizophrenic. The family grimly left the psychiatrist's office and traveled to the local pharmacy to fill a prescription for antipsychotic medications that Jay would probably take for the rest of his life.

What caused Jay's drastic and rather sudden change in mental health? Was Jay destined to be schizophrenic because of his family tree? Did competitiveness with his brother and the feeling that he was less revered than Harry cause Jay's decent into mental disorder? How can psychiatrists and clinical psychologists make accurate diagnoses? Once a diagnosis of mental disorder is made, can the individual ever completely recover?

These and other questions are the emphasis in this unit. Mental disorder has fascinated and, on the other hand, terrified us for centuries. At various times in our history those who suffered from these disorders were persecuted as witches, tortured to drive out demons, punished as sinners, jailed as a danger to society, confined to insane asylums, or, at best, hospitalized for simply being too ill to care for themselves.

Today, some psychologists propose that the view of mental disorders as "illnesses" has outlived its usefulness. We should think of mental disorders as either biochemical disturbances or disorders of learning in which the person develops a maladaptive pattern of behavior that is then maintained by the environment. At the same time, we need to recognize that these reactions to stressors in the environment or to the inappropriate learning situations may be genetically preordained; some people may be more susceptible to disorders than others. Serious disorders are serious problems and not just for the individual who is the patient or client. The impact of mental disorder on the family (just as for Jay's family) and friends deserves our full attention, too. Diagnosis, symptoms, and the implications of the disorders are topics covered in the articles in this section. The following unit will explore further the concept of treatment of mental disorders.

The first article in this unit offers a general introduction to the concept of mental disorder. David Satcher reveals his agenda for better mental health care in the United States. Mental disorder, he concludes, is more widespread than previously thought. Only an active policy of assisting those who need help can change the status of those with mental disorders in this country.

We turn next to some specific disorders. Depression is one of the commonest forms of mental disorder. Depression in its severe form can sometimes lead to suicide. Psychologists recently have been interested in the biochemical mechanisms underlying severe depression. In "Up from Depression," the author looks at the causes, symptoms and treatments for depression. Special attention is paid to the depressed elderly, a group not well studied in psychology. Then, "The Quest for a Cure" details the symptoms of depression and provides a good discussion of the possible treatments, in particular, the revolutionary drug Prozac.

An increasingly common disorder is post-traumatic stress disorder. Some individuals were able to recover from the events of September 11, 2001; others were not. An article in *The Harvard Health Letter* explains why this is the case. It also helps the reader identify post–traumatic stress disorder from reactions to normal stress. The article would be incomplete if it did not also include advice about how to cope with either type of stress—everyday or traumatic.

The next disorder covered in this unit is the one from which Jay suffered—schizophrenia. Sharon Begley in her article "The Schizophrenic Mind" examines the causes, symptoms, and treatments for this baffling and debilitating disorder.

The final disorder described in unit 10 is autism, an intriguing and distressing disturbance of childhood, and one whose numbers are growing dramatically.

MENTAL HEALTH GETS NOTICED

The First-Ever Surgeon General's Report on Mental Health

BY DAVID SATCHER, M.D., PH.D., UNITED STATES SURGEON GENERAL

I am pleased to issue the first-ever Surgeon General's Report on Mental Health. In doing so, I am alerting the American people that mental illness is a critical public health problem that must be addressed immediately. As a society, we assign a high priority to disease prevention and health promotion; so, too, must we ensure that mental health and the prevention of mental disorders share that priority.

Mental illness is the second leading cause of disability in major market economies such as the United States, with mental disorders collectively accounting for more than 15% of all disabilities. Mental disorders—depression, schizophrenia, eating disorders, depressive (bipolar) illness, anxiety disorders, attention deficit hyperactivity disorder and Alzheimer's disease, to name a few—are as disabling and serious as cancer and heart disease in terms of premature death and lost productivity.

Few Americans are untouched by mental illness, whether it occurs within one's family or among neighbors, co-workers or members of the community. In fact, in any one year, one in five Americans—including children, adolescents, adults and the elderly—experience a mental disorder. Unfortunately, over half of those with severe mental illness do not seek treatment. This is mostly due to some very real barriers to access, foremost among them the stigma that people attach to mental illness and the lack of parity between insurance coverage for mental health services and other health care services.

Over the past 25 years, there has been a scientific revolution in the fields of mental health and mental illness that has helped remove the stigma. The brain has emerged as the central focus for studies of mental health and mental illness, with emphasis on the activities that underlie our abilities to feel, learn, remember and, when brain activity goes awry, experience mental health problems or a mental illness. We now know that not only do the workings of the brain affect behavior, emotions and memory, but that experience, emotion and behavior also affect the workings of the brain

As information about the brain accumulates, the challenge then becomes to apply this new knowledge to clinical practice.

Today, mental disorders can be correctly diagnosed and, for the most part, treated with medications or short-term

GREG GIANNINI

I'd describe myself as a regular person.... Most of the time I like taking walks around my house. Before I was living in a group home out in the country and there weren't that many stores or streets to walk on. I like walking to 7-Eleven and Mr. D's fast food.

ROSE CLARK

Sometimes I wake up so sick, but then I go to work and feel better. Being with animals makes me feel 100% better. Does that sound funny?

I love my boss. He's crazy. When he does surgery he dances, does the jitterbug. Sometimes I go into surgery with him to make sure all the animals are lying down straight and not awake. Mostly my responsibilities are taking care of the cages and general cleaning.

I've been with this program for four years. Since then I've gone back to school and gotten a job. I live in my own apartment, got two cats, and have a checking and savings account.

psychotherapy, or with a combination of approaches. The single most explicit recommendation I make in my report is to seek help if you have a mental health problem or think you have symptoms of a mental disorder. It is my firm conviction that mental health is indispensable to personal well-being and balanced living. Overall quality of life is tremendously improved when a mental disorder is diagnosed early and treated appropriately.

My report presents an in-depth look at mental health services in the U.S. and at the scientific research that supports treatment interventions for people with mental disorders. Summarized briefly below, it attempts to describe trends in the mental health field; explore mental health across the human life span; examine the organization and financing of mental health services; and recommend courses of action to further improve the quality and availability of mental health services for all Americans. The report's conclusions are based on a review of more than 3,000 research articles and other materials, including first person accounts from people who have experienced mental disorders.

A Vision for the Future

I cannot emphasize enough the principal recommendation of my report: Seek help if you think you have a mental health problem or symptoms of a mental disorder. But because stigma and substantial gaps in the accessibility to state-of-the-art mental health services keep many from seeking help, I offer the nation the following additional recommendations, which are intended to overcome some of these barriers:

- *Continue to Build the Science Base:* As scientific progress propels us into the next century, there should be a special effort to address pronounced gaps in current knowledge, including the urgent need for research relating to mental health promotion and illness prevention.
- *Overcome Stigma:* An emerging consumer and family movement has, through vigorous advocacy, sought to overcome stigma and prevent discrimination against people with mental illness. Powerful and pervasive, stigma prevents people from acknowledging their mental health problems and disclosing them to others. To improve access

to care, stigma must no longer be tolerated. Research and more effective treatments will help move this country toward care and support of the ill—and away from blame and stigma.

- *Improve Public Awareness of Effective Treatments:* Mental health treatments have improved by leaps and bounds over the past 25 years, but those treatments do no good unless people are aware they exist and seek them out. There are effective treatments for virtually every mental disorder. For more information on how to take advantage of them, call (877) MHEALTH.
- *Ensure the Supply of Mental Health Services and Providers:* Currently, there is a shortage of mental health professionals serving children and adolescents, elderly people with serious mental disorders and those who suffer from mental illness-related substance abuse. There is also a shortage of specialists with expertise in cognitive behavioral therapy and interpersonal therapy—two forms of psychotherapy that have proven effective for many types of mental health problems.
- *Ensure Delivery of State-of-the-Art Treatments:* A wide variety of effective, community-based services—carefully refined through years of research—exist for even the most severe mental illnesses, but they are not yet widely available in community settings. We need to ensure that mental health services are as universally accessible as other health services in the continuously changing health care delivery system. We must speed the transfer of new information from the research setting into the service delivery setting.
- *Tailor Treatment to Individuals, Acknowledging Age, Gender, Race and Culture:* To be optimally effective, diagnosis and treatment of mental illness must be attentive to these factors. Patients often prefer to be treated by mental health professionals who are of the same racial and ethnic background, a fact that underscores the need to train more minorities in the mental health professions.
- *Facilitate Entry into Treatment:* Access to mental health services

can be improved immediately if we enhance the abilities of primary care providers, public schools, the child welfare system and others to help people with mental health problems seek treatment. In addition, ensuring ready access to appropriate services for people with severe mental disorders promises to significantly reduce the need for involuntary care, which is sometimes required in order to prevent behavior that could be harmful to oneself or others.

- *Reduce Financial Barriers to Treatment:* Equality or parity between mental health coverage and other health coverage is an affordable and effective way to decrease the number of ill people who are not receiving proper treatment.

TONY RIVERA

When I first came to the Pastimes Cafe & Antiques I told them that it reminds me of the coffee shops in Baltimore and Maryland. They laughed and we've been friends for two years. They know my name when I walk in. I used to know all their names but I only come every few weeks now and I can't remember. They make me feel comfortable, like I'm not bothering anybody.

KATHY MOLYNEAUX

I didn't know I was depressed until after college. I just thought everyone felt the same way I did. I had problems sleeping, feeling down, overwhelmed, worried and not happy. My graduation from DePaul University in 1983 was a good day. After college, I worked successfully as a nurse for 13 years. I felt like I could relate to the patients because I had been there myself.

The U.S. system is extremely complex; it is a hybrid system that serves many people well, but often seems fragmented and inaccessible to those with the most extensive problems and fewest financial resources. Critical gaps exist between those who need services and those who receive them; only about 40% of those with severe disorders use any services at all.

Although research shows little direct evidence of problems with quality in mental health service programs, there are signs that programs could be better implemented, especially ones that serve children and people with serious impairment. While an array of quality monitoring and improvement methods have been developed, incentives to improve conditions lag behind incentives to reduce costs.

These inequities in insurance coverage for mental and physical health care have prompted 27 states to adopt legislation requiring parity, and compelled President Clinton to order the Federal Employees Health Benefits Program to provide parity for federal employees by the year 2001. Some localized attempts at creating parity so far have resulted in better mental health service access at

---

SHERYL CAUDLE

My family at first didn't understand why I was so depressed. My dad kept asking me why couldn't I be happy?... I never thought I'd be able to work again because of my illness. I've had to quit other jobs in the past, but I don't want to quit cleaning the Roxy [a local movie theater]; I want to have an apartment someday and a job in the community. Both of these things would be special to me because it would mean I've come a long way.

---

negligible cost increases for managed care organizations.

Issues relating to mental health and mental illness have been overlooked or ignored in this country too often and for too long. While we cannot change the past, I am convinced that we can shape a better future.

PATTI REID

I used to live in a house with my family, but I have a rare disorder that makes me think about the past. In 1992, I got this disorder and I couldn't drive my car anymore. I miss driving the most. My two big battles are smiling and taking my medications. Both of these are very hard.

David Satcher, M.D., Ph.D., is the 16th surgeon general of the United States. He is also Assistant Secretary for Health, advising the Secretary on public health matters and directing the Office of Public Health and Science.

Reprinted with permission from *Psychology Today*, January/February 2000, pp. 32-37. © 2000 by Sussex Publishers, Inc.

Up from depression

Wiser diagnosis, better treatment offer new hope

BY PEGGY EASTMAN

In recent visits with your mother, you notice she has lost her customary spark, her sense of humor. She has stopped going out, rarely sees her longtime pals and instead stays at home, staring dully at the TV. Even the grandkids can't cheer her up.

She's just slowing down, you tell yourself. Possibly, but there may be another reason: She may be among the growing number of Americans with serious depression, a draining condition that can ruin the quality of life and often goes unrecognized—especially in older people—by doctors or family members.

Some 19 million Americans experience persistent, or clinical, depression. Of these, 6 million are over age 65, a number that is rising sharply as the older population expands. Experts say the problem, if not brought under control, will only worsen as baby boomers age and confront life changes and losses that can cause depression.

"We're talking about an epidemic," says William E. Reichman, M.D., a psychiatrist at the University of Medicine and Dentistry of New Jersey and president of the American Association for Geriatric Psychiatry (AAGP). "There's a demographic imperative that compels us to pay attention to depression in late life."

On the bright side: In most cases, depression is highly treatable. A deeper understanding of what leads to the disorder is producing better ways to fight it, with everything from self-help measures like exercise and diet to new, more effective drugs.

Overcoming depression "can add years of productivity and happiness to someone who had given up on those aspects of life," says Nathan Billig, M.D., a geriatric psychiatrist in Washington and author of "Growing Older & Wiser" (Lexington Books, 1995).

But fighting depression takes more than the efforts of professionals. "The challenge for baby boomers who may care for an older adult is to gain an understanding of the issue, identify disorders early and help her or him get ap-propriate treatment," says Soo Borson, M.D., director of geriatric psychiatry services at the University of Washington Medical Center in Seattle.

Your Health

Ten warning signs of depression

AS A RULE of thumb, the time has come to seek help when five or more of the following symptoms occur for at least two weeks:
- feeling guilty, worthless, "empty," unloved, hopeless
- no longer enjoying things
- feeling very tired and lethargic
- feeling nervous, restless or irritable
- unable to concentrate
- crying frequently
- sleeping more or less than usual
- eating more or less than usual
- having persistent headaches, stomachaches or pain
- having thoughts of death, especially suicide

NOT JUST THE BLUES

It's normal to be sad after major life events like illness, divorce, losing a job, moving far from home and the death of a spouse or close friend. Most people begin to bounce back after a few days or weeks.

But clinical depression is more than the blues or a reaction to grief. Untreated, the feelings of sorrow, hopelessness and anxiety can last for months or years, leading to impaired functioning, isolation, physical ailments and even suicide.

"[Depression] is a medical disorder, like hypertension or diabetes," says Billig. "It can and must be treated when it interferes with otherwise healthy functioning."

The condition, he stresses, is not a part of normal aging.

Looking for help?...

A FEW OF THE NUMEROUS organizations offering information on depression:

- American Association for Geriatric Psychiatry, 7910 Woodmont Ave., Suite 1050, Bethesda, MD 20814-3004, **www.aagpgpa.org**.
- National Alliance for the Mentally Ill, (800) 950-6264, **www.nami.org**.
- National Alliance for Research on Schizophrenia and Depression, (800) 829-8289, **www.narsad.org**.
- National Institute of Mental Health, (800) 421-4211, **www.nimh.nih.gov**.
- National Mental Health Association, (800) 969-6642, **www.nmha.org**.
- National Depressive and Manic-Depressive Association, (800) 826-3632, **www.ndmda.org**.

But some 90 percent of depressed older adults don't get relief, says the National Mental Health Association, because they are reluctant to seek help or because their doctors don't recognize their illness.

While younger people may be comfortable discussing their troubles, their elders may be more reticent, notes Billig. Depressed older people may hide their true feelings by focusing instead on physical ills or using alcohol.

Thus, experts say, adult children need to know the signs of depression. Asking the older person certain questions—How are you sleeping? Are you seeing your friends?—can yield some clues, too. [See "Ten warning signs."]

If depression is suspected, it's important to help the person recognize the symptoms and seek help from a doctor or psychotherapist (or if the individual is in a nursing home, to ask for a consultation with a mental health professional).

What if the person resists such overtures? One answer is to enlist the persuasive powers of a trusted friend or member of the clergy to encourage him or her to get assistance.

Allan Anderson, M. D. medical director for geriatric psychiatry at Shore Behavioral Health Services in Cambridge, Md., says he tells reluctant patients: "Look, I'm wearing eyeglasses. It's a pain, but I choose to wear them so I can see and not suffer. Depression is an illness. You can get treatment, or you can suffer. I don't want you to suffer."

'MISSING' THE DIAGNOSIS

Primary care doctors generally are not trained in psychiatry and sometimes "miss" depression in their older patients. One study of suicides showed that 20 percent of older adults had seen their doctor about other health conditions on the same day they took their lives, 40 percent had seen their doctor within a week, and 70 percent within one month.

At the least, says Ira R. Katz, M.D., director of geriatric psychiatry at the University of Pennsylvania Medical Center, "the doctor has to ask, 'What have you enjoyed doing lately?' If the answer is 'nothing,' that's very important. The trick is to ask."

... paying for treatment

WHILE DEPRESSION and other mental health problems are gradually being accorded more importance as a public health problem, insurance coverage for treatment is, at best, mixed. Many health plans cover all or some care, but prescription drug coverage varies widely.

Traditional Medicare pays 50 percent of most outpatient mental health care but does not pay for prescription drugs. Coverage in Medicare HMOs varies from plan to plan.

DEPRESSION TRIGGERS

Clinical depression often has no obvious cause but emerges gradually, imperceptibly.

"When I look back on my life and I'm honest with myself, I think I've had this problem all my life," says Pittsburgh resident Marian Schwartz, 85, who recently waged a successful battle against depression.

She went through some hard times that may have set the stage for her condition. She had cared for her invalid husband for about 10 years, and she had had heart surgery. Her son died at age 38, and her daughter struggled with depression.

Over time, Schwartz began having sleep problems and wide appetite swings; she stopped driving and no longer devoured newspapers and books as she once had. She felt lethargic, sad.

Sorrow over misfortune is normal. But it can be compounded in late life, a time when people may become more isolated as they lose spouses and old friends. Without social and emotional support, AAGP's Reichman says, depression can take hold.

Other risk factors:

- family history of the disorder;
- imbalance of brain chemicals that govern mood;
- chronic pain and illnesses like cancer, heart disease and Parkinson's disease;

- dementia (more than half of people with Alzheimer's disease are depressed);
- certain medications, such as beta blockers for heart problems;
- seasonal changes;
- hormonal changes (such as occur at menstruation and menopause); and
- stress.

More than twice as many women experience depression than men. Just why is unclear, but the National Mental Health Association speculates that hormonal changes and the stress of family responsibilities may explain the high rate among women.

Marian Schwartz knows about that kind of pressure. "I was the 'Let Marian do it' person," says Schwartz, a middle child in a family of six children. "All my life I have been the family caregiver."

With counseling, she came to a more realistic understanding of her own needs and the limits of what she can do for others.

DIGGING OUT

Minor depression usually lifts on its own. But it's likely to need active measures to banish a lingering case. As a first step, experts say, get adequate sleep, eat a nourishing diet and spend more time with friends and family.

Exercise is a powerful antidote. A recent Duke University study of 156 people age 50 or older showed that exercise was about as effective as medicine in relieving depression.

In more persistent cases, psychological counseling, or "talk therapy," can reveal underlying causes of depression and help the patient reverse negative attitudes and find better ways of handling problems.

Antidepressant drugs can help, too. Many are available and more are in the pipeline. Selective serotonin reuptake inhibitors (SSRIs), a class that includes Prozac and Zoloft, boost serotonin, a mood-enhancing chemical in the brain.

SSRIs tend to have fewer side effects than the older antidepressants—tricyclics and monoamine oxidase (MAO) inhibitors—and are better tolerated, says Bruce G. Pollack, M.D., director of the Geriatric Psychopharmacology Program at the University of Pittsburgh School of Medicine.

Another new drug is venlafaxine (Effexor), which acts on at least two mood-regulating brain chemicals.

Just as adult children can be key in spotting depression, says the University of Pennsylvania's Katz, they can help determine if a given drug is working for their elder relative or causing side effects like insomnia, loss of balance or sleepiness.

"If Mom is on an antidepressant and she's still depressed, that's a time to speak up," he says, and perhaps change drugs or dosages.

Whatever the drug, relief is not immediate. "It takes a number of weeks for medication to work in treating depression," stresses Anderson of Shore Behavioral Health Services.

The most effective treatment for severe clinical depression may be a one-two punch using drugs and psychotherapy.

Researchers at Brown University said in the New England Journal of Medicine that combined treatment produced an 85 percent positive response rate among the 681 participants in their study. The drug alone elicited a 55 percent positive response rate and talk therapy 52 percent.

Electroconvulsive—or shock—therapy is generally reserved for severely depressed people who don't respond to other treatments. The controversial procedure, in which the brain is electrically stimulated to break the course of depression, is deemed highly effective by some doctors. One possible side effect: temporary memory loss.

Researchers are exploring another treatment in which the vagus nerve in the neck is stimulated with electrical impulses, sending signals to brain areas that control mood.

Says one lifelong sufferer of depression who participated in the University of Texas Southwestern Medical Center's study of the treatment, "For the first time in years, I can feel joy, real joy."

Marian Schwartz is experiencing some joy, too. She has reclaimed her life, beating her depression via therapy and an antidepressant drug. Her message to others who feel depressed: "Please get help. I have benefited greatly. I have more confidence in myself [and] see things in a different perspective now."

AARP would like to learn more about how being denied medical care for depression might affect people. If you or someone close to you has ever been harmed by the inability to get treatment for depression, please write to AARP Foundation Litigation, P. O. Box 50228-D, Washington, DC 20091-0228. All correspondence will be kept confidential.

Peggy Eastman is a Washington-based free-lance writer.

From the *AARP Bulletin*, February 2001, pp. 14-16. © 2001 by the American Association of Retired Persons. Reprinted by permission.

THE QUEST FOR A CURE

BY MARK NICHOLS

Every few weeks, several teenage girls arrive at Halifax's Queen Elizabeth II Health Sciences Centre to take part in a study that may someday ease the crippling misery of depression. For two nights, the girls, a different group each time, bunk down in a sleep laboratory with tiny electrodes attached to their heads. Through the night, electronic equipment monitors their brain activity as they pass through the various stages of sleep, including the periods of rapid eye movement (REM) when dreaming occurs. Half of the roughly 80 girls who will take part in the study have no family history of depression. The others do—their mothers have had major depression and researchers know that these girls have a 30 percent chance of being victims, too. Dr. Stan Kutcher, a Dalhousie University psychiatrist who is involved in the study, wants to see whether a feature of sleep in depressed adults—they reach the REM stage faster than others—shows up in the kids. If it does, doctors for the first time would have a way of predicting depression and starting treatment early. Kutcher has been working with troubled youngsters most of his life. "It's a tremendous feeling to be able to help kids get better," he says. "It's a privilege to be let into their lives."

A pioneer in studying and treating adolescent depression, Kutcher is part of an army of medical researchers whose efforts are bringing new drugs, new therapies and new ways of thinking to bear in the war on the debilitating disorder. One of the biggest breakthroughs came in capsule form when Indianapolis's Eli Lilly and Co. introduced a product called Prozac almost 10 years ago. The first of a new class of drugs that can alleviate depression without the same nasty side effects of many older antidepressants, it profoundly improved the quality of life for millions of people. Thanks to Prozac and drugs like it, says Dr. Sid Kennedy, head of the mood disorders program at Toronto's Clarke Institute of Psychiatry, "depressed people are able to live normal, productive lives in a way that wouldn't have been possible 10 years ago."

Now, drugs that are potentially even better are undergoing tests, while researchers study the intricate universe of the brain in search of clues that could someday banish depression entirely. "Things are really moving quickly," says Dr. Trevor Young, a neuroscientist at McMaster University in Hamilton. "They're really getting close to understanding the biochemical changes that occur in depressed brains."

And doctors are coming closer to the time when they may be able to start treatment, in some cases, even before depression takes hold. After the Dalhousie researchers finish their current series of tests early next year, they will keep track of their young subjects for five years to see whether their REM sleep patterns pinpoint which of them will become depressed. If they do, then doctors in the future may be able to test children from families with a history of depression, and identify potential victims. One possibility, says Kutcher, would be to begin treating those children with antidepressants even before the first bout of depression occurred—in the hope that it never will.

New drugs and therapies join the battle against depression

Underpinning the new wave of research is a quiet revolution that has transformed thinking about depression over the past two decades. As recently as in the 1960s, when Sigmund Freud's psychoanalytic philosophy was still pervasive, depression and most other forms of mental illness were regarded as the consequences of emotional turmoil in childhood. Now, scientists have clear evidence that inherited flaws in the brain's biochemistry are to blame for many mental problems, including manic-depressive illness—with its violent swings between depressive lows and manic highs—and, according to some experts, recurring severe depression. Beyond that, many experts think that damaging events in childhood—sexual or physical abuse, poisoned parental relationships and other blows to the child's psyche—may cause depression later by disrupting development of crucial chemical pathways in the brain. "Losses early in life," says Dr. Jane Garland, director of the mood and anxiety clinic at the British Columbia Children's Hospital in Vancouver, "can raise the brain's level of stress hormones that are associated with depression."

When the dark curtain of depression descends, today's victims have access to quick and effective treatment. Short-term "talk therapies" now in use can help haul a patient out of depression in as little as four months—as opposed to years on a psychoanalyst's couch. The purpose of such therapy, says Dr. Marie Corral, a psychiatrist at the British Columbia Women's Hospital in Vancouver, is "to deal with the skewed thinking that develops when a person has been depressed for a long time." The most widely used methods: interpersonal therapy, which focuses on specific people-related problems, and cognitive therapy, which tries to counter the feelings of worthlessness and hopelessness that plague depressed people. "We try to show the patient that much of this thinking may be unfounded," says Zindel Segal, a Toronto psychologist.

But along with the new approaches to dealing with depression, a treatment introduced nearly 60 years ago that has earned a grim public image—electroconvulsive therapy (ECT)—is still a mainstay. Popularly known as shock treatment, it remains "one of our most potent forms of therapy" for severely depressed patients who do not respond to other treatment, says Dr. David Goldbloom, chief of staff at Toronto's Clarke Institute. ECT is routinely used every year on thousands of depressed Canadians, including older patients who cannot tolerate some of the side-effects of drug therapies.

ECT's bad reputation owes much to the 1975 movie *One Flew over the Cuckoo's Nest*, in which staff members of a mental institution punish a rebellious patient, played by Jack Nicholson, with repeated ECT sessions. Patients *did* endure painful ordeals in the early days of ECT when larger electrical shocks were used to induce a limb-shaking seizure in unanesthetized patients. Electroconvulsive treatment is gentler now. Doctors administer a muscle relaxant and a general anesthetic before subjecting the patient's brain to the amount of current needed to light a 60-watt bulb for one second.

ECT's aftereffects can include painful headaches lasting half an hour or so, and some memory loss. ECT does its job, they add, by altering the brain's electrical and chemical activity. The therapy has some bitter opponents, who claim that it can cause lasting memory loss and impair other brain functions, such as concentration. "ECT damages people's brains—that's really the whole point of it," says Wendy Funk, a 41-year-old Cranbrook, B.C., housewife. Funk says that after receiving electroconvulsive therapy for depression in 1989 and 1990, she lost virtually all memory—she could not recall even her own name or that she was married and had two children.

Meanwhile, for the approximately 70 per cent of patients who respond to them, Prozac and the family of drugs it spawned—Paxil, Zoloft, Luvox and Serzone—are making life far more bearable. Collectively, the drugs are known as SSRIs (for selective serotonin reuptake inhibitors) because they increase the brain's supply of the chemical messenger serotonin. The SSRIs have foes: the Internet bristles with accusations that the drugs can cause panic attacks, aggressive behavior and suicidal tendencies. But most doctors have nothing but praise for the drugs. It's not that they are better than their predecessors at relieving depression—most physicians say they are not.

But SSRIs are easier to live with than some older antidepressants, which often caused dry mouth, daytime sleepiness, constipation, vision problems and other unpleasant side effects. "The SSRIs are better tolerated," says Dr. Russell Joffe, dean of health sciences at McMaster University, "and it is much harder to overdose on them than the older drugs"—a vital consideration in treating people who may be at risk from suicide. The SSRIs can have side effects of their own, including insomnia and a diminished interest in sex that sometimes persuade patients to stop taking them. "You just don't get sexually aroused," says Giselle, a 41-year-old Manitoba resident who requested anonymity. "There's just nothing there."

Another problem with the SSRIs is that patients usually have to take them for three weeks or more before they start to work. The reason: when an SSRI increases the flow of serotonin in the brain, the thermostat-like mechanism that normally controls the flow of the chemical shuts down—and then takes three to six weeks to adapt and allow serotonin to flow again. "If you have a severely depressed patient who may be thinking about suicide," says Dr. Pierre Blier, a professor of psychiatry at Montreal's McGill University, "telling him he may have to wait that long for relief isn't good enough."

Most doctors praise the Prozac-like drugs

After studying the problem exhaustively, Blier and another McGill psychiatrist, Dr. Claude deMontigny, proposed in 1993 that the SSRIs would probably take effect more rapidly if used in conjunction with another drug that could block the brain mechanism causing the delay. Such a drug, a hypertension medication called Pindolol, existed. And the following year, a Spanish physician tried the combination—and found that it worked. Since then, studies have shown that the Pindolol-SSRI combination can cut the waiting time for SSRIs to take effect to about 10 days. Working with that knowledge, several major drug companies now are trying to develop a new generation of fast-acting SSRIs.

Meanwhile, efforts to lay bare the roots of depression are being pursued by a number of Canadian research teams:

• While most antidepressants concentrate on two of the brain's chemical messengers—serotonin and noradrenaline—a research team at the University of Alberta in Edmonton headed by neurochemist Glen Baker is studying a substance called GABA. Another of the brain's neurotransmitters, GABA appears to play a role in quelling the panic attacks that often accompany depression. GABA (for gamma-aminobutyric acid) seems to work in the brain by preventing selected nerve cells from sending signals down the line. To find out more, Baker's team is studying the action of two older antidepressants that are used to treat panic, imipramine and phenelzine. They want to find out whether the drugs work by increasing GABA activity in the brain. A possible payoff: a new class of drugs that could some day stem panic by boosting the flow of GABA in the brain.

•At McMaster, Young's team is focusing on manic-depressive illness in an effort to discover which brain chemicals are involved. One approach to the puzzle involves dosing rats—which have many of the same genes as humans—with antidepressants or mood stabilizers and examining tissue samples to see which genes are activated. Eventually, Young hopes to learn more about the signalling process inside the brain that can go awry and lead to depression or mania. He also wants to identify which defective chemical pathways make that happen. "Once we know more about these things," says Young, "we may be able to correct the problems with drugs."

•In Toronto, a Clarke Institute team co-headed by psychiatrists Sid Kennedy and Franco Vaccarino is using high-tech imaging equipment to look at brain functioning before and after treatment with antidepressants. Images produced by a PET scan machine show that, in depressed people, some parts of the brain's pre-frontal region—an area associated with emotion—are less active than normal. Surprisingly, when antidepressant drugs start acting on the brain, those areas be come even *less* active. Kennedy thinks that may be because in depression, the brain deliberately dampens down pre-frontal activity to cope with high levels of stress, and antidepressants may help the process by reducing activity even further. Kennedy hopes next to study brains in people who had remained well on antidepressants for at least a year, and thinks "we may find that by then activity in the pre-frontal areas has returned to something normal"—meaning that the brain's overstressed condition has been corrected.

The best antidepressants can banish depression—but they do not necessarily protect patients from relapses. Susan Boning, who organizes volunteer services for the Society for Depression and Manic Depression of Manitoba at its Winnipeg headquarters, had been taking Prozac for two years when she felt her mood "dipping" last March. Her condition worsened to the point where she made what she calls "a suicidal gesture" by drinking half a bottle of rum and passing out on her living-room floor. Boning, 37, has stopped taking Prozac and has turned to three other drugs, including Serzone. Boning's experience, like countless others, shows that while medical science is making rapid progress in treating depression, for many in the remorseless grip of the disease it is still not fast enough.

From *Maclean's*, December 1, 1997, pp. 60-62. © 1997 by Maclean Hunter Publishing Ltd. Reprinted by permission.

9/11/01
Post-Traumatic Stress Disorder

September 11th affected all of us, and even at this short interval it seems to mark a new, frightening turn in history. But obviously, anyone who lost a loved one or who was in direct danger that day had an emotional experience that was altogether different than the general reaction. The thousands of rescue workers who dug through the ruins afterward also shouldered special emotional burdens.

Grief, shock, and their elements of disbelief, apathy, and sometimes anger are normal—and healthy—responses to terrible events and sudden loss. Remarkably, many people recover—daunted and with a darker world view perhaps, but ready to continue on with their lives. Studies have shown this to be true of Holocaust survivors, combat veterans, and rape victims. The human psyche is resilient.

Some will have psychiatric problems

But if past experience is any indication, a significant fraction of September 11th survivors and the families of the deceased will have psychiatric problems. The symptoms vary but can include an intense irritability, jumpiness, emotional numbness, flashbacks, and nightmares. Sufferers may struggle with sleep problems. Marriages and personal relationships may fray under the strain.

All of this falls under the heading of *post-traumatic stress disorder* (PTSD), a diagnosis many Americans associate with Vietnam War veterans. Many people diagnosed with PTSD are afflicted with overlapping mental health problems, including depression. *Acute stress disorder* shares some of the same symptoms as PTSD, but is a diagnosis reserved for the first month after a traumatic experience.

It is hard to say how many will suffer from full-fledged PTSD. For Americans, the attacks two months ago have no real parallel either in kind or degree. The closest precedent is the 1995 bombing of the federal office building in Oklahoma City that killed 167 people. A study of survivors of that terrorist attack was published in the Aug. 25, 1999, *Journal of the American Medical Association*. The researchers interviewed approximately 200 people six months after the explosion. A person was eligible for the study if they were within a couple of hundred yards from the blast. Forty-five percent met the criteria for having some kind of psychiatric disorder and 34% had PTSD.

What qualifies as exposure?

By definition, PTSD is a consequence of exposure to a traumatic experience, with trauma being some kind of serious harm. In 1994, the American Psychiatry Association broadened the definition of exposure considerably. In addition to facing a threat of death or serious injury directly, it now includes "witnessing or learning about the unexpected or violent death, serious harm, or threat of death or injury experienced by a family member or close associate."

Who is vulnerable?

It stands to reason that the more direct and severe the traumatic experience, the more likely PTSD will develop. But there isn't a predictable dose-response relationship. Some people with a fairly remote connection to an event will have a strong psychiatric reaction, whereas others will go through a horrifying experience and bounce back.

Researchers have found some patterns. Studies have shown consistently, for example, that women are more susceptible to developing PTSD than men. In the Oklahoma City survivor study, women had twice the PTSD rate as men (45% vs. 23%). A traumatic experience is more likely to trigger PTSD in someone who has had a prior experience. A study done several years ago of women recovering from rape found that those who had been raped before were three times more likely to develop PTSD. Most vulnerable of all are people with prior psychiatric problems such as depression, anxiety, or a personality disorder.

Well shy of mental illness, certain personality traits seem to make PTSD more likely. *Neuroticism* is a tendency to react with strong emotion to adverse events. People with this kind of personality are more sensitive to stress: their response is faster, stronger, and slower to level off than normal. Research has connected high-test scores for neuroticism to PTSD. There may also be a link between PTSD and *impulsivity*, because it leads to recklessness that puts people in harm's way.

Researchers have looked at brain anatomy for clues. Several studies have found that an unusually small *hippocampus*, the part of the brain believed to control the narrative structure of memories, is associated with PTSD. It isn't settled, however, whether that is a cause or an effect.

Acute stress

During the traumatic event itself, some people often enter a *dissociative state,* perhaps as a defense mechanism. They imagine they are elsewhere. In their mind's eye, they see it happening to someone else. People with this kind response are more likely to develop PTSD. If they get stuck in this detached phase, it can turn into total amnesia or various identity disorders. Yet particularly during disasters, many survivors stay amazingly levelheaded and focus on saving themselves—and often others. As horrible as the collapse of the World Trade Center Towers was, it would have been much worse if so many hadn't stayed calm and gotten out of the buildings.

More on PTSD symptoms

PTSD symptoms don't stick to a decipherable time line. They can happen right away or emerge months or years later. After disasters, however, they usually begin within three months, perhaps because there isn't much stigma and people feel freer to express their emotions. In the case of the Oklahoma City bombing, 76% of the survivors said their PTSD started the same day.

The first set of PTSD symptoms includes insomnia, edginess, and irritability. People are easily startled. They have a hard time concentrating. Then, sometimes, an emotional flatness sets in as if the mind is struggling to bury or get rid of the whole experience. People feel listless. They may withdraw socially. They may start to have stomachaches, headaches, dizzy spells, and feel profoundly tired. At odds with this numbness is another set of classic PTSD symptoms that include nightmares, flashbacks, and what psychiatrists aptly term *intrusive thoughts.* The slightest reminder of the traumatic experience can set people off and cause emotional suffering.

How are family members and close friends affected?

The sudden death of a significant other can create a special kind of grief that includes *separation* and *traumatic distress.* People can't stop thinking about the deceased person. They may feel as though part of them has died. Life seems to have no purpose. Some have *facsimile illness symptoms,* which involve reliving the symptoms or pain of the person who died. Relatives of homicide victims may relive the crime, putting themselves in the place of their loved ones. Some psychiatrists believe *traumatic bereavement* should be added as a diagnosis, related to but separate from PTSD. Certainly, normal grief has some of these qualities. The difference is that normal grief tends to

taper off. People adjust and find they can lead meaningful lives again.

Are rescue workers vulnerable?

Technically, the PTSD diagnosis won't apply to rescue workers who are not themselves in serious danger. Several studies have shown, however, that up to 40% of people responsible for body handling and recovery after a disaster show signs of distress and are at risk of developing PTSD.

How can it be treated?

No consensus exists about how to best treat PTSD. A wide range of antidepressants are used. Antiseizure medications like carbamazepine and valproate are sometimes prescribed on the theory that a traumatic experience may lower the arousal threshold of the brain's *limbic system,* which is where seizures originate but it also controls emotions. Beta-blockers, traditionally prescribed to lower blood pressure, may quiet the nervous system and thereby reduce anxiety and restlessness.

Several varieties of psychotherapy have been tried, too, most with some but not complete success. *Cognitive therapy* focuses on memories and breaking negative thought patterns. *Behavioral therapy* aims to cut off a conditioned response that has become automatic.

Many therapists advocate using a technique called *debriefing* right after a traumatic event. It involves getting people to talk, usually in a group, about their experiences and vent their emotions. Some experts believe this is the best way to head off PTSD. Others see it as possibly stirring up thoughts and emotions that people might not otherwise have had.

Are we all suffering from PTSD?

Edgy? The possibility of future attacks has jangled many people's nerves. Waves of bad economic news have added to the background anxiety. Numb? Many Americans say September 11th changed the way in which they look at the world. They no longer feel safe. They are looking for meaning. They pray more. Intrusive thoughts and flashbacks? We don't need to think them up ourselves. Television and other news media bring up plenty of frightening pictures.

No, we don't have PTSD. To say we do trivializes the suffering of others. Still, we're allowed a pang of self-recognition in the broad outlines and descriptions of the condition. These are, after all, disordered times we're living in.

From *Harvard Health Letter,* November 2001, pp. 4-5. © 2001 by President and Fellows of Harvard College. Reprinted by permission.

The Schizophrenic Mind

**A popular movie and a murder trial bring this tragic disease to light.
How can the voices sound so real?**

BY SHARON BEGLEY

THE FIRST TIME CHRIS COLES HEARD THE VOICE, IT SPOKE TO him after midnight. In a gentle tone, it instructed him to meet his friend at a beach cove, right then, and apologize: Chris, the voice told him, had been planning to date the friend's girlfriend. Although Coles was planning no such thing, he did as instructed, arriving at the cove at 2 a.m. It was deserted. He dismissed the incident; imagination, after all, can play tricks in the twilight between waking and dreaming. But the voices kept intruding. Coles saw visions, too. At the beach near his California home, he often saw a profusion of whales and dolphins swimming onto the beach, and a golden Buddha glowing from the bushes by the dunes. "I also had delusions of grandeur," says Coles, now 47. "I felt that I had power over things in nature, influence over the whales and dolphins and waves. I thought I could make things happen magically in the water."

Yates has the **public face** of schizophrenia, gripped by evil forces; Nash has the **hidden one**

Donna Willey's visions came out of a darker world. She saw "bloody images, cut-up people, dismembered people," she says. Voices, too, began haunting her and, despite medication, still won't stop. "They say terrible things," says Willey, 43. "That what I'm doing is not important. They cuss and yell, trying to get me down, saying I shouldn't have done something that way. They're in my head, and they keep yelling." Even as she talks to a reporter in her office at the National Alliance for the Mentally Ill (NAMI) of Greater Chicago, the demons screech "You shouldn't say that," or "Don't say it that way." "The noise, the chaos in my head—it's hard to keep everything separate," she says.

The disease that came to be termed schizophrenia was first described by German psychiatrist Emil Kraepelin in the 1890s, but it remains one of the most tragic and mysterious of mental illnesses. Whether it brings the voices of heaven or of hell, it causes what must surely be the worst affliction a sentient, conscious being can suffer: the inability to tell what is real from what is imaginary. To the person with schizophrenia the voices and visions sound and look as authentic as the announcer on the radio and the furniture in the room. Some 2.5 million Americans have the disease, which transcends economic status, education, geography and even the loving kindness of family. Neither doctors nor scientists can accurately predict who will become schizophrenic. The cause is largely unknown. Although the disease almost surely arises from neurons that take a wrong turn during fetal development, it strikes people just on the cusp of adulthood. Whatever the cause, it seems not to change in frequency: the incidence of schizophrenia has remained at about 1 percent of the population for all the decades doctors have surveyed it. There is surely a genetic predisposition, but not an omnipotent one: when one identical twin has schizophrenia, his or her twin has the disease in fewer than half the cases. Treatment is improving, but a cure is not even on the horizon.

Williamson would eat only **canned food**, so **paranoid** was he that he was being poisoned

Diagnosing schizophrenia can take years. Soon after Andrea Yates confessed that she had drowned her five children, one by one, in a bathtub last year, the prison psychiatrist diagnosed her as having postpartum depression "with psychotic features." So had the psychiatrist who treated Yates after her 1999 suicide attempt. Since psychosis—the inability to distinguish reality from imagination—lies at the core of schizophrenia, both psychiatrists recommended that Yates be tested for that disease. Dr. Phillip Resnick of Case Western Reserve University did so. Last week, taking the witness stand for the defense at Yates's murder trial, he testified that she had a combination of schizophrenia and depression when she killed her children. In 1994, after her first child was born, she said she heard Satan's voice telling her to "get a knife" and hurt baby Noah.

If Yates's is the public face of schizophrenia—bedeviled by voices, gripped by evil forces—then John Nash's is the hidden one. As shown in the Academy Award-nominated picture "A Beautiful Mind," the disease, at least in its early stages, can inspire Olympian leaps of creativity and insight. "That's the wonderful paradox of schizophrenia," says Dr. Nancy Andreasen, professor of psychiatry at the University of Iowa. "People see things others don't, most of which aren't there. But because they perceive the world in a different way, they sometimes also notice things—real things—that normal people don't."

Schizophrenia is marked by the persistent presence of at least two of these symptoms: delusions, hallucinations, frequently derailed or incoherent speech, hugely disorganized or catatonic behavior, or the absence of feeling or volition. If the delusions are especially bizarre, or the hallucinations consist of either a running commentary on what the person is doing or thinking, or multiple voices carrying on a conversation, then that alone qualifies the person as schizophrenic. In one subtype, catatonic schizophrenia, the patient often seems to be in a stupor, resisting all entreaties and instructions, or engages in purposeless movements, bizarre postures, exaggerated mannerisms or grimacing. Yates would sit and stare into space for two hours; she would scratch her head bald and pat her foot obsessively. Before the drownings she rarely spoke, testified family members. Police officers responding to the crime described her as emotionless.

In paranoid schizophrenia, the patient becomes convinced of beliefs at odds with reality, hears voices that aren't there or sees images that exist nowhere but in his mind. Eric Williamson has had paranoid schizophrenia for 15 of his 31 years. As a teen he was terrified that someone would enter his room at night, and so would barricade the door and dangle hangers from the window to alert him to intruders. He would eat only canned food, so paranoid was he that someone was trying to poison him. Once, when his mother walked past the kitchen table as he ate, he cried out, "Why did you put that poison in my soup!?" He soon lost his grip on reality altogether, telling her, "Look how my eyelashes are growing. That's because [my brother] is messing with me."

Despite medication, Willey's voices still **burst** through, especially during **times of stress**

Andrea Yates may have had paranoid as well as catatonic schizophrenia. At the trial, Andrea's mother-in-law, Dora Yates, recalled the time Andrea stood transfixed in front of the television, neither moving nor speaking, for more than half an hour, as her children watched cartoons. Later, Yates told a prison psychiatrist that the cartoon characters were speaking to her, calling her a bad mother and scolding her for allowing her children to consume too much sugar. Yet even after her two suicide attempts, and even after she became nearly mute, her husband, Rusty, testified, he never suspected how severely ill she was.

Neuroscientists have now traced such hallucinations to malfunctions of the brain. In a 1995 study, researchers led by Drs. David Silbersweig and Emily Stern of Cornell Medical School teamed with colleagues in London to scan the brains of schizophrenics in the throes of hallucinations. As soon as an imagined voice spoke, or a vision appeared, a patient pressed a button. That told the scientists when to scrutinize the scans for abnormal activity. They found plenty. When one patient reported seeing dripping colors and severed heads, for instance, the parts of the sensory cortex that process movement, color and objects became active. Still, the complex visions depicted in "Beautiful Mind" are not typical. "The visual hallucinations are usually fragmentary," says Dr. Richard Wyatt, chief of neuropsychiatry at the National Institute of Mental Health, "not the elaborate things in the movie. They're an outline, or a figure without features."

When patients heard voices, the auditory cortex as well as the language-processing areas became active. "These regions process complex auditory, linguistic information, not just beeps or buzzes," says Silbersweig. The voices the patients heard were therefore as real to them as the conversations in the hallways they passed through en route to the lab.

The Chemistry of Mental Chaos

High-tech brain scans and new treatments are beginning to solve the mysteries of this debilitating disease, which affects 1% of the population. But much remains unknown.

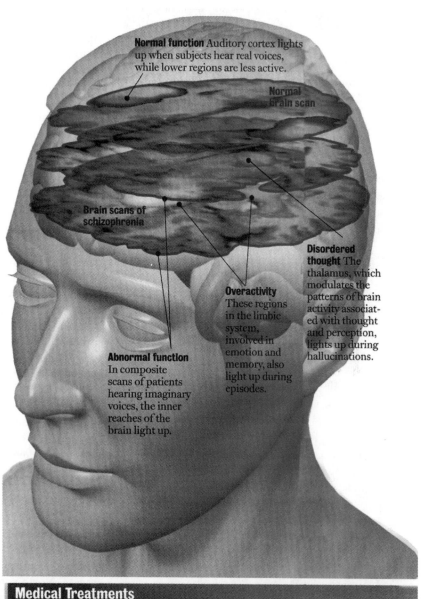

Normal function Auditory cortex lights up when subjects hear real voices, while lower regions are less active.

Normal brain scan

Brain scans of schizophrenia

Disordered thought The thalamus, which modulates the patterns of brain activity associated with thought and perception, lights up during hallucinations.

Overactivity These regions in the limbic system, involved in emotion and memory, also light up during episodes.

Abnormal function In composite scans of patients hearing imaginary voices, the inner reaches of the brain light up.

Neurological Roots

Schizophrenia is associated with overactivity in the part of the brain normally involved in arousal and motivation, known as the mesolimbic pathway. This can produce hallucinations and delusions.

Nerve cells line the mesolimbic pathway

Neuron

Neuron

Dopamine receptors

The disease has been linked to an excess of the brain chemical dopamine, which helps signals pass between nerve cells.

Normal dopamine system In healthy people, the flow of dopamine between brain cells is carefully regulated.

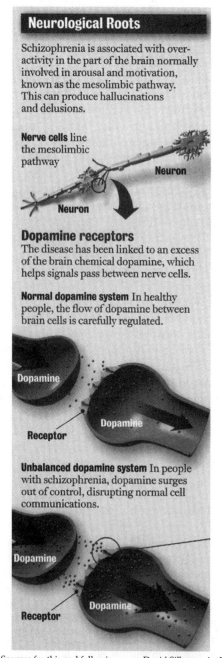

Dopamine

Dopamine

Receptor

Unbalanced dopamine system In people with schizophrenia, dopamine surges out of control, disrupting normal cell communications.

Dopamine

Dopamine

Receptor

Medical Treatments

Traditional antipsychotics blocked dopamine in the mesolimbic pathway, but they also blocked it in other parts of the brain, creating troublesome side effects.

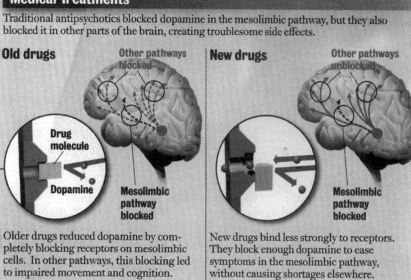

Old drugs

Other pathways blocked

Drug molecule

Dopamine

Mesolimbic pathway blocked

Older drugs reduced dopamine by completely blocking receptors on mesolimbic cells. In other pathways, this blocking led to impaired movement and cognition.

New drugs

Other pathways unblocked

Mesolimbic pathway blocked

New drugs bind less strongly to receptors. They block enough dopamine to ease symptoms in the mesolimbic pathway, without causing shortages elsewhere.

Sources for this and following page: David Silbersweig, M. D., and Emily Stern, M. D., Cornell University Medical School. Sources: Jeffery Lieberman, M.D. University of North Carolina Medical School. Images courtesy of David Silbersweig M. D. and Emily Stern M. D.; Text and research by Josh Ulick, Graphic by Kevin Hand—Newsweek.

Taking Pictures

By scanning the brains of people with schizophrenia in the midst of auditory and visual hallucinations, scientists can pinpoint the overactive regions that cause these symptoms.

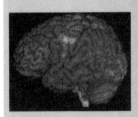

In this image of a hallucinating brain, taken from PET scans, the parts of the outer shell (known as the cerebral cortex) involved in vision and hearing light up.

Statistical Snapshot

Schizophrenia afflicts an estimated 2.5 million Americans, and cuts across all segments of society. Direct treatment costs run about $20 billion a year.

Age
% WHO HAD AN EPISODE IN THE PREVIOUS YEAR

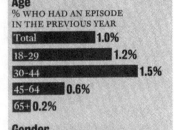

Total	1.0%
18-29	1.2%
30-44	1.5%
45-64	0.6%
65+	0.2%

Gender
% WHO HAD AN EPISODE IN THE PREVIOUS YEAR

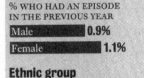

Male	0.9%
Female	1.1%

Ethnic group
% WHO HAD AN EPISODE IN THE PREVIOUS YEAR

White/other	0.9%
Black	1.6%
Hisp.	0.4%

Employment status
% OF LIFETIME SCHIZOPHRENIA SUFFERERS

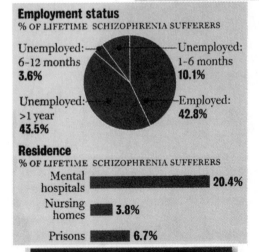

Unemployed: 6-12 months **3.6%**

Unemployed: 1-6 months **10.1%**

Unemployed: >1 year **43.5%**

Employed: **42.8%**

Residence
% OF LIFETIME SCHIZOPHRENIA SUFFERERS

Mental hospitals	20.4%
Nursing homes	3.8%
Prisons	6.7%

How to Get Help

National Schizophrenia Foundation
Provides information about the disease and support groups. Call 800-482-9534 or log on to sanonymous.org.

National Mental Health Association
Lobbies federal and state governments on mental-health issues. Call 800-969-6642 or check out www.nmha.org.

National Alliance for the Mentally Ill
Supports a help line. Call 800-950-6264 or go to www.nami.org.

American Psychiatric Association
Provides referrals to psychiatrists around the country. Call 888-357-7924 or log on to www.psych.org.

Deep within the brain during hallucinations, structures involved in memory (the little sea-horse-shaped hippocampus), in emotions (the amygdala) and in consciousness (the thalamus) all flick on like streetlights at dusk. That suggests why hallucinations are packed with rare emotional power—the power to make Chris Coles ashamed enough to venture to a deserted beach at night, the power to make Eric Williamson so terrified he ate only canned food. Sensory signals are conveyed deep into the brain, where they link up with memories and emotions. The neuronal traffic might go the other way, too, with activity in the emotional and memory regions triggering voices and visions.schizophrenia.

Why one person sees whales and another sees severed heads remains poorly understood. But the content of hallucinations probably reflects personal experience: in one patient the neuronal pathways activated during a hallucination run through the memories of seashore visits, while in another they intersect memories of pain and terror. Yates, who has a deeply religious background, had satanic hallucinations. Soon after a relative tried to rape her at the age of 11, Joanne Verbanic became convinced that strangers were trying to break into her house. Fourteen years later ominous voices started telling her that her brother would be killed. "I thought I was being followed and my phone was being tapped," she says. "There was a hole in the ceiling of my closet, and I thought there was a wire up there. I thought they had installed microphones in my eyeglasses and a dental filling." Other voices told her to kill herself; at 25 she tried to throw herself from a moving car, but her husband yanked her back.

"What's so cruel about voices is that they come from your very own brain," says Carol North, now a respected psychiatrist and researcher at Washington University, who first heard voices when she was 16. "They know all your innermost secrets and the things that bother you most." North's voices tormented her about failing a neurophysiology exam. "That was a horrible thing for me. The voices said, 'Carol North got an F.' They'd say things like, 'She can't do it [get into medical school],' 'She's just not smart enough'."

Another key brain area involved in schizophrenia is nearly silent. The Cornell/London brain-imaging study showed that schizophrenia is marked by abnormally low activity in the frontal lobes (just behind the forehead). These regions rein in the emotional system, provide insight and evaluate sensory information. They provide, in other words, a reality check. "You may need a double hit to suffer the psychotic symptoms of schizophrenia," says Silbersweig. "You need the aberrant sensory and emotional functioning, but you also need aberrant frontal-lobe function, which leaves you with no inhibition of these hallucinations and no reality check. That makes the hallucinations so believable."

The absence of a reality check makes "willing" yourself out of schizophrenia just about impossible. "It is very unlikely for somebody to will themselves to get better,"

Famous Figures, Troubled Minds

Throughout history, many well-known people, diagnosed or not, have exhibited some of the bizarre behaviors that are now associated with schizophrenia.

David Helfgott: His doctor says the famed pianist with the strange speech and other odd behaviors has schizoaffective disorder, not schizophrenia.

Vaslav Nijinsky: After six weeks of nearly nonstop diary writing, the Russian ballet dancer was diagnosed with schizophrenia by Eugen Bleuler, who coined the term.

Mary Todd Lincoln: The president's wife said she was haunted, wandered hotel hallways in her nightgown and sewed large sums of money in her clothes to foil imaginary thieves.

Zelda Fitzgerald: Hospitalized with nervous exhaustion at 27 and diagnosed with schizophrenia by Karl Jung, she received an early form of shock therapy.

Vincent van Gogh: Besides famously slicing off his ear, the erratic genius suffered hallucinations and memory lapses and once swallowed paint.

says NIMH's Wyatt. Toward the end of the film, when Nash recognizes that he has a mental illness, he says, "I just choose not to acknowledge" the figures he hallucinates. The reality is grimmer. Even among people who have had their illness for decades, and who have periods of clarity (thanks to medication), only some learn to discriminate between the voices everyone hears and the voices only they can hear. Verbanic, who founded Schizophrenics Anonymous in 1985, had been hospitalized often enough to recognize her symptoms. While working on bankruptcies for Ford Motor Credit, "I thought the attorneys weren't really attorneys and the files were phony," she says. She asked a supervisor to take her to the hospital.

Some **2.5 million** Americans have the disease, which eludes even the **lovingkindness** of family.

Identifying what happens in the brain during schizophrenic hallucinations is one step short of understanding why they happen. The old theory that cold, rejecting mothers make their children schizophrenic has long been discredited. Although the actual cause remains elusive, scientists know a few things. The age of the father matters. A 25-year-old has a 1-in-198 chance of fathering a child who will develop schizophrenia by 21, finds Dr. Dolores Malaspina of Columbia University. That risk nearly doubles when the father is 40, and triples when he passes 50. Viruses or stresses that interfere with a fetus's brain development also raise the risk; mothers who suffer rubella or malnutrition while pregnant have a greater chance of bearing children who develop the disease. And if there is schizophrenia in your family, you run a higher-than-average risk of developing it. Last year researchers led by NIMH's Dr. Daniel Weinberger linked a gene on chromosome 22 to a near-doubled risk of schizophrenia. When the gene, called COMT, is abnormal, it effectively depletes the frontal lobes of the neurochemical dopamine. That can both unleash hallucinations and impair the brain's reality check.

The seeming authenticity of the voices means that people with schizophrenia can be barraged by commands that, they are convinced, come from God or Satan. That inference is not illogical: who else can speak to you, unseen, from inside your head? Some patients have heard commands to shoplift, some to commit suicide. Believing she was possessed by Satan, Yates thought that her children "were not righteous." If she killed them while they were young, she told a psychiatrist, then "God would take them up" to heaven. Legally, "insanity" means the inability to tell right from wrong. There is no evidence that people with schizophrenia have impaired moral judgment. Then why do some obey commands to break the law, or worse? Perhaps one need look no further than Genesis 22. When Abraham heard God's command to sacrifice his only son, Isaac, he did not hesitate to take the boy up the mountain to the place of sacrifice and raise the knife.

Another misconception about schizophrenia involves creativity. In real life, bipolar disorder, with its alternating mania and depression, is more closely associated with creativity than schizophrenia is. "Most of John Nash's inventiveness came before his illness," says NIMH's Wyatt. "With schizophrenia, you can have brilliant thoughts, but they're hard to translate into something others understand." Untreated schizophrenia is so crippling that patients can barely buy groceries or pay bills, let alone pen a novel or compose a concerto. It may, however, inspire feats of genius in math and physics. "Creativity in these fields doesn't require sustained discipline," notes Iowa's Andreasen. "Many insights come as intuitions rather than brute proof by empirical evidence." Sadly, though, many of the creative breakthroughs that people with schizophrenia claim are not: thanks to delusions of grandeur, a crazy doodle can seem a Nobel Prize-winning insight. "I thought there were 10,000 universal truths that I needed to understand, that there were messages in the pattern of paint on the wall and in the pattern of concrete," recalls Carol North.

There is, as yet, no cure for schizophrenia, for drugs cannot unscramble tangled neuronal circuits. But drugs can quiet them. Those that give rise to the delusions and

'Is There Trouble With Jim?'

When someone you love hears voices through walls

By Dirk Johnson

THREE YEARS AGO, MINDY GREILING SAT IN A PSYCHOL-ogist's office and listened to her son, Jim, talk about wanting to kill her. "I want to shoot you in the face," he said, "because you look so evil." As a boy growing up in suburban Minneapolis, Jim Greiling was a Cub Scout, a Little Leaguer, a math whiz. Now 24, he suffers from schizophrenia, a disease that tortures families as it haunts the ill. Like millions of American families with a sufferer at home—or one who is off wandering some-where in the world—Mindy and Roger Greiling are on intimate terms with this disease. They know the help-lessness of trying to force treatment on an adult who re-fuses. They know the grief of letting go of dreams. "When he is young, you think about what the future might be for him," his father said. "It wasn't this."

Schizophrenia rains down guilt on some families—old notions held that poor parenting was to blame, with a finger usually pointed at the mother. Today it is believed to have a strong genetic component, leaving some relatives feeling as though they handed down a curse. The disease still brings shame, and it can ruin a family's finances. The Greilings were in a better posi-tion than most. They are well-educated and prosper-ous—and enlightened enough to know that schizophrenia is nobody's fault. But they also know the feeling of standing in the living room of their split-level home amid the wreckage of their son's hallucina-tions: smashed flowerpots, holes punched in the wall, kitty litter kicked across the floor. Their son's bouts have meant calling the police, with his terrified mother pleading: "He's 6-foot-4, and I'm afraid of him."

For Jim's sister, Angela Greiling Keane, a journalist in Washington, it means feelings of helplessness, a thousand miles from crisis. Unexpected telephone calls trigger anxiety. "When it's 7 a.m., and the caller ID says it's my parents, I automatically worry: is there trouble with Jim?"

Theirs are ghastly struggles. After one of Jim's ram-pages at home his parents called the police and asked them to take him to the hospital. But the police refused, since the mentally ill cannot be committed until they pose a threat. "You reach the point," said Mindy, "where you're actually hoping for something to hap-pen, so he'll be forced to go to a hospital."

There had been worries for years—during high school Jim smoked marijuana, and the family wanted to believe drugs were behind his erratic behavior. But while he was a student at the University of Montana he called home and said something that gave his mother chills. "He said he could hear the voices of women through the walls of the next apartment," said Mindy. "He said they were talking about him."

Mindy Greiling, a state representative, was busy at a late-night legislative session last year when another call came from Montana. Jim had been arrested. "After the session adjourned, she drove through the night to the jail. She felt "heart-broken," she says, as she saw her son behind the glass wearing an orange prisoner's suit, looking gaunt and whiskered. Jim had broken a window in a neighboring apartment, then climbed in-side, lay down on a sofa and fell asleep. The judge in Montana released Jim, who entered a state mental hos-pital where he underwent treatment for three months. Now he lives in a house in St. Paul with four other pa-tients. Everybody is assigned a job; Jim drives a van on the late shift. He is taking his medicine and seems to have gotten accustomed to his routine.

But for his family, the worries have scarcely stopped. Just the other day, the old voices came back. Jim was sit-ting on the sofa with his father, when he turned and asked: "Did you just say that you didn't like me?" The father said no. Jim smiled, reassured. For his parents, it is frightening to know that Jim still hears those voices. They can only hope that he ignores them.

hallucinations of schizophrenia are awash in the neuro-chemical dopamine. Thorazine, an early antipsychotic, blocked dopamine receptors, with the result that dopam-ine had no effect on neurons. But since dopamine is also involved in movement, Thorazine leaves patients slow and stiff, "doing the Thorazine shuffle," says Suzanne Andriukaitis of NAMI. Dopamine also courses through circuits responsible for attention and pleasure, so Thora-zine puts patients in a mental fog and deadens feelings. "The old drugs are a nuclear weapon against dopamine,"

says Dr. Peter Weiden of Downstate Medical Center in Brooklyn, N.Y. "They eliminate your sense of pleasure and reward. Patients lose their joy."

People with schizophrenia can be **barraged** by commands that, they are convinced, come from **God**

The new antipsychotics, called "atypicals," are more like smart bombs. Drugs including Clozaril, Risperdal,

Zyprexa, Geodon and Seroquel target mainly the dopamine-flooded regions, so patients no longer feel as if the voices of 40 radio stations, as different as NPR and the local hip-hop station, are blaring in their ears. "The volume is softer, the speed is slower, it's making more sense," says Donna Willey. Although the voices and visions don't always disappear, the new drugs can allow people with schizophrenia to hold jobs and have families. Still, they increase appetite, and may alter metabolism, resulting in what NIMH's Wyatt calls "the enormous problem" of huge weight gain. Willey gains 20 pounds a year on Zyprexa, and has ballooned from 120 pounds to her current 280. That makes some reluctant to take the drugs. Another side effect is foggy thinking, the feeling that brain signals are trying to push through caramel. Patients may also lose their libido. For all the power of the new drugs, they are treatment and not cure.

Sometimes Chris Coles misses the angelic voices. "They said complimentary things," he remembers. "They were sweet voices, telling me about the sunrise or sunset." But Zyprexa and Seroquel have stilled the angels. Willey wishes her voices would fall silent. Although Zyprexa has hushed them, they still burst through perhaps once a day, especially during times of stress. And she still, 20 years after she first heard the voices, isn't always completely, totally sure that they're not real.

With ANNE UNDERWOOD *in New York*, KAREN SPRINGEN *in Chicago and* ANNE BELLI GESALMAN *in Houston*

From *Newsweek*, March 11, 2002, pp. 44-51. © 2002 by Newsweek, Inc. All rights reserved. Reprinted by permission.

SCIENCE

THE SECRETS OF AUTISM

THE NUMBER OF CHILDREN DIAGNOSED WITH AUTISM AND ASPERGER'S IN THE U.S. IS EXPLODING. WHY?

By J. MADELEINE NASH

TOMMY BARRETT IS A DREAMY-EYED FIFTH-GRADER WHO lives with his parents, twin brothers, two cats and a turtle in San Jose, Calif., the heart of Silicon Valley. He's an honor-roll student who likes math and science and video games. He's also a world-class expert on Animorph and Transformer toys. "They're like cars and trains and animals that transform into robots or humans—I love them!" he shouts exuberantly.

And that is sometimes a problem. For a time, in fact, Tommy's fascination with his toys was so strong that when they weren't around he would pretend to *be* the toys, transforming from a truck into a robot or morphing into a kitten. He would do this in the mall, in the school playground and even in the classroom. His teachers found this repetitive pantomime delightful but disturbing, as did his mother Pam.

Autistic disorders may afflict nearly 300,000 kids in the U.S. alone

By that point, there were other worrisome signs. Pam Barrett recalls that as a 3-year-old, Tommy was a fluent, even voluble talker, yet he could not seem to grasp that conversation had reciprocal rules, and, curiously, he avoided looking into other people's eyes. And although Tommy was obviously smart—he had learned to read by the time he was 4—he was so fidgety and unfocused that he was unable to participate in his kindergarten reading group.

When Tommy turned 8, his parents finally learned what was wrong. Their bright little boy, a psychiatrist informed them, had a mild form of autism known as Asperger syndrome. Despite the fact that children with

Asperger's often respond well to therapy, the Barretts, at that moment, found the news almost unbearable.

That's because just two years earlier Pam and her husband Chris, operations manager of a software-design company, had learned that Tommy's twin brothers Jason and Danny were profoundly autistic. Seemingly normal at birth, the twins learned to say a few words before they spiraled into their secret world, quickly losing the abilities they had just started to gain. Instead of playing with toys, they broke them; instead of speaking, they emitted an eerie, high-pitched keening.

Up to 20 genes may be involved in autism, but they're not the only factors

First Jason and Danny, now Tommy. Pam and Chris started to wonder about their children's possible exposure to toxic substances. They started scanning a lengthening roster of relatives, wondering how long autism had shadowed their family.

The anguish endured by Pam and Chris Barrett is all too familiar to tens of thousands of families across North America and other parts of the world. With a seeming suddenness, cases of autism and closely related disorders like Asperger's are exploding in number, and no one has a good explanation for it. While many experts believe the increase is a by-product of a recent broadening of diagnostic criteria, others are convinced that the surge is at least in part real and thereby cause for grave concern.

In the Barretts' home state of California, for instance, the number of autistic children seeking social services has more than quadrupled in the past 15 years, from fewer than 4,000 in 1987 to nearly 18,000 today. So common are

The Geek Syndrome

At Michelle Winner's social-skills clinic in San Jose, Calif., business is booming. Every week dozens of youngsters with Asperger syndrome file in and out of therapy sessions while their anxious mothers run errands or chat quietly in the waiting room. In one session, a rosy-cheeked 12-year-old struggles to describe the emotional reactions of a cartoon character in a video clip; in another, four little boys (like most forms of autism, Asperger's overwhelmingly affects boys) grapple with the elusive concept of teamwork while playing a game of 20 Questions. Unless prompted to do so, they seldom look at one another, directing their eyes to the wall or ceiling or simply staring off into space.

Yet outside the sessions the same children become chatty and animated, displaying an astonishing grasp of the most arcane subjects. Transformer toys, video games, airplane schedules, star charts, dinosaurs. It sounds charming, and indeed would be, except that their interest is all consuming. After about five minutes, children with Asperger's, a.k.a. the "little professor" or "geek" syndrome, tend to sound like CDs on autoplay. "Did you ask her if she's interested in astrophysics?" a mother gently chides her son, who has launched into an excruciatingly detailed description of what goes on when a star explodes into a supernova.

Although Hans Asperger described the condition in 1944, it wasn't until 1994 that the American Psychiatric Association officially recognized Asperger syndrome as a form of autism with its own diagnostic criteria. It is this recognition, expanding the definition of autism to include everything from the severely retarded to the mildest cases, that is partly responsible for the recent explosion in autism diagnoses.

There are differences between Asperger's and high-functioning autism. Among other things, Asperger's appears to be even more strongly genetic than classic autism, says Dr. Fred Volkmar, a child psychiatrist at Yale. About a third of the fathers or brothers of children with Asperger's show signs of the disorder. There appear to be maternal roots as well. The wife of one Silicon Valley software engineer believes that her Asperger's son represents the fourth generation in just such a lineage.

It was the Silicon Valley connection that led *Wired* magazine to run its geek-syndrome feature last December. The story was basically a bit of armchair theorizing about a social phenomenon known as assortative mating. In university towns and R.-and-D. corridors, it is argued, smart but not particularly well-socialized men today are meeting and marrying women very like themselves, leading to an overload of genes that predispose their children to autism, Asperger's and related disorders.

Is there anything to this idea? Perhaps. There is no question that many successful people—not just scientists and engineers but writers and lawyers as well—possess a suite of traits that seem to be, for lack of a better word, Aspergery. The ability to focus intensely and screen out other distractions, for example, is a geeky trait that can be extremely useful to computer programmers. On the other hand, concentration that is too intense—focusing on cracks in the pavement while a taxi is bearing down on you—is clearly, in Darwinian terms, maladaptive.

But it may be a mistake to dwell exclusively on the genetics of Asperger's; there must be other factors involved. Experts suspect that such variables as prenatal positioning in the womb, trauma experienced at birth or random variation in the process of brain development may also play a role.

Even if you could identify the genes involved in Asperger's, it's not clear what you would do about them. It's not as if they are lethal genetic defects, like the ones that cause Huntington's disease or cystic fibrosis. "Let's say that a decade from now we know all the genes for autism," suggests Bryna Siegel, a psychologist at the University of California, San Francisco. "And let's say your unborn child has four of these genes. We may be able to tell you that 80% of the people with those four genes will be fully autistic but that the other 20% will perform in the gifted mathematical range."

Filtering the geeky genes out of the high-tech breeding grounds like Silicon Valley, in other words, might remove the very DNA that made these places what they are today.

—By J. Madeleine Nash.
With reporting by Amy Bonesteel/Atlanta

cases of Asperger's in Silicon Valley, in fact, that *Wired* magazine coined a cyber-age term for the disorder, referring to its striking combination of intellectual ability and social cluelessness as the "geek syndrome." *Wired* went on to make a provocative if anecdotal case that autism and Asperger's were rising in Silicon Valley at a particularly alarming rate—and asked whether "math-and-tech genes" might be to blame (*see box*).

Yet the rise in autism and Asperger's is hardly confined to high-tech enclaves or to the children of computer programmers and software engineers. It occurs in every job category and socioeconomic class and in every state. "We're getting calls from school systems in rural Georgia," observes Sheila Wagner, director of the Autism Resource Center at Atlanta's Emory University. "People are saying, 'We never had any kids with autism before, and now we have 10! What's going on?'"

It's a good question. Not long ago, autism was assumed to be comparatively rare, affecting as few as 1 in 10,000 people. The latest studies, however, suggest that as many as 1 in 150 kids age 10 and younger may be affected by autism or a related disorder—a total of nearly 300,000 children in the U.S. alone. If you include adults, according to the Autism Society of America, more than a million people in the U.S. suffer from one of the autistic disorders (also known as pervasive developmental disorders or PDDs). The problem is five times as common as Down syndrome and three times as common as juvenile diabetes.

No wonder parents are besieging the offices of psychologists and psychiatrists in their search for remedies. No wonder school systems are adding special aides to help teachers cope. And no wonder public and private research institutions have launched collaborative initiatives aimed at deciphering the complex biology that produces such a dazzling range of disability.

In their urgent quest for answers, parents like the Barretts are provoking what promises to be a scientific revolution. In response to the concerns they are raising, money is finally flowing into autism research, a field that five years ago appeared to be stuck in the stagnant backwaters of neuroscience. Today dozens of scientists are racing to identify the genes linked to autism. Just last month, in a series of articles published by *Molecular Psychiatry*, scientists from the U.S., Britain, Italy and France reported that they are beginning to make significant progress.

Meanwhile, research teams are scrambling to create animal models for autism in the form of mutant mice. They are beginning to examine environmental factors that might contribute to the development of autism and using advanced brain-imaging technology to probe the deep interior of autistic minds. In the process, scientists are gaining rich new insights into this baffling spectrum of disorders and are beginning to float intriguing new hypotheses about why people affected by it develop minds that are strangely different from our own and yet, in some important respects, hauntingly similar.

AUTISM'S GENETIC ROOTS

AUTISM WAS FIRST DESCRIBED IN 1943 BY JOHNS HOPKINS psychiatrist Leo Kanner, and again in 1944 by Austrian pediatrician Hans Asperger. Kanner applied the term to children who were socially withdrawn and preoccupied with routine, who struggled to acquire spoken language

GUIDE FOR PARENTS
How do you tell if your child is autistic? And what should you do if he or she is?

WHAT TO LOOK FOR

SIGNS OF AUTISM

(Usually apparent in toddlers; watch for cluster of symptoms)
- No pointing by 1 year
- No babbling by 1 year; no single words by 16 months; no two-word phrases by 24 months
- Any loss of language skills at any time
- No pretend playing
- Little interest in making friends
- Extremely short attention span
- No response when called by name; indifference to others
- Little or no eye contact
- Repetitive body movements, such as hand flapping, rocking
- Intense tantrums
- Fixations on a single object, such as a spinning fan
- Unusually strong resistance to changes in routines
- Oversensitivity to certain sounds, textures or smells

SIGNS OF ASPERGER'S

(Usually diagnosed at 6 or older)
- Difficulty making friends
- Difficulty reading or communicating through nonverbal social cues, such as facial expressions
- No understanding that others may have thoughts or feelings different from his or her own
- Obsessive focus on a narrow interest, such as reciting train schedules
- Awkward motor skills
- Inflexibility about routines, especially when changes occur spontaneously
- Mechanical, almost robotic patterns of speech

(Even "normal" children exhibit some of these behaviors from time to time. The symptoms of autism and Asperger's, by contrast, are persistent and debilitating.)

—By Amy Lennard Goehner

yet often possessed intellectual gifts that ruled out a diagnosis of mental retardation. Asperger applied the term to children who were socially maladroit, developed bizarre obsessions and yet were highly verbal and seemingly

GUIDE FOR PARENTS *continued*

Snapshots from the Autistic Brain

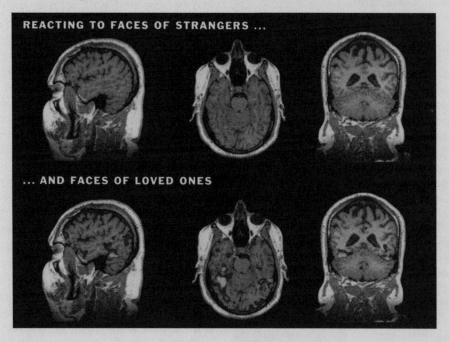

Neuroimaging studies confirm what scientists long suspected: autistic brains don't react to facial cues the way normal brains do. But in one regard the conventional wisdom was wrong. In a breakthrough study, Karen Pierce at the University of California at San Diego has shown that when faces of strangers are replaced by faces of loved ones, the autistic brain lights up like an explosion of Roman candles.

WHERE TO START

GET AN EVALUATION: Take your child to a developmental pediatrician with expertise in autism or Asperger syndrome. The pediatrician will evaluate your child with a team of specialists (speech therapists, occupational therapists, behavior therapists) to determine the areas in which your child needs help.

EARLY INTERVENTION: Every state is mandated to provide a free evaluation and early-intervention services for children. To find out whom to contact in your state, consult the National Information Center for Children and Youth with Disabilities (funded by the Department of Education) at 800-695-0285 or *nichcy.org/index.html*. Ask about support groups in your area.

HOW TO TREAT IT

There is no cure for autism, but there are many treatments that can make a difference:
SPEECH THERAPY: Can help overcome communication and language barriers
OCCUPATIONAL THERAPY: Helps with sensory integration and motor skills
BEHAVIORAL THERAPY: Improves cognitive skills and reduces inappropriate behavior
EDUCATIONAL THERAPY: A highly structured approach works best
MEDICATION: Can reduce some symptoms
SPECIAL DIETS: Eliminating certain food groups, such as dairy, helps some children

HELPFUL WEBSITES
ONLINE ASPERGER SYNDROME INFORMATION AND SUPPORT *www.aspergersyndrome.org*
AUTISM SOCIETY OF AMERICA *autism-society.org*
FAMILIES FOR EARLY AUTISM TREATMENT *www.feat.org*
AUTISM RESOURCES *autism-info.com*
YALE CHILD STUDY CENTER *info.med.yale.edu/chldstdy/autism*

Network: Other parents can be great sources in finding the right treatments.

quite bright. There was a striking tendency, Asperger noted, for the disorder to run in families, sometimes passing directly from father to son. Clues that genes might be central to autism appeared in Kanner's work as well.

VACCINES
Are the Shots Safe?

Ask the parents of autistic children whether they believe childhood vaccines can cause autism, and the answer will probably be yes. They have heard of too many cases of babies who were perfectly normal until they got their measles, mumps and rubella (MMR) shot and then, within weeks—if not days—started throwing tantrums, losing language skills and generally tuning out.

Ask doctors the same question, and they are likely to cite the panel of experts convened by the Institute of Medicine last year. They studied the evidence but found no explanation for how vaccines might possibly cause autism. Included in the review were studies that showed no significant difference in the incidence of autism disorders before and after MMR immunization became routine in 1988 in Britain. "We bent over backward to look for the biological mechanisms that would support a link," says the panel's chairwoman, Dr. Marie McCormick of the Harvard School of Public Health.

But failing to prove that something can happen is not the same as proving it doesn't, and the issue is still a matter of furious debate. The only scientific evidence against childhood vaccines comes from Dr. Andrew Wakefield, formerly at the Royal Free Hospital in London. His theory is that autism stems from a severe immune reaction to something in the vaccine. In February he published a paper showing that immunized children with autism and bowel disorders have higher levels of measles particles in their intestinal tissue than normal children do. The evidence is not entirely persuasive, however; measles particles in the tissues do not necessarily mean that the virus—or the vaccine—causes autism.

What about all the children whose symptoms appeared shortly after their MMR? The association may be purely coincidental. The shots are given at 15 months, which is when behavior and speech patterns in babies usually become sufficiently pronounced for parents to start noticing that something is wrong. Most of the evidence suggests that autism is primarily a genetic disorder. It may be that some symptoms appear immediately after birth but are too subtle to be spotted in the first year or so of life.

To get more definitive answers, the National Institutes of Health and the Centers for Disease control have each launched their own investigations. Karyn Seroussi of Poughkeepsie, N.Y., for one, supports this research. "If it's the shots, I want to know," says Seroussi, an autism advocate and parent of an autistic son. "If it's not, I want to know what the heck it is that's causing autism." On that, both parents and doctors can agree.
—*By Alice Park*

But then autism research took a badly wrong turn. Asperger's keen insights languished in Europe's postwar turmoil, and Kanner's were overrun by the Freudian juggernaut. Children were not born autistic, experts insisted, but became that way because their parents, especially mothers, were cold and unnurturing.

In 1981, however, British psychiatrist Dr. Lorna Wing published an influential paper that revived interest in Asperger's work. The disorder Asperger identified, Wing observed, appeared in many ways to be a variant of Kanner's autism, so that the commonalities seemed as important as the differences. As a result, researchers now believe that Asperger and Kanner were describing two faces of a highly complicated and variable disorder, one that has its source in the kaleidoscope of traits encoded in the human genome. Researchers also recognize that severe autism is not always accompanied by compensatory intellectual gifts and is, in fact, far likelier to be characterized by heartbreaking deficits and mental retardation.

Perhaps the most provocative finding scientists have made to date is that the components of autism, far more than autism itself, tend to run in families. Thus even though profoundly autistic people rarely have children, researchers often find that a close relative is affected by some aspect of the disorder. A sister may engage in odd repetitive behavior or be excessively shy; a brother may have difficulties with language or be socially inept to a noticeable degree. In similar fashion, if one identical twin has autism, there is a 60% chance that the other will too and a better than 75% chance that the twin without autism will exhibit one or more autistic traits.

How many genes contribute to susceptibility to autism? Present estimates run from as few as three to more than 20. Coming under intensifying scrutiny, as the papers published by *Molecular Psychiatry* indicate, are genes that regulate the action of three powerful neurotransmitters: glutamate, which is intimately involved in learning and memory, and serotonin and gamma-aminobutiric acid (GABA), which have been implicated in obsessive-compulsive behavior, anxiety and depression.

Those genes hardly exhaust the list of possibilities. Among the suspects are virtually all the genes that control brain development and perhaps cholesterol and immune-system function as well. Christopher Stodgell, a developmental toxicologist at New York's University of Rochester, observes that the process that sets up the brain resembles an amazingly intricate musical score, and there are tens of thousands of genes in the orchestra. If these genes do what they're supposed to do, says Stodgell, "then you have a Mozart's *Concerto for Clarinet*. If not, you have cacophony."

A DIFFERENCE OF MIND

AUTISTIC PEOPLE OFTEN SUFFER FROM A BEWILDERING ARRAY of problems—sensory disturbances, food allergies, gas-

FIRST PERSON

My Brother

KARL TARO GREENFELD

My autistic brother Noah and I once played together. He was two, and I was a year older. We wrestled, and I tickled him. He responded in a high-pitched giggle, halfway between a baby's gurgle and a child's laughter. I can't remember ever playing with him again. Noah stayed forever a baby, profoundly retarded, always dependent, never very communicative. And my role changed, much too early, from playmate to steward. There was barely any sibling rivalry. There were no battles to be fought. He would always be the center of attention.

I was treated as a sort of supporting player. Because my father had written a trilogy of books about our family with Noah as the title character (starting with *A Child Called Noah*; 1972), I would often be asked what it was like having an autistic brother. I never figured out how to respond. The answer I always gave—that I had never known any other life or any other brother—seemed cryptic and somehow unsatisfactory.

But that remains the only answer I can give. Noah, who can't speak, dress or go to the bathroom completely unassisted, will always be the center of our family. He never earned that role; his needs dictated it. I wasn't consciously resentful of this as a child. There was no more reason to be angry about this than there was about the rigid laws of basic arithmetic.

I accepted the fact that Noah and his problems could fill a battleship of parental duty and obligation, leaving my mother and father too spent to worry about the more banal problems of their normal son. But at some point in my early teens, in the confusing years of adolescence, I stopped having friends over. Noah's condition dictated what we ate and when we slept and to a great degree how we lived. We never had fancy furniture because he chewed on the couch cushions and spit on the carpets. He would pull apart anything more complicated than a pencil. I was ashamed of our home and family. Already marked as different by virtue of being Asian American in a predominantly white community, I came to see Noah as an additional stigmatizing mark.

My father used to say every family has a skeleton in its closet. Only ours was out in the open. I don't even remember if I talked about Noah in school. My friends knew about him, but after the first few questions, there wasn't much to say. Noah didn't change. Autism is a condition, I knew from close up, for which there are no miraculous cures. So he always stayed Noah. This kid who shared the same black hair and brown eyes as I had but couldn't talk and wanted to be left alone. So what was there to say about Noah? He was my brother who was never going to grow up.

Noah is 35 now and has been living in institutions since he was 18. My parents visit him every weekend at the state-run Fairview Developmental Center in Costa Mesa, Calif. I go whenever I am in town. (Currently I live in Hong Kong.) We bring Noah his favorite foods: sushi, fresh fruit and Japanese crackers and take him for a walk or a ride. Sometimes he lashes out at me. Spitting. Scratching. Pulling hair. but he knows me; I can tell by the wary squint he gives me. We're brothers, after all.

My parents are now in their 70s. My father underwent open-heart surgery a few years ago. Eventually, the responsibility for Noah will fall solely upon me. I imagine I may have to move my own family back to California to visit him every weekend, so that those caring for him will know that despite Noah's temper tantrums and violent outbursts, he is loved; he is a brother and part of a family. He is still the center of my life. My travels, from Los Angeles to New York City to Paris to Tokyo to Hong Kong, will always bring me back to him. I don't know any other life. I have no other brother.

Greenfeld is the editor of TIME ASIA.

trointestinal problems, depression, obsessive compulsiveness, subclinical epilepsy, attention-deficit hyperactivity disorder. But there is, researchers believe, a central defect, and that is the difficulty people across the autistic spectrum have in developing a theory of mind. That's psychologese for the realization, which most children come to by the age of 4, that other people have thoughts, wishes and desires that are not mirror images of their own. As University of Washington child psychologist Andrew Meltzoff sees it, the developmental stage known as the terrible twos occurs because children—normal children, anyway—make the hypothesis that their parents have independent minds and then, like proper scientists, set out to test it.

Children on the autistic spectrum, however, are "mind blind"; they appear to think that what is in their mind is identical to what is in everyone else's mind and that how they feel is how everyone else feels. The notion that other people—parents, playmates, teachers—may take a different view of things, that they may harbor concealed motives or duplicitous thoughts, does not readily occur. "It took the longest time for Tommy to tell a lie," recalls Pam Barrett, and when he finally did, she inwardly cheered.

FIRST PERSON

My Son

AMY LENNARD GOEHNER

I didn't know the world that my friends with normal—or, as we call them, typically developing—kids live in until recently. Two and a half years ago, my husband and I adopted our second child, Joey. And as he has grown to be a toddler, every milestone he has reached has been bittersweet—a celebration but also a painful reminder of all the milestones our 8-year-old son Nate has never reached.

Before Joey could talk, he pointed—as if to say, "Hey, Mom, look at that dog over there"—the way kids do to engage you. I flashed back to the evaluation forms we filled out for Nate when we were taking him to specialists. One question that appeared on every form was "Does your child point?" It's a major developmental step, a gesture that communicates a child's desire to share something outside himself. Nate never pointed.

When Nate was 2 and not talking, we took him to a big New York City hospital to get him evaluated. The neurologist gave us his diagnosis almost apologetically, in a very quiet voice. I remember just two words: "Maybe autistic."

When I stopped crying, I went to my office and called everyone I had ever met who was in any way connected to the world of special-needs kids. We made a lot of mistakes before finding the perfect match for Nate (and us)—a wonderful speech therapist whom we later dubbed our captain. When she met Nate, he was nonverbal and running around her office like a self-propelled buzz saw. She looked at us calmly and said, "Let's get busy. We've got work to do."

We've been working ever since. In addition to continual speech, behavior and occupational therapy, we have dabbled in what one of our doctors called "the flavor of the week"—vitamins and supplements and other "can't miss" cures. We shelled out a small fortune for every must-have tool that Lori, Nate's occupational therapist, mentioned even casually, including weighted vests (to help "ground" Nate) and special CDs (to help desensitize him to loud sounds). "Every time Lori opens her mouth, it costs me a hundred bucks," my husband once said.

Recently I read Joey a picture book that contained illustrations of fruit. Joey pretended to pick the fruit off the page and eat it, offering me a bit. Again I flashed back to those evaluation forms: "Does your child engage in pretend/imaginative play?" Nate's idea of play is to drop sticks and small stones into a drain at the playground. He could do this for hours if we let him. Last week Joey took a long noodle from his bowl of soup, dragged it across the table and said, "Look, it's a train. There's the freight car." Then Nate took a noodle from his soup. He tossed it onto the ceiling.

Yet maybe because I entered motherhood through the special-needs world, I somehow feel more a part of it than I do the "normal" one. The challenges in this world are greater, but the accomplishments—those firsts—are that much sweeter.

The other day I heard Joey singing a song about trains, and I realized that I couldn't remember the first time I heard my second son sing. I just took it for granted. With Nate, I never take anything for granted.

When Nate was 6, I was invited to hear his class put on a concert. I had no idea what to expect, as Nate doesn't sing. What he does do is make loud, repetitive noises, occasionally while rocking back and forth. But I went anyway. And when the music teacher approached Nate and began to sing a song Nate loved to listen to, Nate looked down, stared at his hands and very quietly chimed in, "A ram sam sam, a ram sam, gooly, gooly, gooly… " The other moms rushed to hand me tissues as tears streamed town my face. I was listening to Nate sing. For the first time.

Goehner is head arts reporter at TIME

Meltzoff believes that this lack can be traced to the problem that autistic children have in imitating the adults in their lives. If an adult sits down with a normal 18-month-old and engages in some interesting behavior—pounding a pair of blocks on the floor, perhaps, or making faces—the child usually responds by doing the same. Young children with autism, however, do not, as Meltzoff and his colleague Geraldine Dawson have shown in a series of playroom experiments.

The consequences of this failure can be serious. In the early years of life, imitation is one of a child's most powerful tools for learning. It is through imitation that children learn to mouth their first words and master the rich nonverbal language of body posture and facial expression. In this way, Meltzoff says, children learn that drooping shoulders equal sadness or physical exhaustion and that twinkling eyes mean happiness or perhaps mischievousness.

For autistic people—even high-functioning autistic people—the ability to read the internal state of another person comes only after long struggle, and even then most of them fail to detect the subtle signals that normal individuals unconsciously broadcast. "I had no idea that other

FIRST PERSON

Myself

TEMPLE GRANDIN

I was 2 ½ years old when I began to show symptoms of autism: not talking, repetitive behavior and tantrums. Not being able to communicate in words was a great frustration, so I screamed. Loud, high-pitched noises hurt my ears like a dentist's drill hitting a nerve. I would shut out the hurtful stimuli by rocking or staring at sand dribbling through my fingers.

As a child, I was like an animal with no instincts to guide me. I was always observing, trying to work out the best ways to behave, yet I never fit in. When other students swooned over the Beatles, I called their reaction an ISP—interesting social phenomenon. I wanted to participate but did not know how. I had a few friends who were interested in the same things I was, such as skiing and riding horses. But friendship always revolved around what I did rather than who I was.

Even today personal relationships are something I don't really understand. I still consider sex to be the biggest, most important "sin of the system," to use my old high school term. From reading books and talking to people at conventions, I have learned that autistic people who adapt most successfully in personal relationships either choose celibacy or marry someone with similar disabilities.

Early education and speech therapy pulled me out of the autistic world: Like many autistics, I think in pictures. My artistic abilities became evident when I was in first and second grade, and they were encouraged. I had a good eye for color and painted watercolors of the beach.

But words are like a foreign language to me. I translate them into full-color movies, complete with sound, which run like a videotape in my head. When I was a child, I believed that everybody thought in pictures. Not until I went to college did I realize that some people are completely verbal and think only in words. On one of my earliest jobs I thought the other engineer was stupid because he could not "see" his mistakes on his drawings. Now I understand his problem was a lack of visual thinking and not stupidity.

Autistics have trouble learning things that cannot be thought about in pictures. The easiest words for an autistic child to learn are nouns because they relate directly to pictures. Spatial words such as *over* and *under* had no meaning for me until I had a visual image to fix them in my memory. Even now, when I hear the word under by itself, I automatically picture myself getting under the cafeteria tables at school during an air-raid drill, a common occurrence on the East Coast in the early 1950s.

Teachers who work with autistic children need to understand associative thought patterns. But visual thinking is more than just associations. Concepts can also be formed visually. When I was little, I had to figure out that small dogs were not cats. After looking at both large and small dogs, I realized that they all had the same nose. This was a common visual feature of all the dogs but none of the cats.

I credit my visualization abilities with helping me understand the animals I work with. One of my early livestock design projects was to create a dip-vat and cattle-handling facility for a feed yard in Arizona. A dip vat is a long, narrow, 7-ft.-deep swimming pool through which cattle move in single file. It is filled with pesticide to rid the animals of ticks, lice and other external parasites. In 1978 dip-vat designs were very poor. The animals often panicked because they were forced into the vat down a steep, slick decline. They would refuse to jump into the vat and would sometimes flip over backward and drown.

The first thing I did when I arrived at the feedlot was put myself inside a cow's head and see with its eyes. Because their eyes are on the sides of their head, cattle have wide-angle vision. Those cattle must have felt as if they were being forced to jump down an airplane escape slide into the ocean.

One of the first steps was to convert the ramp from steel to concrete. If I had a calf's body and hooves, I would be very scared to step on a slippery metal ramp. The final design had a concrete ramp at a 25° downward angle. Deep grooves in the concrete provided secure footing. The ramp appeared to enter the water gradually, but in reality it abruptly dropped away below the water's surface. The animals could not see the drop-off because the dip chemicals colored the water. When they stepped out over the water, they quietly fell in because their center of gravity had passed the point of no return.

Owners and managers of feedlots sometimes have a hard time comprehending that if devices such as dip vats and restraint chutes are properly designed, cattle will voluntarily enter them. Because I think in pictures, I assume cattle do too. I can imagine the sensations the animals feel. Today half the cattle in the U.S. are handled in equipment I have designed.

Grandin is an assistant professor of animal sciences at Colorado State University.

people communicated through subtle eye movements," says autistic engineer Temple Grandin, "until I read it in a magazine five years ago" (*see box*).

At the same time, it is incorrect to say autistic people are cold and indifferent to those around them or, as conventional wisdom once had it, lack the high-level trait known as empathy. Last December, when Pam Barrett felt overwhelmed and dissolved into tears, it was Danny, the most deeply autistic of her children, who rushed to her side and rocked her back and forth in his arms.

Another misperception about people with autism, says Karen Pierce, a neuroscientist at the University of California at San Diego, is the notion that they do not register faces of loved ones as special—that, in the words of a prominent brain expert, they view their own mother's face as the equivalent of a paper cup. Quite the contrary, says Pierce, who has results from a neuroimaging study to back up her contention. Moreover, the center of activity in the autistic mind, she reported at a conference held in San Diego last November, turns out to be the fusiform gyrus, an area of the brain that in normal people specializes in the recognition of human faces.

In a neuroimaging study, Pierce observed, the fusiform gyrus in autistic people did not react when they were presented with photographs of strangers, but when photographs of parents were substituted, the area lit up like an explosion of Roman candles. Furthermore, this burst of activity was not confined to the fusiform gyrus but, as in normal subjects, extended into areas of the brain that respond to emotionally loaded events. To Pierce, this suggests that as babies, autistic people are able to form strong emotional attachments, so their social aloofness later on appears to be the consequence of a brain disorganization that worsens as development continues.

In so many ways, study after study has found, autistic people do not parse information as others do. University of Illinois psychologist John Sweeney, for example, has found that activity in the prefrontal and parietal cortex is far below normal in autistic adults asked to perform a simple task involving spatial memory. These areas of the brain, he notes, are essential to planning and problem solving, and among their jobs is keeping a dynamically changing spatial map in a cache of working memory. As Sweeney sees it, the poor performance of his autistic subjects of the task he set for them—keeping tabs on the location of a blinking light—suggests that they may have trouble updating that cache or accessing it in real time.

To Sweeney's collaborator, University of Pittsburgh neurologist Dr. Nancy Minshew, the images Sweeney has produced of autistic minds in action are endlessly evocative. They suggest that essential connections between key areas of the brain either were never made or do not function at an optimal level. "When you look at these images, you can see what's not there," she says, conjuring up an experience eerily akin to looking at side-by-side photographs of Manhattan with and without the Twin Towers.

A MATTER OF MISCONNECTIONS

DOES AUTISM START AS A GLITCH IN ONE AREA OF THE brain—the brainstem, perhaps—and then radiate out to affect others? Or is it a widespread problem that becomes more pronounced as the brain is called upon to set up and utilize increasingly complex circuitry? Either scenario is plausible, and experts disagree as to which is more probable. But one thing is clear: very early on, children with autism have brains that are anatomically different on both microscopic and macroscopic scales.

For example, Dr. Margaret Bauman, a pediatric neurologist at Harvard Medical School, has examined postmortem tissue from the brains of nearly 30 autistic individuals who died between the ages of 5 and 74. Among other things, she has found striking abnormalities in the limbic system, an area that includes the amygdala (the brain's primitive emotional center) and the hippocampus (a seahorse-shaped structure critical to memory). The cells in the limbic system of autistic individuals, Bauman's work shows, are atypically small and tightly packed together, compared with the cells in the limbic system of their normal counterparts. They look unusually immature, comments University of Chicago psychiatrist Dr. Edwin Cook, "as if waiting for a signal to grow up."

An intriguing abnormality has also been found in the cerebellum of both autistic children and adults. An important class of cells known as Purkinje cells (after the Czech physiologist who discovered them) is far smaller in number. And this, believes neuroscientist Eric Courchesne, of the University of California at San Diego, offers a critical clue to what goes so badly awry in autism. The cerebellum, he notes, is one of the brain's busiest computational centers, and the Purkinje cells are critical elements in its data-integration system. Without these cells, the cerebellum is unable to do its job, which is to receive torrents of information about the outside world, compute their meaning and prepare other areas of the brain to respond appropriately.

Several months ago, Courchesne unveiled results from a brain-imaging study that led him to propose a provocative new hypothesis. At birth, he notes, the brain of an autistic child is normal in size. But by the time these children reach 2 to 3 years of age, their brains are much larger than normal. This abnormal growth is not uniformly distributed. Using MRI-imaging technology, Courchesne and his colleagues were able to identify two types of tissue where this mushrooming in size is most pronounced.

These are the neuron-packed gray matter of the cerebral cortex and white matter, which contains the fibrous connections projecting to and from the cerebral cortex and other areas of the brain, including the cerebellum. Perhaps, Courchesne speculates, it is the signal overload caused by this proliferation of connections that injures the Purkinje cells and ultimately kills them. "So now," says Courchesne, "a very interesting question is, What's driving this abnormal brain growth? If we could understand that, then we might be able to slow or stop it."

A proliferation of connections between billions of neurons occurs in all children, of course. A child's brain, unlike a computer, does not come into the world with its circuitry hard-wired. It must set up its circuits in response to a sequence of experiences and then solder them together through repeated neurological activity. So if Courchesne is right, what leads to autism may be an otherwise normal process that switches on too early or too strongly and shuts off too late—and that process would be controlled by genes.

Currently Courchesne and his colleagues are looking very closely at specific genes that might be involved. Of particular interest are the genes encoding four brain-growth regulators that have been found in newborns who go on to develop mental retardation or autism. Among these compounds, as National Institutes of Health researcher Dr. Karin Nelson and her colleagues reported last year, is a potent molecule known as vasoactive intestinal peptide. VIP plays a role not only in brain development but in the immune system and gastrointestinal tract as well, a hint that other disorders that so frequently accompany autism may not be coincidental.

The idea that there might be early biomarkers for autism has intrigued many researchers, and the reason is simple. If one could identify infants at high risk, then it might become possible to monitor the neurological changes that presage the onset of behavioral symptoms, and someday perhaps even intervene in the process. "Right now," notes Michael Merzenich, a neuroscientist at the University of California, San Francisco, "we study autism after the catastrophe occurs, and then we see this bewildering array of things that these kids can't do. What we need to know is how it all happened."

The genes that set the stage for autistic disorders could derail developing brains in a number of ways. They could encode harmful mutations like those responsible for single-gene disorders—cystic fibrosis, for instance, or Huntington's disease. They could equally well be garden-variety variants of normal genes that cause problems only when they combine with certain other genes. Or they could be genes that set up vulnerabilities to any number of stresses encountered by a child.

A popular but still unsubstantiated theory blames autism on the MMR (measles, mumps and rubella) vaccine, which is typically given to children at around 15 months (*see box*). But there are many other conceivable culprits. Researchers at the University of California at Davis have just launched a major epidemiological study that will test the tissues of both autistic and nonautistic children for residues of not only mercury but also PCBs, benzene and other heavy metals. The premise is that some children may be genetically more susceptible than others to damage by these agents, and so the study will also measure a number of other genetic variables, like how well these children metabolize cholesterol and other lipids.

Drugs taken by some pregnant women are also coming under scrutiny. At the University of Rochester, embryologist Patricia Rodier and her colleagues are exploring how certain teratogens (substances that cause birth defects) could lead to autism. They are focusing on the teratogens' impact on a gene called HOXA1, which is supposed to flick on very briefly in the first trimester of pregnancy and remain silent ever after. Embryonic mice in which the rodent equivalent of this gene has been knocked out go on to develop brainstems that are missing an entire layer of cells.

In the end, it is not merely possible but likely that scientists will discover multiple routes—some rare, some common; some purely genetic, some not—that lead to similar end points. And when they do, new ideas for how to prevent or correct autism may quickly materialize. A decade from now, there will almost certainly be more effective forms of therapeutic intervention, perhaps even antiautism drugs. "Genes," as the University of Chicago's Cook observes, "give you targets, and we're pretty good at designing drugs if we know the targets."

Paradoxically, the very thing that is so terrible about autistic disorders—that they affect the very young—also suggests reason for hope. Since the neural connections of a child's brain are established through experience, well-targeted mental exercises have the potential to make a difference. One of the big unanswered questions, in fact, is why 25% of children with seemingly full-blown autism benefit enormously from intensive speech- and social-skills therapy—and why the other 75% do not. Is it because the brains of the latter are irreversibly damaged, wonders Geraldine Dawson, director of the University of Washington's autism center, or is it because the fundamental problem is not being adequately addressed?

The more scientists ponder such questions, the more it seems they are holding pieces of a puzzle that resemble the interlocking segments of Tommy Barrett's Transformer toys. Put the pieces together one way, and you end up with a normal child. Put them together another way, and you end up with a child with autism. And as one watches Tommy's fingers rhythmically turning a train into a robot, a robot into a train, an unbidden thought occurs. Could it be that some dexterous sleight of hand could coax even profoundly autistic brains back on track? Could it be that some kid who's mesmerized by the process of transformation will mature into a scientist who figures out the trick?

—With reporting by Amy Bonesteel/Atlanta

From *Time*, May 6, 2002, pp. 46-56. © 2002 by Time, Inc. Magazine Company. Reprinted by permission.

UNIT 11

Psychological Treatments

Unit Selections

47. **Are We Nuts?** Mary McNamara
48. **Support Groups: Study Casts Some Doubts**, *Harvard Health Letter*
49. **Treating Anxiety**, Sarah Glazer

Key Points to Consider

• Are Americans "nuts"? Why do you agree or disagree? What varieties of psychotherapy are commonly available to your knowledge? Does psychotherapy work? Why are Americans "in love with psychotherapy"? Do you think that supportive lay persons can be as effective as psychotherapists? Is professional assistance for psychological problems always necessary? How and why is psychotherapy replacing spirituality, according to Mary McNamara?

• Can people successfully change themselves? Why do people turn to self-help groups rather than to professionals? What disorders are amenable to intervention by support groups? What does research show about the efficacy of support groups? Can support groups be dangerous? How can we be sure that we are receiving good advice from self-help groups? Do you think support groups should include a trained professional or trained facilitator? Why or why not?

• How does chronic anxiety differ from the everyday anxiety we sometimes experience? What are some of the effects of anxiety, severe or not? What are some of the treatments for severe anxiety? Can you differentiate anxiety from phobias and other forms of fear?

• If you had to pick a disorder to "suffer from," which one would you pick and why? Have you ever recognized in yourself some of the symptoms discussed in the book? Do you think you have any mental disorders? If you think you do, what will you do about it? If a friend came to you for advice about a common disorder, what advice would you offer?

 **Links: www.dushkin.com/online/**
These sites are annotated in the World Wide Web pages.

The C.G. Jung Page
http://www.cgjungpage.org

Knowledge Exchange Network (KEN)
http://www.mentalhealth.org

NetPsychology
http://netpsych.com/index.htm

Sigmund Freud and the Freud Archives
http://plaza.interport.net/nypsan/freudarc.html

Have you ever had the nightmare that you are trapped in a dark, dismal place? No one will let you out. Your pleas for freedom go unanswered and, in fact, are suppressed or ignored by domineering authority figures around you. You keep begging for mercy but to no avail. What a nightmare! If you are fortunate, you awake to your normal bedroom and to the realities of your daily life. For the mentally ill, the nightmare of institutionalization, where individuals can be held against their will in what are sometimes terribly dreary, restrictive surroundings, is a reality. Have you ever wondered what would happen if we took perfectly normal individuals and institutionalized them? In one well-known and remarkable study, that is exactly what happened.

In 1973, eight people, including a pediatrician, a psychiatrist, and some psychologists, presented themselves to psychiatric hospitals. Each claimed that he or she was hearing voices. The voices, they reported, seemed unclear but appeared to be saying "empty" or "thud." Each of these individuals was admitted to a mental hospital, and most were diagnosed as being schizophrenic. Upon admission, the "pseudopatients" or fake patients gave truthful information and thereafter acted like their usual, normal selves.

Their hospital stays lasted anywhere from 7 to 52 days. The nurses, doctors, psychologists, and other staff members treated them as if they were schizophrenic and never saw through their trickery. Some of the real patients in the hospital, however, did recognize that the pseudopatients were perfectly normal. Upon discharge almost all of the pseudopatients received the diagnosis of "schizophrenic in remission," meaning that they were still clearly defined as schizophrenic; they just weren't exhibiting any of the symptoms at the time of release.

What does this study demonstrate about mental illness? Is true mental illness readily detectable? If we can't always pinpoint mental disorders (the more professionally accepted term for mental illness), how can we treat them? What treatments are available and which treatments work better for various diagnoses? The treatment of mental disorders is a challenge. The array of available treatments is ever increasing and can be downright bewildering—and not just to the patient or client! In order to demystify and simplify your understanding of various treatments, we will look at them in this unit.

We commence with two general articles on treatment. In the first, Mary McNamara asks, "Are We Nuts?" If one examines the popularity of psychotherapy today, then one might indeed conclude that, yes, Americans appear to be crazy because so many of us are in therapy. Some therapy clients consider psychotherapy to be fashionable. Why are we in love with psychotherapy? Is therapy truly helpful? Both questions are explored in McNamara's article.

In a companion article, support groups are put under the scientific microscope. Such groups are becoming more and more popular. Do such groups work? Do they result in positive change? The answers are not easy. Support groups may or may not be beneficial, according to recent research.

In the third article, the common cold of mental health—anxiety—is explored with a special eye on its treatment. Anxiety afflicts many of us. Some individuals suffer from chronic and intense anxiety, known as generalized anxiety disorder. Other individuals suffer from very specific forms of anxiety, such as phobias or intense fears of objects that are not normally harmful. Sarah Glazer in "Treating Anxiety" not only details the symptoms of chronic anxiety but also provides a good discussion of the possible treatments for it.

ARE WE Nuts?

By Mary McNamara Los Angeles Times

Americans have long been in love with the idea of psychotherapy. When Sigmund Freud made his first and only visit to the United States in 1909, American intelligentsia flocked to his lectures. Since then, psychotherapy has spread like kudzu, morphing from the medical treatment of specific, diagnosable mental illnesses into a sort of societal support system offered by psychiatrists, psychologists, counselors, therapists, self-help gurus and TV talk-show hosts.

"Seek professional help" is our standard answer to everything from episodes of psychotic rage to dating problems, and "self-help" has become its own industry. We use terms like "manic depressive," "obsessive compulsive" and "neurotic" to describe the most benign, everyday sort of behaviors.

And should true tragedy occur, the psychologists and counselors are there on the front lines, elbowing out the friends and clergy if not the paramedics. No other area of science or medicine so informs our national discussions or perceptions of who we are and who we should be.

But is it working? Are we getting any better? Is our mental health improving? And is our increased self-awareness benefiting society?

"It's difficult to gauge, compared to other parts of medicine," says Rochester, N.Y., psychiatrist John McIntyre. "There's no question that treatment of specific mental disorders is very effective—the efficacy rate is often higher than in other medical procedures. But when you broaden it to other issues, it gets fuzzy. It's had the overall beneficial effect of increasing knowledge of human nature, but are people better? How do you measure that?"

'Hysterical misery'

There is no arguing the fact that psychotherapy and psychiatry have improved the lives of millions suffering from often devastating chemical and mental imbalances. And, certainly, Freud had no personal illusions about transforming the human condition. He was content, he once said, to turn people's "hysterical misery into ordinary human unhappiness."

But here in America, we want to teach the world to sing, in perfect harmony. And so we look to psychology to provide us with answers and solutions to everything from a president's mendacity (there was that abusive stepfather) to relations between the sexes (which planet am I from?) to a baseball player's overt racism and homophobia (don't fire him, send him to a therapist).

According to Surgeon General David Satcher, the next decades will put the effectiveness of psychotherapy and psychiatry to the test. One out of five baby boomers can expect to suffer a mental disorder, from substance abuse to late-onset schizophrenia, while almost 21 percent of children ages 9 to 17 suffer from diagnosable mental disorders.

But measuring a nation's mental health is a difficult thing to undertake. One traditional method is to look at a society's tendency toward "social deviance"—its rates of crime, divorce, suicide, drug use and out-of-wedlock births. Most of these have decreased in recent years, although the divorce rate is significantly higher than it was even half a century ago.

But how valid are these numbers as indicators of mental health?

"Crime is not a good measure because there are a lot of social and economic reasons for crime," says Wendy Kaminer, pop psychology critic and author of "I'm Dysfunctional, You're Dysfunctional" and more recently "Sleeping With Extraterrestrials." "And to use divorce, well, if you have a sick norm [of troubled marriages], what is mentally healthy? To conform or rebel?"

Even using drug use as an indicator of mental instability is dangerous, she says, because there are many possible reasons for drug abuse; many in the scientific community believe the propensity for abuse is genetic.

Political movements have a complex relationship with the psychoanalytical movement. At one level, political movements by definition reject the psychological paradigm, their premise being that discontent stems not from our selves but from the System. On the other hand, Freud's identification of the id and the unconscious had a profound effect, particularly on the youth movements of the '60s and '70s.

Age of the id

"The id really came out in the '60s," says Peter Wolson, a Beverly Hills, Calif., psychoanalyst. "Suddenly, the thing is to be happy, not to lead a good life. Have fun, have orgasms, and this leads into the '70s and '80s, which is about getting ahead, still about 'me,' and then you have a backlash, mainly from fundamentalists. But even the backlash is very self-centered, very much of the id."

The United States has a long, complicated relationship with the culture of self—with self-government, self-actualization, self-discovery, self-aggrandizement. We celebrate nonconformity in a way that absolutely defines conformity and claim to treasure individualism while mass-producing more products than any other country in the world. "I gotta be me," we say, and if that "me" doesn't work out, well, we'll just try on a new one.

Psychology seems to provide both the means and the motive for the culture of self, and therein lies its greatest strength and its greatest failings.

"In a way, psychology has replaced religion," says David Blankenhorn of the Institute for American Values, based in New York. "It is who we are, the air we breathe. And it can truly help people who suffer and can yield important insights. But the assumptions of the paradigm are so relentlessly centered on self, all other structures of meaning and authority evaporate. 'What do I want?' becomes the governing question."

Much of Blankenhorn's work centers on marriage and fatherhood, two areas greatly affected by the mass marketing of psychological theories in very different ways.

"For men, there are clearly advantages," he says. "They are more able to express emotions. Most fathers today hug their children and say, 'I love you.' For our fathers and grandfathers, such emotional intimacy was not there, and there is a whole generation of men walking around wounded from that."

But while fatherhood has benefited, he says, marriage has not.

"If talking about marriage and relationships was the basis of good marriage and relationships, we'd have the best in the history of the world," he says. "But they are now more fragile than they have ever been. Men and women seem unhappier with each other than ever."

Self-invention

Freud argued that it is pointless to try to make people happy because that's not what they want. Yet happiness seems to be the carrot at the end of psychology's stick—if you know yourself, you can change yourself and you can be happy. All the time. The creation of such expectations may be one of the psych-culture's greatest drawbacks.

"It's a mixed blessing," says University of Washington sociologist Pepper Schwartz. "We've hugely increased our sensitivity to each other. We understand, for example, how much damage words can do. More people take responsibility for their actions, and if they don't, someone makes them. But we've also created whole new categories of what people should worry about, hundreds of new ways in which we can fail or people can fail us."

Our expectations from relationships have become much higher.

"Just look at the area of sex therapy," she says. "We have a hundred new ways to create inadequacies."

On the other hand, we have become more informed consumers, of theories as well as products.

"It used to be if Dr. So-and-So said something in the newspaper, readers would assume it was true," Schwartz says. "Not anymore. An easy example is how we have examined and rejected corporal punishment."

Like Blankenhorn, Schwartz believes the successes of the psychological movement are most evident in our attitudes toward parenting.

"If nothing else, I know we've made better fathers, although the numbers of fathers who leave is an area where we have possibly slid. But the ones who stay are much more participatory. No one's shocked to see a man in the grocery store alone with his kids. When I was a young woman, you would have assumed the mother was dead."

But again, are such changes the result of psychologically increased self-awareness, or the women's movement?

"The only real answer to 'Are we better yet?' " says Kaminer, "is, 'We don't know yet.' "

From *Minneapolis Star Tribune*, February 8, 2000. © 2000 by the Los Angeles Times. Reprinted by permission.

Cancer
Support Groups: Study Casts Some Doubt

In the past decade or so, many people have come to believe that healing can be a question of mind over matter. The notion that medical fate can be determined not only by the power of positive thinking but also through focused mental efforts of friends, relatives, and even strangers was once confined to "alternative" medicine. But scores of scientific studies have documented that support groups, social connectedness, and even prayer are not just effective in improving life but extending it. Mainstream medicine hasn't embraced all of these studies by any means, nor should it. But, at a minimum, most doctors acknowledge that psychosocial support has real consequences for health beyond just making people feel better.

The first study

If this phenomenon can be traced to a single source, it is a study in the Oct. 14, 1989, *Lancet* led by Stanford psychiatrist David Spiegel. He randomly assigned women with advanced breast cancer to either a support group and standard care, or standard care alone. Before the study, Spiegel and his team thought that participating in the support group would improve the quality of life, but they doubted it would affect survival. To their surprise, women in the support group lived, on average, 18 months longer than the women who received just standard care.

Other researchers have attempted to duplicate Spiegel's findings. The results are split down the middle. Half of the 10 investigations on record suggest that participating in a support group could, in fact, increase survival time. The others found no such effect. But the positive results seem to have gotten more attention. Support groups have sprung up everywhere. The promise of living longer isn't the only reason people join, but it has been dangling out there as a possible benefit.

No survival benefit

Now the largest study to date seems to have dashed the notion that support groups make patients live longer. In a multicenter investigation in Canada, 255 women with metastatic breast cancer were randomly assigned to two groups—158 attended support groups, 77 didn't. All the women received similar medical care. The women who went to a support group reported less pain and greater improvement in depression and other psychological symptoms. And those who were in the greatest distress

when they entered the study got the most benefit. But a key finding was that the support groups didn't add extra months to the lives of participants. With or without support group participation, the women lived for about a year and a half.

In an editorial in the Dec. 13, 2001, *New England Journal of Medicine* in which the Canadian study appeared, Spiegel said that the disparity between these results and his findings a dozen years ago might say as much about the state of breast-cancer treatment as it does about the value of support groups. He pointed to the substantial strides in breast-cancer detection and therapy. Indeed, the breast-cancer death rate finally started to drop in the 1990s.

Attitudes have changed

Maybe more importantly, attitudes about breast cancer have changed. No longer is it a condition that invokes an embarrassed silence. It's discussed in every conceivable forum, motivates powerful advocacy groups, and garners millions of research dollars each year. When women faced breast cancer virtually alone, joining a support group may have been one of the few ways to escape demoralizing—and unhealthy—isolation. Now breast cancer is out of the closet. With friends and family more likely to be understanding, the support group may be less of a lifeline. While participating in one might have been enough to tip the balance in the 1980s, it is now just one of several factors that can improve a patient's well-being.

Still helpful

Although a support group may not guarantee a longer life, it may mean a happier one. At the very least, support groups—whether for breast cancer, heart disease, emphysema, or myriad other conditions—offer an opportunity to vent about your condition without the fear of burdening or boring friends and family. They can spawn new friendships, offer coping strategies, and alleviate stress.

For people who prefer to keep their problems to themselves, a support group may just be a source of practical advice that is hard to find elsewhere. What better place to learn where to get a decent wig or a dentist with experience in treating people who are undergoing chemotherapy than a room of cancer survivors? Who is more likely to know which supermarket in your community has the best supply of sugar-free foods than a group of people with diabetes? It usually doesn't take long to tell if a support group is for you. If it isn't, you can drop out.

If you have a common condition like breast or prostate cancer, obesity, diabetes, emphysema, arthritis, diabetes, or heart disease, or are caring for someone with Alzheimer's disease, a support group is likely to be as close as the nearest hospital. You may need to travel farther, but an increasing number of groups exist for people with rare conditions. A host of other organizations, including health plans, foundations, advocacy groups, wellness centers, and adult education programs run them, partly because it's in their self-interest to do so. Support groups bring in potential customers or patients. Regardless of the sponsor, it's best to find a group run by a health professional. They can keep the discussion on track and ensure that the medical information exchanged is accurate.

Support online

If you want to communicate with others who have your condition, but don't want to do it in person, you may want to look into an Internet chat room or bulletin board. They are usually "hosted" by a Web site of some kind. You don't have to wait until the next scheduled meeting to voice a new concern or to pick up the thread of an ongoing discussion. Online interaction is also attractive to the many people who prefer to share their thoughts in writing.

But the Internet is also a free-for-all, especially when it comes to health information. Also, remember that while you may enjoy Internet anonymity, there's the danger that others will abuse it to peddle half-baked ideas or lie about who they are. For that reason, it's safest to start with the chat rooms or discussion groups on the Web sites of reputable non-profit organizations like the American Heart Association or the American Cancer Society. Such groups have experts who monitor the discussion boards to check that the information posted is sound.

Not do or die

Some people just aren't joiners. Perhaps they get the support they need from friends, family, or a particularly strong inner life. But if you believed the research findings that support groups extended life, not to join a support group seemed almost reckless. This latest study should send the message that support groups are a matter of choice, not a do-or-die-sooner situation. At the same time, both science and common sense say people in almost any dire circumstances can help each other out in innumerable ways. What's more, the more comfortable you are in a group, whether in person or through a computer hookup, the more you'll get out of it.

From *Harvard Health Letter*, April 2002, pp. 1-2. © 2002 by President and Fellows of Harvard College. Reprinted by permission.

Treating Anxiety

BY SARAH GLAZER

The Issues

Last December, Arlene Gellman got stuck in a mysteriously long traffic jam in New York's Brooklyn-Battery Tunnel. Suddenly terrified that a new terrorist attack had occurred, her heart began to race, and she felt as if the tunnel walls were closing in on her. She thought she was about to die.

As a psychotherapist, Gellman recognized the symptoms immediately: She was experiencing a panic attack for the first time in her life.

Moving into survival mode, she knocked on the door of the bus stalled next to her and asked the driver to talk her down from the panic. He confessed that he was suffering the same symptoms. The last time he had been stuck in the tunnel, he said, was the day the World Trade Center collapsed.[1]

Five months after the Sept. 11 terrorist attacks on the twin towers and the Pentagon killed more than 3,000 people, New Yorkers and other Americans are suffering lingering symptoms of anxiety and trauma. Children's author Rachel Leventhal, who ran for her life from the falling debris with her 3-year-old daughter in tow, is still haunted by vivid recollections of the horrifying moments and has had trouble returning to work. Miramax films executive Jennifer Horowitz, who arrived at work in time to watch the second tower collapse, avoided subways and buses for weeks and still avoids midtown Manhattan, convinced it's the next target of terrorists. (*See box, "The Day the Sky Fell—A Mother's Story."*)

Experts say these feelings are normal in the days and weeks immediately after a traumatic event. Physical and psychosomatic symptoms common after a trauma—including heart palpitations and hypertension—help explain why New York physicians reported a rise in patients since Sept. 11 complaining of symptoms like heart trouble or head pain.

But if certain symptoms continue for more than three months following a traumatic event, they could signal more serious psychological consequences, such as depression, anxiety disorders characterized by panic attacks and post-traumatic stress disorder (PTSD).[2]

America's largest mental health emergency to date has turned the spotlight on a debate over which treatments are most effective for treating PTSD and anxiety disorders. Many experts say studies show that cognitive-behavioral therapy (CBT) is the most effective, but others put their faith in so-called talk therapy. Still, others believe drugs and group therapy show promise.

A diagnosis of PTSD, according to the American Psychiatric Association, requires that the person must have been exposed to an event that triggered a sense of "fear, helplessness or horror" and must experience three types of symptoms. The symptoms must persist at least one month past the event or in the case of long-term chronic PTSD, at least three months past the event. The three symptoms are:

- repeated re-experiencing of the event—including distressing nightmares, flashbacks or intrusive mental images;

- avoiding reminders of the event—such as places, persons or thoughts associated with the event; and

- physiological symptoms such as insomnia, irritability, impaired concentration and increased "startle" reactions.[3] (*See table, "How Men and Women Respond to Trauma".*)

Before Sept. 11, studies showed that about 6 percent of American men and 10 to 14 percent of women experienced PTSD at some time in their lives, making it the fourth most common psychiatric disorder. While women are twice as likely as men to develop PTSD, it is not clear whether women are more psychologically vulnerable or whether they suffer more PTSD because they are more likely to be sexually molested than men. (*See table, "How Men and Women Respond to Trauma".*)

In addition, personal violence is more likely to cause PTSD than events like earthquakes or car accidents. For example, PTSD developed in 55 percent of people who reported being raped, compared with 7.5 percent of those involved in accidents. The disorder also develops more often in women than men after a physical assault, such as a mugging. Some experts believe that if trauma victims feel some sense of mastery over the situation, they are more likely to come through it without developing PTSD.

A recent article in the prestigious *New England Journal of Medicine* suggested that PTSD rates among men and women touched by Sept. 11 may be similar to those experienced by men and women in accidents, natural disasters or the sudden loss of loved ones.[4]

How Men and Women Respond to Trauma

Men and women often develop post-traumatic stress disorder (PTSD) at different rates in response to similar traumatic events.
In the case of physical assaults, for example, only about 2 percent of the men developed PTSD, compared with 21 percent of the women.

Overall, men experienced more traumatic events than women, but women's PTSD rates were twice as high
as shown by data collected by two researchers (bottom two categories).

Traumatic Event	Prevalence of Event		Rate of PTSD in Response to Event	
	Men	Women	Men	Women
Rape	0.7%	9.2%	65.0%	45.9%
Molestation	2.8	12.3	12.2	26.5
Physical assault	11.1	6.9	1.8	21.3
Accident	25.0	13.8	6.3	8.8
Natural Disaster	18.9	15.2	3.7	5.4
Combat	6.4	0.0	38.8	-
Witnessed death or injury	40.1	18.6	9.1	2.8
Learned about traumatic event	63.1	61.8	1.4	3.2
Sudden death of loved one	61.1	59.0	12.6	16.2
Any traumatic event*	60.7	51.2	8.1	20.4
Any traumatic event**	92.2	87.1	6.2	13.0

*Data from Kessler et. al.

**Data from Breslau et. al.

Source: Rachel Yehuda, "Post-Traumatic Stress Disorder," The New England Journal of Medicine, Jan. 10, 2001

Judging from the rates of PTSD that occurred after the 1995 bombing of the Oklahoma City federal building, about 35 percent of those directly exposed to the Trade Center tragedy will suffer from PTSD. Since tens of thousands of people fled the Sept. 11 attacks, and an estimated 100,000 people directly witnessed the event, the toll could be substantial. And that's not counting the tens of millions worldwide who watched it on television.[5] The risk of developing PTSD increases with the observers' proximity to the traumatic event, whether the observers lost a loved one or felt their own lives were in danger and their experience with previous traumas.

In New York, city, state and federal officials are gearing up to provide mental health services to an unprecedented number of potential patients. As many as 2 million New Yorkers may need some form of counseling, ranging from a one-time talk with a minister or a group-counseling session to more extended psychotherapy, according to the New York State Office of Mental Health.

The New York City Police Department in November ordered all of its 55,000 employees and officers to attend group-therapy sessions to relieve stress in the aftermath of the disaster.[6] "By making it mandatory, no one has to be the macho guy who doesn't show up, but who really needs it and is home beating his wife or drinking too much or who takes his gun and kills himself. Those things happen," says JoAnn Difede, director of Acute Trauma Response at New York Weill Cornell Medical Center, who is advising the department.

To help remove the stigma often associated with mental health counseling, city and state health departments in mid-January plastered advertisements on the city's subway cars urging New Yorkers still experiencing classic PTSD symptoms to seek help. Some of the ads profiled regular New Yorkers seeking counseling. One ad shows a list of things that helped relieve the stress for "William," 35, of Brooklyn. It includes such things as "talked with my co-workers about everything" and "went to three

sessions with a therapist to talk with other men about our feelings."

Chip Felton, director of mental health disaster-related services at the New York State Office of Mental Health, says the ads—some of which feature New York celebrities like Yankees manager Joe Torre—are intended to send the message, "If it's OK for them to ask for help, it's OK for me to do it too."

Some city residents call the effort overkill. "This must be unique in human history—that an entire town has been pathologized and treated like the walking wounded," says Andrew J. Vickers, a British researcher at the Sloan-Kettering Memorial Cancer Institute in New York. During German bombing raids on London in World War II, he points out, "We had the blitz. It was all about the indomitable spirit. It's a very different time psychologically."

But experts in treating PTSD say not treating the syndrome can have dangerous and costly consequences, including alcohol and drug abuse to numb unbearable feelings, wrecked family relation-

The Paralyzing Power of Anxiety Disorders

Most people have experienced anxiety before a big exam, a job interview or a first date. Unlike such brief bouts of intense worry, anxiety disorders are illnesses that fill people's lives with overwhelming anxiety and fear. According to the National Institute of Mental Health, anxiety disorders are "chronic" and "relentless" and potentially disabling, in some cases keeping a sufferer housebound. More than one anxiety disorder can be experienced at a time, and some people may suffer from an anxiety disorder along with other kinds of illnesses, such as depression.

Five major types of anxiety disorders are:

- ***Panic disorder**—Repeated episodes of intense fear that strike often and without warning. Physical symptoms include chest pain, heart palpitations, shortness of breath, dizziness, feelings of unreality and fear of dying.*
- ***Post-traumatic stress disorder**—Persistent symptoms, including nightmares, numbing of emotions and being easily startled, that occur for more than one month after experiencing or witnessing a traumatic event.*
- ***Generalized anxiety disorder**—Constant, exaggerated, worrisome thoughts and tension about routine life events, lasting at least six months.*
- ***Obsessive-compulsive disorder**—Repeated, unwanted thoughts or compulsive behaviors that seem impossible to stop or control.*
- ***Phobias**—Extreme disabling fear of something that poses little or no actual danger. People with social phobia, for example, have an overwhelming fear of humiliation in social situations.*

Source: National Institute of Mental Health

ships and suicide. Children and teenagers may also express anxiety and depression through substance abuse, pre-marital sex or even avoiding attending a college far from home, say experts at the New York University (NYU) Child Study Center. The center is treating children who attended school near the trade center, now known worldwide as "Ground Zero."[7]

Psychotherapist Gellman's first experience with PTSD was with Vietnam veterans while she was in training at a veterans' hospital in Philadelphia in the early 1970s. Of the survivors of the Sept. 11 tragedy she has been treating, she says, "I am seeing the same symptoms. Here some people are having nightmares and awakenings with night terrors, but I think we're yet to see what the full reaction is going to be. We're still in the grief stage."

Gellman says that one reason people who have been exposed to horrifying events like Sept. 11 have nightmares or awaken in terror is that while they are asleep, they slip into an unconscious state and their normal defenses are relaxed. Some people have vivid reimaginings during the day that are like nightmares while awake.

Survivors who were at the World Trade Center on Sept. 11 tell Gellman they keep visualizing people throwing themselves out of the buildings. "That seems to be the most recurring thought," she says. "Among people who lost loved ones, it's different," she adds. "The most prominent thought seems to be: 'What was it like for their loved ones burning to death in there?'"

As policy-makers, researchers and mental health professionals debate how best to treat PTSD and anxiety disorders, here are some of the questions being asked:

Is cognitive-behavioral therapy the most effective treatment for PTSD?

Research on treating PTSD overwhelmingly points to cognitive-behavioral therapy (CBT) as the most effective approach. Through a technique known as "exposure," the victim of a trauma retells the story of the traumatic incident repeatedly—sometimes even revisits the scene of the trauma—in order to become desensitized to the painful memories.

"The whole point of the treatment is to explain that a memory can't hurt you,"

says Rachel Yehuda, director of the Division of Traumatic Stress Studies at Mt. Sinai School of Medicine/Bronx Veterans Affairs Medical Center in New York.

For example, firefighters recovering from severe burns have reported flashbacks in which they feel the searing pain of their flesh burning and smell the odors of smoke and flames, according to Difede, who specializes in treating New York firefighters with burn injuries.

A common response among such trauma victims is to avoid anything that reminds them of the event. Avoidance can range from a firefighter feeling unable to return to work, a raped woman refusing to walk in the neighborhood where she was attacked, or—in extreme cases—experiencing difficulty leaving one's home. When a person goes to such lengths to avoid painful memories of the event, Yehuda explains, "they're not open to corrective information" such as the fact that the event is unlikely to happen again. And that information is considered crucial to helping the person get used to remembering the event without being paralyzed by it.

The process of getting used to the memory is sometimes termed "desensitization." One approach is to assign a pa-

The Day the Sky Fell—A Mother's Story

On Sept. 11, Rachel Leventhal had planned to shop for clothes for her 3-year-old daughter at the World Trade Center's underground mall, a mere six blocks from her home.

Her daughter Zoe was still in her pajamas when they both heard a plane fly directly overhead, so low that they could see a bizarre shadow cross the front window. Three seconds later, Leventhal and her daughter were startled by an unusually loud sound. Unbeknown to them, it was the first plane crashing into the famous skyscraper.

The scene from their window looking onto Broadway resembled a Superman movie. Hundreds of people were streaming down the street gasping and pointing downtown in horror. Downstairs on the street to investigate, Leventhal felt an earthquake-like boom.

"Time started to move really slowly. We looked and there was a gigantic hole in the Trade Center," Leventhal recalls. Neighbors on the street were saying it must have been a drunken pilot, but Leventhal had a terrible feeling it wasn't over yet.

She took her daughter upstairs and tried to keep her busy making crafts. Then she turned on the TV news. As the second plane was striking the second tower on live TV, she heard and felt the explosion. Her floor shook. There was another huge rumble.

"I screamed to Zoe to get away from the windows and threw her down on the floor," she remembers shielding her daughter with her body. "I thought we were being bombed and the house was about to come down on top of us. You couldn't see outside; it was blackened with smoke and debris."

Her husband called from his office and told her to get out of their Tribeca neighborhood right away. Grabbing a toothbrush and thrusting Zoe in her stroller, Leventhal fled the building. Just as they reached the street the second tower came down. "I was worried it was a nuclear bomb. Debris was snowing all over us," Leventhal recalled. "Smoke and clouds of debris enveloped us."

At first, Zoe looked up at her mother and smiled, saying, "A bad Pokemon hit the building." Her mother answered, "No, this is a real thing."

They began a long, terrible run uptown, away from the trade center, weaving their way through thousands of New Yorkers who were looking back at the towers gasping and crying.

Zoe became hysterical, crying, "Don't stop here!" each time her mother stopped.

Finally, Leventhal reached a church where parishioners were standing outside offering help. "I'm Jewish, but I thought, 'This is what churches are for.'" A group of African-American women standing on the church steps, greeted her with: "Praise the Lord, you're OK." Leventhal stayed with them until her husband, whom she reached by cell phone, arrived.

Leventhal and her family spent the next two weeks in her mother's apartment uptown. That's when she and her daughter started to experience classic signs of traumatic stress.

"I couldn't eat. I lost 15 pounds," she recalls. "If my mom was 10 minutes late getting back from her health club, I was scared. I couldn't sleep at all." The fear had gripped her so deeply, she says, that her sleep felt more like restless hallucinations than dreams. Her daughter obsessively replayed the Twin Towers' collapse in the form of Pokemon figures knocking down towers of blocks. Such repetitive reenactments are a classic sign of trauma in children.

Gradually, Leventhal started taking her daughter to nursery school in their Lower Manhattan neighborhood even though their apartment was still off-limits. For the first three weeks, Leventhal stayed at the school for six hours a day, afraid of another terrorist or anthrax attack. "I didn't know if I would have to save Zoe," she explains.

Eventually the teachers started sending Leventhal to the local coffee shop at lunch time, pleading with her to eat something. She started volunteering, making food for Ground Zero workers at a local restaurant.

The family has finally moved back to their Tribeca apartment. "I'm doing really well now," she says. But her plans to go back to work as a children's book writer are on hold. She says she cleans house and exercises "obsessively."

And some days, if she hears a tale like the one about the Catholic priest who administered last rites to firemen entering the towers on Sept. 11, it sets her back a few days. "I feel very sad, depressed. I have vivid imagery of the firemen. I can imagine the scene as they went to their deaths. I think maybe I'll leave the city. It's hard."

---

tient "homework" of listening several times a week to a tape recording of herself recounting her rape, for example, until it loses some of its emotional impact.

The International Society for Traumatic Stress Studies (ISTSS) strongly recommends exposure therapy as the first line of treatment for PTSD. "[N]o other treatment modality has such strong evidence for its efficacy," the groups said in recently published guidelines for treating PTSD. The guidelines noted that in a dozen high-quality studies of various therapies, patients treated with exposure consistently showed more improvement in PTSD and anxiety symptoms—after as few as nine to 12 sessions.[8]

Joseph LeDoux, a neuroscientist at NYU and a leading expert in anxiety, says his brain research helps explain why cognitive-behavioral therapy works better in the short run than insight-oriented psychoanalytic therapy. His work has found that an almond-shaped structure deep inside the brain, called the amygdala, plays a role in generating the kinds of persistent memories that haunt survivors of traumatic events.

He says the part of the brain activated during cognitive-behavioral condition-

Several Treatments Target Anxiety Disorders

Alison Scherr, a 30-year-old Manhattan artist, has been plagued with panic attacks since college. They would come on suddenly, often when she felt overwhelmed by work. She would hyperventilate, shake uncontrollably, feel disconnected from her surroundings, lose a sense of time and, most of all, feel incredibly frightened.

Over the years, she has seen therapists and tried anti-depressants. Nothing really helped, she says, until she began seeing a clinical psychologist who uses cognitive-behavioral therapy (CBT).

Steven Phillipson explained to Scherr that her panic attacks tended to snowball because she was so afraid of them. "He said to let it take over," Scherr recalls. "It was really scary at first, but it was the only way that ever got through to me." Together, in weekly sessions over six months, Alison and Phillipson practiced talking back to the internal force that was causing the panic attacks as if it was another person.

Today, as soon as Scherr feels a panic attack coming on, she acknowledges the power of the attack and then takes a confrontational attitude. She addresses her panic as if it were a person: "You can make me start hallucinating," she says. "You can make me convulse. I'm just going to continue walking down the street, and then I'm going to my meeting."

Scherr says this challenging bring-it-on attitude was "very empowering in a weird way," and usually causes the attack to dissipate. And although she still has panic attacks, she says she's "not running around afraid of them, and they don't last as long."

Experts see anxiety attacks as a form of the primitive "fight or flight" response developed by humans as a response to danger. A person jumping out of the path of an oncoming truck will feel many of the same physical symptoms, such as a racing heartbeat or rapid breathing.

But panic attacks are scary because they seem to occur "out of context," explains Manhattan psychologist Ethan Gorenstein. People experiencing them often think they are dying or suffering a heart attack because their physiological responses are so overpowering. Physical symptoms similar to those accompanying panic attacks are one reason traumatic memories can be so frightening to people suffering from post-traumatic stress disorder (PTSD).

Originally developed to treat obsessive-compulsive disorder, CBT also has been found effective with other anxiety disorders. The method has been most successful in treating adult rape victims with PTSD, which is typically characterized by intrusive flashbacks of a traumatic event and avoiding reminders of the event for more than one month after the event.

Trauma patients undergoing CBT "exposure" treatment confront the traumatic event by repeatedly describing the experience or physically revisiting places and routines associated with it. The International Society for Traumatic Stress Studies (ISTSS) recommends CBT exposure as the method with the strongest research evidence for effectiveness in reducing trauma symptoms.[1]

In addition to CBT, several other treatments, some traditional and others in the "alternative" category, have been developed to treat post-traumatic stress disorder and related problems, including:

Eye Movement Desensitization and Reprocessing (EMDR) was developed by California psychologist Francine Shapiro in 1987. It shares some aspects of CBT but asks patients to remember a traumatic image while the therapist moves a finger back and forth in front of the patient's face. Some EMDR therapists tap a patient's hand rhythmically, have the patient listen to audio tones, or follow flashing lights. EMDR has been found effective in treating civilian post-traumatic stress. But no one can really explain how it works, which is a matter of hot debate. Some proponents suggest it taps into non-verbal memories or produces a form of hypnosis. But some studies suggest the treatment works equally well without the eye movements.

Group therapy, often used by Vietnam veterans to deal with traumatic memories of warfare, is considered helpful, but there is little research on it.

Antidepressant drug therapy has been found to help reduce PTSD symptoms, particularly two drugs similar to Prozac, Zoloft and Paxil. Other antidepressants may also help.

Individual psychotherapy, the "talk therapy" developed by the founder of psychoanalysis, Sigmund Freud, has been studied in only a few clinical trials, but many case studies support its efficacy. Some studies also find that short-term, trauma-focused talk therapy is also effective with PTSD.

Psychological debriefing, originally developed for emergency workers, typically involves a single group session immediately after a traumatic event, in which those involved are asked to retell their experience. There is little research supporting the method, and some research has found that it can re-traumatize those involved.

Hypnosis has been used for more than a century to treat trauma symptoms. Practitioners included Freud and his colleague Joseph Breuer. Studies suggest that hypnosis can help PTSD patients remember traumatic events and can relive nightmares and dissociation—the emotional numbing and sense of detachment felt by some trauma victims. However, experts warn that hypnosis can also lead to "false memories" among suggestible patients. More studies are needed to determine whether hypnosis enhances the benefits of CBT, psychodynamic and drug therapies.[2]

Massage, acupuncture and yoga also can reduce anxiety symptoms, according to Andrew J. Vickers, a research methodologist in the Integrative Medicine Service at Memorial Sloan-Kettering Cancer Center in New York City. It is unknown whether the techniques can also relieve more serious anxiety disorders.

1. Edna B. Foa *et al.*, *Effective Treatments for PTSD: Practice Guidelines from the International Society for Traumatic Stress Studies* (2000), p. 78.
2. *Ibid.*, pp. 352–3.

ing has a direct connection to the amygdala. By contrast, the parts of the brain involved in the kind of thinking and reasoning crucial to psychoanalytic therapy are not directly connected to the amygdala and must follow a more complex neural pathway.

"So in order for insight into your problem to gain control over the amygdala [in psychoanalysis], it has to go through the back roads and side streets; whereas the medial prefrontal cortex, [the part of the brain involved in behavioral regulation], has a superhighway to the amygdala," LeDoux says.

But only a fraction of therapists have training in CBT. Most use traditional talk therapy, also known as psychodynamic therapy, which some experts say isn't good enough.

"It's pretty clear from research that you can't do regular old counseling. You're much better off if you do this trauma-focused [CBT] therapy," says Randall D. Marshall, director of Trauma Studies and Services at the New York State Psychiatric Institute/New York State Office of Mental Health. Marshall is coordinating a four-hospital consortium to train New York City mental health professionals in CBT techniques for treating Sept. 11 mental health victims.

Talk therapy, whose historical roots lie in the case-history approach of its founder, Sigmund Freud, has been subjected to very few studies of the type of ISTSS considers the gold standard. These "gold standard" studies enroll large numbers of trauma patients and randomly assign them to different types of treatment or a placebo. The studies then compare how the patients rate on standard tests of anxiety and PTSD symptoms.

For psychodynamic therapy, the number of such studies can be counted on one hand, compared with a score of CBT trials and about a dozen trials of promising drugs like antidepressants, according to Matthew J. Friedman, executive director of the National Center for Posttraumatic Stress Disorder at the Department of Veterans Affairs (VA).[9]

"There is a rich literature on psychodynamics used with World War I veterans and by Freud, but it's a descriptive literature," Friedman says. "It does not conform to current standards for randomized clinical trials." Nevertheless, Friedman maintains, "to say, 'The only treatment worth a damn is that with effective research behind it' is to throw out work by very creative thinkers."

One randomized trial comparing 18 sessions of psychodynamic therapy to hypnosis and desensitization therapy found little difference in benefits among the 112 patients immediately after the treatment. However, when patients were followed up over a longer period, the psychodynamic treatment group showed greater improvement than the other two groups. They had fewer symptoms like nightmares or disturbing memories. Psychodynamic therapy may help patients develop coping mechanisms that continue long after the therapy ends and may have a broader impact on their lives, suggests Harold S. Kudler, assistant chief of psychiatry at the VA Medical Center in Durham, N.C.[10]

"It's harder to study the long-term effects of psychodynamic treatment, which aims more at personal growth and development than specific symptom reduction," says Kudler, who was trained in psychoanalysis and authored the ISTSS guidelines chapter on psychodynamic therapy. "Psychodynamic therapy attempts to help the survivor deal with individual responses to trauma, which may be broader than the symptoms listed in the *Diagnostic and Statistical Manual Of Mental Disorders*. I think CBT is helpful; it's a useful and effective treatment," Kudler agrees. "But it will not serve some patients as well, and other patients feel a need to take a deeper look—where they play more of a role in initiating the conversation."

Some researchers suggest that CBT's effectiveness may be limited to certain kinds of patients—those with a specific traumatic experience in adulthood and those who are willing to confront their disturbing memories. So far, most of the successful trials of CBT have been done with adult female sexual-assault victims, notes Charles R. Marmar, vice-chairman of the department of psychiatry at the University of California, San Francisco.

"There still needs to be more research on how CBT generalizes with a whole range of other kinds of trauma victims," Marmar says. "There's not a lot of convincing evidence that CBT is safe and effective for the majority of combat veterans." Marmar is affiliated with the VA clinic in San Francisco, one of the largest VA facilities treating PTSD in war veterans.

Compared with the victim of a single rape, combat veterans with PTSD have typically suffered repeated traumas in war, often have longstanding drug- and alcohol-abuse problems and may have other psychiatric illnesses complicating the picture, Marmar notes.

"They're less able to tolerate the exposure component"—where the patient is forced to confront memories of the trauma—Marmar says. "They get very flooded with overwhelming and unmanageable anxiety and get very phobic about it." Veterans also tend to have a lot of anger about their experience, and studies find that traumatized patients who are also angry tend to respond poorly to CBT.

"CBT is aimed at anxiety and fear; it's fear deconditioning; it's not anger deconditioning," Marmar points out.

In addition, specific types of trauma may produce idiosyncratic responses, such as the belief among some victims of childhood sexual abuse that they have multiple personalities.[11] Dori Laub, a psychoanalyst and trauma expert at Yale University, describes patients sexually abused in childhood who take on as many as 100 personalties in adulthood, such as the persona of an imaginary teenager who kicks her abuser. "What can CBT say to all this? Nothing in my opinion," Laub says. "CBT is a limited approach to damaging behavior; it can be effective but it tucks the [behaviors] away in some way and the traumatic experience is still there."

A study published by Marmar in 1988 found that short-term psychodynamic therapy was helpful for widows who had lost husbands in traumatic or lingering deaths and who still suffered prolonged grief years after the death. Widows don't necessarily suffer the terror and helplessness that characterizes the rape victim at the time of the event—it's more the horror of getting the news, Marmar suggests.

The death of a close relationship often activates a longstanding psychological conflict, which is tailor-made for psychodynamic therapy, Marmar notes. He cites the case of a woman patient whose husband was killed by a tour bus, a traumatic accident that she witnessed. At first, it seemed to be the core of her problem. Underlying her grief, however, was the fact that years before the husband had had a love affair. "She'd never dealt with it; she was angry [about the affair] and guilty about the anger. Those issues were successfully dealt with in dynamic psychotherapy," Marmar recalls.

The kind of short-term psychodynamic therapy Marmar has found effective for trauma is "very different" than

Chronology

1880s–1890s

Austrian psychoanalyst Sigmund Freud theorizes that mental disorders are often rooted in traumatic events and that symptoms can be alleviated when memories are put into words—forming the basis for modern psychotherapy.

1880

French neurologist Jean-Martin Charcot demonstrates that the symptoms of female "hysteria"—similar to modern-day post-traumatic stress disorder (PTSD)—are psychological, since they can be induced or relieved through hypnosis.

1895

Joseph Breuer, an Austrian physician, and Freud publish *Studies on Hysteria,* proposing that mental disorders are sometimes rooted in psychological trauma.

1896

Freud publishes *The Aetiology of Hysteria,* claiming that childhood sexual abuse is at the root of every case of hysteria, a claim he later modifies.

Early 1900s

Mental breakdowns, known as "shell shock," represent 40 percent of British battle casualties in World War I.

1919

W. H. R. Rivers, a psychiatrist in Scotland, begins to treat returning veterans by having them recall traumatic events.

1940s

During World War II, 25 percent of evacuations from the front are for psychiatric reasons. Psychiatrists pioneer talking cures to return men to battle quickly.

1941

American psychologist Abraham Kardiner publishes *The Traumatic Neuroses of War,* outlining the traumatic syndrome known as "battle fatigue." He successfully treats hundreds of combat veterans.

1960s

Studies of Holocaust and Hiroshima survivors reveal the impact of massive trauma on civilians.

1967

Robert Jay Lifton publishes *Death in Life: Survivors of Hiroshima,* demonstrating that overwhelming events can numb basic human capacities.

1970s

Psychologists begin to recognize that survivors of war and rape show many of the same symptoms.

1972

Ann Burgess and Lynda Holmstrom coin the term "rape trauma syndrome" to describe symptoms resembling those of traumatized combat veterans, such as nightmares and numbing.

1975

A center for research on rape is created within the National Institute of Mental Health.

1979

Lenore Walker publishes *The Battered Women.*

1980s

Post-traumatic stress disorder is officially recognized by the psychology profession.

1980

Post-traumatic stress disorder first appears as a diagnosis in the American Psychiatric Association's *Diagnostic and Statistical Manual of Mental Disorders.*

1990s

The definition of PTSD is expanded to include short-lived symptoms and reactions to common life events like the sudden death of a loved one.

1994

The revised *Diagnostic and Statistical Manual* includes "acute stress disorder" for post-traumatic stress symptoms that last less than three months after a traumatic event.

2000s

New York City is faced with the largest mental health emergency in recent U.S. history.

Sept. 11, 2001

The World Trade Center and the Pentagon are hit by terrorists who hijacked airliners, killing more than 3,000. Experts predict tens of thousands of civilians who witnessed the events will suffer PTSD, depression and other mental disorders.

Helping Children Deal With Fears

Sept. 11 was the first day of school at the Washington Market School, a preschool just seven blocks north of the World Trade Center. Virtually every parent and child walking to school that morning saw the first hijacked plane hit the north tower.

Many of the parents arrived dazed, shaking or hysterical, recalls school head Ronnie Moskowitz, who promptly corralled the parents off to a separate room to express their fears and tears.

"I didn't want the children to see their parents out of control, because then the children would lose it," says Moskowitz, who is also a psychotherapist. "The children would not know who would keep them safe."

Research shows that parents' responses to a violent event strongly influence their children's ability to recover.[1] A parent's anxious reaction is one of the best predictors of whether a child will develop an anxiety disorder, according to Tamar Chansky, a child psychologist and director of the Children's Center for Obsessive-Compulsive Disorder and Anxiety in Plymouth Meeting, Pa.

"Children will look to their parents' faces as a guide to how hopeless this is," Chansky says. It's reasonable for parents to express their alarm, she says. "Kids need to know it's normal to feel upset. But when a parent lays off discipline or bedtime [rules]—that's not a good message. Children need to feel they are getting back to normal."

Research after previous large-scale disasters, like the 1995 bombing of the federal building in Oklahoma City, suggests that children who still show symptoms of post-traumatic stress disorder (PTSD)—like having repeated nightmares or being too easily startled—for more than three months after the event are likely to have them a year later. Other children exhibit what experts call a "sleeper" effect: They seem fine until they have to do something that reminds them of the event, like getting on a plane or returning to the school where the disaster occurred.

While this research suggests children should be screened for PTSD soon after a traumatic event, experts note that it's important not to force children to talk about a trauma. Elissa J. Brown, a trauma expert at New York University Child Study Center, worries about approaches like "drama therapy," where schoolchildren are instructed to act out a traumatic event in a one-shot session. That approach, she cautions, can stir up feelings of anxiety related to the event without giving children skills to cope with them.

In Oklahoma City, children watched a lot of TV coverage after the bombing were more likely to demonstrate PTSD symptoms, Brown says. Throughout the New York area, child experts reported that preschoolers who watched the repetitive news footage of the towers collapsing thought they were being attacked repeatedly or that multiple buildings were being attacked.

"Let's turn off that TV," Brown told a group of teachers and mental health professionals assembled in December at NYU.

Here are some additional guidelines the NYU Child Study Center issued for parents shortly after Sept. 11:

- Parents can show children that they themselves are sad, but they should temper their own intense emotions.
- Don't be afraid to talk about the attack. Children are likely to be concerned about things of immediate importance, such as whether or not their school is safe.
- Be truthful and honest in answers. Hiding information causes children to feel confused, reluctant to turn to adults for help and mistrustful of other information.
- Allow and encourage expression in private ways, such as through journals or art.
- Maintain as much of a normal routine as possible.
- Determine your child's risk for problems. Those at most risk are children who have some personal experience with the tragedy. They may have been close to the area or have family or friends who have been hurt or killed.
- Reassure children of their safety and that you and many others are working to make sure they are safe.[2]

Chansky concedes the last recommendation can be tricky in the case of terrorists. "No one wants to lie to a child and say, 'It will never happen again,' but you can say, 'Millions of people, the president and the Army are working to make sure it will never happen again.'"

1. "Helping Children and Adolescents Cope with Violence and Disasters," National Institute of Mental Health, updated at www.nimh.nih.gov
2. *Helping Children and Teens Cope with Traumatic Events and Death; Manual for Parents and Teachers,* New York University Child Study Center, Sept. 25, 2001.

general psychodynamic psychotherapy, he stresses. "It is very tightly trauma-focused, and it deals more with the event and the meaning of the event," he says. "In that sense, it may be more like CBT than other forms of psychotherapy."

Some trauma experts argue that forcing a patient to confront a memory can be dangerous in extreme cases. Asher Aladjem, chief psychiatrist at the Program for Survivors of Torture at New York University-Bellevue Hospital, says

he frequently sees patients from foreign countries who have no memory of being tortured although their bodies bear the evidence—scars of unspeakable physical abuse. Amnesia about a traumatic event is a well-recognized symptom in

The Warning Signs of PTSD

*Diagnostic experts say post-traumatic stress disorder oc-
curs only after a person has been exposed to a traumatic
event that involved either a perceived or actual threat to the
person or another person. Moreover, the person's response
to the event involved fear, helplessness or horror. People diagnosed with PTSD have clinically significant distress or
impairment in social, occupational or other areas. Furthermore, the following three symptoms must be present together for at least one month:*

I. The person persistently re-experiences the event in
at least one of several ways, such as:

- Intrusive recollections of the event
- Nightmares
- Flashbacks
- Intense physiological reaction to reminders of the
event, such as palpitation and other panic responses

II. The person avoids reminders of the event and has
generalized numbness of feeling as evidenced by any
of the following behaviors:

- Avoids pursuits, people and places that remind him
or her of the event
- Unable to recall aspects of the event
- Restricted range of emotions
- Loss of interest in, or less participation in, activities

III. The person has increased physical symptoms, such as:

- Difficulty falling or staying asleep
- Irritability or outbursts of anger
- Becomes more vigilant and concerned about safety
- Exaggerated startle reactions to sounds or movements

Source: Diagnostic and Statistical Manual of Mental Disorders, *4th ed.*

---

the avoidance category of PTSD symptoms, he notes.

In a recent case of a refugee who
could not remember his own torture and
who was under pressure from the U.S.
government to come up with an account
to qualify for refugee status, Aladjem's
hospital team decided against adminis-
tering sodium amytal, a truth serum that
is used to help people remember repressed memories.

"The feeling was that if the patient is
defending himself so much he can't remember, once you bring up that memory, what happens? Then the patient gets
stuck with the memory, and you basically strip them of their defense," Aladjem says. That defense could be standing
between a patient and psychosis, some
experts believe.

Challenging the view that a memory
cannot hurt trauma victims, Aladjem
counters, "I cannot say for sure that the
memory could not kill them. They could
become suicidal; the memory itself
could be very dangerous." He adds,
"CBT is not the panacea for PTSD. If it
were, it would have helped a lot more
people. It's one theory and one way that
is helpful but it's not the only way to approach the problem."

In fact, concedes the New York State
Psychiatric Institute's Marshall, many

patients who start out with CBT drop out
before completing the treatment because
they find the prospect of their memories
too frightening. And about 20 to 30 percent of people who stick with the therapy
find it to be of only minimal benefit, he
says.

Therapists from both the CBT and
psychoanalytic camps generally share
the view that antidepressants can be a
useful adjunct to therapy, particularly as
a way of calming a patient's fears sufficiently to permit them to talk about distressing memories.[12] "If someone starts
therapy and can't do it, we'll suggest
medication; if they do medications, we'd
raise psychotherapy again and maybe it
won't seem so scary to them," Marshall
says.

Are children's anxieties being adequately identified and treated?

In September 1991, when a fire at a
chicken-processing plant in Hamlet,
N.C., killed 15 people and injured 57,
virtually every child in the small, mostly
poor community was affected, according
to Duke University researchers who
studied the impact of the fire on schoolchildren. Almost every child either knew
someone who was killed or injured or

witnessed bodies falling out of the door-
way to the plant.

Children who had experienced previous traumas in their lives were far more
likely than their classmates to develop
PTSD after the fire.[13] Many had experienced prior horrifying events, including
the rape of a mother or the violent death
of a parent or loved one. Yet none had
ever been diagnosed or treated, according to John S. March, a professor of psychiatry at Duke University and author of
a study of the incident.[14]

Experts say children suffering from
PTSD, anxiety and depression often go
undiagnosed because they typically respond to trauma by being quiet or just
withdrawing. "These are silent sufferers," says NYU Child Study Center Director Harold S. Koplewicz. "These are
children who may stop attending school
or have trouble concentrating but will
rarely be rambunctious. In a class of 30,
you can see four or five kids who don't
look good: They're inattentive, they look
sad. Yet, if you ask the teacher, they
wouldn't have picked out those kids."

In New York City, because public
schools had only been in session a few
days before the terrorist attacks, many
teachers did not have time to get to know
the children in their classes well enough
to detect changes that could signal

PTSD, such as setbacks in toilet training or increased aggression, pointed out Elyssa J. Brown, assistant director of the NYU Institute for Children at Risk.

"I encourage you to look at past records," Brown urged school and mental health professionals at a December symposium sponsored by NYU. Children who had previous psychological or behavior problems could be predisposed to PTSD, she said.

For sheer scale, Sept. 11 will be the largest exposure of U.S. children to a traumatic event in recent history. About 8,000 children were evacuated from schools near the World Trade Center on Sept. 11, according to Spencer Eth, medical director of behavior health services for St. Vincent Catholic Medical Centers and a professor of psychiatry at New York Medical College. "Many of these children saw buildings burning, saw people falling from buildings, and they were evacuated in a time of great crisis and turmoil," Eth says.

Based on what happened after the Oklahoma City bombing, Eth estimates that about a third of the children will experience such symptoms as nightmares or bad memories, although not necessarily enough symptoms to be diagnosed with full-blown PTSD. Koplewicz estimates that another 5,000 children not evacuated were traumatized by the deaths of parents, relatives or adult friends.

Because of the magnitude of the problem in New York, finding and treating children who are suffering will be an enormous undertaking. Since January, child experts from NYU's Child Study Center and from St. Vincent's have been working with teachers at schools near Ground Zero to help identify children who may need mental health services. In the process, they hope to learn more about how children respond to a trauma of such magnitude and to cognitive behavioral therapy—the primary treatment they will be offering.

Under the screening program, mental health professionals spend a class period asking children whether they are having any post-traumatic symptoms, such as anger, depression, difficulty sleeping or concentrating, recurrent nightmares or physical sensations like choking or a

racing heartbeat. During preliminary screening, about 25 percent of the children reported symptoms and asked for help.

However, it wasn't only the youngsters near the Twin Towers who were affected by the attacks, according to Koplewicz. Another 50,000 of the city's children—about 5 percent of the child population—were suffering from anxiety or depression beforehand, he says, making them vulnerable to PTSD. "In New York City alone, we're talking about 70,000–80,000 kids who are at risk and are more vulnerable than the rest of the population," Koplewicz says.

Kids in neighboring towns were affected, too, says Leslie Bogan, a child psychologist in suburban Westchester County. Since Sept. 11, she has been seeing increased anxiety disorders among her child patients, including regressive behavior in toilet training, irritability, difficulty sleeping and eating. In addition, child experts say numerous schoolchildren in the area have complained of psychosomatic pains like headaches or stomach aches.

Bogan, who is affiliated with Cornell University and the Yale Child Study Center, says that since Sept. 11 she and colleagues have offered their help to suburban schools. "They don't want our help," she says. "The schools will tell you they're very well prepared and their kids are having no difficulty whatsoever."

Bogan is skeptical of that assessment. "I'm not sure school personnel are well-trained" to recognize signs of PTSD or anxiety, she says. "They tend to react to acting out. Kids who are sad go underdiagnosed."

Although schools in Lower Manhattan have been receptive to help from mental health professionals, child trauma experts say large-scale school screening for PTSD in the rest of the country would raise some delicate questions.

Screening can be potentially harmful if children are asked to describe a traumatic event and aren't given coping skills to deal with it, says John A. Fairbank, co-director of the National Center for Child Traumatic Stress, a federally funded center located at Duke University

and the University of California-Berkeley. The center is planning to study better ways to identify children who suffer sexual abuse, family violence or who live in neighborhoods assaulted by violent crime.

Yet, Fairbank acknowledges that many children with problems go unnoticed unless they are brought to the attention of a school official or a physician. "There isn't any systematic screening" in most of the country, he points out. Schools and parents are often resistant to taking time from academic learning to deal with social issues like childhood trauma.

The debate over how best to treat traumatized children mirrors that for treating adults—except that for children the debate centers on whether CBT is better than play therapy, which springs from the same roots as psychoanalysis.

The mental health experts from St. Vincent's and NYU plan to treat the World Trade Center youngsters with CBT pegged to the child's developmental level. Treating a child with CBT typically involves having the child tell the story of the traumatic event—through pictures, for young children, or through writing, for older children—until they can repeat it without disabling sensations of fear. They then discuss the event in individual sessions with a therapist and/or in a group of other children in order to correct mistaken ideas, often of self-blame, which continue to haunt them.

Although CBT has more research supporting it than other methods of treating traumatized children, Fairbank notes that, in general, far fewer studies have been conducted on trauma treatment for children than for adults.

"The most common treatment children get is child-centered play therapy, which is a dinosaur... mostly worthless," says March, a strong CBT advocate. If play therapy includes such CBT components as narrating the story of the trauma and facing one's fears, it can be helpful, March says. "But [if] it involves shooting basketball outside with kids—which most therapists end up doing—or focusing on the parent-child relationship, it's not very helpful at all," he maintains. March's study of the impact of the Hamlet fire found that CBT was effective in reducing symptoms for children and teens across a variety of age and school settings.[15]

But Fairbank maintains that the verdict is still out on competing therapies, since there has been so little research to date. "I wouldn't call [play therapy] a dinosaur at all," he says. "There's art therapy; there is play therapy. They may be effective. I don't think we should toss them out without evaluating them." He also thinks Prozac-like antidepressants constitute another promising therapy, particularly for teens, that needs further testing.

A $10 million federal initiative, funded by the Department of Health and Human Services' Substance Abuse and Mental Health Services Administration, created the National Center for Child Traumatic Stress in September before the terrorist attacks. It was established to identify the most effective treatments for traumatized children and to funnel information about those techniques to mental health professionals around the nation. The initiative includes funding for 17 other institutions treating children across the country.

Notes

1. For background, see David Masci and Kenneth Jost, "War on Terrorism," *The CQ Researcher*, Oct. 12, 2001. pp. 817–848.

2. For background, see Kathy Koch, "Childhood Depression," *The CQ Researcher*, July 16, 1999, pp. 593–616, and Sarah Glazer, "Boys' Emotional Needs," *The CQ Researcher*, June 18, 1999, pp. 521–544.

3. American Psychiatric Association, *Diagnostic and Statistical Manual of Mental Disorders*, 4th edition, 1994.

4. Rachel Yehuda, "Post-Traumatic Stress Disorder," *The New England Journal of Medicine*, Jan. 10, 2001, pp. 108–114.

5. *Ibid.*

6. Richard Lezin Jones, "All in Police Dept. Face Counseling," *The New York Times*, Nov. 30, 2001, p. A1.

7. For background, see Sarah Glazer, "Preventing Teen Drug Use," *The CQ Researcher*, July 28, 1995, pp. 657–680, and Karen Lee Scrivo, "Drinking on Campus," *The CQ Researcher*, March 20, 1998, pp. 241–264.

8. Edna B. Foa, *et al.*, eds., *Effective Treatments for PTSD: Practice Guidelines from the International Society for Traumatic Stress Studies*, p. 78.

9. For background, See Mary H. Cooper, "Prozac Controversy," *The CQ Researcher*, Aug. 19, 1994, pp. 721–744.

10. Harlod S. Kudler, *et al.*, "Psychodynamic Therapy," in Foa, op. cit., pp. 186–187.

11. For background, see Kathy Koch, "Child Sexual Abuse," *The CQ Researcher*, Jan. 15, 1993, pp. 25–48.

12. Tamar Nordenberg, "Escaping the Prison of a Past Trauma: New Treatment for Post-traumatic Stress Disorder," *FDA Consumer Magazine*, May-June 2000, at www.fda.gov.

13. John S. March *et al.*, "Posttraumatic Symptomatology in Children and Adolescents After an Industrial Fire," *Journal of the American Academy of Child and Adolescent Psychiatry*, August 1997, pp. 1080–1088.

14. *Ibid.*

15. John S. March, *et al.*, "Cognitive Behavioral Psychotherapy for Children and Adolescents with Posttraumatic Stress Disorder After a Single-Incident Stressor," *Journal of the American Academy of Child and Adolescent Psychiatry*, June 1998, pp. 583–593.

From *CQ Researcher*, February 8, 2002, pp. 99-111. © 2002 by CQ Press, A Division of Congressional Quarterly, Inc. Reprinted by permission.

Index

Index

Test Your Knowledge Form

We encourage you to photocopy and use this page as a tool to assess how the articles in *Annual Editions* expand on the information in your textbook. By reflecting on the articles you will gain enhanced text information. You can also access this useful form on a product's book support Web site at *http://www.dushkin.com/online/*.

NAME: DATE:

_____

TITLE AND NUMBER OF ARTICLE:

_____

BRIEFLY STATE THE MAIN IDEA OF THIS ARTICLE:

_____

LIST THREE IMPORTANT FACTS THAT THE AUTHOR USES TO SUPPORT THE MAIN IDEA:

_____

WHAT INFORMATION OR IDEAS DISCUSSED IN THIS ARTICLE ARE ALSO DISCUSSED IN YOUR TEXTBOOK OR OTHER READINGS THAT YOU HAVE DONE? LIST THE TEXTBOOK CHAPTERS AND PAGE NUMBERS:

_____

LIST ANY EXAMPLES OF BIAS OR FAULTY REASONING THAT YOU FOUND IN THE ARTICLE:

_____

LIST ANY NEW TERMS/CONCEPTS THAT WERE DISCUSSED IN THE ARTICLE, AND WRITE A SHORT DEFINITION:

We Want Your Advice

ANNUAL EDITIONS revisions depend on two major opinion sources: one is our Advisory Board, listed in the front of this volume, which works with us in scanning the thousands of articles published in the public press each year; the other is you—the person actually using the book. Please help us and the users of the next edition by completing the prepaid article rating form on this page and returning it to us. Thank you for your help!

ANNUAL EDITIONS: Psychology 03/04

ARTICLE RATING FORM

Here is an opportunity for you to have direct input into the next revision of this volume.
We would like you to rate each of the articles listed below, using the following scale:

1. **Excellent: should definitely be retained**
2. **Above average: should probably be retained**
3. **Below average: should probably be deleted**
4. **Poor: should definitely be deleted**

Your ratings will play a vital part in the next revision.
Please mail this prepaid form to us as soon as possible.
Thanks for your help!

RATING	ARTICLE
_____	1. A Dance to the Music of the Century: Changing Fashions in 20th-Century Psychiatry
_____	2. Good and Evil and Psychological Science
_____	3. Exploring a Controversy
_____	4. The Tangled Skeins of Nature and Nurture in Human Evolution
_____	5. Altered States of Consciousness
_____	6. Brain-Based Learning
_____	7. The Senses
_____	8. Sight Unseen
_____	9. It's a Noisy, Noisy World out There!
_____	10. An Ear for Color: Exploring the Curious World of Synesthesia, Where Senses Merge in Mysterious Ways
_____	11. Phantom Sensations: Understanding the Pain Felt by an Amputee
_____	12. Pain and Its Mysteries
_____	13. Brains in Dreamland
_____	14. Memory and Learning
_____	15. Understanding Our Differences
_____	16. New Evidence for the Benefits of Never Spanking
_____	17. The Seven Sins of Memory: How the Mind Forgets and Remembers
_____	18. Memory's Mind Games
_____	19. Cognitive Development in Social and Cultural Context
_____	20. Mind in a Mirror
_____	21. Intelligence: The Surprising Truth
_____	22. The Inner Savant
_____	23. Fundamental Feelings
_____	24. Medical Detection of False Witness
_____	25. What's Your Emotional IQ?
_____	26. How to Multitask
_____	27. The Biology of Aging
_____	28. Fetal Psychology
_____	29. Parenting: The Lost Art
_____	30. Living to 100: What's the Secret?
_____	31. Start the Conversation
_____	32. Psychoanalyst: Sigmund Freud

RATING	ARTICLE
_____	33. Positive Psychology: An Introduction
_____	34. Oldest, Youngest, or In Between
_____	35. Got Time for Friends?
_____	36. Rational and Irrational Fears Combine in Terrorism's Wake
_____	37. Whodunit—The Media?
_____	38. The Feminization of American Culture
_____	39. The Emperor Has No Clothes, or, Do You See Individualist-Collectivist Societies?
_____	40. Disarming the Rage
_____	41. Mental Health Gets Noticed
_____	42. Up From Depression
_____	43. The Quest for a Cure
_____	44. Post-Traumatic Stress Disorder
_____	45. The Schizophrenic Mind
_____	46. The Secrets of Autism
_____	47. Are We Nuts?
_____	48. Support Groups: Study Casts Some Doubts
_____	49. Treating Anxiety

(Continued on next page)

BUSINESS REPLY MAIL
FIRST-CLASS MAIL PERMIT NO. 84 GUILFORD CT

POSTAGE WILL BE PAID BY ADDRESSEE

McGraw-Hill/Dushkin
530 Old Whitfield Street
Guilford, Ct 06437-9989

NO POSTAGE
NECESSARY
IF MAILED
IN THE
UNITED STATES

ABOUT YOU

Name _____ Date _____

Are you a teacher? ☐   A student? ☐
Your school's name _____

Department _____

Address _____ City _____ State _____ Zip _____

School telephone # _____

YOUR COMMENTS ARE IMPORTANT TO US!

Please fill in the following information:
For which course did you use this book?
_____

Did you use a text with this ANNUAL EDITION?   ☐ yes   ☐ no
What was the title of the text?
_____

What are your general reactions to the *Annual Editions* concept?
_____

Have you read any pertinent articles recently that you think should be included in the next edition? Explain.
_____

Are there any articles that you feel should be replaced in the next edition? Why?
_____

Are there any World Wide Web sites that you feel should be included in the next edition? Please annotate.
_____

May we contact you for editorial input?   ☐ yes   ☐ no
May we quote your comments?   ☐ yes   ☐ no

DAVID GLENN HUNT
MEMORIAL LIBRARY
GALVESTON COLLEGE